Mathematics for Dyslexics and Dyscalculics

Mathematics for Dyslexics and Dyscalculics

A Teaching Handbook

Fourth Edition

Steve Chinn and Richard E. Ashcroft

WILEY Blackwell

This edition first published 2017

Edition history: 1e Whurr Publishers Ltd, 1993; 2e Whurr Publishers Ltd. 1998; 3e John Wiley & Sons, Ltd. 2007

Registered Office
John Wiley & Sons Ltd, The Atrium, Southern Gate, Chichester, West Sussex, PO19 8SQ, UK

Editorial Offices
350 Main Street, Malden, MA 02148-5020, USA
9600 Garsington Road, Oxford, OX4 2DQ, UK
The Atrium, Southern Gate, Chichester, West Sussex, PO19 8SQ, UK

For details of our global editorial offices, for customer services, and for information about how to apply for permission to reuse the copyright material in this book please see our website at www.wiley.com/wiley-blackwell.

Library of Congress Cataloging-in-Publication data applied for

Paperback ISBN: 9781119159964

A catalogue record for this book is available from the British Library.

Cover image: Violka08/Gettyimages

Set in 10/12.5pt Galliard by SPi Global, Pondicherry, India

Printed in Singapore by C.O.S. Printers Pte Ltd

10 9 8 7 6 5 4 3 2 1

Dedicated to the memory of our dear friend and colleague, Lyn Rawles

Contents

Foreword

Steve Chinn's newest edition of the 1993 Chinn and Ashcroft book *Mathematics for Dyslexics* is an important and timely addition to the dyscalculia or mathematical learning disabilities literature. As Chinn notes in his introductory chapter, basic and applied research on dyscalculia has lagged behind that of dyslexia for decades. The gap has closed somewhat in recent years, but children's and adults' struggles with basic mathematics remain relatively neglected. This seemingly benign neglect can have largely unrecognised long-term consequences for students and ultimately the communities within which they reside (National Mathematics Advisory Panel, 2008), independent of their reading skills, cognitive abilities, or ethnic background. For instance, adults who have difficulty solving word problems that require whole number arithmetic, fractions, simple algebra and measurement have compromised employment prospects (Bynner, 1997; Parsons and Bynner, 1997; Rivera-Batiz, 1992), and difficulties in other areas of life that require quantitative knowledge (e.g. Reyna *et al.*, 2009).

These adults would be considered innumerate – either because of an underlying difficulty with mathematical learning (e.g. low working memory capacity), poor instruction, poor motivation, or some combination – and now include 20–25% of adults in the United Kingdom and the United States. Unfortunately, the path to adult innumeracy starts early, probably before the beginning of formal schooling (Duncan *et al.*, 2007; Ritchie and Bates, 2013). One recent study suggested that children who start school with a poor understanding of Arabic numerals, the magnitudes they represent and the relations among them [e.g. $7 = (6 + 1) = (5 + 2) = (4 + 3)$] score poorly on numeracy tests as adolescents (Geary, Hoard, Nugent, and Bailey, 2013). In this study, six-year-olds who started school in the bottom 15–20% in this number knowledge were four times more likely to score as innumerate in adolescence on tests that have been shown to predict later employability and wages in young adults. By eight years of age, these at-risk children learned basic arithmetic as quickly as other children, but they never narrowed the school-entry gap. This is not to say that they could not catch up with the right remediation approaches, but it does emphasise the importance of catching and addressing potential difficulties early.

The questions then become, what are the early precursors of school-entry quantitative knowledge and what are the key mathematical competencies that must be developed to ensure students have functional numeracy skills by the time they leave school? The foundation is a solid understanding of Arabic numerals and the relations among them, and in Chapter 5 Chinn does an admirable job of identifying these core number skills and how they should become elaborated over the course of schooling (i.e. organized around the base-ten system). Strong arithmetic skills are just as important as the number skills on which they are built, and Chinn devotes chapters 6–14, inclusive, to various aspects of arithmetic, from learning the multiplication tables (or learning backup strategies for children who have difficulties memorising facts), to rational numbers (i.e. fractions, decimals, and percentages). Each of these chapters is organised around learning issues detailed in the introductory chapters and is presented with detailed examples, explanations and advice on how to approach the instruction of each of these critical topics. The final chapters expand the discussion to applied topics, such as time telling, lay out the basics for approaching algebra and geometry, and provide very useful teaching tips.

In all, this is not just a much-needed book for remedial approaches to dyscalculia, but a book that identifies critical number and arithmetic skills that are important for all students to learn. The focus of course is on instruction and remediation, and the approaches detailed herein will be particularly useful for instructing children with one form of cognitive difficulty (e.g. in memorizing basic facts) or another (e.g. poor working memory capacity), but these same approaches should be helpful for any child who is struggling with basic mathematics. Our best estimate, at this point, is that any child in the bottom 25% on mathematics achievement tests is in need of remedial attention, whether or not they have cognitive difficulties, and this book provides the roadmap for this remediation.

David C. Geary,
Curators' Professor, Thomas Jefferson Fellow,
Department of Psychological Sciences,
Interdisciplinary Neuroscience Program, University of Missouri

1

Dyscalculia, Dyslexia and Mathematics

Introduction

In 1981, when we moved from working in mainstream schools and began teaching in schools for dyslexic learners, our initial expectation was that teaching mathematics would be much the same as before. At that time we could not find any source of guidance to confirm or contradict this expectation. We thought dyslexia meant difficulties with language, not mathematics. Experience would, very quickly, change this impression.

Over the last 35 years, and the 23 years since we published the first edition of this book, we have accumulated experience, tried out new (and old) ideas, researched, read what little appropriate material was available (there is still far less published on learning difficulties in mathematics than on language (Gersten *et al.*, 2007)), learned from our learners and have become convinced that difficulties in mathematics go hand in hand with the difficulties of dyslexia and, especially, that a different teaching attitude and approach is needed.

The first four chapters of this book look at some of the background that influenced the evolution of these teaching methods and continues to underpin their ongoing development. This requires a look at the learner, the subject (mathematics), the teacher and the pedagogy. The main mathematical focus of this book is number, primarily because this is the first area of mathematics studied by children and thus provides the first opportunity to fail. Our experience suggests that number remains the main source of difficulty for most of the learners we have worked with, even in secondary education. We also know that the foundations for all

Mathematics for Dyslexics and Dyscalculics: A Teaching Handbook, Fourth Edition.
Steve Chinn and Richard E. Ashcroft.

work to GCSE (the national examination for 16-year-old students in England), and beyond, are based in these early learning experiences. The evaluations and expectations of a child's mathematical potential are often based, not always correctly, on performance in early work on number (e.g. Desoete and Stock, 2011). The remaining chapters describe some of the methods we use to teach our dyslexic learners, with the ever-present caveat, that no one method will work for all learners.

One of the main reasons for the first four chapters is to address the complexity of learning profiles. This will explain why the methods described in the subsequent chapters are effective, but still will not meet the needs of every single child, and why teachers need the skill of responsive reactivity. There are now a number of researchers who have referred to this complexity and from a number of perspectives. Watson (2005) states:

> There is no standard recipe for mathematical success. The joyous range of characteristics that make each child an individual ensure that this is true, so teachers need an understanding of the child and the subject to be able to adjust methods and improvise, from secure foundations and principles, to meet those individual needs.

Mabbott and Bisanz (2008) note that, 'Children who experience difficulties in mathematics are a heterogeneous group' and as Zhou and Cheng (2015) express so elegantly and succinctly, 'mathematical competence is a constellation of abilities'. Kaufmann and a collection of international researchers (2013) writing together say that heterogeneity is a feature of developmental dyscalculia. Chapter 2 provides more detail on some of the reasons for this heterogeneity.

We also believe that a greater understanding of the ways dyslexic and dyscalculic students learn and fail mathematics will illuminate our understanding of how other children learn and fail mathematics. In other words, the reasons for failure are unlikely to be specific to dyslexic and dyscalculic learners. Poor performance in maths spreads beyond students identified as dyscalculic, for example Rashid and Brooks (2010) found low levels of attainment in a significant percentage of the population of 13–19-year-old students in England. The extrapolation from this is that many, if not all of the methods advocated in this book will also help many non-dyslexic and non-dyscalculic students to learn mathematics. We have long been advocates of the principle of learning from the 'outliers' (Murray *et al.*, 2015).

Our aim has always been to teach mathematics in a mathematical way rather than seek out patronising collections of mnemonics and one-off tricks.

Definitions of Dyslexia

The year 2016 marks the 120th anniversary of the publication of the first paper (Pringle-Morgan, 1896, reproduced in the *BDA Handbook* 1996) describing a 14-year-old student with specific difficulties with reading, which Pringle-Morgan labelled, based on Kussmaul's study in 1878, as 'congenital word blindness'. Pringle Morgan also described idiosyncratic difficulties for the young student in maths: 'Interestingly he could multiply 749 by 867 quickly and correctly as well as working out $(a+x)(a-x)=a^2-x^2$, yet failed to do $4 \times \frac{1}{2}$.'

The issue of mathematics disappeared from definitions of dyslexia for a while, for example in 1968 the World Federation of Neurology defined dyslexia as: 'A disorder manifested by a difficulty in learning to read, despite conventional instruction, adequate intelligence and socio-cultural opportunity. It is dependent upon fundamental cognitive difficulties that are frequently of a constitutional character.'

But, by 1972 the Department of Education and Science for England and Wales included number abilities in its definition of specific reading (sic) difficulties. In the USA, the Interagency Conference's (Kavanagh and Truss, 1988) definition of learning disabilities included 'significant difficulties in the acquisition of mathematical abilities' and, in the UK, Chasty (1989) defined specific learning difficulties as: 'Organising or learning difficulties, which restrict the students competence in information processing, in fine motor skills and working memory, so causing limitations in some or all of the skills of speech, reading, spelling, writing, essay writing, numeracy and behaviour.'

In 1992 Miles and Miles, in their book *Dyslexia and Mathematics*, wrote: 'The central theme of this book is that the difficulties experienced by dyslexics in mathematics are manifestations of the same limitations which also affect their reading and spelling.'

In 1995 Light and Defries (1995) highlighted the comorbidity of language and mathematical difficulties in dyslexic twins, one of the earliest mentions of the possibility of comorbid dyslexia and dyscalculia.

In the new millennium, it seems that the definitions of dyslexia are moving back to focus solely on language. This is likely to be due to the current interest in and awareness of dyscalculia and comorbidity and the trend in the UK to see 'specific learning difficulties' used as an umbrella term to cover dyslexia, dyscalculia, dyspraxia (developmental coordination disorder) and dysgraphia, rather than a label that was solely interchangeable with dyslexia. This is relevant for our perceptions of dyscalculia and mathematical learning difficulties. So, recently in the UK, the Rose Report's (2009) definition of dyslexia focused on reading and spelling, with no mention of arithmetic or numeracy skills: 'Dyslexia is a learning difficulty that primarily affects the skills involved in accurate and fluent word reading and spelling. Characteristic features of dyslexia are difficulties in phonological awareness, verbal memory and verbal processing speed.' However, within the report, there are discussions on co-occurring issues, which include difficulties with mental calculation.

In the USA, the International Dyslexia Association adopted a definition of dyslexia (2002), which also focused on language:

> Dyslexia is a specific learning difficulty that is neurobiological in origin. It is characterised by difficulties with accurate and/or fluent word recognition and by poor spelling and decoding abilities. These difficulties typically result from a deficit in the phonological component of language that is often unexpected in relation to other cognitive abilities and the provision of effective classroom instruction. Secondary consequences may include problems in reading comprehension and reduced reading experience that can impede growth of vocabulary and background knowledge.

If dyslexia and dyscalculia are now to be defined as separate, distinct specific learning difficulties, then the concept of comorbidity (e.g. Cirino *et al.*, 2015; Shin and Bryant, 2015) becomes very relevant. An important question for researchers is to decide whether the comorbidity is causal, independent or a different outcome resulting from the same neurological basis. The study by Moll *et al.* (2014) suggests that deficits in number skills are due to different underlying cognitive deficits in children with reading disorders compared to children with mathematics disorders. These deficits are, for reading disorders, a phonological deficit and, for mathematics disorders, a deficit in processing numbers.

Our classroom experience is that most of the dyslexics we have taught have had difficulties in at least some areas of mathematics. It should be noted that, in our school, the results from our specifically designed intervention, in terms of grades achieved in GCSE (the national exam for 16-year-old students in England) were from A* to D and with one ex-student, who was severely dyslexic, obtaining a degree in mathematics. The theme of this book is of positive prognosis.

In her seminal book, Yeo (2002) looked at the issues surrounding dyspraxia, dyslexia and mathematics difficulties. The specific learning difficulty, dyspraxia (developmental coordination disorder) brings another set of issues to a pupil's attempts to learn mathematics.

Finally in this section, we should be aware that dyslexia is a problem internationally (as dyscalculia certainly is). Although the English language is probably the most challenging language to learn, especially for the mastery of spelling, dyslexia occurs in many languages. For example, the Yemen Dyslexia Association (Al Hakeemi, 2015) defines dyslexia as: 'A functional disorder of the left side of the brain. It causes difficulty in reading, writing or mathematics associated with other symptoms such as weakness in short-term memory, ordering, movements and directions awareness.'

The Evolution of Definitions of (Developmental) Dyscalculia

At the time (2015) of writing this, the fourth edition of our book, the idea of a specific mathematics disability, now known as dyscalculia in the UK, had slipped out of common usage in our government documents, whereas at the time of the third edition it had recently slipped in. This observation draws attention to the influence of governments on the recognition of and provision for learning disabilities. A search for 'dyscalculia' on the gov.uk website on 10 April 2015 yielded no results, suggesting instead that we try to search for 'calculi'.

The term dyscalculia remains not well defined, or at least without a consensus, though there have been some recent proposals as to what the definition should be (e.g. Kaufmann *et al.*, 2013). However, it does now seem agreed that it is a specific learning difficulty that is solely related to mathematics, that is, there is no mention of a comorbid language difficulty. As one would expect, the prevalence of dyscalculia will be dependent on how it is defined.

It should be stated at this stage that, erroneously, for some people 'dyscalculia' suggests a dire prognosis, that of a *permanent inability* to do mathematics. This would be 'acalculia', a complete loss of the ability to work with numbers and caused by a stroke or a traumatic injury to the brain. The two terms are not interchangeable.

It remains the situation that much less research exists in comparison to dyslexia. When David Geary spoke at the 2002 IDA conference he compared our knowledge of dyslexia to being close to adulthood and our knowledge of maths learning difficulties to being in its early infancy. Gersten *et al.* (2007) give data on the ratio of papers on reading disability to mathematical learning disability for five subsequent decades. For 1966–1975 the ratio was 100:1 and for 1996–2005 it was 14:1. Desoete *et al.* (2004) note that from 1974 to 1997 only 28 articles on maths learning difficulties were cited in Psyc-Info, whereas there were 747 articles on reading disabilities.

The work of Kosc, a pioneer in the field of dyscalculia, plus a review of the early literature on dyscalculia can be found in *Focus on Learning Difficulties in Mathematics* (Kosc, 1986). Ramaa and Gowramma (2002) provide a comprehensive review of the literature to that time and Gersten *et al.* (2007) provide a more recent review, taking in a range of different perspectives. The various authors in *The Routledge International Handbook of Dyscalculia and Mathematical Learning Difficulties* (Chinn, 2015) provide a wealth of references. The international nature of the research tells us that dyscalculia is an international problem (e.g. Faber, 2014).

The earliest reference to a specific learning difficulty in maths that we could find is by Bronner (1917), referred to in Buswell and Judd (1925): 'Frequent references have been made to children whose ability seems to be normal or even superior as far as general mental capacity is concerned, but who have special difficulties in arithmetic. Bronner has proposed the hypothesis that there are special disabilities in such subjects as arithmetic.'

Little happened for dyscalculia and specific learning difficulties in the next 60 years. Indeed, it was not until the third edition of this book (2007) that the word 'dyscalculia' was included in the title. However, there have been a few definitions of dyscalculia proposed over the past 50 years, with one of the earliest from Kosc (1974) who defined it in terms of brain abnormalities: 'Developmental dyscalculia is a structural disorder of mathematical abilities which has its origin in a genetic or congenital disorder of those parts of the brain that are the direct anatomico-physiological substrate of the maturation of the mathematical abilities adequate to age, without a simultaneous disorder of general mental functions.'

Weinstein (1980), quoted in Sharma (1986) considered dyscalculia as, 'A disorder of the abilities for dealing with numbers and calculating which is present at an early age and is not accompanied by a concurrent disorder of general mental functions.'

Magne (1996) published a bibliography of the literature on dysmathematics.

The definition of dyscalculia from the UK's Department for Education and Skills booklet (DfES, 2001, now archived) on supporting learners with dyslexia and dyscalculia in the National Numeracy Strategy is: 'Dyscalculia is a condition that affects the ability to acquire mathematical skills. Dyscalculic learners may have difficulty understanding simple number concepts, lack an intuitive grasp of numbers, and have problems learning number facts and procedures. Even if they produce a correct answer or use a correct method, they may do so mechanically and without confidence.'

There does seem to be a long-standing consensus that dyscalculia should be perceived as a specific difficulty, for example:

> The World Health Organisation (2010) uses the term 'Specific disorder of arithmetical skills' which 'involves a specific impairment in arithmetical skills that is not solely explicable on the basis of general mental retardation or of grossly inadequate schooling. The deficit concerns mastery of basic computational skills of addition, subtraction, multiplication and division rather than of the more abstract mathematical skills involved in algebra, trigonometry, geometry or calculus.'

The American Psychiatric Association (2013) also uses 'specific' in their definition of Developmental Dyscalculia (DD) as: 'A specific learning disorder that is characterised by impairments in learning basic arithmetic facts, processing numerical magnitude and performing accurate and fluent calculations. These difficulties must be quantifiably below what is expected for an individual's chronological age, and must not be caused by poor educational or daily activities or by intellectual impairments.'

It is of interest that an international team of experts (Kaufman *et al.*, 2013) proposed a definition that suggests two sub-types of Developmental Dyscalculia (DD), 'Primary DD is a heterogeneous disorder resulting from individual deficits in numerical or arithmetic functioning at behavioral, cognitive/neuropsychological and neuronal levels. The term secondary DD should be used if numerical/arithmetic dysfunctions are entirely caused by non-numerical impairments (e.g. attention disorders).'

Also working with a hypothesis of sub-types, Karagiannakis and Cooreman (2015) propose a classification model of mathematical learning difficulties:

> Core number. Difficulties in the basic sense of numerosity and subitising (Butterworth, 2005; 2010).
>
> Visual-spatial. Difficulties in interpreting and using spatial organisation and representation of mathematical objects.
>
> Memory. Difficulties in retrieving numerical facts and performing mental calculations accurately.
>
> Reasoning. Difficulties in grasping mathematical concepts, ideas and relations and understanding multiple steps in complex procedures/algorithms.

These may be taking us onwards from Butterworth's 2005 single core deficit model. The interactions between the complexity of maths and the heterogeneous nature of individuals makes the situation highly complex.

Thus, we may have to seek some key patterns whilst being open to variations on these core themes. We should not risk failing children (and adults) by simply saying, 'If people can't agree to the definition, then it doesn't exist.'

There seem to be two components to the various definitions that have been proposed. One is a description of the mathematical difficulties. This component tends to focus on basic maths, that is, numeracy and arithmetic, sometimes with a focus on the very basic skills, for example numerosity (Butterworth, 2010), core number deficits (e.g. Reeve and Gray, 2015) and number sense. Even here there are complexities. Berch (2005) found 30 alleged components of number sense in the literature.

The other component focuses on the neurological causes. As technology grows at an exciting pace, then the possibilities of watching the brain at work (e.g. Bugden and Ansari, 2015; Reigosa-Crespo and Castro, 2015) are in stark contrast to the early days of examining the brains of dyslexics post-mortem (Gallaburda, 1989). However, even with this amazing capacity to watch brains at work, the situation remains complex, as Bugden and Ansari (2015) observe: 'Neuroimaging studies investigating the cognitive mechanisms that contribute to DD deficits have yielded an inconsistent and hard to interpret pattern of data. Given the early stages of functional MRI and EEG research, it is difficult to interpret from the current set of data what neurobiology underlies cognitive deficits in children with DD.'

Returning to the mathematical behaviours that might contribute to that aspect of definitions of dyscalculia, our experience and the relevant research, suggests that the list below covers many of these:

- Difficulty when counting backwards.
- A poor sense of number and estimation.
- Difficulty in remembering 'basic' facts, despite many hours of practice/rote learning.
- The only strategy used to compensate for lack of recall is to count in ones.
- Difficulty in understanding place value.
- No sense of whether any answers that are obtained are right or nearly right.
- Slow to perform calculations.
- Forgets mathematical procedures, especially when complex, for example 'long' division.
- Addition is often the default operation.

- Avoids tasks that are perceived/predicted as likely to result in a wrong answer.
- Weak mental arithmetic skills.
- High levels of mathematics anxiety.

As a footnote to this section, we suggest that if one views dyslexia and dyscalculia as similar in nature, then it would follow that many of the problems of learning maths can be circumvented. They may well still persist into adulthood, with the danger of regression if hard-won skills are not regularly practised. This optimistic view would not preclude great success in maths for some 'dyscalculics' in the same way that dyslexia has not held back some great writers and actors.

Comorbidity

An awareness of the co-occurrence (termed comorbidity in the medical field) of two or more educationally relevant disorders in the same individual, has grown in the past 30 years. The first edition of this book was titled *Mathematics for Dyslexics.* It was the third edition that saw the introduction of 'Dyscalculia' into the title. We now have a wider recognition of learning difficulties, including Asperger syndrome (though that term may soon be subsumed into autistic spectrum disorders), dyspraxia/developmental coordination disorder (Yeo, 2003; Pieters *et al.*, 2015), attention deficit hyperactivity disorder, hearing impairment (Gowramma, 2015) and, indeed, dyscalculia.

But the authors' interest in learning difficulties was born out of our experiences of working with children who had been diagnosed as dyslexic, so that will be a starting point for this section.

In terms of the co-occurrence of difficulties in language and maths, Joffe's pioneering paper (1980a) on maths and dyslexia included a statistic that has been applied over enthusiastically and without careful consideration of how it was obtained, that is, '61% of dyslexics are retarded in arithmetic' and thus, many have since assumed, 39% are not). The sample for this statistic was quite small, some 50 dyslexic learners. The maths test on which the statistic was primarily based was the British Abilities Scales Basic Arithmetic Test, which is, as its title suggests, predominantly a test of arithmetic skills. Although the test was untimed, Joffe noted that the group that achieved well would have done less well if speed had been a consideration. She also stated the extrapolations from this paper would have to be cautious. Other writers seem to have overlooked Joffe's own cautions and detailed observations. For example she states, 'Computation was a slow and laborious process for a large proportion of the dyslexic sample.' The results from mathematics tests can depend on many factors and speed of working will be one of the most influential of these factors for a population that is often slow at processing written information.

Joffe (1980a; 1980b; 1983) provided an excellent overview of the relationship between dyslexia and mathematics. Within these three relatively short papers Joffe provided many observations that create a clearer understanding of difficulties in mathematics. Most notably Joffe drew attention to a deficit in the essential skill of generalising, an observation rarely seen in other research.

Miles (Miles and Miles, 1992) suggests that mathematical difficulties are likely to occur concurrently with language difficulties. Lewis *et al.* (1994) provide data on co-occurrence from a large sample of 9 and 10-year-old pupils. More recently Landerl and Moll (2010) concluded that: 'Comorbidities of learning disorders are not artificial. They are the result of a complex interplay between both general and disorder-specific aetiological factors.'

It has been our combined experience of 50 years of teaching maths to dyslexics that the percentage of co-occurrence is close to 100, though obviously with a range of levels of impact on learning.

One of the key beliefs for interventions for dyslexia is that the teaching and learning are multisensory. However, there is an inclination in maths teaching in UK schools, as compared to, say teaching physics (SC's initial teaching role), to drop experiments and demonstrations in the early years and move to the sole use of symbols and 'talk and chalk'. One of the earliest papers to suggest a multisensory approach to the teaching of mathematics to dyslexics was from Steeves (1979), a pioneer in this field. Steeves advocated the same teaching principles for mathematics as Samuel Orton had suggested for language.

There are many other parallels at many levels between dyslexia and dyscalculia and all that surrounds these specific learning difficulties, for example prevalence, definition, teaching methods, aetiology, perseveration, attitude of academics and governments and so forth.

Prevalence

Perhaps it is not surprising, given that we do not have a clear agreed definition of the problem, that there is a range of figures given for the prevalence of dyscalculia. For example, in the study by Lewis *et al.* (1994) of 1200 children aged 9–12, only 18 were identified as having specific mathematics difficulties in the absence of language difficulties. Lewis *et al.*

did not find any one pattern or reason why this was so. The same distinction is made by Ramaa and Gowramma (2002) in a fascinating study of children in India. Ramaa and Gowramma used both inclusionary and exclusionary criteria to determine the presence of dyscalculia in primary school children. Both experiments suggest that the percentage of children identified as potentially dyscalculic was between 5.5% and 6%. Ramaa and Gowramma also list 13 observations from other researchers about the nature and factors associated with dyscalculia, including persistent reliance on counting procedures and extra stress, anxiety and depression. Sutherland (1988) states that on the basis of his study, few children have specific problems with number alone. Badian (1999) has produced figures for the prevalence of persistent arithmetic, reading or arithmetic and reading disabilities, from a sample of over 1000 children, suggesting that for grades 1–8, 6.9% qualified as low in arithmetic, which included 3.9% low only in arithmetic.

Hein *et al.* (2000) studied samples from rural and urban areas in Germany and found that 6.6% of their third grade sample performed significantly worse in arithmetic than in spelling tests. Shalev *et al.* (2001) working in Israel, have suggested that developmental dyscalculia, taking a discrepancy model, has a significant familial aggregation. They estimate the prevalence of developmental dyscalculia to be between 3% and 6.5% of children in the general school population and conclude that there is a role for genetics in the evolution of this disorder. Inevitably this will raise a mathematical learning disabilities version of the nature/nurture debate. A study which offers a further perspective on the nature/nurture aspect was conducted by Ramaa (2015), who has investigated arithmetic difficulties among socially disadvantaged children and children with dyscalculia.

Desoete *et al.* (2004) found prevalence rates of dyscalculia, from a study of a large sample of pupils in Belgium, that were 2.2% of second graders, 7.7% of third graders and 6.6% of fourth graders.

Reigosa-Crespo *et al.* (2012) take an interesting perspective, looking at what they term as arithmetical dysfluency (AD) alongside developmental dyscalculia (DD). They estimated the prevalence and gender ratio of arithmetical dysfluency and dyscalculia in the same cohort. The estimated prevalence of DD was 3.4%, and the male to female ratio was 4:1. However, the prevalence of AD was almost three times as great (9.35%) and with no gender differences found (the male to female ratio was 1.07:1). They conclude that, based on these contrasting findings, DD, defined as a defective sense of numbers, could be a distinctive disorder that affects only a portion of children with AD. The difference in these findings could also be explained by the restriction of the definition of DD to a defective sense of numbers.

What is mathematics?

Mathematics is not just arithmetic or manipulating numbers. It is possible that a person could be good at some topics in maths and a failure in other topics? Does dyscalculia imply an inability to succeed in all of the many topics that make up mathematics?

In terms of subject content, early maths is primarily about numbers and thus about our number system. Later it becomes more varied, with new topics introduced such as measure, algebra, and shape and space. So the demands of maths can be quite varied. This can be very useful from the perspective of intervention. We believe that intervention for maths difficulties should also include some time doing parts of maths that the learner can do, so that intervention sessions are not all about the things the learner cannot do. It is a problem that number is a disproportionate part of early learning experiences (and of 'everyday' maths). So it seems logical that poor number skills are a key factor in dyscalculia. It also seems logical that we have to consider the match between the demands of the task and the skills of the learner.

In terms of approach, maths can be a written subject or a mental exercise. It can be formulaic or it can be intuitive. It can be learnt and communicated in either way, or in a combination of ways by the learner and it can be taught and communicated in either way or a combination of ways by the teacher. Maths can be concrete and visual, but fairly quickly moves to the abstract and symbolic. It has many rules and a surprising number of inconsistencies, particularly in the early stages. In terms of judgement, feedback and appraisal, maths is unique as a school subject. Work is usually a blunt 'right' or 'wrong' and that judgement is a consequence of the mathematics itself, not of how the teacher chooses to appraise the work.

And one has to ask, 'Why is it such an entrenched part of mathematics culture that it has to be done quickly?'

What is the role of memory?

We often pose the question in lectures: 'What does the learner bring (to maths)?' We have already mentioned some factors such as anxiety. But what about memory? We know that Krutetskii (1976) lists mathematical memory as a requirement to be good at maths. We are certain that short-term and working memory are vital for mental arithmetic, particularly for those sequential, formula based maths thinkers, but can a learner compensate for difficulties in some of these requirements and thus 'succeed' in maths?

However excellent a maths curriculum, it is virtually impossible for it to meet the needs of every learner, for example in the dictated pace of progress. It is certain that a component of the curriculum will be mental arithmetic. This activity needs effective memories, long, short and working. So a learner with poor short-term and working memories could fail maths when it is mental maths, even though he may have the potential to become an effective mathematician. If failure is internalised as a negative attributional style by the learner then that potential may never be realised.

It is possible that Krutetskii's *mathematical memory* draws a parallel with Gardner's (1999) multiple intelligences. Perhaps there are multiple long-term memories. That would explain some of the discrepancies we see in children's memory performances. Like any subject, there is a body of factual information for maths and if a learner can remember and recall this information then he will be greatly advantaged and, if he can't, then failure is likely. Just how much that is the case depends on the curriculum and how it is taught.

So, good memories may be required for doing maths in general. Short-term and working memories may be essential for mental maths and mathematical long-term memory will be very important for the number facts and formulae needed when doing mental arithmetic. Geary considers memory to be a key contributing factor in mathematics learning difficulties (Geary, 2004).

There is an accumulation of evidence in the UK that the teaching of maths is heavily reliant on pupils having good memories, often at the expense of developing understanding. We suspect that this is not unique to the UK.

Counting

The first number test on Butterworth's Dyscalculia Screener (2003) is for subitising. Basically, this means an ability to look at a random cluster of dots and know how many are there, without counting. Most adults can do this at six dots plus or minus one.

A person who has to rely entirely on counting for addition and subtraction is severely handicapped in terms of speed and accuracy. Such a person is even more handicapped when trying to use counting for multiplication and division. Often their page is covered in endless tally marks and often they are just lined up, usually untidily, not grouped as, for example ~~IIII~~, that is, the gate pattern for five. Maths for them is done by counting in steps of one. If you show them patterns of dots or groups, they prefer rows and rows of tallies.

But maths is not just the ability to 'see' and use five. It's the ability to see other chunks, patterns and inter-relationships, for example to see nine as one less than ten, to see $6+5$ as $5+5+1$, to count on in twos, fives and tens, especially if the pattern is not the basic one of 10, 20, 30, 40… but, for example, 13, 23, 33, 43…. It seems to us from our teaching experiences that the ability to work with numbers in chunks is vital for progression.

An over-reliance on counting puts a much greater load on working memory and makes computations much more difficult, especially for mental arithmetic.

It seems to be an assumption that, because a child can count forwards, then they can, with equal facility, count backwards, too. This is not the case for many children and the ability to reverse a procedure extends to other areas of maths, too. For example, we teachers often instruct children to reverse a process in algebra in order to 'solve' an equation. Counting backwards, reversing a procedure requires an effective working memory capacity.

However, at the root of all this is the need for students to progress beyond the 'counting in ones' strategy (Chinn and Ashcroft, 2004).

What distinguishes the dyscalculic learner from the garden-variety poor mathematician?

Stanovich (1991) asked: 'How do we distinguish between a "garden variety" poor reader and a dyslexic?' The equivalent key question to ask for maths is 'How do we distinguish between a "garden variety" poor mathematician and a dyscalculic?' Of course, part of the answer will depend on how dyscalculia is defined. However, in the classroom situation, we would suggest that the answer to this latter question has a lot to do with perseveration of the difficulty in the face of skilled, varied and conventional intervention and the stage in the curriculum at which that intervention is targeted.

This leads to further questions, such as, 'Can you be a good reader and still be a dyslexic? Can you be good at some areas of maths and still be dyscalculic?' Our hypothesis is that the answer to both questions is 'Yes', but that is partly because maths is made up of many topics, some of which make quite different demands (and for both these questions, good and appropriate teaching can make such a difference). It is also to do with this difficulty being a continuum and it is the interaction between a learner's position on that spectrum and the way he is taught that creates the potential to move forwards or backwards along that spectrum of achievement.

The temptation is to return to the thought that problems with numbers are at the core of dyscalculia. And it is numbers that will prevail in real life, when school algebra is just a distant memory. And it is likely that the main problem is in accessing these facts accurately and quickly, usually straight from memory, rather than via inefficient strategies such as counting. There is also the practice among some educators to hold learners at the number stage in the mistaken belief that mastery of number, often judged in terms of mechanical recall of facts and procedures, is an essential prerequisite for success in mathematics.

Not all factors involved in learning difficulties are solely within the cognitive domain and the child. A difficulty may be exacerbated by a bureaucratic decision. For example, some bureaucrats stipulate a level of achievement, often specifying this level precisely, that defines whether or not a child's learning difficulties may be addressed in school or even assessed. This decision may be influenced, at least in part, by economic considerations. But, even then, is a child's dyslexia or dyscalculia defined solely by achievement scores? Is there room to consider the individual and what he brings to the situation? For example, an 11-year-old pupil I assessed in 2015 had been scored on the Number Skills Test of the British Ability Scales as 1 y 10 m behind chronological age when she was nine years old. This did not even come near to quantifying her current difficulties. By the age of 11 years, she was below the 5th percentile in low-stress tests of the four operations. She was in the top 5% of students of her age for maths anxiety. She struggled to repeat four digits forward and reversed under ideal and quiet lab conditions. Her standardised score on a 15-minute maths test (Chinn, 2017a) placed her at the 2.5th percentile. She struggled to match the symbols for the operations with the appropriate vocabulary. She had little understanding of place value.

If we take an assumption that maths learning difficulties are on a normal distribution or even a spectrum, then our view is that it is the severity and the multi-manifestations of contributing difficulties coupled with very limited impact from individualised instruction (which may not always be as skilled as is necessary) that distinguishes a child with dyscalculia from a child with mathematical learning difficulties.

What are the predictors?

We have to keep in mind the fact that children develop at different rates. So when should we have concerns about learning and what signs should we be looking for? A number of researchers have identified potential predictors.

Keeler and Swanson (2001) found that significant predictors of maths achievement are verbal and visuospatial working memory and knowledge of strategies (e.g. clustering or rehearsal) to enhance working memory.

Gersten *et al.* (2005) identify fluency and proficiency with number combinations (also known as basic number facts).

Gathercole and Alloway (2008) found that working memory capacity at age four years can be predictive of low attainment levels in maths. Children in the low working memory group in their study were more than seven times more likely not to reach expected levels in maths 30 months later.

Desoete (2011; 2015) has studied predictive indicators in children in kindergarten. Whilst finding that 87.5% of children at risk for dyscalculia/MLD can be detected, it seemed easier to screen the children who are not at risk. The central executive component of working memory and digit recall were important predictors. Siegler *et al.* (2012) found that primary schoolchildren's knowledge of fractions and division predicted their overall achievement in maths in secondary school five or six years later. Since many of the children with dyscalculia are unlikely to have mastered fractions and division in primary school, this negative prediction is likely to be apposite for them.

Geary's (2013) warning is that: 'Children's quantitative competencies upon entry to school can have lifelong consequences. Children who start behind generally stay behind.' He suggests that explicit direct instruction of core numerical relations may be particularly important. We have to confess that our agreement with this recommendation on direct instruction is wholehearted.

Chan *et al.* (2014) found that for Hong Kong children first graders' place value understanding in the first semester was the strongest predictor of their mathematical achievement at the end of first and second grades.

The first of the three Key Findings of The National Research Council's study on *How People Learn* (Bransford *et al.*, 2000) supports our use of the Buswell and Judd (1925) observation on the first learning experience: 'Students come to the classroom with preconceptions about how the world works. If their initial understanding is not engaged, they may fail to grasp the new concepts and information that are taught, or they may learn them for the purpose of a test, but revert to their preconceptions outside the classroom.'

The message is that predictors matter, but we must not underestimate the power of the first learning experiences to influence later learning.

(Note: There is a special volume of the *Journal of Learning Disabilities*, 38 (4), 2005, dedicated to early identification and intervention for students with difficulties in mathematics.)

What is appropriate teaching?

For many teachers the first reaction to hearing of a child's diagnosis will be, 'So he's dyscalculic, how can I teach him?' We are certain that using the range of methods and strategies we developed and used during our years working with students with dyslexia and mathematical difficulties will also be effective with dyscalculic learners. Indeed we have probably taught many, many learners who have the comorbid problems of dyslexia and dyscalculia. What we address as teachers is the way the learner presents, not a learner defined solely by some stereotypical attributes or, even more summarily, by a label.

The majority of the chapters in this book are about methods for teaching maths to students who have maths learning difficulties and dyscalculia.

A good question to ask is, 'Where do I begin? How far back in maths do I go to start the intervention?' This may be a difference, should we need one, between the dyscalculic and the dyslexic who is also bad at maths. It may be that the starting point for the intervention is further back in the curriculum for the dyscalculic than for the dyslexic. (This is yet another topic needing research.) It may also be that the subsequent rates of progress are different. Kaufmann *et al.* (2003) advocate a numeracy intervention programme that involves both basic numerical knowledge and conceptual knowledge, and suggest that there is a need for explicit teaching of numerical domains that often have been neglected in school mathematics. In other words they are asking, 'How far back do you start to explain mathematics?' The answer is almost always, 'At the beginning.'

And for a final thought in this section, we ask, 'What is the influence of the style of curriculum?' We know, for example, from a European study in which S.C. was involved (Chinn *et al.*, 2001), that the pedagogy behind the maths curriculum certainly affects thinking style in maths for many pupils.

What are the interactions and factors? (See also Chapter 2)

There are many reasons why a child or an adult may fail to learn maths skills and knowledge. For example, a child who finds symbols confusing may have been successful with mental arithmetic, but finds written arithmetic very challenging. There may be other examples of an onset of failure at different times, which will most likely depend on the match between the demands of the curriculum and the skills and deficits of the learner, for example a dyslexic will probably find word problems especially difficult (though good reading skills do not solve many of the issues with word problems). Even a child who is not dyslexic or dyscalculic, but is learning at the concrete level, may find the abstract nature of algebra difficult. A child who is an holistic learner may start to fail in maths if his new teacher uses a sequential and formula-based inchworm teaching style (see Chapter 3). A learner may have a poor mathematical memory and the demands on memory may build to a point where they exceed his capacity. For example, Skemp (1971) commented on rote learning:

> The problem here is that a bright and willing child can memorise so many of the processes of elementary maths so well that it is difficult to distinguish it from learning based on comprehension. Sooner or later, however, this must come to grief, for two reasons. The first is that as maths becomes more advanced and more complex the number of different routines to be memorised imposes an impossible burden on the memory. Second, a routine only works for a limited range of problems.

This quote is not exclusive to dyslexics and dyscalculics. It illustrates the commonality of many of the difficulties across a broad spectrum of learner, but, of course, not the commonality of the severity of these difficulties.

Among the many hypotheses we have generated between us as to why our dyslexic students have such extraordinary difficulty in retaining basic multiplication facts in long-term memory is the powerful influence of the first learning experience. Buswell and Judd (1925) explained how the first experience of learning something new is a dominant entry to the brain, then going further by suggesting that re-learning the information, even to the point of apparent mastery, will only revert to the original erroneous recall. This critical finding, now 90 years old, can be related to recent work on understanding the role of inhibition in learning maths, that suppressing distracting information and unwanted responses plays a critical role in the development of mathematics proficiency (Borst and Houde, 2014; Cragg and Gilmore, 2014).

For many people the perception of maths is that it is a consistent and logical subject. The report, *Key understandings in mathematics learning* (Nunes *et al.*, 2007) states: 'The evidence demonstrates beyond doubt that children must rely on logic to learn mathematics.' The reality is that there are many instances where there are challenges to consistency and logic. Children build beliefs about maths, for example that four is bigger than two. Fractions appear to contradict this belief when ½ is bigger than ¼. Morsanyi and Szucs (2015) note that 'when we reason about belief-inconsistent materials we have to actively inhibit the effect of our beliefs.' In his fascinating book, *Influence: The Psychology of Persuasion*, Cialdini (2007) maintains that the desire for consistency is a central motivator of our behaviour.

What happens in the classroom with learning difficulties will depend on the interactions between the demands of the task, the skills of the teacher, and the skills and attitudes of the learner. Sometimes the interaction is harsh in its impact on the learner, for example if one of the demands of mental arithmetic is that it be done quickly, then any learner who retrieves and processes facts slowly will fail as a consequence of this one factor alone.

However, none of the underlying contributing factors discussed above and in Chapter 2 are truly independent. Anxiety, for example, is a consequence of many influences. Our hypothesis is that the factors mentioned earlier in this chapter and in the next chapter are the key ones. There may well be others and the pattern and interactions will vary from individual to individual, and possibly even from day to day in that individual, but these are what we consider to be the difficulties at the core of dyscalculia and mathematical learning difficulties.

The Nature of Mathematics and the Ways it is Taught

In order to teach successfully, you need a knowledge of the learner and a knowledge of the subject. You may not need to be a degree level mathematician, but to teach mathematics effectively, even at its earliest stages, you must have a deep understanding of the nature of mathematics and its progression beyond the immediate topics being taught and an ability to communicate that understanding. Mathematics is a subject that builds on previous knowledge to extend knowledge. We are convinced of the need for teachers to be flexible and responsive in their ways of teaching and doing maths and to recognise and accept this flexibility in their pupils, too. Teaching is a hugely complex skill. At its best it is an art.

Number and arithmetic are the first experience of mathematics for most children and are the areas of mathematics most people use in later life. Early experience of success or failure at this stage sets the scene for later, both academically and emotionally (Geary, 1990; 1994; Desoete and Stock, 2011). Some learners learn competence in limited areas of arithmetic, for example they are comfortable with addition, but cannot carry out subtractions. Indeed SC's recent research (Chinn, 2012) has suggested that addition is the default operation for many learners. The developmental nature of maths is key to success and failure for learners. Any gaps in the precursors for new topics will make learning unsuccessful.

As a strategy to address this issue of pre-requisite knowledge, there is currently in the UK a keen interest in 'mastery'. Whilst much depends on the interpretation of this approach, there is always a danger that a new pedagogy for teaching can be over-applied. What can create significant problems for many learners are programmes that require mastery before progression (e.g. Kumon mathematics), because mastery, especially of rote learning tasks, and even more especially under the pressure of working quickly, is, despite its name, a transient stage for many dyslexics. There is no doubt that the developmental nature of maths makes it essential for children to understand each new concept as they build their knowledge of maths. However, we have to be careful about what has to be 'mastered' and whether that involves understanding as well as recall, and how that will be used to dictate subsequent progress.

In terms of subject content, early maths is primarily numbers. Much of the work on dyscalculia has focused on very early number sense, 'approximate number sense' (ANS), for example Landerl *et al.* (2004). Later, maths becomes more varied, with new topics introduced such as measure, data and spatial topics. Up to GCSE (the national examination in England for children aged 16 years), despite the different topic headings, the major component remains as number. So although the demands of maths can be quite broad, which can be very useful for many learners, number can remain a disproportionate part of early learning experiences.

Numbers can be exciting, challenging tools (McLeish, 1991), or the cause of great anxiety (Ashcraft *et al.*, 2007; Chinn, 2009; Devine *et al.*, 2012; Lyons and Beilock, 2012). Mathematics is a sequential, interrelating subject, building on early skills and knowledge to take the student on to new skills and knowledge whilst reflecting on previous learning. It is a subject of organisation and patterns (Ashcroft and Chinn, 2004), of abstract ideas and concepts. Gaps in the early stages of understanding can only handicap the learner in later stages, for example in the speed of processing number problems.

Mathematics is a subject where the child learns the parts; the parts build on each other to make a whole; knowing the whole enables the learner to reflect with more understanding on the parts; that in turn strengthens the whole. Knowing the whole also enables one to understand the sequences and interactions of the parts and the way they support each other, so that the getting there clarifies the stages of the journey. Teachers are (usually) in the fortunate position of being conversant with the subject and can bring to their work knowledge and experience beyond the topic they are teaching. The learner is rarely in this position and thus is vulnerable to assumptions about his levels of knowledge and experience, often made unconsciously by the teacher or based on the child's fluency in reciting maths facts and procedures.

It is important that the learner develops a clear, broad and flexible understanding of number and processes at each stage, that he begins to see the interrelationships, patterns, generalisations and concepts clearly and without anxiety. To teach a child to attain this understanding of mathematics requires in teachers a deep understanding of mathematics and numbers to a level where their communication is effective with children of a wide range of abilities. They also need to understand where mathematics is going beyond the level at which they teach, as well as where it has come from, so that what they teach is of benefit to the child at the time and helps, not hinders, him later on as his mathematics develops. Teachers need to be mindful of what is coming after what they have taught, because the development of a concept starts long before it is addressed directly. There is a vital role for teacher training here and that role will depend on how it is defined and executed. We would wish to see significant elements on the manifestations and consequences of difficulties in learning maths in all initial teacher training.

To illustrate the point of where a topic is rooted and where it is leading, consider the strategy advocated in this book for teaching the nine times table (see Chapter 6). The method uses previous information (the ten times table), subtraction, estimation, refinement of the estimation and patterns. Although a child may not need to realise that he is doing all these things when he learns how to use a strategy to work out 6 × 9, the processes are being used, concepts are being introduced and foundations are being laid. We agree with Madsen *et al.* (1995) that instruction should be conceptually oriented. Two key observations from a 2008 Ofsted Report (Ofsted are the official inspectors of schools in England) were, 'Their (the pupils) recall of knowledge and techniques was stronger than their understanding.... The pupils' view that mathematics is about having correct written answers rather than about being able to do the work independently, or understand the method, is holding back pupils' progress.' These are from observations of mainstream students. Many of the problems of maths are not exclusive to dyslexic and dyscalculic students.

A second illustration of the influence of early ideas involves a subtraction such as:

$$\begin{array}{r} 93 \\ -\underline{47} \end{array}$$

A frequent error is the answer 54, which occurs when the child subtracts 3 from 7. This is an easier process than the correct one, but can also be the consequence of earlier subtraction experience where the child is told to: 'Take the smaller number from the larger number.' Dyslexics have a tendency to take instructions literally and feel safer when procedures are consistent. There is also (again) the problem that a first learning experience is often a dominant learning experience (Buswell and Judd, 1925), which means that the consequences of that experience being incorrect are very detrimental.

Rawson (1984) said of teaching English to dyslexics, 'Teach the language as it is to the child as he is.' Chasty (1989) said, 'If the child does not learn the way you teach, then you must teach the way he learns.' This advice is apposite for teaching mathematics to all children, but most especially to those with maths learning difficulties. One of the attributes of an effective teacher is the ability to communicate clearly. This is usually a consequence of knowing the child, usually enhanced by listening to the child, and presenting work in a way that pre-empts as many of the potential difficulties as is possible. Thus, the teacher needs to understand the way each child learns and fails to learn, though the different ways individuals learn can be frustrating in that a lesson which works superbly with one child may not work at all with another (see Chapter 2). This combined understanding of the child and all his strengths, weaknesses and potentials plus a knowledge of the nature, structure and concepts of mathematics will help to pre-empt many of the potential learning problems. It can often sustain the child whilst at the lowest stage of school intervention.

We believe that there are certain key concepts in the maths taught to most children up to the age of 16 years and that these concepts reappear regularly to be developed throughout a child's progression through his school years. The benefit of this is that the child may strengthen that concept as each new manifestation appears. The drawback is that the child may never develop the concept if he has not generalised and internalised all or even some of the preceding experiences. It is a vital part of the teacher's role to ensure that as many children as possible develop a sound understanding of these concepts, rather than a rote learned regurgitation of a mass of unconnected memories.

Finally, it should be remembered that an insecure learner values consistency. This characteristic is linked to automaticity, in that automaticity allows the brain to devote more capacity to what is different or an extension of what is known. Consistency will also reduce anxiety.

2

Factors that may Contribute to Learning Difficulties in Mathematics

Different children bring different combinations of strengths and weaknesses to mathematics. These will interact with each other, the mathematical topic and the learning situation to create different levels of success and failure, probably with different impact on different maths topics. As Zhou and Cheng (2015) note: 'Mathematical competence is a constellation of abilities which might have different origins. Disabilities in mathematics would be diagnosed with different screening measures and successfully intervened by using different approaches.'

Chinn (1995a; 1995b) has conducted studies on error patterns, speed of working, basic fact knowledge, cognitive style, auditory sequential memory and IQ, and has extended this to studies on children from two other European countries, with Dutch and Irish colleagues (Chinn *et al.*, 2001). Bryant *et al.* (2000) list 33 characteristic behaviours of students with LD who have teacher identified maths weaknesses.

It is worth noting that maths learning difficulties are an international issue, for example Faber (2014), no matter what the PISA ranking of the country. It is a consequence of the normal distribution. The average scores may differ from country to country, but the tail remains a tail.

The deficits and difficulties interrelate and combine to form a large part of the picture of what the child brings to the problem. Each deficit may make a different contribution to the overall problem and the contribution may affect the situation at different times and in different maths situations, so, for example, reading may not be a major problem until the child reaches word problems. Interactions between factors are also varied and influential. As a consequence there is an enormous individuality among

Mathematics for Dyslexics and Dyscalculics: A Teaching Handbook, Fourth Edition.
Steve Chinn and Richard E. Ashcroft.

dyslexic and dyscalculic children, a fact that most specialist teachers readily recognise. Comorbid conditions such as ADHD (Marshall *et al.*, 1999) and, we suspect, particularly dyspraxia (Yeo, 2003), will complicate the situation even more. A knowledge of the deficits and difficulties and, of course the strengths, provides a general background which you, the teacher must have firmly fixed in mind as you individualise your approach to each child or as you work with a group. Empathy is a key characteristic of an effective teacher.

Potential Areas of Difficulty in Learning Mathematics

There are many factors that might contribute to a child's failure to master mathematics. Some of these are within the child, for example a poor working memory. Some are a consequence of the maths, for example any inconsistency in the patterns a child seeks to support his learning. Some are interactions of two or more factors.

Directional confusion

The issue of consistency arises here, for example we learn to count and then write the numbers 1–10 from left (smallest value) to right (biggest value) but we write multi-digit numbers such as 45, 291 with the largest (value) digit on the left and the smallest to the right. Traditionally we carry out written computations of addition, subtraction and multiplication from left to right with the answer appearing at the bottom, and division from right to left with the answer appearing at the top.

Dyslexic learners often rely on the consistency of work. Changes which seem irrational to the learner will confuse as, for example with the 'teen' numbers, where the syllable used to represent the 'ten' comes after the word used to represent the 'ones'. Thirteen will illustrate this. The 'teen' syllable infers a ten and the 'thir' infers three. The order infers 31 when compared to the words used for the other decades, for example 'sixty four' (six tens and four) is written as 64. The use of patterns and generalisations, whilst dealing with inconsistencies, will support weak memories. Whilst such problems may be addressed in isolation, there is always the possibility that they will re-appear when the child is dual tasking, such as adding two digits in the process of carrying out a three-digit plus three-digit computation.

This situation is further illustrated in the four operations. In the procedure for addition it does not affect the answer whether the top number is added to the bottom number or vice versa. Although it is normal practice to add from right to left, if the sum does not involve 'carrying' and the child adds from left to right the answer will still be correct, as in example A. (Indeed some children scan the sum to see if this is the situation and then add left to right.)

A 362
+431

This will not work as well, although I have seen learners do this successfully, with 'carry backwards', as in examples such as B.

B 578
+266

'500 plus 200 is 700. 70 plus 60 is 130. Add this to 700 to get a running total of 830. 8 plus 6 is 14. Add this to 830 to achieve the answer 844.'

Subtractions are less open to flexibility, partly because subtraction facts are not commutative. It now matters which number is taken from which, but the normal practice for subtraction of starting from the right (ones) column is not necessary if there is no renaming required, as in example C.

C 875
−562

'8 take away 5 is 3. 7 take away 6 is 1. 5 take away 2 is 3. The answer is 313.'

This operation is also susceptible to early experience where it is tempting to describe subtraction as 'taking the little number from the big number' creating problems with examples such as D.

D 643
−276

'6 take away 3 is 3. 7 take away 4 is 3. 6 take away 2 is 4. The answer takes the three digits and reverses the order, to give an incorrect answer of 433.'

An example of the interactions of factors was provided by a learner who found difficulty with decimals. From his perception it seemed illogical that, using the decimal point as a focus, the place values to the left are ones, tens, hundreds, thousands, and so on, increasing by a factor of ten each time, whereas to the right of the decimal point the place values are tenths, hundredths, thousandths and so on, deceasing by a factor of ten each time.

He perceived an inconsistency in the absence of oneths. There are implications here for concept, direction and language. The sounds, for example, of 'tens' and 'tenths' and 'thousand' and 'thousandths' are very similar and thus easily confused. There are mathematical implications, too, in the frequent tendency to focus on the decimal point when manipulating decimal numbers.

Whilst addition and multiplication fact squares have many benefits, they do make directional demands (which may be alleviated by the use of an L-shaped piece of card).

Some learners find the directional demands of negative co-ordinates (e.g. (−3, −7)) significantly harder to master than positive co-ordinates. This is the first example we have used to illustrate an interesting and challenging characteristic of many dyslexic and dyscalculic learners doing maths, that is, the surprising impact of what may be perceived as a minor change in difficulty by a teacher could be a major difficulty for the child.

Sequencing problems

There are many sequences in mathematics. Indeed the numbers 1–9 are the first experience of a maths sequence for most children. Being able to recognise and remember sequences is a useful skill. Children often manage safe, familiar sequences such as 10, 20, 30, 40, but fail to recognise a variation such as 12, 22, 32, 42. Such automatic extension and/or transfer of knowledge cannot be assumed. They may recite 2, 4, 6, 8, readily but be more hesitant with 1, 3, 5, 7, 9.

Place value, one of the most important concepts in maths, demands the ability to sequence according to set rules. Young children learning to count to ten are unlikely to understand the underlying implication of writing the digits 1 and 0 as 10 to represent 'ten'.

Some children find one-to-one correspondence difficult when counting and have to rely on strategies such as touching the nose with one finger while touching the objects to be counted with the other hand. The ability to master one-to-one correspondence is fundamental to the development of maths skills.

Many of the sequences of maths are not automatised by dyslexic learners as demonstrated in an interesting exercise (Fawcett and Nicholson, 1999) where dyslexics could balance successfully on one foot, but lost their balance when asked to count backwards from one hundred at the same time, that is, to dual task. It is not uncommon to find children for whom counting backwards is difficult, raising issues around any change to the demands of a task. It may be assumed by a teacher that counting back is as easy a task as counting forwards, but for some learners the difference in difficulty is huge. It is easy to underestimate the impact of a modification to a task for a dyslexic learner. Gray and Tall (1994) noted that the cognitive complexity of counting back is enormous.

For example, one of the exercises in a recent curriculum variation for England was to count forwards in 5 s to a target number, which would be quite a difficult task in itself for many dyslexics, but then the curriculum required the child to count backwards in 5 s. It may seem that these two tasks are of almost equivalent difficulty, but the counting backward task is very much harder and may result in the child withdrawing from the task. Indeed the reversal of any sequence may be very challenging for children with maths learning difficulties. In the new (DfE, 2013) programme of study for children in England they were expected to count to and across 100, forwards and backwards. They also faced missing number problems such as $7 = ? - 9$, where the 'normal' sequence is changed. This is not to say that these objectives should be avoided for children with learning difficulties, but that any unrealistic expectations on how easily these will be learned should be made realistic and extra input provided.

There may also be a difficulty in remembering the sequence of steps to follow for algorithms, particularly long division, which may be in part due to the difficulty for children in trying to build some understanding to support their recall of this particular procedure (see Chapter 10).

A sub-skill for developing an understanding of place value is the ability to sequence numbers. The English language is not as supportive as we may assume, as already mentioned with the teen numbers. With bigger numbers, too, there can be problems, as illustrated by the not uncommon error, where a pupil writes 600300050 for six hundred and three thousand and fifty or by the less common, but equally logical answer of 3650. Ho and Cheng (1997) have shown that training in place value can improve children's addition skills, which is another example of taking intervention back to an early stage in the curriculum for learning maths.

The understanding of a sequence is often related to the ability to generalise, see patterns, and sometimes to recognise and discount irrelevant information. It is one of the many decisions that teachers have to make to decide when and which materials and visual images support the understanding and recognition of sequences.

Visual difficulties

These may include perceptual difficulties, for example the learner may confuse +, ÷ and × (especially if written carelessly) or 6 and 9 or 3 and 5 or x2 and x^2 or the learner may just not see a decimal point in a number.

The presentation style of a worksheet or exercise can be confusing and even overwhelming, especially if items are written too closely together, where the interaction between short-term memory difficulties and spatial tracking of the place on the page may cause the student to copy information inaccurately. Some form of separation, for example lining off or highlighting, will help reduce this aspect of visual confusion. Sometimes a coloured overlay (available from Crossbow Education, see Appendix 2) can help to change the black/white contrast of normal worksheets, handouts and books, and help the student to maintain a more focused image of the page. Sometimes it helps if a card can be used as a cover of irrelevant information to help pinpoint the helpful information. This has the added benefit of screening off some of the text, helping to make the task look less daunting. The process of copying from a board to an exercise book may be even more problematic, since screening off information is less available and the time lag involved in moving from looking up at a board then back down onto a desk is longer. There is a strong argument for any text written in quantity on a board to be written using different colours to separate different lines or sections.

Whilst some text books overwhelm the user with the density of the text presented on a page, some more modern books, in an attempt to look more appealing to the student, use a layout that is too busy or one where it is difficult for the reader to track through the information in the correct order. This will also create problems in using assistive technology. This problem is also particularly true of many computer programmes for maths, where the temptation to use every visual known to the programmer is just too strong. The result is a blur of images that distract focus from the necessary maths message.

The pressure of having to work quickly in maths may exacerbate the problems of visual discrimination and students may fail to notice that the operation symbol has changed in the work they are doing, for example from + to ×, and consequently they perseverate with addition. Lining off or highlighting different sections of a worksheet may help prevent this problem. One of the reasons for doing this is that you, the teacher, do actually test/evaluate what you are intending to test/evaluate.

The selection of appropriate worksheets and textbooks is vitally important for a dyslexic student. These materials tend to be used independently by the student. An older student may not wish to draw attention to himself in class by constantly asking for help with accessing the text, so the text should be critically appraised by the teacher to ensure it is at a level commensurate with the reading ability of the pupil.

Spatial awareness

Spatial awareness can be considered as being closely linked to visual difficulties and sequencing. Spatial awareness is needed for work such as geometry, place value, algebra (distinguishing between 2x, ×2 and x^2, for example, where it could also be classed as problems with visual discrimination). Questions such as $2x(x^2+2)$ can be a real challenge as the location in space of each 2 in this expression is very significant in terms of its mathematical meaning.

The student may not be able to relate two-dimensional drawings to the three-dimensional shape they represent. He may not be able to track across graph paper for co-ordinates and this may be particularly noticeable in negative co-ordinates (e.g. (−3, −7)), when the direction of the tracking changes. The same problem may be true for information presented in the form of a timetable. Teachers should look for a pattern in difficulties in these areas as the child himself may not be aware that he has problems.

Spatial awareness also affects organisation of work on paper so that what seems straightforward may in fact be a very demanding task. For example, the computation:

$$\begin{array}{r} 11 \\ 638 \\ \underline{+794} \\ 1432 \end{array}$$

needs to have the digits lined up correctly according to their place value, the 'carry' numbers in the right place (and remembered) and the relevant numbers have to be added together.

It may be that (appropriately sized to the child's individual needs) squared paper or vertically lined paper helps to address this issue.

Short-term and working memory

An awareness of the impact of working memory on the ability to succeed in maths has grown quite dramatically since the first edition of this book, for example Ashcraft and Krause (2007), Gathercole and Alloway (2008) and Hoffman (2010).

Poor short-term and working memory can create several areas of difficulty and have a strong influence on how a learner processes numbers. Deficits in short-term memory and working memory combine with long-term memory deficits to create significant difficulties for learners. For example, a child trying to add 47 and 78 mentally has to hold the numbers in his memory, probably work out 7+8 (poor long-term and retrieval memory for basic facts means he may well have to count on, thus increasing the time the original sum has to be held in memory), remember 5, carry 1, remember that he has to add 4 and 7 (and the carried 1), work out 7+4+1, recall the 5 and put them all together in the right (reverse) sequence as 125. There is a belief among too many people who influence the structure and style of maths curricula that mental arithmetic is 'good' for children. Indeed, not so long ago, in England it was a requirement that maths lessons in junior schools start with ten minutes of mental arithmetic. Unless this activity is carefully differentiated it will not be a motivating experience for some learners.

Short-term memory difficulties may even prevent a learner from starting a problem (see also anxiety, stress and self-image). He may simply forget some or most of the teacher's instructions, especially if distracted in some way. Short-term memory does not store information. If the child forgets what he has been told he has no way of retrieving that information other than asking a fellow pupil, or the teacher. The situation will be exacerbated if dual tasking is involved, for example any of the many distractions that can be experienced in a classroom.

If a learner's short-term memory is overloaded, he may be so confused as to have no clues as to where to start. The learner may not be able to 'hold' the visual image of the question he is trying to solve. He may not be able to hold the question in auditory memory while he searches for a necessary number fact. (Indeed the working out of that fact, say 9+6 by counting on, may overload the memory and leave him not remembering the initial question). It is not uncommon to see children sub-vocalising the information in order to help retain it. Often sub-vocalising is an indication that the child is concentrating on the task.

A poor short-term memory is detrimental to the task of copying information from a board or a screen. A child may only be able to copy a few digits or letters at one time. This will make copying slow, but can also make it inaccurate in that the child has to constantly return to the appropriate point to pick up the next information to copy.

Short-term memory may also handicap the interpretation of a series. For example, if the series has five items before repetition as in abcdeabcde-abcdeab… and the child analyses within his (low) short-term memory capacity of three items, he gets abc, dea, bcd, efa… and thus not see the sequence. A similar problem for this child would occur with numbers over three digits.

Short-term memory obviously creates a problem with mental computations, but it also impacts on written work, causing the learner to use extra notations, such as tally marks, which may lead to confusion and will certainly lead to slower work. Ackerman *et al.* (1986) make an interesting speculation on differential achievement in reading and arithmetic, observing that the child's acquisition of reading is monitored more closely (by adults) than the acquisition of number facts. The child reads aloud and the teacher corrects him on the spot when he falters compared to more independent practice in arithmetic. (See also Buswell and Judd's observations on the influence of the first learning experience, page 16.)

Whilst a poor short-term memory may prevent a child from starting a task, a poor working memory will stop him executing it. There is now an increasing body of evidence as to the critical role working memory plays in learning maths. The problems can be as basic as in place-keeping whilst counting or task abandonment (Gathercole and Alloway, 2008).

Gathercole and Alloway found that teachers view children with low working memory as being poor at monitoring the quality of their work and making careless errors. They suggest that a likely cause of these behaviours is that children forget crucial information part way through a task and fail to remember how far they have progressed with the task.

In a classic example of the interactions between the factors that impact on learning maths, Ashcraft *et al.* (1998) have shown that anxiety adversely affects working memory used for mathematics tasks, and more recently (Ashcraft and Krause, 2007) have confirmed that it compromises the functioning of working memory.

Long-term memory

Rote learning as a means of loading information such as spellings, times table facts or algorithms into long-term memory is often ineffective with dyslexics (Pritchard *et al.*, 1989; Chinn, 1994; 2003) though teachers still persist in trying, often under 'back to basics' pressure. The 2013 maths programme for England had the expectation that: 'By the end of year 4, pupils should have memorised their multiplication tables up to and including the 12 multiplication table and show precision and fluency in their work.'

However, multisensory methods can make significant improvements. Parents are often encouraged to use ingenious methods to teach their children, such as convoluted mnemonics (McDougal, 1990), or presenting multiplication facts tables as songs or as raps, with varying degrees of success. The reality is that many dyslexics (and many other learners if S.C. is to believe the many hundreds of teachers who have answered his question, 'How many pupils at age ten years have learned all the times table facts?') have significant difficulties learning basic facts such as times tables (Pritchard *et al.*, 1989; Chinn, 1995a; 2003). Geary (2004) suggests that a retrieval deficit resistant to instructional intervention might be a useful diagnostic indicator of arithmetical forms of maths learning difficulties. This problem of poor retrieval of basic facts is particularly frustrating for parents (and many teachers) who encourage the child to practise until he achieves mastery one day, only to find that the child has forgotten again soon after, often by the next day. If this issue is not recognised and actively acknowledged by educators then many children will be demotivated and condemned to failure in maths.

Poor long-term memory may also handicap other areas of mathematics, such as recall of algorithms/formulae and mathematics vocabulary. At university level, an ex-student, extremely dyslexic, who went on to achieve a degree in mathematics had problems remembering the names of formulae even though he could easily manipulate and use them mathematically.

Geary (2004) recognises the important role that memory plays in maths learning difficulties, noting that children who have lower than expected maths achievement scores over successive academic years often have some form of memory or cognitive deficit, and that a diagnosis of mathematics learning difficulty is often warranted.

As an illustration of a memory difficulty in relation to a possible circumvention, in a 1994 pilot study, Chinn presented basic addition facts (e.g. $4+7$, $6+5$) at four-second and twelve- second intervals, using a tape recorder and working with 11–13-year-old learners in mainstream and specialist dyslexia schools. Dyslexic learners scored much lower on average than their mainstream counterparts on the four-second (instant recall) tasks for both addition and multiplication facts. For addition, given twelve seconds, the dyslexic learners could use strategies (even that most basic of strategies, finger counting, is effective in twelve seconds for addition) to score almost on a par with the mainstream learners. However, this was not the case for the times table facts, where there seemed to be less availability of appropriate strategies. For example, finger counting, when used for facts such as 8×7, is not effective. This deficit will affect accuracy and speed in so many areas of mathematics.

Chinn and Kay (2003) conducted a classroom study on errors in recall of multiplication facts and found that the more errors a student made, the more likely his errors were to be inconsistent, that is, not the same type of error for each mistake. The hypothesis is that when information has no meaning for the learner then his recall will have no patterns and no rationale, even for his errors.

In their book, *How People Learn*, based on the findings of a two-year study for the National Research Council (USA), Bransford *et al.* (2000) give three key findings. The second of these is pertinent in this section:

To develop competence in an area of enquiry, students must:

a. have a deep foundation of factual knowledge,
b. understand facts and ideas in the context of a conceptual framework, and
c. organise knowledge in ways that facilitate retrieval and application.

Whilst this finding specifies the need for a deep foundation of factual knowledge, it mediates this by placing it in the context of understanding facts and organising knowledge to facilitate retrieval. It is this mediation that is so important for dyslexic and dyscalculic learners. It allows them ways to access information that may not be directly retrievable from long-term memory. It is one of the foundations for the pedagogy outlined in this book.

Speed of working

Many of the factors described in this section, such as speed of writing, affect the speed of work in mathematics, and speed of working is often an issue in mathematics. For example, the Kumon mathematics scheme looks for 'demanding but realistic standards for speed and accuracy', times table practice books often define success on the basis of completing an exercise in quick time and mental arithmetic often has to be carried out at (an arbitrary) speed. Speed of working is a classic example of the interaction between a characteristic of the learner and an unnecessary, yet firmly established requirement of the subject.

Chinn (1995b) compared the average time to stop work on 21 basic numeracy questions for a mainstream school population and a specialist dyslexia school population. The results of this pilot study showed that, on average, dyslexic learners took 50% longer to complete or to stop attempting the task.

Ackerman and Dykman (1996) suggest that slowness impedes automatisation in reading, spelling and arithmetic.

For the tests of mental arithmetic, given to all pupils aged 11 years in the UK in 2014 and 2015, the administrators did not allow extra time for each item on the basis that a 25% increase in time normally allocated to pupils with dyslexia for examinations changes, for example, 10 seconds to 12.5 seconds and this difference is not considered to be of any practical value to the pupil. There is a temptation to write a short dissertation on the logic of that situation.

The issue of speed is a good example of interacting and indeed cyclic factors. The demand for speed can induce anxiety, and this can reduce the effectiveness of working memory (Ashcraft *et al.*, 1998) and reduced memory impacts on accuracy and speed of working.

Hunt *et al.* (2014) found that maths anxiety was a significant predictor of response time to both carry and no-carry addition problems and was related to a higher error rate on carry problems.

Ackerman *et al.* (1986) drew attention to a contrary effect of speed of working, '… standardised arithmetic tests may fail to reveal automatisation failure in younger school children because of over generous time limits.' Although it is our experience that often the pressure of working quickly for tests depresses performance.

Many of the dyslexic students we have worked with over some 25 years were slow processors of mathematical work. This has many implications, including, for example, the potential for a misdiagnosis on the Dyscalculia Screener (Butterworth, 2003) where there is encouragement to 'work faster'. And the new (2013) maths curriculum for English primary children has within its aims, 'the ability to recall and apply knowledge *rapidly* and accurately.'

The vocabulary and language of mathematics

Mathematics has its own vocabulary and language, and it has 'word problems' (Grauberg, 1998; Leong and Jerred, 2001; Kibel, 2004; E. Miles, 2004; Molina, 2012; Donlan, 2015; Jitendra, 2015). Much of its vocabulary is shared with non-mathematical applications (Morgan, 1999; Chinn, 2004), for example 'operation' can be ÷, −, × or + in maths or, in everyday language, take place in a hospital. The semantics and language of mathematics can be very peculiar to maths and, in children's minds, totally divorced from the language or realities of everyday life (Boaler, 2015): 'Students come to know this about maths class, they know they are entering a realm in which common-sense and real world knowledge are not needed.'

This brings further problems for the dyslexic, whose language skills may be weak. To complicate the issue even further, mathematics has its own collection of symbols, which are vital to an understanding of mathematics. 'It is largely by the use of symbols that we achieve voluntary control over our thoughts' (Skemp, 1971).

In addition to having to master the subtle differences in the appearance of three of the key symbols in early number work, +, ×, ÷, the same symbol has different names, for example + can be read as 'add, more, plus, positive, and' (Henderson, 1989; Chinn 2017b). Perhaps, because the use of addition and all of the four operations is a common and everyday activity they have acquired a varied and inconsistent vocabulary, which is also an issue with much of early number work including, for example, the teen numbers. This situation is exacerbated by the compilers of word problems manipulating the semantics of a word problem so that the operation required to solve the problem is the opposite of the key word built into the problem.

Even when the vocabulary is not inconsistent or misleading, apparent mastery can create an illusion of learning. The ability of a young child to count from one to ten does not mean that he understands the quantities associated with each number, nor that he understands the place value structure of the two digits 10. Yet: 'Mastery of the spoken number sequence provides a foundation for the development of notational understanding, and thereby establishes the necessary foundation for the development of arithmetic skills' (Donlan, 2015).

It is problematic that this confusing choice of vocabulary is most apparent in early numeracy, the area of mathematics the child meets first. It is particularly apparent in the vocabulary used for time (Chinn, 2001). The need for consistency is again threatened. 'Language is the key to learning' (Rothman and Cohen, 1989). Later in mathematics, the language becomes more mathematically specific, for example 'parabola', although education has given new meaning to differentiation and integration. Not even calculus is safe from the jargon vendors.

Another example of the dual use of vocabulary, which must create bewilderment for many children, is to describe a runner as being third in a race and then to use third for the fraction ⅓.

The vocabulary used by teachers to explain a topic is critical and may give rise to different aspects of a concept. For example, 'six eights' is a statement that does not convey its mathematical meaning, whereas, 'six lots of eight' has more meaning, but still does not completely convey the maths. Many children must see, 'simplify 6/8' and wish it was simple.

The vocabulary of word problems beyond the maths terms can also create difficulties. For example, the choice of the words 'pens' or 'apples' or 'Jim' are accessible, whereas 'digestive biscuits' or 'Nathaniel' are less so. The overall variability of vocabulary facing students as they tackle word problems makes it difficult for a teacher to pre-empt all possibilities. If only questions and problems were designed to test the maths they were intending to test.

A child needs to be able to read a problem with accuracy, speed and comprehension. He also needs to be sufficiently sophisticated in his skills to be able to adjust his style of reading to the task in hand. The wording for mathematics problems tends to be precise, rarely truly related to everyday life and sometimes deliberately confusing. All this requires accurate reading and interpretation. In addition to these problems, a child who misses key words or small words such as 'not' will be greatly disadvantaged.

In an interesting study by Smith (1996), the dyslexic learners' error rate compared to controls on word problems revealed that even subtle changes had an effect. For example, the error rate was much greater for the question, 'How many is 6 less than 28?' than for, 'What is 7 more than 32?' A possible reason for this is the greater importance of the sequence of numbers in the subtraction question than in the addition question.

Harries and Sutherland (1999) carried out an international comparison of primary school textbooks. Their observations focus more on the ways that the structure of numeracy is developed in books from different countries than the design, layout and language, but they do make the interesting observation that the use of colour in the UK and the USA is more for decorative purposes than for instructional gains.

It seems obvious that the vocabulary of worksheets and textbooks should not be a barrier to the mathematics content.

Siegel and Fonzi (1995) looked at the diversity of reading tasks in a secondary setting, emphasising its contribution to the learning environment. A child who has difficulties with reading will be disadvantaged, perhaps more than we might think in a subject that is usually considered to be less intensive in its use of words. However, the semantic structure of mathematics questions can be a long way from everyday English. Rothman and Cohen (1989) discuss the importance of teaching the vocabulary and language of mathematics. Molina (2012) provides a comprehensive analysis of the role of language in maths.

Fuchs and Fuchs (2002) looked at the performance of students with just maths disabilities, students with comorbid maths and reading disabilities and controls, when faced with word problems at three levels of increasing complexity. (The paper is also a useful source of references for research into word problems.) The lowest level of difficulty was for arithmetic story problems, which were one-step story problems that involved minuends of nine or less. The students were provided with a box of pennies (one unit coins) and instructed to use whatever strategy would get the right answer. The next level was the complex story problems, based on the problems taught in the third grade curriculum. These involved shopping list problems and pictograph problems. The answers were scored on the basis of accurate computations and problem-solving skills, such as identifying the relevant information. These questions included one to three-step operations. The third level was real-world problem solving, based on the third-grade skills which teachers identified as essential. Students were presented with tabular and graphic information and then answered questions that involved selecting relevant information and using ten essential problem-solving skills. Again, these took one to three-step operations to solve.

Not surprisingly the scores decreased from level 1 to level 3 problems. What is interesting is the comparison of the scores for the three categories of students. For the students with maths difficulties only, the scores for level 1 were 75%, level 2, 14% and level 3, 12%. For the students with comorbid maths and reading difficulties the figures were, respectively 55%, 8% and 5%. For the typical students, the scores at level 2 were 30% and level 3, 19%. None of the groups showed great success with more complex word problems, which we suspect on the basis of lecturing for teachers around the world, is an international problem, but the combination of maths disability with reading disability has a highly detrimental effect on problem-solving skills, even though the problems were read to students.

There are a number of strategies that can be taught to improve performance in word problems, including learning how to rephrase a question, learning how to illustrate the problem, using the Singapore Model Method (Kho *et al.*, 2009) or using one of the multi-read strategies, such as: read through to overview, read through to identify relevant and irrelevant information, read through to understand what is being asked, identify the operation(s), solve and read through to check if the answer obtained makes sense in the original question. Students may benefit from an awareness of the role of inhibition and meta-cognition in solving word problems. For example, Borst and Houde (2014) use the problem, 'Bill has 20 marbles. He has 5 more marbles than John. How many marbles does John have?' to illustrate the role of inhibition of 'more than' meaning addition, but in this problem the operation is subtraction. The student has to think about the problem and be able to think about that thinking. Problem-solving skills require reflection and time in contrast with the culture of quick work for much of the previous maths students have met. Students need to be encouraged to make this adjustment.

Sharma (1985) advocates the use of a reverse 'translation', that is the learner translates a number statement into a word problem as well as vice versa. We have found this a very effective technique, particularly when structured to show how problems of increasing complexity can be written (Chinn, 2017b).

Finally, Bryant *et al.* (2000) have produced a list of 33 characteristic behaviours of students with learning difficulties who have teacher-identified maths weaknesses, for example, 'Takes a long time to complete calculations' comparing the frequency of occurrence in the study group with LD pupils without maths difficulties. Not too surprisingly, the top three difficulties were, 'Difficulty with word problems. Difficulty with multi-step problems. Difficulties with the language of maths.'

Cognitive style or thinking style (see Chapter 3)

The child's cognitive style or thinking style, the way he works out a problem, is significantly influenced by the factors above. To be a successful mathematician a child needs to be flexible in his cognitive style (Krutetskii, 1976), but this goal may not be achieved because of the child's learning experiences, which in turn may be controlled by the style of the maths curriculum (Chinn *et al.*, 2001). If a learner's cognitive style is inflexibly set at one extreme he is at risk of failure. There is an additional problem if the teacher's style is also inflexible and unresponsive to the learner's style. For example, marks awarded for different problem-solving styles may vary from teacher to teacher (Chinn, 1994).

This particular facet of mathematics learning and teaching was highlighted by Cockcroft (1982), who stated (number 242): 'We are aware that there are some teachers who would wish us to indicate a definitive style for the teaching of mathematics, but we do not believe this is either desirable or possible.' And (number 256): 'The now well established fact that those who are mathematically effective in daily life seldom make use in their heads of the standard written methods which are taught in the classroom.' Once again we return to *How People Learn* (Bransford *et al.*, 2000) for their third key finding: 'A "metacognitive" approach to instruction can help students learn to take control of their own learning by defining learning goals and monitoring their progress in achieving them.'

Conceptual ability

In a 1996 study, Chinn looked at the WISC scores and the GCSE mathematics grades for 26 dyslexic boys. The (expected) relationship between full IQ and grades was found, with a grade C or above achieved by all learners whose IQ was above 115. However, for learners with IQs in the average range the controlling factor seemed to be motivation and confidence (all 26 subjects were learners at our school and so we could estimate these somewhat unquantifiable factors). Interestingly, verbal IQ gave better correlation than performance IQ and, although showing a low average score (8.65), the arithmetic sub-test showed high correlation (also it must be recognised that this sub-test focuses on mental arithmetic). The study also showed that it would be very unwise to make predictions for individuals on the basis of any full or sub-test score, an observation echoed by Ackerman *et al.* (1986):

> We likely will never find one-to-one associations between hypothesised cognitive weaknesses and achievement outcomes. In part, this is because we can never be certain people are giving their best effort, especially children and adolescents. But, even more there is the problem of devising tasks that measure only one aspect of cognitive processing. It is difficult to control the variables when working with humans!

A child's ability to form concepts will be aided by the range and extent of the experiences he receives. 'Drill and practice' is often used to reinforce a new topic, but it may not help the development of a concept. A dyslexic or dyscalculic student typically has a slower working rate and will often manage less practice for this reason alone. A child who continually fails in mathematics will also have a smaller range of successful experiences and consequently will be less likely to be able to see patterns and to generalise, and thus to form concepts. This has the effect of compounding his difficulties and retarding his progress. Piaget's belief was that a child's building up of mathematical knowledge developed as a result the more general growth of the child's activities and thought discoveries (Hughes, 1986). It is more logical to believe that children with learning difficulties in mathematics will fare better if given more explicit instruction.

We have similar doubts over children's ability to deal, without appropriate support, with the conceptual development from the concrete manipulatives to the abstract symbols of maths, for example Hiebert, as quoted in Hughes (1986):

> Many children do not connect the mathematical concepts and skills they possess with the symbols and rules they are taught in school. We shall argue that it is the absence of these connections that induces the shift from intuitive and meaningful problem-solving approaches to mechanical and meaningless ones.... Even though teachers illustrate the symbols and operations with pictures and objects, many children will have trouble establishing important links.

This point is also made by Hart (1989), warning us that materials may not necessarily generate the same links and learning images in the learner as in the teacher.

To reiterate another problem faced by dyslexic and dyscalculic children, they are also at risk from a phenomenon described by Buswell and Judd (1925). They point out a potential consequence of unsupervised practice. Say a child misunderstands a new idea and then uses the wrong procedure or method in his first practice at this new topic, then subsequent remediation and even mastery will not be sustained. The child will return to the first method he used. It is advisable to check the first few examples a learner tries before an incorrect procedure or concept becomes embedded in his brain.

The slow speed of working of many dyslexic learners usually means they are likely to attempt fewer practice examples of any new topic. Carnine (quoted in Kelly *et al.*, 1990) demonstrated that presenting a limited number of examples of a concept causes students to form misconceptions about that concept.

Anxiety, withdrawal, self-image and the affective domain

There is enough research and information available on the affective domain, particularly anxiety, and maths to fill a book of its own.

Lundberg and Sterner (2006) give a perspective: 'Over and above common cognitive demands and neurological representations and functions, performance in reading and arithmetic is influenced by a number of motivational and emotional factors such as need of achievement, task orientation, helplessness, depression, anxiety, self-esteem, self concept, locus of control, goal commitment, psychological adjustment, metacognition and self-regulation.'

Anxiety can be facilitative or debilitative. Unfortunately maths anxiety is almost always debilitative and even, painful. Lyons and Beilock (2012) found that regions in the brain associated with threat and pain are activated on the anticipation of maths (but, interestingly, not once the maths is started). They suggest that this is one explanation as to why students with high maths anxiety avoid maths courses. Young *et al.* (2012) found brain activity in areas that were specific to math anxiety and unrelated to general anxiety, intelligence, working memory or reading ability.

Risk taking is an important part of the learning process. Too many pupils learn to avoid risk taking in maths lessons and homework by opting out (Houssart, 2005). An ex-student of the authors (who studied mathematics at degree level) told us that one of the biggest causes of anxiety for him was to be told, on failing at some task, 'Never mind, you did your best.' He would anticipate potential failure and not do his best so that when he did fail he could say, 'Well, I didn't try.' This situation was further illustrated in two studies, one on dyslexic students and the other on low achievers in maths, of the errors they made on arithmetic problems (Chinn, 1995b; 2012). The most notable difference in the errors made between dyslexic and mainstream learners was the percentage of no attempts. If you are anxious about trying something a 'no attempt' strategy is a simple, but effective way of dealing with the fear of negative evaluation. (A strategy we have found helpful is to use white boards for some work so that students can delete any wrong answers and thus the record of any error is only temporary.) We have always tried to develop in our students an understanding of maths facts and procedures as a way of reducing this problem, a philosophy endorsed by Madsen *et al.* (1995), who investigated the effect of conceptually oriented teaching on mathematical competence. One of their outcomes was the decrease in 'no attempts'. This 'no attempt' situation is somewhat compounded by (Western) society's attitude to mathematics and its belief that being unable to 'do' mathematics is a common characteristic in people and thus acceptable. Such beliefs shape our expectations.

There are other beliefs associated with these attitudes to maths (Mtetwa and Garofalo, 1989; Chinn, 2012) such as, 'mathematics problems have only one answer' (and you have to find that answer) and, 'only geniuses are capable of creating mathematics.' 'Fractions are impossible.' 'If the two numbers in a word problem are relatively close in value, for example, 2300 and 2050, then you either add or subtract them. If the two numbers are not relatively close, for example, 33 and 497, then you multiply or divide them.' Beliefs can exacerbate anxiety in that often they imply inflexibility and restricted access to success in mathematics.

There is also the influence of expectations; for example we know that many teachers and parents expect that their children will learn the times table facts. This appears to be unrealistic from the response to SC's question to many hundreds of teachers from around the UK, 'What percentage of children aged ten years do not know all the times table facts?' Most responses suggest a figure above 60%. We find this quite depressing and possibly indicative of the failure of rote learning to take children to success with this goal.

Our expectation in Western societies that people may not be good at maths means that a low ability in maths, or in fact being 'hopeless' at maths may well attract much mutual sympathy among other adults. The social consequences of difficulties with maths have a much better acceptance than the consequences of reading or writing difficulties. However, schools, of course, rarely reflect life. In school there may well be significant consequences of being bad at maths, for example a learner could be allocated to a teaching group which may limit the levels of work in several other subjects as well as maths. Also in school, unlike life, it's hard to completely avoid the mathematics you feel you can't do. This is now true even after school in England. From 2013 all teenagers who fail to get a high grade in maths have to continue to study maths until the age of 18 years. For those who still fail to achieve a qualification finding work or any course of further study will be extremely difficult.

It is a challenging to address the negative expectations of such students, which, if not challenged, result in self-fulfilling prophecies that, sadly, confirm the expectations.

Two key factors that aid learning are ability and attitude. Hattie (2009) states, 'Whereas cognitive ability reflects what an individual *can* do, personality traits reflect what an individual *will* do.' The latter can go a long way towards compensating for the former, but then the two factors are pretty closely inter-linked, for example when success encourages good attitude. A teacher from one of our post-graduate certificate courses investigated the concerns that mathematics teachers had about their pupils. She found that when the pupils were younger, up to around age eight, the main concern from teachers was that some pupils could not learn the basic maths facts. The main concern of teachers of older pupils was low motivation and poor attitude. It would not seem an unreasonable hypothesis to see a causal link between these two concerns.

It seems that maths creates anxiety for many learners and it usually seems to be an anxiety that does not facilitate learning. Ashcraft *et al.* (1998) and others have shown that anxiety in maths can impact on working memory and thus depress performance even more. Skemp (1986) suggested that it is the reflective activity (the activity of introspective analysis) of intelligence that is most easily inhibited by anxiety.

Vukovic *et al.* (2013) found that: 'Higher levels of mathematics anxiety in second grade predicted lower gains in children's mathematical applications between second and third grade, but only for children with higher levels of working memory. Overall, our results indicate that mathematics anxiety is an important construct to consider when examining sources of individual differences in young children's mathematical performance.'

Students with good working memory are usually less at risk in maths, but anxiety can change that relationship. Ramirez *et al.* (2013) found:

> A negative relation between math anxiety and math achievement for children who were higher in WM. High-WM individuals tend to rely on WM-intensive solution strategies, and these strategies are likely disrupted when WM capacity is co-opted by math anxiety. We argue that early identification

> and treatment of math anxieties is important because these early anxieties may snowball and eventually lead students with the highest potential (i.e. those with higher WM) to avoid math courses and math-related career choices.

The anxiety many dyslexic and dyscalculic (and other) pupils have with examinations can be partly addressed by rehearsing and practising under examination conditions. Indeed, many special needs children, as well as dyslexic pupils, can experience anxiety when facing any change or new situations. Levels of anxiety can be reduced by flagging up the change by telling the pupils that it will be occurring and what will be the likely outcomes. One of the main reasons we had school-based examinations twice a year at our school was to give pupils a carefully controlled experience of examinations and thus, it was hoped, reduce the stress and anxiety levels when they finally reached the national exams. This strategy was targeted at the students' trait anxiety about examinations. Trait anxiety resides in the individual at all times, whereas state anxiety is aroused at specific times and in specific situations, so, for example, trait anxiety could occur when a student is asked to answer a mental arithmetic question in front of her classmates.

Richardson and Shuinn (1972) devised a Mathematics Anxiety Rating Scale, used by Ashcraft *et al.* (1998) for their study on anxiety and working memory. Chinn (2009) devised a Mathematics Anxiety Questionnaire for the secondary school age range, obtaining scores for mainstream and dyslexic students. 'Taking an end-of-term maths examination' was ranked as the highest anxiety item for all ages, males and females and dyslexic students.

There is a recurring theme in this book, that is, our concerns regarding an over-emphasis on rote learning in mathematics. Skemp (1971) explains how over-reliance on this strategy can result in anxiety. 'The increasing efforts the student makes will inevitably use the only approach which he knows, memorising. This produces a short-term effect, but no long-term retention. So further progress comes to a standstill, with anxiety and loss of self-esteem.'

There are those who believe that persistence with rote learning will eventually lead to mastery and reduced anxiety. That simple, over-optimistic belief is based on a limited interpretation of education in general and the learning and understanding of maths in particular.

More worrying even than debilitating anxiety or low self-esteem is that some learners develop an attributional style (Seligman, 1998) for maths, which makes their attitude to maths personal, as in, 'I'm too stupid to do maths', pervasive, 'I can't do any maths' and permanent, 'I'll never be able to do maths.' An attribution is the way we explain the causes of success or failure. An individual with a combination of the three attributions identified above could well present as a dyscalculic, even if he started his maths experiences with optimism and some successes. It is an important part of a teacher's role in the maths classroom to listen for the clues that reveal the development of negative attributions and to challenge them (positively). The interchanges of communications within a classroom have a huge impact on attributions. We suspect it is the uniquely judgemental nature of mathematics, often exacerbated by those who design teaching programmes and those who actually teach maths that makes maths a topic that makes a major contribution to negative attributional style in so many students (and thus in adults).

We are aware that school reports on dyslexic and dyscalculic children sometimes contain comments from teachers where the blame for lack of progress is placed on the child. One such example was, 'He must learn to take advantage of the excellent teaching he receives.' A comment that reinforces a negative personal attribution onto the child.

Anxiety, self-esteem, self concept and attribution are a cumulative and cyclic problem – more failure, more anxiety, poorer self-image, more failure, more anxiety, more helplessness and thus onwards.

General Principles of Intervention

Looking at the factors that may lead to difficulties in mathematics sets up a background awareness of the characteristics of the learners. This has to be matched to the subject being taught, mathematics, and the present level of knowledge of the learner. The combinations of all these variables ensure that no one method will work for all. We despair each time we see some dictate which says all children will be taught by some new method or despair even more over, because the lesson should have been learnt last time around, the promotion of some recycled method.

Our principles are based on:

- Using what the child does know to take him to what he can know (as opposed to demanding facts and procedures he doesn't know so that he no longer wishes to meet anything else that he might not know).
- Acknowledging the pupil's thinking style and teaching him in a way that takes account of the need to teach to that style whilst attempting to develop a more harmonious approach (as opposed to imposing your own, or the programme's thinking style on every child).

- Making the maths developmental, so that, in building on what he does know, he constantly revisits it and it provides an increasingly secure base on which to build further new learning (as opposed to seeking the quick plaster to stick on the one problem… plasters fall off after a while).
- Using the language that communicates the idea to the child and backing up that language with appropriate visual images whenever possible (as opposed to telling a child that 'this works so just do it' even if some children are complicit in that attitude).
- Acknowledging that even our absolute best ever method for doing a particular part of maths will not successfully teach every child (so we need to be responsively flexible in our selection of methods, yet keep in mind that, although some children will need the alternative method, other children may be confused by it).
- Using the same core/key numbers to build an understanding of each process or concept (not a mixture of mnemonics, recipes and 'tricks').
- Teaching 'why' as well as 'how'.
- Keeping a responsive balance in all teaching.

These principles are applicable to any child, but to paraphrase Miles and Miles (1992), the consequences of not applying them for dyslexics and dyscalculics will be disastrous. We would like learning to be robust and based on understanding, not transitory and based solely on a number of unrelated memorised facts and procedures. This pragmatic philosophy has been advocated by several researchers (see Kaufmann *et al.*, 2003) who postulate the need for an integration of procedural (knowing how to) and conceptual (knowing why) knowledge.

Consequently most interventions discussed in this book are very much built on the typical fact knowledge levels of dyslexics and dyscalculics, for example with times tables facts the usual knowledge base is 0×, 1×, 2×, 10× and 5×. Other times tables are addressed by using these facts, for example the four times table can be computed from twice the two times table, which also introduces the idea of staged multiplications. 'Experts don't store answers, but they do store key facts and strategies that help them get answers' (K. Anders Ericsson, quoted by Doidge, 2007, p. 203).

Our intervention plan is aimed to help the learner to 'catch up' with his peers. There are some cautionary notes to this ideal. Some areas of mathematics will remain a considerable challenge, for example instant recall of times table facts. The teacher has to look at the objective, the investment required (by teacher and learner) and make a decision as to how much time (and frustration) can be expended on the objective and whether it can be by-passed without undue impact on general development. Teaching has to be efficient and effective for the child, not just for the teacher. And 'catch-up' may not always be achieved by taking the most direct route.

Second, it is almost always the case that the intervention has to be taken back a long way in the developmental structure of maths. It may not take a long visit to the basic topic that is a key precursor for the current topic, but it will be necessary if the understanding is to be consolidated.

Third, the intervention needs to be developmental rather than a patch to stick on a single issue. This helps students to understand concepts by ensuring frequent revisiting and reinforcement of ideas and strategies. The programme we used in our schools has a spiral (or helix) structure, but concepts can often occur obliquely as well. We try to capitalise on this. For example, breaking down a times table fact such as 7×8 into 5×8 plus 2×8 is the same principle, that is, partial products, which we will use for 23×47 (breaking it down into 20×47 plus 3×47). Generally, we try to check a teaching idea by asking ourselves if it is leading anywhere else, that is, is it developmental mathematically?

Finally, this book is not about games or activities. We feel that a teacher knows his or her group enough to be the best judge of what games or activities may best suit to reinforce knowledge.

Summary

Despite a new focus on language in some of the recent definitions of dyslexia and the omission of difficulties with arithmetic, it has not changed the situation that arithmetic difficulties are likely to co-occur for the majority of dyslexic learners. The definition from the UK's Rose Report (2009), however, does, in its notes, include mental arithmetic as a potentially co-occurring difficulty.

> Dyslexia is a learning difficulty that primarily affects the skills involved in accurate and fluent word reading and spelling. Characteristic features of dyslexia are difficulties in phonological awareness, verbal memory and verbal processing speed.
>
> Dyslexia occurs across the range of intellectual abilities. It is best thought of as a continuum, not a distinct category, and there are no clear cut-off points. Co-occurring difficulties may be seen in aspects of language, motor co-ordination, *mental calculation*, concentration and personal organisation, but these are not, by themselves, markers of dyslexia. A good indication of the severity and persistence of dyslexic difficulties can be gained by examining how the individual responds or has responded to well-founded intervention.

We have focused on areas that may create difficulties in learning mathematics. Chinn (1995a; 1996) has tried to investigate the influence of individual factors and is now convinced that any prediction, either of success or failure, is not a simple matter. Learners are heterogeneous. Not only are there the interactions between areas of difficulty, but also the learning environment, the learner's ability to adapt to his problems and circumvent them, (often a learner is unaware of his differences and abilities) and, of course, motivation and attitude. These latter influences are effectively impossible to quantify. Thus, it is possible to say that a particular factor, for example, auditory sequential memory (Chinn, 2000), will impact on learning. It is not possible to predict levels of success or failure based on even a quantified deficit.

Mathematics is a sequential subject, so if early difficulties are not addressed effectively then 'classroom-acquired' difficulties will be added to innate difficulties and compound the child's failure. If the remediation is started at the right time but is too slow, or continues for too short a time, the extent of the child's problems will still be increasing for, whilst his peers make progress, the dyslexic or dyscalculic child will be marking time (or even regressing). Lack of knowledge and skills will develop into a lack of confidence, which will develop into reluctance to become involved in learning. We suspect that this final stage can occur as early as seven years old for far too many pupils.

Thus, it seems accepted that many dyslexics have difficulty in at least some aspects of mathematics, but this is not necessarily in all areas of mathematics. Indeed some dyslexics are gifted problem solvers, despite persisting difficulties in, for example, rote learning of basic facts. An inappropriate education may leave such a child floundering in early numeracy when he has the ability to leapfrog over these difficulties into more advanced aspects of mathematics. If the problem is not appropriately (and continuously) addressed, these learning difficulties may reduce the extent of the child's mathematical experiences, making it harder for him to develop concepts and to progress past the very basic levels of knowledge. The difficulty may create a cumulative effect beyond its original potential if it is not addressed at an early stage (and thereafter).

The problems for dyscalculics are going to be both wider in their manifestations and more severe in their impact.

As the teacher, you require empathy, that is, an understanding of the strengths and weaknesses which the child brings to each lesson. Our experience is that a child often knows more than he realises he knows, but has not generalised or organised his knowledge of the developmental structure and interrelating nature of mathematics, a situation also observed by Askew and William (1995). It is the successful interaction of these two areas of knowledge, the learner and the subject, which helps to make an effective teacher.

3

Cognitive (Thinking) Style in Mathematics

Introduction

We use the term cognitive (or thinking) style in mathematics to refer to the way a person thinks through a problem. Allport (1937, quoted in Riding and Rayner, 1998) describes cognitive style as a person's typical or habitual mode of problem solving, thinking, perceiving and remembering. We have the optimistic attitude of many teachers and would challenge the word 'habitual'. Mathematically, its history can be dated back as far as Descartes (1638, cited in Krutetskii, 1976), who described two styles of problem solver. The first solves problems by a succession of logical deductions, whilst the second uses intuition and immediate perceptions of connections and relationships. These two contrasting styles are described again in later literature. Boltevskii (1908, cited in Krutetskii, 1976) and Harvey (1982) labelled the two styles geometers and algebraists, where the algebraist links most closely to the logical, sequential thinker and the geometer to the intuitive style. Kovalev and Myshishchev (in Krutetskii, 1976) used the term 'intuitive' to describe a person who is not conscious of every step in his thought processes, but who perceives essential connections more clearly and quickly than his complementary stylist, the 'discursive' thinker. Skemp (1981 and 1986, also Choat, 1982) describes relational and instrumental understanding. Marolda and Davidson (2000) describe 'Mathematical Learning Profiles' looking at how students learn and how teaching can be differentiated to meet preferred profiles

Although in his classic book *How to Solve It*, Polya (1990) identified four styles of problem-solver, the four can readily be combined in pairs, reducing

Mathematics for Dyslexics and Dyscalculics: A Teaching Handbook, Fourth Edition.
Steve Chinn and Richard E. Ashcroft.

them to two distinct styles. Polya called the four styles groping, bright idea, algebra and generalisation. The first two describe intuitive thinkers and the last two describe sequential thinkers. This reduction down to two distinct styles seems a possibility for all models of thinking styles.

More recently, Kahneman (2011) described two modes of thinking: 'System 1 operates automatically and quickly, with little or no effort and no sense of voluntary control. System 2 allocates attention to the effortful mental activities that demand it, including complex computations. The operations of System 2 are often associated with the subjective experience of agency, choice and concentration.' Kahneman uses a maths example, working out 17×24, to illustrate the modes and provides a further example of the interaction of the many factors that are involved in doing maths: 'Your muscles tensed up, your blood pressure rose and your heart rate increased. Someone looking closely at your eyes while you tackled this problem would have seen your pupils dilate.'

In terms of learning, Riding and Cheema (1991) provided a good overview of cognitive styles as applied to all areas of learning. Duffin and Simpson (2006) suggested four types of mathematical learners: alien (preference for absorbing new information without trying to link it with the existing knowledge), natural (preference for integrating new and old knowledge in a coherent 'global' structure), coherence (preference for finding a 'local' structure in the new knowledge) and flexible (preference for adopting different ways of thinking depending on the situation).

There is an obvious overlap here with meta-cognition. Returning to *How People Learn* (Bransford *et al.*, 2000), the third key finding is: 'A "metacognitive" approach to instruction can help students learn to take control of their own learning by defining learning goals and monitoring their progress in achieving them.' Taking a perspective that is broader than just thinking style Mortimore (2008) provides an excellent overview of learning styles and dyslexia.

We believe that the reality is that people use flexible cognitive styles. This belief is not rocket science.

Qualitative and Quantitative Style

Sharma (1986; 1989) identified and labelled two extreme styles of learning personalities (again taking a broader construct than thinking style) as quantitative and qualitative. The characteristics of the quantitative style are essentially sequential/logical and those of the qualitative are intuitive and holistic. Sharma also suggested that most personalities lie on a

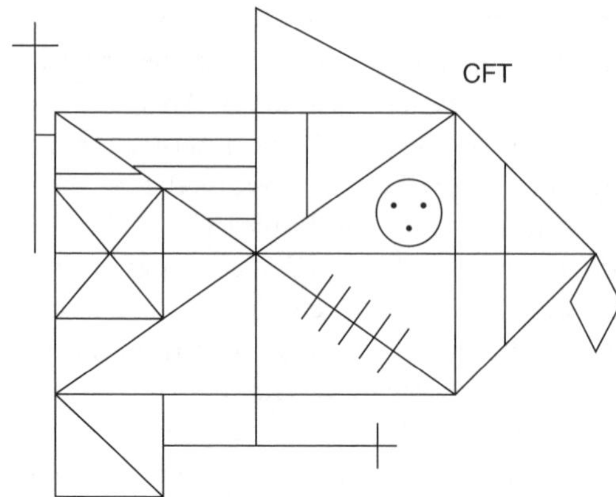

Figure 3.1 The Rey Osterrieth Complex Design Test.

continuum between these two extremes. He used the order in which the Rey Osterrieth Complex Figure is copied as one of the instruments to diagnose the preferred learning personality. This figure (Figure 3.1) is detailed and Sharma looks to see if the detail takes precedent over the outline, or vice versa, when the figure is reproduced.

Sharma's qualitative learner approaches problems holistically and is good at recognising patterns. He uses an intuitive approach, tends not to show his working and does not like practice exercises. This contrasts with the quantitative learner, who processes information sequentially, looking for formulae, methods and 'recipes'. This learner attempts to classify problems into types and to identify a suitable process to use in solving the problem.

It is worth noting that the intuitive style is not always viewed favourably. For example, Skemp (1971) considered it a hit-and-miss method, a method that is not always reproducible. Most people have experience of the teacher who says, 'I am not marking that mathematics until I can see some method written down.' (Whilst there are some very valid reasons for this to be a reasonable comment, it can indicate a lack of understanding of thinking style.)

The brain

The rapid and dramatic advances in ways that the brain can be studied have changed much of what we thought we knew in the earlier editions of this book. The broad characterisation of behaviours as left brain and right brain may well have to be abandoned. So we will take what we wrote in those editions as an historical introduction.

Some writers have linked cognitive style to hemispheric specialisation. Kane and Kane (1979) suggested the roles played by each hemisphere in a variety of different modes. For thinking, the right brain is described as deductive, divergent, intuitive, holistic, relating to concepts, simultaneity and geometry, whilst the left brain is described as inductive, convergent, segmented, logical and algebraic. Wheatley (1977) and Wheatley *et al.* (1978) linked problem-solving styles with left and right brain specialisations. He described the right brain as all-at-once and gestalt and the left as one-at-a-time and serial. Wheatley also concluded that a good problem solver achieves a smooth integration of the two modes of thinking.

The interpretation (or speculation) as to what the brain is doing is of interest, in that it gives a neurological perspective on different thinking styles. It seems somewhat dismissive to describe the 'global' thinker as intuitive, which seems to infer little conscious thought (though see Kahneman's System 1), when the intuitive process is probably based on rapid consideration of possibilities, experiences and knowledge rather than being a sort of inspired, unconsidered guess.

Even when our knowledge of the brain was in its infancy Springer and Deutsch (1993) added notes of caution to those who claim that schools fail to educate the right side of the brain: 'But are these right-hemisphere functions? We do not think it is as simple as that and there is certainly no conclusive evidence to that effect. Our educational system may miss training or developing half of the brain, but it probably does so by missing out on the talents of both hemispheres.' Pioneering work by cognitive neuroscientists such as Bugden and Ansari (2015) is now offering the possibilities of detailed and accurate studies of the brain at work and the scope of neuronal plasticity.

Although the location of brain activity is a fascinating area which modern technology is making more accessible to investigation, the way the student presents in class, his observable behaviours, may provide enough information for a teacher when planning appropriate responses and interventions. Cognitive style is often easy to identify if teachers just take time to observe the student as he works and possibly to reinforce those observations with some carefully chosen diagnostic questions and comments.

Cognitive (Thinking) Style in the Classroom

The work of Bath and Knox (1984) and Bath *et al.* (1986) on cognitive style arose from work and observations in the classroom, more specifically from teaching dyslexic (and probably dyscalculic) children of secondary school age. It therefore has its roots in the observation of children with specific learning difficulties as they studied mathematics. Bath *et al.* labelled the two extremes of the continuum of cognitive styles as grasshoppers, basically intuitive and answer oriented, and inchworms, basically step by step and formula oriented. The characteristics of the two styles are summarised in Table 3.1 (Chinn, 2004) by looking at the three stages of solving a problem: identification, solving and verification.

Table 3.1 Cognitive styles of the inchworm and the grasshopper.

	Inchworm	*Grasshopper*
First approach to a problem (identification)	1. Focuses on the parts and details.	1. Overviews, holistic, puts together.
	2. Looks at the numbers and facts to select a suitable formula or procedure.	2. Looks at the numbers and facts to estimate an answer, or narrow down the range of answers. Uses controlled exploration. This is far more cerebral than guessing.
Solving the problem	3. Formula, procedure oriented.	3. Answer oriented.
	4. Constrained focus. Uses one method.	4. Flexible focus. Uses a range of methods.
	5. Works in serially ordered steps, usually forward.	5. Often works back from a trial answer.
	6. Uses numbers exactly as given (numerically literal).	6. Adjusts, breaks down/ builds up numbers to make the calculation easier.
	7. More comfortable with paper and pen. Documents method.	7. Rarely documents method. Performs calculations mentally (and intuitively).
Checking and evaluating answers (verification)	8. Unlikely to check or evaluate answers. If a check is done it will be by the same procedure/method.	8. Likely to appraise and evaluate answers against original estimate. Checks by an alternate method/ procedure
	9. Often does not understand procedures or values of numbers. Works mechanically.	9. Good understanding of number, methods and relationships.

The teacher's role

Bath *et al.* (1986) investigated cognitive style by classifying answers to a series of carefully designed mathematics questions, thus directly taking into account how a child actually does mathematics. One of the main recommendations of our book is the necessity for teacher and child to be flexible in their approach to mathematics – Krutetskii (1976) uses the wonderful word 'harmonious' to describe the blending of styles – yet to be aware that learners (and teachers) may not always achieve this goal. Sharma (1989) commented on the need for teachers to be aware of cognitive style:

> All of us show and use different and unique mixtures of the two (personalities) but one approach is more dominant than the other in different individuals. And that is what the teacher should be aware of almost constantly. Since you, the teacher, are usually in the controlling role, then the source and sanction for this flexibility must come predominantly from you.

This situation is well expressed by Cobb (1991): 'We do not mean to imply that the teacher's beliefs are simply transferred to the student. Rather, the teacher has the authority to legitimise what is acceptable and to sanction what is not acceptable.'

The structure of mathematical abilities

Krutetskii (1976), in presenting a broad outline of the structure of mathematical abilities during school age, specifies a need for flexible thinking and some other skills which dyslexics and dyscalculics may find difficult. He specifies:

- The ability for logical thought in the sphere of quantitative and spatial relationships, number and letter symbols; the ability to think in mathematical symbols.
- The ability for rapid and broad generalisation of mathematical objects, relations and operations.
- Flexibility of mental processes in mathematical activity.
- Striving for clarity, simplicity, economy and rationality of solutions.
- The ability for rapid and free reconstruction of the direction of a mental process, switching from a direct to a reverse train of thought.
- Mathematical memory (generalised memory for mathematical relationships), and for methods of problem solving and principles of approach.

- These components are closely interrelated, influencing one another and forming in their aggregate a single integral syndrome of mathematical giftedness.

Although Krutetskii makes these observations concerning giftedness in mathematics, they are equally apposite for competence and for avoiding failure. The reader can see within these observations where dyslexics and dyscalculics may typically be at a disadvantage and where learning difficulties may create problems.

There are other sources of support for different learning styles (e.g. and in more general terms, de Bono, 1999), but the emphasis of the remainder of this chapter is to paint a clearer picture of the background reasons for, and consequences of, different cognitive styles in mathematics.

Thinking styles

To expand and clarify the picture of the two extremes of the cognitive style continuum, consider some mathematics problems and the solutions which an inchworm and a grasshopper might use. There is no implied value judgement on the two (extremes) of style. Indeed Kubrick and Rudnick (1980) suggested that teachers should encourage a wide variety of approaches, ideas and solutions. As has been already quoted, Krutetskii looks for a 'harmonious' approach. If for no other reason, the ability to generate more than one way of solving a problem allows the student to be more effective when checking his own work.

Examples

Some of the questions below are taken from the Test of Cognitive Style in Mathematics (Bath *et al.*, 1986) now included in Chinn's (2017a) book on diagnosing and assessing mathematical learning difficulties. When using questions such as these with learners, the key diagnostic question is, 'How did you work that out?' or, 'How did you do that?' A supplementary question that explores the flexibility in problem solving skills is, 'Can you think of another way of doing this problem?'

$2 \times 4 \times 3 \times 5$ (to be done mentally; no writing)

An inchworm will see first the 2 and the times sign. He tends not to overview the problem. Also he tends to take the problem 'literally', that is, if it says $2 \times 4 \times 3 \times 5$, then that is the order and it is not to be changed, and since 2 is an easy times table, he will begin: $2 \times 4 = 8$.

The next stage may be a little more challenging for times table facts, but $8 \times 3 = 24$.

The last stage (24×5) may be too much of a challenge because of the load on working memory in multiplying 4 by 5, remembering that the ones digit is 0, carrying the 2, holding it in memory while multiplying 2 by 5, remembering the 2, knowing where to incorporate it, remembering the ones digit 0 and putting it all together to give 120. Some children will just say 'That's as far as I can get.'

A grasshopper, especially if he knows he has limited times table knowledge, will overview the problem, reading through to the end to see if there are any short cuts or easy strategies or rearrangements. He may also be trying to get an estimate of the value of the answer.

He is likely to rearrange the problem to $(3 \times 4) \times (2 \times 5)$, that is, $12 \times 10 = 120$. Thus he has taken a more global and flexible view of the question. In doing so he has reduced the demand on his times table knowledge and the load on his working memory.

Find three consecutive numbers that add up to make 60

An inchworm with some algebra skills will develop an equation:

Let the first number be n:

then the second number is $n+1$
and the third number is $n+2$.

So $n+(n+1)+(n+2)=60$ which is then solved:

$$\begin{aligned} 3n+3&=60 \\ 3n&=60-3=57 \\ n&=57/3 \\ n&=19, n+1=20, n+2=21 \end{aligned}$$

The three numbers are 19, 20 and 21. The process is logical and sequential and is (effectively) independent of the value of the numbers involved; it will work for any similar problem. It takes the solution almost directly from the way the question is presented.

An inchworm without algebra skills will find it difficult to make a reasonable guess at a starting number. His subsequent adjustments to his guess will most probably be step by step, one at a time. So if his first guess is 10, his next guess is likely to be 11, irrespective of and without any appraisal of the answer generated with 10.

A grasshopper will start with a controlled exploration, leading to an estimate. He will see that the three numbers are approximately equal and that a good estimate of their value is given by 60/3 = 20. It is only a short and easy step (easy for the grasshopper, but not necessarily as easy for the numerically literal inchworm) to 19, 20, 21. Again the strategy is holistic/global and peculiar to these numbers. It is an answer-oriented strategy.

How many squares in Figure 3.2 are black?

The pattern of 7 × 7 squares in Figure 3.2 is not equally divisible into black and white squares, which makes the problem less straightforward.

The inchworm will probably resort to counting each square, thus focusing on the parts of the square.

In a formula mode, an inchworm may see a square, count the number of black squares on each side as 4, multiply 4 × 4 and say '16'. Sometimes if the tester says, '49 squares and 16 are black?' hinting that 16 does not match the almost half relationship. The inchworm will feel secure in the use of the formula (4 × 4 = 16) for a square and not see the obvious inaccuracy of the solution.

Figure 3.2 The squares.

The grasshopper is holistic in his initial overview. The 7×7 squares make 49 and 'half' will be seen to be 25 since observation (of the corners or number of black rows) shows that the larger number of squares are black.

This problem illustrates the 'whole to parts' against the 'part to whole' contrast in the two styles.

$$37+85+36+19+43$$

The inchworm will rewrite the sum in vertical form:

$$\begin{array}{r} 37 \\ 85 \\ 36 \\ 19 \\ \underline{+43} \end{array}$$

The addition may be carried out with tallies to mark progress and help the child keep count as he moves down the numbers. The child is unlikely to use a pre-estimate or a check.

The inchworm will work in the order in which the numbers are given.

The grasshopper is likely to look for pairs and clusters of numbers which add to 10 or 20, for example in the ones column there is $7+3=10$ and $9+6+5=20$. In the tens column there is $3+3+4=10$ and from $8+1+3$ (carried from units) he can extract $8+2$, leaving 2. Answer 220.

The grasshopper will probably have already grouped 85 and 19 as a little over 100 and 36, 37 and 43 as a bigger bit over 100, estimate 200 and a bit. He is using numbers as parts of a whole, where the whole is 10 or 100 or 1000. He is taking the numbers out of the order in which they are presented.

Inferences from the examples

These examples are used to show how learners with the two styles approach problems. Our experience of teaching dyslexic and dyscalculic students leads us to some observations:

- There are some learners at the extremes of the continuum.
- An individual learner may (and should) use both styles sometimes for different questions and sometimes for the same question.
- The style an individual learner uses can depend on the type of question or even on the level of difficulty of the same type of question.

- The type of compensatory strategy (e.g. finger counting or inter-relating facts) that is used relates to cognitive style.
- Prescriptive curricula create more inchworms than grasshoppers.
- Inchworms with a poor memory for basic facts and procedures are at risk in mathematics.
- Inchworms with a poor working memory are at risk in mathematics.
- Insecure learners are more likely to favour the inchworm style.
- Grasshoppers in the school system need to learn how to document their work.
- Inaccurate grasshoppers are at high risk in mathematics.
- Some questions favour grasshoppers, others favour inchworms, particularly multiple choice questions for grasshoppers.
- Having a dominant style does not mean that the learner is successful in using that style.
- Inchworms want to know 'How?' Grasshoppers want to know 'Why?'

Chinn *et al.* (2001) in a European study of dyslexic pupils found that, overall, there is a greater tendency for dyslexics to use the inchworm strategies, not because they relate to this thinking style better, but for security and for a perceived minimisation of risk in another manifestation of the tendency to try and avoid errors and thus negative feedback. The study also showed that at that time, before the new Primary Curriculum was introduced in Ireland, the prescriptive nature of the maths curriculum gave the Irish sample a heavy inchworm bias. This would suggest that children can be indoctrinated towards an inchworm thinking style in mathematics by a prescriptive, formula-oriented curriculum.

You, the teacher, have to be aware of these different styles and the fact that the child may not use the style he has been taught (Hart, 1978) or may, as Duffin (1991) observed, use his own method first and then diligently reproduce for the teacher the standard method he has been taught. Some children may have their enthusiasm for maths crushed if an inflexible cognitive style approach is demanded by the teacher or the curriculum. This is yet another characteristic of learners as individuals, which should warn us that there is no such thing as one method for all.

We could speculate which of the sub-skill deficits listed in Chapter 2 affect the way a child would solve such problems. For example, poor long-term memory for basic facts could contribute to a grasshopper style, in that a child may have to overview and combine data in order to avoid facts that he cannot recall. What is clear is that the way a child (or adult) solves a question depends on the blend of deficits and strengths he brings to the problem. You can usually go a long way to finding out how a child solves a problem by asking the simple question, 'How did you do that?' This question also encourages meta-cognition. An interest in how the student is working, rather than a judgement, will be a major source of help for many learners, especially when combined with an awareness of what the child brings to the question.

Contrary to their natural inclination, particularly for examinations, grasshoppers need to learn to know and communicate how they achieved an answer, not just what the answer is. Contrary to their natural inclination, inchworms need to learn, where appropriate, the appropriateness of an answer and why a procedure works.

Zarzycki (2001) explains that almost all school students in Poland are taught only one written method for dealing with the addition, subtraction, multiplication and division of whole numbers. His research supports the claim that there can be detrimental side effects stemming from this restriction in instruction and learning. As mentioned above, our own research with regard to a similar situation in Ireland pre-1999 also supports this. There is, however, a benefit in having consistency over the years in that parents are not alienated from the way their children are taught mathematics.

Cognitive style and problems

Cognitive style can be used to compensate for some of the difficulties mentioned in Chapter 2. It also can be used to reinforce the connections and links between number facts and between operations and help students interpret word problems. For example, in the question below:

'Sam wins £96 at bingo and decides to share it equally between his six grandchildren. How much does each child receive?'

At the least sophisticated level of analysis, the word 'share' implies that the operation to use is divide. Most children will assume from previous experience that divide will infer a big number divided by a small number, so they will arrive a 96 ÷ 6.

This has now changed a (contrived) real-life problem into an abstract number statement. An inchworm will try to divide the numbers as they are. It is unlikely to occur to him that both numbers can be divided by 2, making the problem 48 ÷ 3, and, indeed, this may not have made the problem any easier for him.

It is likely that the numbers will be re-written in the bus stop form 6)96 and a short division attempted (or not attempted, if anxiety takes over). However, if the student has all these skills and facts at his disposal, then the method is effective.

A grasshopper may picture the problem, the £96 being shared out between the six children, visualising the notes and coins being given out in six piles. So, if six £10 notes are given out, then 6 × £10 has been distributed, so £96 − £60 leaves £36 to distribute. Now six £5 notes can be given out, so 6 × £5 has gone, with £36 − £30 leaving £6 to share. So each grandchild has received £10 and £5 and £1, a total of £16. This may be done by variations on this theme, such as sharing £6 as £1 each, which leaves £90 which shares as £15.

The 'division' question has been changed into a question about the subtraction of chunks or partial products. It has been re-interpreted linguistically and mathematically. The student has been able to use facts within his memory bank. An inchworm is highly unlikely to tackle a division problem by involving multiplication.

Teachers and cognitive style

A learner may not have the same cognitive style as his teacher. If neither party is aware of this there are likely to be consequences, not least in communication and in judgement of work. For example, the marks awarded for a method could be affected. Chinn (1995) has carried out a survey of teachers' marks for three very different methods, which all resulted in a correct answer, used to solve a word problem. The range of marks for each answer varied from 0 to 10 (out of 10), so a child could be with one teacher and receive an encouraging 10 or be with another teacher and score 0 out of 10. The awarding of a particular mark can usually be rationalised by the teachers concerned. This could be a very good reason for a mathematics department to meet and discuss marking policies. Mackay (1994) noted the restricted range of methods accepted for mathematics tests at Key Stage 2 (age 7–10 years) of the English National Curriculum at that time.

Teachers should be aware of their own cognitive style. If they are towards the extreme ends of the continuum, then they will need to make a conscious effort to ensure they are communicating with learners from the other end of the spectrum. This mismatch of cognitive style between learner and teacher could be one of the reasons why students say, 'I could understand algebra the way Mrs Jones explained it last year, but I can't understand the way Mrs Smith explains it this year.'

Sometimes when we lecture for teachers we may ask them to try some questions which can identify their own cognitive style. It is interesting to note in that almost every group that we have done this with, internationally, there is no dominant style within the group, rather a close to even split between the two styles.

Sharma (1989) and Marolda and Davidson (2000) have noted that quantitative and qualitative personalities prefer different learning materials, distinguishing between discrete or quantitative materials (e.g. number lines, bead strings) and continuous or qualitative materials (e.g. Cuisenaire rods, empty number lines). This is just one of the factors teachers have to take into account when choosing concrete materials to illustrate a mathematics concept. Choosing appropriate materials is another teaching skill with, once again, a range of responses from the learners.

Summary

If you are to teach effectively and diagnostically then you must be aware of and respond to the nature, variety and consequences of the child's strengths, weaknesses and cognitive style. An awareness that there is a range of cognitive styles in any teaching group can help the teacher present a lesson more effectively and to a broader spectrum of learners.

The inchworm needs to learn how to overview a problem before embarking on a procedure and how to appraise and evaluate an answer, preferably by using an alternative approach. He needs to move towards knowing 'Why?' The grasshopper needs to learn how to document his methods and how to focus on the detail as one way of checking the validity of his answers. He needs to move towards knowing 'How?' Krutetskii's advice of harmonious use of both styles makes for good problem solvers.

4

Testing and Diagnosis

Teaching and diagnosis are inextricably intertwined. If you are working with an individual student, then a diagnostic approach to teaching must be inevitable. You need to appraise the student's skills and deficits in mathematics as an ongoing activity. As soon as teaching begins, diagnosis begins.

It is the authors' experience that children often know more than most tests reveal; for example an algorithm may be almost mastered, but a small misunderstanding causes failure and it is only the failure that is noted. As we have said before, intervention often needs to start further back than one might initially think, but not necessarily always from square one, and testing should bear this in mind and try to find the optimum place to start the intervention.

If you are working with a group of students you can still build in an ongoing diagnostic approach to much of the work you do by designing at least some of the exercises, worksheets and tests you use to give you that diagnostic information. One way of doing this is by examining error patterns (Engelhardt, 1977; Ashlock, 2010).

After considering some theoretical background, this chapter suggests a testing procedure. There could be many other equally valid procedures (e.g. Dowker 2001) and any procedure should be flexible enough in structure to respond to the child's answers rather than rigidly following a fixed protocol.

Chinn (1992) has discussed the use of testing, in particular the benefits and disadvantages of norm-referenced and criterion-referenced tests. Kubiszyn and Borich (2007) provide an interesting overview of performance tests. However, before returning to this discussion, we should step

Mathematics for Dyslexics and Dyscalculics: A Teaching Handbook, Fourth Edition.
Steve Chinn and Richard E. Ashcroft.

back and ask the obvious and fundamental question, 'Why test?' Some of the answers to this question include:

- Parents may wish to know how their child's achievements compare with those of his/her peers.
- A teacher may wish to monitor the progress of his or her group and/or identify those who need extra help and/or collect data with which to stream groups.
- There may be a need to measure rates of progress of an individual or a group.
- To measure the efficacy of the teaching programme/intervention.
- There may be some mandatory requirement to test.
- The test may be used to assess the ability of the child to progress to higher levels of study or to a new school.
- The test may be used to award a certificate recording a level of achievement.
- It may be used for diagnostic reasons (e.g. to find the child's strengths, weaknesses, knowledge base and learning style) and thus identify a pupil's special needs.

It is understandable for a parent, or indeed a concerned educator, to wish to have an idea of the depth of a child's problems, measured in terms of a direct comparison with his peers. Tests which are 'normed' against a large population of children are used for these comparisons, for example the Mathematics Competency Test (Vernon *et al.*, 2002), the Basic Number Screening Test (Gillum *et al.*, 2012), the Wide Range Achievement Test: 4 (Wilkinson and Robertson, 2006) or the 15-minute Screener Test (Chinn, 2017a) (see the References and Appendix I for details). It is not the function of these tests to provide a diagnosis of 'dyslexic' or 'dyscalculic' problems. If the examiner wishes to derive a diagnostic profile of the child's strengths, weaknesses and learning style, additional testing will have to be done. The standardised test only sets the baseline for the diagnosis.

Criterion-referenced tests are more diagnostic (by design) than norm-based tests. Interpretation of a criterion-based test can identify particular tasks that the child can and cannot do, but not necessarily his error patterns (Young and O'Shea, 1981; Ashlock, 2010) or why he can or cannot do a particular task. Such tests can be lengthy if they are designed to be thorough and/or cover much ground (see Wilson and Sadowski, 1976).

If these tests are used with groups, say as a class test, then the accurate interpretation of an individual child's errors can be uncertain and relies heavily on how much of his method the child has documented. Of course, if the test is administered to an individual, then diagnostic questioning can be used to supplement the written evidence. As in the *Test of Thinking Style in Mathematics* (Chinn, 2017a), the key question is, 'How did you do that?' possibly followed by, 'And can you think of another way it can be done?' Careful, knowledgeable, well-timed and informed questioning is usually non-threatening.

Bryant and Reivera (1997) sum up the assessment structure with four questions:

> When push comes to shove, the following questions should guide our assessment practices:
>
> Where do students stand in relation to their peers?
>
> What do students know and what don't they know?
>
> Why do students perform as they do (i.e. how on earth did they come up with that answer)?
>
> Is what I am teaching working?

Gillum (2012) offers guidance on assessment of dyscalculia and maths learning difficulties for educational psychologists, the group that are so often at the front line for diagnosis of specific learning difficulties.

We are avoiding entering the debate on the use of labels. It is an interesting debate. The stakes are high for some children and adults and there are many arguments and counter-arguments for their use. We believe that key considerations are the child (adult) and the situation. It is a very real issue for the person concerned and academic theorising may sometimes overlook the realities.

A Diagnostic Test Protocol

In our ideal world the diagnosis/assessment would be carried out by a skilled and experienced person rather than a computer. So much of the information gathered comes from the nuances.

This diagnostic procedure, structured for a dyslexic or dyscalculic child, links back, as does all the work in this book, to a knowledge of the child and what he brings to the subject. The procedure is designed to be appropriate to the child and to the mathematics he is likely to encounter. It also relates to the teaching strategies described in this book, indicating which are likely to be more effective for the child. Although the test items suggested here have been carefully selected, they are by no means meant to be definitive and thus should be modified to suit the individual. The structure and rationale of the test should, however, act as a guide.

The diagnostic procedure will examine the child's knowledge of basic facts, his levels of understanding of fundamental concepts (such as place value), his use of strategies and his thinking style, and it should provide the examiner with enough information to construct a teaching programme appropriate to the child's needs.

The basic structure of the test protocol suggested below is designed to measure the child's present level of achievement and to ascertain why and in what ways the child is having difficulty. Although the basic premise must be that each child is a unique individual, there are certain common areas that are likely to create difficulty for the dyslexic or dyscalculic learner (see Chapter 2). The protocol is designed to investigate these areas and to provide the examiner with a profile of the child's mathematical abilities. The test is aimed at early mathematics and therefore concentrates on numeracy. It is primarily designed for an age range from around 8 to about 15 years, depending on the extent of the deficit, but it should be easy to modify some of the content to extend this range upwards. The test need not be given in one session, but may be spread over whatever time the examiner considers manageable for the child. Some items will be easier than others (which is information in itself). The examiner should unobtrusively encourage the child to try his best and certainly avoid any pressure with regard to speed of working.

Structure of the Diagnostic Protocol

The test structure includes most or all of the following components:

- A norm-based (standardised) test (see Appendix 1)
- Counting/adding on tasks
- Number bonds (combinations)
- Times table and division facts
- Place-value tasks
- Mathematics vocabulary and language
- The four operations
- Money
- Word problems

- Anxiety
- A thinking style test
- Working and short-term memory

There are several standardised tests to choose from (see Appendix 1 for suggestions). The individual requirements of each examiner will probably reduce the choice. It is worth having several tests at the ready as many dyslexic children have a long history of being tested and may well have done your first choice recently.

Counting and adding on tasks

A good starting point is to scatter about 30 one pence coins or chunky counters on a table top and ask the child to estimate how many are there and then ask the child to count them. The test is looking at sense of number (estimation), one-to-one correspondence, speed of counting, accuracy and whether or not the child groups the counters/coins and in what size of group.

This is a good introductory item since there is not a right or wrong answer.

The examiner can also ask the child to count a (smaller) number of dots on a card, a task where he cannot handle and move the items he is counting. The dots can be presented in a regularly spaced line and then at random.

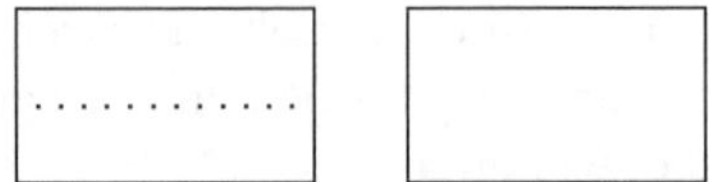

A series of fact cards may be made (on index or blank playing cards) and used to check basic addition and subtraction skills. When testing for basic addition and subtraction fact knowledge and strategies, the examiner should also be aware of the Einstellung effect (Luchins, 1942), which is the lack of flexible interchange between operations (add, subtract, multiply and divide) and which is observed when a child stays with the original operation even after the operation sign has changed (a behaviour that is different to misreading signs).

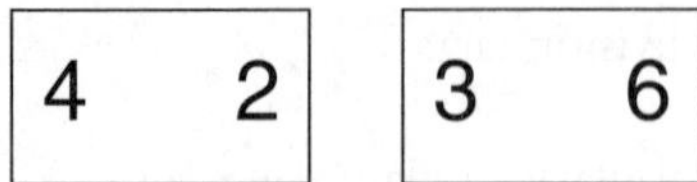

- 4 + 2 checks a basic, low number addition fact and whether the child counts on to 4, counts from 1 to 4 and then on to 6 or just knows the answer.

- 3 + 6 checks as above and to see if the child changes the order to the easier counting on task of 6 + 3.
- 4 + 3 = □ introduces the child to the 'box' for an answer, a number to make the question right. The examiner says, 'What number goes in the box to make the right answer?'
- 5 + □ = 9 checks if the child is flexible enough in his knowledge of addition (and subtraction) to understand what is required, that is, does he count on or subtract 5 from 9 to obtain 4. The examiner asks 'What number goes in the box to make this sum right?'
- 6 + 4 = □. The number bonds for 10 are an important set of data to learn, so the child's level of knowledge of these facts needs to be checked.
- 'Can you write three more pairs of numbers that add up to 10, like 6 and 4?' Does the child immediately give you 4 + 6, or does he have a strategy such as the sequence 9 + 1, 8 + 2, 7 + 3?
- Give the child two 5p, six 2p and ten 1p coins and ask him to show you some ways of making 10p. Here the test is examining how many ways he produces 10p and whether he works to a system, for example 5 + 5 to 5 + 2 + 2 + 1 to 5 + 2 + 1 + 1 + 1, etc.
- 10 = 7 + □. Can the child use his number bonds for 10 in a different (subtraction) format?
- 8 + 7 = □. Many children, even if they say they 'just know' the answer, can be gently persuaded to tell you exactly how they worked it out. Some children will simply count on, using their fingers or objects in the room. The finger movements may be very slight, so the examiner will have to be observant. Some children extend their limited lexicon of facts by interrelating number facts. So 8 + 7 becomes 1 less than 2 × 8, or 2 less than 10 + 7.
- 9 + 8 = □, 9 + 6 = □, 9 + 4 = □. In asking this sequence (one at a time) the examiner is trying to see if the child has a consistent strategy for adding onto 9. Has the child started to see patterns?
- 17 – 8 = □. Checks a problem similar to those above, but presented as a subtraction.
- 60 – 6 = □. Can the child extend his number bonds for 10 to other 'ten' situations?

Times table facts

Pritchard *et al.* (1989) found that dyslexics had better retrieval of the two times, five times and ten times tables, so the protocol can acknowledge this. The examiner can resort to straightforward questions, especially if he has established a good rapport with the child. He can simply ask, 'Which of your times tables do you know? ' and maybe prompt, 'The twos?' The most frequent response is, 'The 2s, the 5s and the 10s' with some 'smart' kids adding on 'The 1s and the 0s'.

If the child says he does know the two times table the examiner should ask, 'What are seven twos, what is seven times two?' The examiner must observe whether the child has instant recall or if he counts up 2, 4, 6, 8, 10, 12, 14 or if he uses a strategy, such as 5 × 2 and 2 × 2, added to make 7 × 2. Similar, careful diagnostic questioning can be used to establish a broad picture of the child's times table knowledge.

The examiner may also wish to determine how many (if any) strategies the child uses to work out times table (and addition) facts. For example, if he knows that 2 × 8 = 16, does he add on a third 8 for 3 × 8, or if he knows 5 × 8 = 40, does he add another 8 to obtain 6 × 8? This can be checked by some leading questions. Another common strategy is to halve ten times table facts to obtain five times table facts. A child who has developed his own strategies is more likely to be aware of the interrelationships between numbers.

The commutative property is expressed as $a \times b = b \times a$, or in numbers, 7 × 8 = 8 × 7, that is, it does not matter whether a rectangle is 9 × 4 or 4 × 9, the area is the same (36). The commutative property is useful knowledge and worth including in a test procedure. If nothing else, it effectively halves the number of facts the child needs to remember. So a child may be asked to give the answer to 4 × 8 if he is told 8 × 4 = 32.

Formal, low-stress, norm-referenced tests for each of the four operations can be found in *More Trouble with Maths* (Chinn, 2017a).

Place value

The child is asked a series of questions. The numbers should be written on cards and shown to the child.

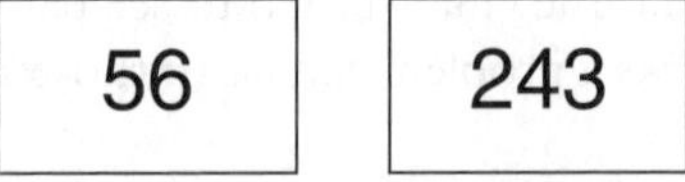

- If this number is fifty-six (56), what is this number? 243.
- What is this number? 8572. Which digit tells us how many hundreds in the number?
- What is this number? 4016.
- Write (as digits) the number four thousand, two hundred and thirty-three.
- Write the number sixteen thousand and seventeen in digits.

- What is the value of each digit in this number? 5656
- Work out 14 × 2, 14 × 20, 14 × 200

The vocabulary and language of mathematics

- The examiner needs two sets of cards, one set with each of × ÷ + − = the other set with add, divide, subtract, times, multiply, share, minus, plus, equals, same as, take away, more, less, difference. The child is asked to match the sign to the name. He can be told that there may be more than one name per sign. Make sure that the child can read the words. This checks the ability to relate the word to the symbol.

  One of the most severely mathematically handicapped students we have ever assessed had significant speech and language difficulties.

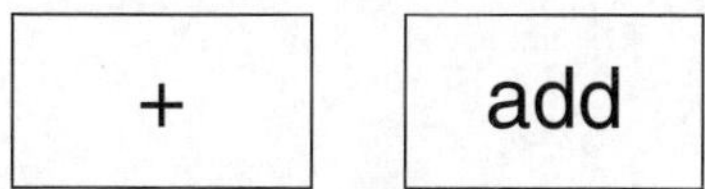

- Ask the child to make up an addition (and possibly subtraction, multiplication and division) problem. The examiner may need to talk the child into this (e.g. 'If we had 5 + 6, can we make that into a problem that uses words?')

Concepts/understanding

- 'Explain what you understand by the word divide (or multiply). Tell me how you would explain to someone what divide is.' The examiner will have different levels of expectation for this depending on the child and may find that discussion can lead to a clearer picture of the child's understanding of these deceptively simple concepts.
- 'Give me an estimate, an easier number to use, for 97.' The child may be bold enough to go to 100, but many will only go as far as 98. I have even known an answer of 76. The examiner is looking to see if the child has understood the need to make the estimate a number that is easy to use in calculations.
- Make up a word problem using in a mathematical way the word 'share'.

The four operations (+ − × ÷)

Ashlock's (2010) book *Error Patterns in Computation* introduces the idea of analysing a child's errors and then providing appropriate remedial instruction. Careful selection of computation items should give useful diagnostic information, although it may not be possible to identify every error a student makes. This stage of the protocol also allows the examiner to introduce some criterion-referenced items.

Chinn (1995b) has studied the errors made by 11–13-year-old dyslexic students. The one error type that dyslexic students made at a rate far above that of non-dyslexics was the error of the 'No attempt'. If there is no answer to a question then, obviously there can be no diagnostic information. This is a very important reason to keep the whole test protocol low stress. Smith (1996) also makes some interesting observations on errors, as do Young and O-Shea (1981).

Some examples of basic criterion-referenced tests are given below, but a teacher should set up their own criterion test battery based on their own circumstances, such as the type of student, the syllabus and the requirements for record keeping.

Addition

These questions can be presented on a worksheet. The questions must be well spaced out and preferably ruled off from each other. The child can be asked to make an estimate for each question first. The use of a worksheet format does not preclude the continued use of the question, 'How did you do that?'

1. $\begin{array}{r} 36 \\ +21 \\ \hline \end{array}$ Checks two digit plus two digit with no 'carrying'

2. $\begin{array}{r} 20 \\ +47 \\ \hline \end{array}$ Checks adding to a zero

3. $\begin{array}{r} 357 \\ +469 \\ \hline \end{array}$ Checks three digit plus three digit with two 'carries'

4. 8 + 5 + 7 + 5 + 1 + 9 + 2 checks if the child uses number bonds for ten and pairs the numbers, rewrites the problem vertically, finger counts, tries to use memory as he adds in order, uses tallies, either to count each unit or as 'carries for tens'. In other words, does the child overview the question or simply start adding at the first two numbers.

Subtraction

Another example of helping the examiner to look at methods and errors instead of just whether the answers are right or wrong. Indeed both sets of questions were chosen to investigate the typical errors a dyslexic or dyscalculic student may make.

1. 46 −23 Checks two digit minus two digit with no renaming (renaming refers to changing 46 to 30 and 16)

2. 73 −44 Checks two digit minus two digit with renaming

3. 840 −427 Checks three digit minus three digit with subtraction from zero

4. 1000 −699 Checks use of the renaming algorithm as opposed to rounding up the 699 to 700 and then adjusting the (interim) answer

Again the questions are designed to investigate the typical errors dyslexics, dyscalculics and many other children may make.

Multiplication

1. 23 ×2 Checks two digit times one digit with no carrying (using easy number facts)

2. 37 ×2 Checks two digit times one digit with carrying

3. 23 ×20 Relates to the first example to see if child can extend times 2 to times 20

4. 42 ×22 Checks two digit times two digit

5. 624 ×203 Checks three digit times three digit; also if the middle line of the 'traditional' method is written as 000, that is, unthinking/mechanical use of an algorithm

Note that, although these examples are 'easy' they allow the child to demonstrate his ability to solve the problem without failing because he does not know times table facts beyond two, five and ten. They also provide the examiner with information about the way the child solves basic multiplication problems and his error patterns beyond not retrieving basic facts.

Division

1. 2)46 Checks two digit divided by one digit with no carrying
2. 2)74 Checks two digit divided by one digit with one carry
3. 5)56 Checks two digit divided by one digit with remainder (or decimal
4. 2)4008 Checks dividing into numbers which include zeros

Again the information required centres on methods and number concepts rather than basic fact knowledge.

Word problems

Word problems should not be solely a test of reading ability, although the examiner needs to know if this is another barrier to success in mathematics. Again, the worksheet should be designed to be clear, uncluttered and accessible. The following examples are progressively more challenging.

The child is asked to read and solve the problems.

1. What is 7 add 3?
2. What is 49 minus 7?
3. Take 12 from 25.
4. If six boxes contain 2 pens each, how many pens altogether?
5. Mike has ten red pens, three paper clips and seven pencils. How many things can Mike use for writing?
6. Pat goes to the shop and buys two sweets at 5p each and ten sweets at 3p each. How much does she pay?
7. Sally and Kath have twenty-two model cars to share equally between them. How many do they each get?

- Questions 1 and 2 are the simplest and most straightforward.
- Question 3 reverses the order in which the numbers are to be subtracted.
- Question 4 mixes numbers as digits and numbers as words.
- Question 5 contains extraneous information.
- Question 6 has more than one stage.
- Question 7 is asking the child to divide and does not include any digits, the numbers are written as words.

Thus, each question probes a different aspect of the child's knowledge and abilities. His answers should give the examiner a good picture of the child's expertise with basic word problems. Although the questions are presented as a written exercise, once again the examiner can ask, 'How did you do that?' It is worth noting that word problems that require two stages/steps are often very problematic for dyslexics, dyscalculics and indeed many other learners, too.

Money

Knowledge of money is a survival skill. It is also interesting to see how a child's ability to solve money problems compares with his ability to solve equivalent number problems. Later, the child's knowledge of money problems can be used, for example, to work with decimal fractions (see Chapter 10).

1. How many pence in one pound?
2. How much is half of a pound?
3. Show the child a card with £1.00 – 24p and ask him 'How much change is there from a pound if a bar of chocolate costs 24p?'
4. Show the child a card with £100 and £19 written on it and ask, 'If you have £100, how many computer games can you buy if each game costs £19? Do you have any change? How much?'
5. You have £5 and you want to buy four things that cost (show the child a card with £1.50, £2.50, 75p, 70p). Have you enough money to buy all four things?

- Question 1 checks basic knowledge (essential to complete the other questions).
- Question 2 is asking if the child has absorbed what 50p is.
- Question 3 is 'real' life mathematics and looks at subtraction.
- Question 4 is asking if the child has a concept of the value of money. Does he know that £100 is an identifiable amount of money.
- Question 5 is looking at another typical 'shopping' exercise and requires two stages.

Attitude and Anxiety

It may also help and encourage the child if he is asked questions such as the following:

> 'How do you like mathematics?'
>
> 'Do you think you are any good at mathematics?'

'Are there any bits you are quite/especially good at?'

'Which bits of maths do you like best?'

'Are there any areas where you think you could do with a little extra help?'

Of course, the child may have given many clues during the interview, such as, 'I could never do division.' The teacher should be particularly observant of any comments that give clues as to the child's attributions (see Chapter 2).

Note that there is a standardised test of maths anxiety in secondary age students in *More Trouble with Maths* (Chinn, 2017a).

Thinking Style or Cognitive Style

For diagnostic ideas see Chapter 3.

Tests for Dyscalculia

Currently this remains an area where there is little choice of tests. Butterworth's (2003) Dyscalculia Screener is exactly that, a screener, administered individually via a computer and based on Butterworth's model of dyscalculia. Emerson and Babtie's (2010) The Dyscalculia Assessment offers a comprehensive collection of diagnostic activities for primary-aged children.

As the concept evolves, as it will, as new researchers follow Butterworth's pioneering work, then the testing is likely to evolve, too.

More Trouble with Maths. A Complete Guide to Identifying and Diagnosing Mathematical Difficulties (Chinn, 2017a) contains a number of tests, some standardised, covering many of the factors that will contribute to dyscalculia (and mathematical learning difficulties) so that a decision is based on a range of data. It is closely structured around the test protocol outlined in this chapter.

Summary of the Test Protocol

The answers to the questions from the various strands of the protocol, combined with a knowledge of the way the child solves each question, should provide the examiner with a comprehensive picture of what the child can do and how he does it, so that the examiner has a measure of the child's number and operation sense, basic knowledge and his appropriate use of numeracy skills. The child's cognitive style can be deduced from such behaviours as to whether he finger counts to solve 8 + 7 or if he uses (2 × 8) – 1 or 7 + 7 + 1, his estimate for 97, or how he solves 1000 – 699. As well as providing a picture of the child's strengths and weaknesses, the protocol helps you as the teacher to obtain a clearer idea as to what strategies the child is likely to find easy to adopt and which he will find hard to absorb.

The protocol described here is a guide to a structure for diagnosis. As a tester gains experience he will adapt these ideas and introduce new questions, which enable him to follow where the child's responses lead. It should be the goal of the teacher/tutor to construct a diagnostic protocol that is appropriate to their own educational environment.

5

Concept of Number

Introduction

When a child has problems learning the basic facts of number, then his problems may be compounded by his consequent failure to develop an understanding of the values and interrelationships of numbers. Of course, it does not automatically follow that a child who successfully rote learns the basic facts will develop an understanding of numbers. It is important that any child should develop a 'feel' or 'facility' for number, that is, he needs to learn:

- A sense of the size or value of a number (Berch, 2005).
- A recognition of the other numbers which it is near to.
- How near a number is to other numbers, particularly the key/core numbers such as one, two, five, ten, twenty, fifty, hundred, thousand and so on.
- Whether the number is larger or smaller than other numbers, and by roughly how much.
- The relationship of the number to key/core numbers, which infers an understanding of the operations and their effect.

For children with dyslexia/dyscalculia/learning difficulties in mathematics, the development of this last facility is a likely alternative route for coping with the memory demands of early numeracy as suggested in the NRC's Key Finding 2 (Bransford *et al.*, 2000). An early failure to learn basic number facts from memory or by using efficient strategies can keep

Mathematics for Dyslexics and Dyscalculics: A Teaching Handbook, Fourth Edition.
Steve Chinn and Richard E. Ashcroft.

them from the range and quality of experiences needed to develop number concept. Of course, memorising the basic facts does not guarantee the development of a concept of number, so the compensatory ideas advocated here may benefit a wider population than just dyslexics and dyscalculics. We are trying to take the child beyond a total reliance on counting on and fallible memory.

The first number test on the NFER-Nelson Dyscalculia Screener (Butterworth, 2003) is for subitising. This means an ability to look at a random cluster of dots and know accurately how many are there, without counting. It is the direct perceptual apprehension of the numerosity of a group. Most adults can do this with confidence for four items. The subtest is about a fundamental knowledge of number. The approximate number system (ANS) is what it says it is, an ability to approximately appraise the magnitude of a quantity or compare the magnitude of quantities without relying on language or symbols.

Using consistent and recognisable patterns for objects enhances the ability to recognise quantity, for example ten:

A person who has to rely entirely on counting for addition and subtraction is severely handicapped in terms of speed and accuracy. Such a person is even more handicapped when trying to use counting for multiplication and division. Often their maths work sheets are covered in endless tally marks and often they are just lined up, neither neatly nor grouped in fives as in the gate pattern ~~IIII~~. Their maths is done by counting in steps of one. If you show these learners patterns of dots or groups as on dominoes or playing cards, they prefer lines of tallies. This is not just about the ability to 'see' and use five as a cluster. It is also the ability to see other number relationships such as nine being one less than ten, to see $5+6$ as $5+5+1$, to count on in twos, tens and fives, especially if the pattern is not the basic one of 10, 20, 30… but 13, 23, 33, 43…

As teachers we are trying to develop the ability to go beyond counting in ones by seeing the patterns and interrelationships in numbers (Chinn and Ashcroft, 2004).

This chapter looks at the very early stages of number work. These are the stages where a dyslexic or dyscalculic child may have started to fail or is failing to progress conceptually. Thus, even an older child may need to return to these early topics to recover the experiences he had not taken on board earlier. As with much of the material in this book, the work described is not age-specific, but rather achievement specific. As a tutor/teacher, you need to adjust the style and approaches of your presentation of the work to avoid patronising the learner.

Early Recognition of Numbers and Their Values

To return to 'subitising', a small number of objects can usually be recognised instantly by using a visual sense of number, so that a child seeing two different clusters of, say, four spots will recognise them as the same quantity. This ability disappears with larger numbers (though some children and adults have been able to extend the skill to remarkably large numbers).

Slightly larger numbers may be more quickly recognised if:

1. The objects are arranged in a recognisable patterns, or
2. The number can be seen as a combination of other numbers. Thus, even at this early stage of development, the child can be introduced to the use of patterns and inter-relationships.

So, for example, ten can be shown as in the two arrangements of five squares (as also shown above).

Teachers (or parents) can also introduce certain special numbers that can be used as landmarks, reference points or stepping stones towards understanding other numbers, for example ten. Then five can be seen as half of ten, nine can be seen as one less than ten, twelve can be seen as two more than ten and twenty as two times ten. Coinage the world over uses key numbers for its values, almost always using 1, 2, 5, 10, 20, 50, 100 and so on. Other numbers and values are constructed from these key coins. For example, the lack of a coin worth 7 does not handicap the manipulation of money for something that costs 7. A 5 coin and a 2 coin can be used.

The Language of Mathematics (see also Chapter 2)

In this chapter, we use the word 'number' to mean one of the following:

- The mathematical symbol for the number, for example 8
- The written form of the number word, for example eight
- The sound of a number word, for example 'ate'

So already we are using three interpretations of even such a basic word as 'number'.

For most of the dyslexics and dyscalculics we teach, the problem of mathematics as a 'foreign' language becomes particularly acute when there is a necessity to write numbers down. The situation is exacerbated by the conventions of place value (base ten). As an example, we have seen 11-year-old boys write 'six hundred and five thousand and twenty' as:

> 600500020 and as a slightly less obvious error, but still based on a rationale, 5620.

It is worth remembering the linguistic confusion that surrounds the first two digit numbers, ten to nineteen. Sadly the inconsistencies of these ten numbers confuse many children and act as the first (and thus possibly dominant) experience of a failure to understand a mathematics topic.

Early Number Work

Sorting/classifying

An important mathematical pre-skill is the ability to differentiate objects and group together those with common attributes, such as colour, size or function. This activity is the first stage towards counting the objects in a set. Piaget emphasised the importance of classification, that is, the ability to sort objects according to a characteristic similarity such as size, colour or shape and seriation, the ability to arrange objects (and numbers) in increasing or decreasing size.

The number zero is an important concept to introduce, even at this early stage. It can be introduced here to represent the complete absence of any objects in the set (or group). This early exposure is important to introduce to a child in a clear way the concepts built around zero.

Correspondence between sets of objects

Understanding that two sets contain the same number of objects can be achieved by matching each object from the first set with each object from the second. If there are any objects left after such a matching process, then one set contains more objects and the other contains fewer objects.

This level of understanding allows sets of objects to be compared, even though the actual number in either set is established. This acts as an early introduction to the concept of 'more than' and 'less than' and to the question, 'Is it bigger or smaller?' The same approach can be extended to compare more than two sets and thus the idea of rank orders.

There are some benefits in using the patterns we use in this book, though they should not be used exclusively. The goal is to get the child to recognise a quantity with absolute consistency. They can also be used to compare two sets without using numbers, for example:

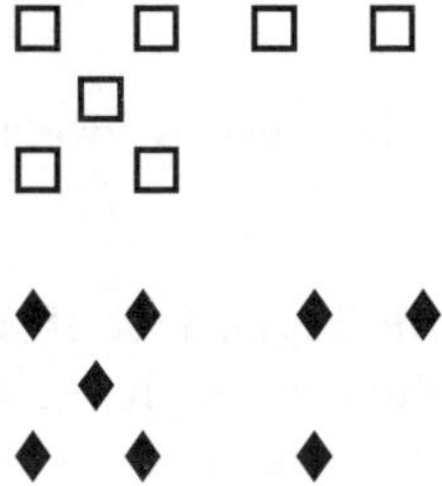

Correspondence between objects and numbers: counting

Stage 1

Introducing the number words and number symbols gives, in effect, abstract sets, which can be matched with sets of actual objects. For example, when the set of three objects is seen to correspond with the symbol '3', we can begin to call the number of objects 'three'.

It can then be seen that if the objects are counted in any different order, the correspondence shows that there are still three. Furthermore, if other sets of different objects are also seen to correspond with 3, then the relationship of a constant 'three-ness' for the two 'different' sets can be developed. Another important move forward comes if the child can be encouraged to explore the arrangement of objects within a set to discover that the number is conserved even though the arrangement is different. In this way the child learns the interrelationship of numbers, for example $3 = 2 + 1$ or $1 + 2$ and then later 3 as $5 - 2$ so that the interrelationships between key numbers, 1, 2, 5, 10 is an early experience.

Stage 2

At this stage the child is starting to relate the objects, the symbol for the number of objects, and the word (sight and sound) for the number, and the 'break down' of the number (Table 5.1).

It is necessary for the number symbols and sounds in the above table to be known by heart. The exact spelling of the number words is of less importance (and likely less achievable) for children with dyslexia. The ARROW strategy (Lane, 1992; 2012) may well be of use to help achieve this target. ARROW is a multisensory learning and teaching approach developed in schools and researched under the auspices of Somerset County Council and the University of Exeter. ARROW uses a child's own voice, the self-voice, to develop skills central to reading, spelling, speaking and listening. ARROW is an acronym for Aural-Read-Respond-Oral-Written in which the self-voice, replayed on audio-CD or via a PC, is linked to looking, writing, listening and speech skills.

Stage 3

Counting can be used to associate the movement from object to object with a movement to the next number. In the early stages, while counting aloud, a child cannot always synchronise these movements and it may help if he counts against a regular rhythm or beat (e.g. a metronome).

This is also an introduction to addition.

Stage 4

The extension of the skill of counting forwards to the skill of counting backwards is not easy for the dyslexic or dyscalculic child. More practice in the reverse operation of removing one object at a time while counting the numbers backwards (and seeing the digits) will almost certainly be needed.

This is also an introduction to subtraction.

Table 5.1 Tallies, symbols and words representing numbers.

Objects	♦	♦ ♦	♦ ♦ ♦	♦ ♦ ♦ ♦	♦ ♦ ♦ ♦ ♦	♦ ♦ ♦ ♦ ♦ ♦
Number symbols (Digits)	1	2	3	4	5	6
Words (Sounds)	one	two	three	four	five	six

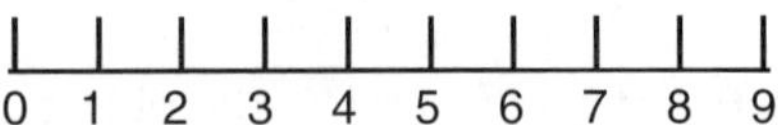

Figure 5.1 The number line.

Stage 5

The Number Line (Figure 5.1) is useful at all levels of mathematics. Here it associates each extra mark with the next number and confers regularity and proportionality on the counting process. It also establishes the order of the numbers, as well as the convention for counting of increasing to the right and decreasing to the left. But beware. The converse is true for place value, another of the inconsistencies of early maths.

Furthermore, the regular spacing of the numbers begins the connection between numbers and length. This can be reinforced by using apparatus such as Dienes blocks or Cuisenaire rods. Cuisenaire rods are continuous, that is they do not have any gradations, so they give a different, but supportive perspective.

Number lines act as an intermediate stage between images of materials such as bead strings and Cuisenaire rods and symbols. Counting in both directions along the number line is beneficial for linking addition and subtraction.

Visual Sense of Number

Experiments can show that the visual sense of quantity (randomly arranged objects) is limited to about four or five. That is to say, most children will immediately recognise the number of objects in sets of one, two, three, four or five (without time for counting). This seems to imply that children have an in-built 'feel' for the sizes or values of these numbers. Indeed some researchers believe the skill of realising a difference between one object and two objects exists in neonates.

From about six objects onwards, an accurate visual sense of number is less reliable and the objects have to be counted, unless there are other clues in the arrangement of the objects. In other words, the child has to use a one-to-one correspondence, treating each number as a separate identity. Thus he begins to relate numbers, build them up and see constituent parts.

Visual Clues to Number Concept

Numbers can more easily be 'assessed and accessed' if they form a recognisable pattern or if they can be seen as a combination of simpler numbers (this can be done in the early stages without a formal understanding of addition or multiplication). At this stage such an exercise adds further reinforcement to the idea of breaking down and building up numbers. The work can then be extended to bigger numbers, as shown in Figure 5.2. The numbers should become instantly recognisable through their patterns,

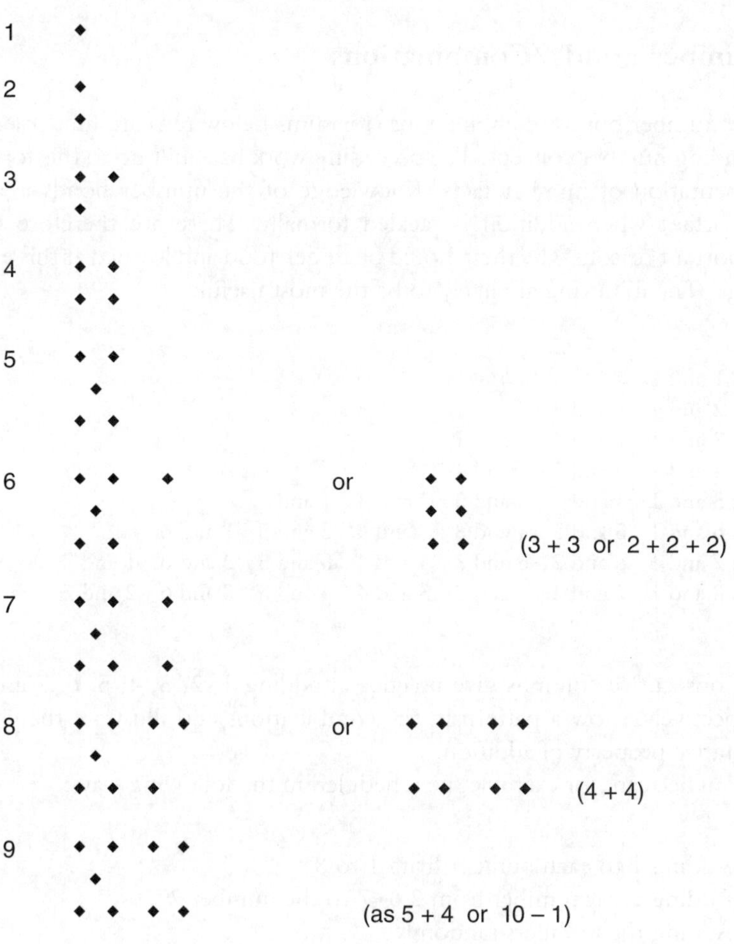

Figure 5.2 Breaking down and building up numbers.

familiar from dice and dominoes, though the authors are less happy with the pattern used on dice, dominoes and playing cards for six, that is two rows of three, rather than the 5 + 1 pattern advocated in this book for developing number sense.

Any attempt to 'standardise' on a particular version is likely to be counterproductive, because each child will feel happiest with the version that suits him individually. Despite our principle that the best version is the one that works for a particular child, sometimes a little intrusion helps to rationalise and organise the child's ideas, for example in guiding them towards use of the key numbers, 1, 2, 5 and 10.

Number Bonds/Combinations

The number bonds/combinations (for sums below ten) are fundamental in aiding number concept. The preceding work has built up to this formal presentation of number facts. Knowledge of the number bonds is also important when addition is tackled formally. There are therefore two important reasons why they should be understood and learned at this early stage. The following are likely to be the most useful:

2 as 1 and 1							
3 as 2 and 1	1 and 2						
4 as 3 and 1	2 and 2	3 and 1					
5 as 4 and 1	3 and 2	1 and 4					
6 as 5 and 1	4 and 2	3 and 3	2 and 4	1 and 5			
7 as 6 and 1	5 and 2	4 and 3	3 and 4	2 and 5	1 and 6		
8 as 7 and 1	6 and 2	5 and 3	4 and 4	3 and 5	2 and 6	1 and 7	
9 as 8 and 1	7 and 2	6 and 3	5 and 4	4 and 5	3 and 6	2 and 7	1 and 8

Consecutive columns give practice at adding 1, 2, 3, 4, 5, 6, 7 and 8 respectively, show a pattern in the combinations and illustrate the commutative property of addition.

Practice can, for example, be scheduled in the following ways:

- Adding 1 to each number from 1 to 8
- Adding every number from 2 to 7 to the number 2
- Adding the numbers randomly
- Adding numbers in every possible way to make a given sum, such as 7

The practice can be supported by using 'concrete' materials:

1. Any form of counters that remain separate, so that the child sees the 'ones' in each part and the resultant whole, possibly arranged in recognisable patterns.
2. Blocks, like centicubes, which can be joined together and separated, so that the child starts to see the numbers holistically.
3. Cuisenaire rods, where each number is represented by a rod of different length and colour, so that the child visualises the 'sizes' of the numbers, rather than counting in ones. They are a 'continuous' material.
4. A number line, which links the numbers to a sense of proportionality and sequencing and allows the child to track forwards and backwards.

An important consequence of this work should be the establishment of the commutative law, which states that the order in which the numbers are added does not affect the answer, in other words $2 + 5 = 5 + 2 = 7$. This also reinforces what will be an important component of the developmental structure of our philosophy, that is, the learner is encouraged to look and consider before starting to compute. For example, in adding a small number such as 2 to 7, it is better to start with the 7 and count on the 2, than start with the 2 and count on 7. This does require teachers to ease back on the demand for instant answers or instant reactions.

You will need to establish the commutative law by reminding and organising the child to see the logic of the demonstrations he has just undertaken.

This latter concept, plus the actual number bonds/combinations is summarised below:

+	*1*	*2*	*3*	*4*	*5*	*6*	*7*	*8*
1	2	3	4	5	6	7	8	9
2	3	4	5	6	7	8	9	
3	4	5	6	7	8	9		
4	5	6	7	8	9			
5	6	7	8	9				
6	7	8	9					
7	8	9						
8	9							

This table can be used for reference by the child and as a compact source from which to memorise the data. The patterns and sequences help the memorising.

Place Value

Number sense and place value understanding are found to be core numerical abilities for Chinese children learning early mathematics. Deficiencies in these two numerical skills, together with fact-retrieval and procedural skills could predict Chinese children having difficulties learning mathematics in the first few school years (Ho *et al.*, 2015). (See also Ho and Cheng, 1997.)

The use of base ten and the consequent place value of numbers are conventions that lie at the heart of our number system. The most frequent, and predictable, difficulty that occurs is that the child does not understand that the value of a digit depends on its place in a string of digits. This difficulty is not to be confused with the transposal of numbers (e.g. 34 for 43). There are also some problems with misunderstanding the language of these conventions. For example, a number such as 'three hundred and fifteen thousand' could be 30015000. Many problems that appear in later numeracy can be traced back to a lack of understanding of place value. It therefore needs careful attention, particularly when zeros are involved.

Grouping in tens

The number ten owes its significance to the number of fingers we have and their use in counting. This use of ten as a collective unit has significance in the written symbols we use for numbers. We have ten fingers and ten different number symbols. When we ran out of fingers for counting a quantity bigger than ten, we had to use something else, for example a second person's fingers, likewise when we ran out of number symbols we had to use a second, additional symbol. Using this in another column or place was a crucial concept in the history of mathematics.

The following approach attempts to show a logical connection between a number of objects and the symbols used to write the numbers. The approach moves from the concrete to the abstract, 'foreign language', written form in progressively more abstract/representative forms.

Step 1 Physically grouping

Objects do not naturally form themselves into groups of ten. Practice in doing this can be the first step towards understanding. The type of exercise here is simply to provide a group of items and let the child group them in tens, possibly as two groups of five. What the child sees are groups of tens which are numerically proportional to their value (Figure 5.3).

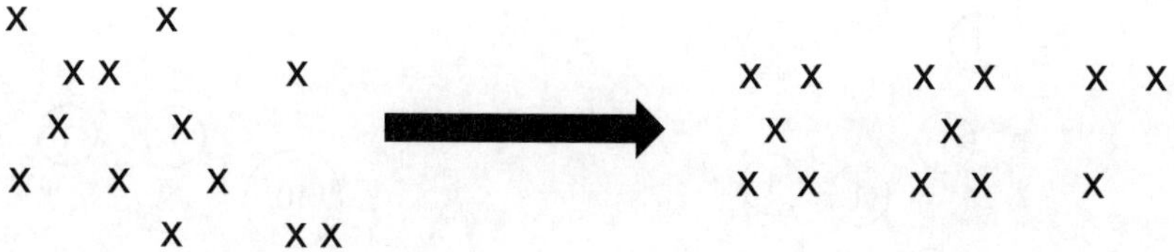

Figure 5.3 Physically grouping.

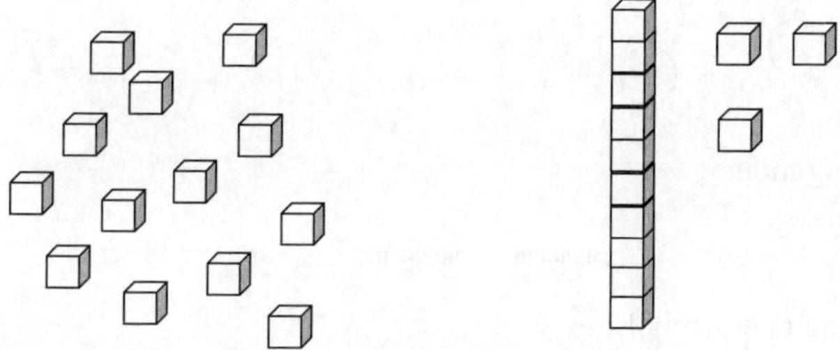

Figure 5.4 Base ten blocks.

Step 2 Using base ten blocks
Dienes (or base ten) blocks have a different block for ten, which is in direct proportion to the length of ten ones blocks (Figure 5.4).

Step 3 Using money
Although a 10p coin is physically larger than a 1p coin, it is not proportionally ten times bigger, but it is a different colour. The use of money therefore moves the child towards non-proportional representation of quantity (Figure 5.5a).

Step 4 Using written tally symbols
The use of different tally symbols for ten and one, such as used in ancient Egypt and for Roman numbers, gives a written symbol version of the money activity above (Figure 5.5b) and shows that grouping into tens has a long history.

Another suitable manipulative type of object here is bundles of ten cocktail sticks or straws and single cocktail sticks or straws. The material retains proportionality, but emphasises the 'collecting together' of ones into tens.

Step 5 Recording in words
Writing numbers down can be achieved using the words 'Tens' and 'Ones' as labels (Figure 5.6).

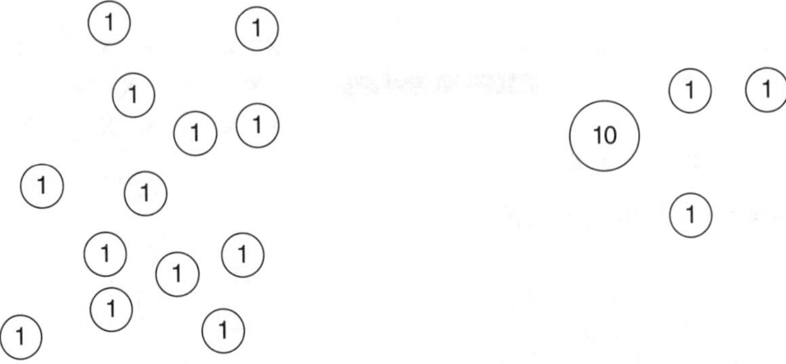

5.5a Using money.

IIIIIIIIIIIII   ~~IIIIIIIIII~~ III   X III

5.5b Using tally symbols.

1 Tens   3 Ones

Figure 5.6 Recording in words.

Tens	Ones
1	3

Figure 5.7 Using headings.

1 3

Figure 5.8 Omission of headings.

Step 6 Using place value columns
Writing these labels for each number is inefficient and time consuming, but using them as headings (Figure 5.7) saves some of this effort, while leaving a clear reminder of the existence and value of the number places. Later we will use the place value cards to help maintain the concept during addition and subtraction.

Step 7 Omission of the headings
Eventually, the headings can be dropped once their role in defining the place value of the digits is understood (Figure 5.8).

This is a highly structured progression and care must be taken before leaving any step out. It may be that the teacher simply moves through a particular step more quickly according to the learner's response.

Tens alone

When we write 10, we are conveying that these two digits represents 1 ten and 0 ones. In some number systems, it would be redundant to mention the 0 ones, because zero means there are no objects there. The Hindu-Arabic system use of zero is a very sophisticated concept. The Romans did not feel the need for a symbol for nothing. Place value uses fixed relative positions. So an understanding of the role of 0 as marking that a particular 'place' is empty is essential, as is its role of maintaining the place and thus value of the other digits. One good way of demonstrating this with children is to make each child a place value and his fingers the digits, so that 30 looks like Figure 5.9. The teacher can discuss with the children why the second (ones) child is needed to demonstrate 30.

Figure 5.10 shows three ways of depicting four tens. They must be identified as tens, classified, counted and recorded together. The 0 in the written version 40 makes it quite clear that:

- The 4 objects are tens, and
- * There are no ones

Figure 5.9 Hands showing place value.

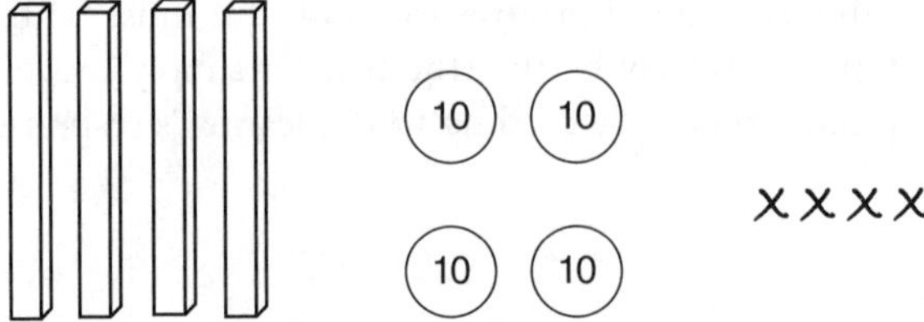

Figure 5.10 Three ways of depicting four tens.

In the spoken form, ten became abbreviated to -ty. Hence six tens became sixty, etc. Although it is obviously incorrect and contrived there is some good teaching value in the use of 'tenty' for one hundred. For example, it is a logical extension of the pattern of the other '-ty' numbers and helps the child realise something new is happening if we change the rule/pattern to a new word – hundred. It is also useful if renaming from the hundred column is used.

Grouping in hundreds

After 10, 20, 30, 40, 50, 60, 70, 80, 90, it is, if we understand the use of ten as the base number, impossible to record any more tens in the tens column. We have run out of number symbols again, using all the digits 1–9. If this counting in tens was demonstrated using 10p coins, there could also be an argument against having too many coins. The solutions to the two situations are parallel; we use another collective unit, hundred, in another column, or we use another coin. In each case, the hundred can be seen as 10 tens. Dienes blocks or cocktail sticks may again be used here, especially if the sticks are available in boxes of 100. In Figure 5.11 the number 235 is represented in various ways.

Grouping in thousands

Thousand is the next collective unit, composed of 10 hundreds. The next collective units are ten thousand and hundred thousand. The analogues of money, tally symbols and labels are less effective in contributing to an understanding of numbers above a thousand, although discussions about how many base ten thousand blocks would be needed to construct these higher value numbers are helpful, particularly as they continue to follow a pattern of 'long', 'flat' and 'cube'. Usually, if place value has been properly understood up to this point, further extension of the system offers no further fundamental problems.

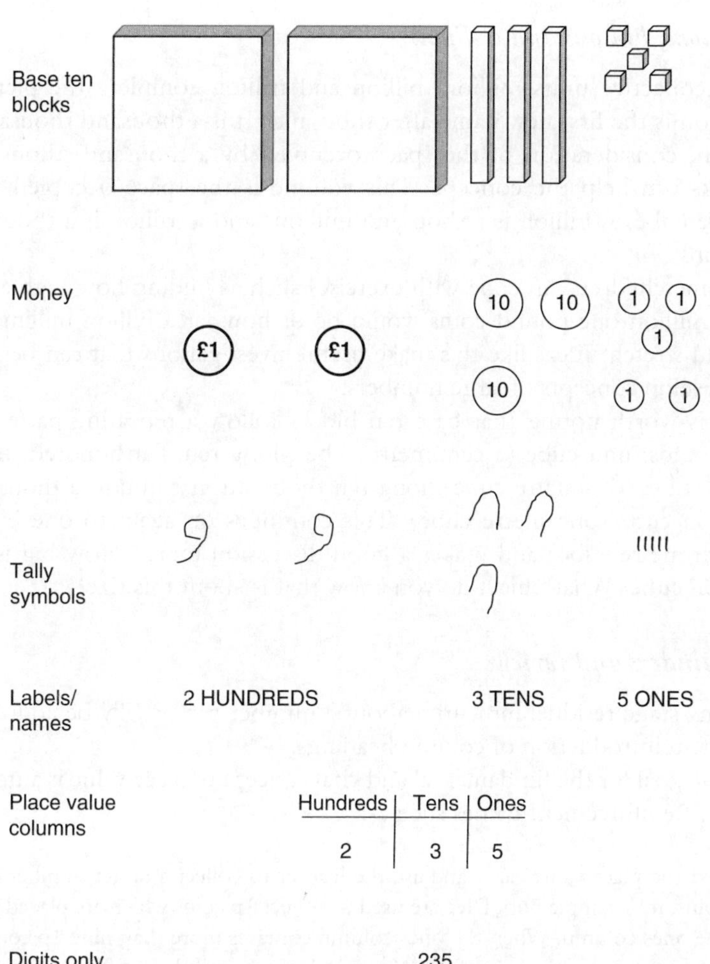

Figure 5.11 Representations of the number 235.

Certain large numbers with thousands can cause problems because of language, the word 'ten' used in 'ten thousand' and 'hundred' used in 'hundred thousand' and the large number of digits, many of which can be zeros. For example, the number two hundred and six thousand and fifty can be incorrectly written as 200600050, 2006050, 20600050, 2060050, 6250, etc. It can be helpful to consider the number in two parts: the thousands separate from the rest, which must fill three places (for hundreds, tens and ones) set aside in advance, for example for the above number the first step would be 206 □□□, then 206 □50, then 206 050.

Millions, billions and trillions

The collective units million, billion and trillion complete the picture. Million is the first new name after thousand. It is a thousand thousands. Again, consideration of the space occupied by a thousand 'thousand' blocks can help the concept. This volume is the space occupied by a metre cube. A billion is a thousand millions and a trillion is a thousand billions.

Some children can cope with exercises such as finding how high a pile of a million one pound coins would be or how far a billion millimetres would stretch. Ideas like this make useful investigations that can be used to develop concepts of large numbers.

It is worth noting that base ten blocks follow a repeating pattern in thousands: unit cube (a centimetre cube), long ten, flat hundred, thousand cube, (decimetre cube), long ten thousand, flat hundred thousand, million cube (one metre cube). This continues on again to one billion (a ten metre cube) and makes a good discussion topic. 'How big is the billion cube? What object do you know that is about this size?'

Reminders and reviews

At any stage residual insecurity about a number can usually be addressed by the reintroduction of column headings.

The goal for the fundamental and vital concept of place value is automaticity. Reinforcement games such as:

> Use the place value cards and ask the learner to collect a target number of coins, for example 56p. Dice are used to collect 1p coins which are placed in the ones column. When the ones column contains more than nine 1p coins then trading ten 1p coins for a 10p coin is used until the target is reached. The game then continues taking away 1p coins back to zero, using trading again, but now trading down from a 10p coin to ten 1p coins.
>
> (It is possible to buy six-sided dice with 1p, 2p, 5p, 10p, 20p, 50p and with 0, 1, 2, 5, 10, 20. See the Resources List.)

Diagnostic ideas

Questions such as the following can be used for practice, and for diagnosing difficulties:

- What is the value of the 7 in the number 4725?
- Write in figures thirty thousand and five.

- Write the numbers seventeen and then seventy-one.
- Write in words 12,065.
- Write down the largest and smallest three-digit numbers you can make with the three digits 2, 6 and 9.

Number Bonds/Combinations for Ten

Because of its universal significance, it is essential for a child to have a good understanding of ten (and its role in the base ten system). It is worth making a special study of the number bonds for ten and helping the child to learn these facts. They are core facts and, if rote learning a lot of facts is difficult, these are one of the key collections of facts that do need to be learned. Focus on learning the facts with the most value/mileage. There are several illustrations and exercises that can be used to help the child understand and visualise these facts.

10 + 0
9 + 1 }these are especially useful for estimation / mental arithmetic
8 + 2 }
7 + 3
6 + 4
5 + 5 {some children readily understand and remember 'doubles' (and also see that 5 is exactly half of 10)
4 + 6
3 + 7
2 + 8
1 + 9
0 + 10

All the different ways of making ten can be found, for example, by:

- Joining together ten centicubes, then breaking them up in various ways
- Using a ten-bead bead-string which is an excellent model for emphasising the conservation of 10 as the beads can't get off, nor can any be added as it breaks down into different number bonds
- Laying down a Cuisenaire rod for ten, then laying down beside it combinations of other rods to give the same length

987654321
123456789

Figure 5.12 Different font sizes to illustrate the number combinations for ten.

- Using an abacus
- Using coins or poker chip or chunky counters
- Using the pattern for ten

x x   x x
 x   x
x x   x x

Diagrams like those in Figures 5.12 can help the memory.

The number bonds/combinations for ten can be used and extended into many areas of numeracy, for example when adding a column of numbers by 'casting out tens' and the number bonds for 100. They are facts with high usage potential and thus worth a concentrated learning effort.

Numbers Near Ten, Hundred or Thousand

Ten, hundred and thousand are major 'landmarks' and reference points in the base ten system.

- From them, steps outwards can give meaning to numbers nearby, above or below. For example, the number 8 is just 'less than' 10, and the number 1010 is just 'more than' 1000. Later this can be quantified, as in 8 is 2 less than 10 and 1010 is 10 more than 1000.
- A question like 4×98 can be seen as just 'less than' 4×100. This can give the approximate answer 'just below 400', or can form the starting

point for estimation work and mental calculations in the grasshopper style:

$$\begin{aligned} 4\times98 &= 4\times100-4\times2 \\ &= 400-8 \\ &= 392 \end{aligned}$$

The appraisal question, 'Is the answer bigger or smaller?' can be used again in this context.

- Dienes/base ten blocks are designed to give visual, and kinaesthetic perspectives on these quantities and their relative values. It is not safe to assume that children will immediately make the relationship between blocks, symbols and quantities. You will have to demonstrate this.
- There are many examples of carefully chosen and presented visual images within the 'Maths Explained' video tutorials (www.mathsexplained.co.uk).

Summary

This chapter has looked at the concept of numbers and their values, concentrating on place value and the importance of key numbers, especially ten. The remaining chapters will continue to develop number concept and facility by extending the child's experiences into the interrelationships of numbers and operations. What is important at this stage is that the child has some clear ideas as to the values of the low numbers, their relationship to the key numbers and an understanding of number bonds/combinations in the light of the conservation of number and the commutative law, and a clear concept of place value. This knowledge will form a sound base for the remaining development of maths skills and knowledge and thus the foundations for the developmental programme.

6

Addition and Subtraction

Basic Facts/Number Combinations

One of our key beliefs is that interventions must have mathematical structure and credibility.

Introduction

If you ask dyslexic or dyscalculic children, or indeed any child, to add 8 and 7 and explain how they reached their answer you will get a selection of methods, depending on each child's experiences and own idiosyncratic ideas. Ackerman *et al.* (1986) call them 'inconsistent', for example:

- Counting all: the child counts to 8 and then counts on the 7 (probably counting on fingers or on objects in the room).
- Counting on: the child holds 8 in his head and counts on 7 counting through 9 to 15 (again, probably counting on fingers or on objects in the room). This strategy is prone to the common error where the child starts counting at 8.
- Using 10: the child breaks 7 into $2+5$, uses the 2 with the 8 to make 10, then adds 5, or works via $7+3$.
- Using doubles: the child uses $(2\times8)-1$ or $(2\times7)+1$.
- Straight recall: the child 'just knows'.

Carpenter and Moser, quoted in Thompson (1999) identify five levels of sophistication of addition strategies used by young children when solving simple word problems:

Mathematics for Dyslexics and Dyscalculics: A Teaching Handbook, Fourth Edition.
Steve Chinn and Richard E. Ashcroft.

- Count all.
- Count on from the first number.
- Count on from the larger number.
- Recall/retrieval of a known fact.
- Deriving the fact from a known fact (as in using 5 + 5 to access 5 + 6).

In their research on basic addition, Gray and Tall (1994) observed that children rated as above average in maths by their teachers either accessed facts by direct recall or used 'mathematical' strategies to work them out, often very quickly. The children rated as below average had poor recall and little or no use of these compensatory strategies. The above average group rarely used counting. Counting was the only resort for the below average group.

More recently there has been an increased interest from researchers such as Torbeyns *et al.* (2004) and Smith and Teague (2014) in children's use of strategies, although some have only looked at a limited range of strategies. Generally speaking, these studies suggest that children with learning difficulties in maths, not surprisingly, continue to use the counting-on strategy longer than their age equivalent 'normal' peers. Torbeyns *et al.* comment on the potential benefits that: 'early and frequent intervention directed toward facilitating the development of these children's procedural skills might reduce the difference in the rate of development.' If children are left to devise their own survival strategies, then we must not be surprised if these lack mathematical sophistication; nor must we be surprised if it is very difficult to replace these established methods with new ones. In other words, the intervention should start before it is needed. It should be pre-emptive and based on what we know about the reasons for children to start to fail in maths.

It is of note that, increasingly in the USA, the term *arithmetic, or number combinations* is replacing the term *number facts* (Gersten *et al.*, 2005) recognising that the 'facts' are not always accessed by simple retrieval.

In this chapter we will look at strategies for working out basic facts efficiently and in ways that enhance and interrelate numbers, number concept, concept of ten and place value and facility with number and number operations. We are assuming that a child will have great difficulty in rote learning the facts and, even if he should succeed, difficulty in holding those facts in memory for more than a few hours. Threlfall and Frobisher (1999) argue that 'the short-term gains that give rote learning its appeal are illusory and are less efficient in the longer term' and we should note that Threlfall and Frobisher are not referring to a special needs population, where their comments are even more apposite. Children will be able to access more facts if they have strategies to use when memory fails them and leaves them with no way to obtain an answer, that is, helpless. Some strategies will be used in their entirety by a child, but others will be mastered to the stage where they become memory 'hooks' and are only used in part to supplement a half-known fact and give a security in the validity of the answer. Since the strategies involve the same key facts each time, this procedure automatically rehearses these key facts over and over again. However, just because we choose to label them 'key' facts does not mean they are guaranteed a secure place in long-term memory.

The strategy of counting on is an ineffective strategy beyond counting on one or two or maybe three. It is a method that requires too much time to operate and it tends therefore, to be susceptible to poor short-term memory and may overload working memory. It is also susceptible to counting errors. Furthermore, it does not support number concept or the relationships between numbers; neither does it encourage seeing patterns in numbers. We advocate strategies that use number relationships wherever possible. Chinn (1994) looked at the knowledge of basic addition facts presented at four-second intervals and twelve-second intervals to a dyslexic population of 11–13-year-old students and found that, although dyslexic pupils scored significantly less well than a mainstream population in the four-second addition task, their scores in the twelve-second addition task were virtually equivalent. This is not surprising, as one would expect any of the facts asked to be accessible in twelve seconds by finger counting (although other strategies were used by both groups).

The relative ease, and accuracy, of counting on in ones as a strategy for accessing addition facts may be a major contributor to addition being the default operation for many learners (Chinn, 2013). Counting back in ones is often done for subtraction, less efficiently. Counting forwards and backwards in other numbers, say three, is even less efficient for multiplication and division facts.

It is easy to underestimate just how much early experience and information a dyslexic or dyscalculic student has missed, which makes it difficult to know how far back to go when starting a teaching programme. One of the key ideas that this chapter advocates is the breaking down and building up of numbers. So, if a child did not receive and absorb work such as looking at 6 as in Figure 6.1, then strategies which suggest that $8+6$ can be added as $(8+2)+4$ will be less easy to teach (or learn). As ever, you have to 'read' the child to know how much material to provide. Ashlock (2010) provides an excellent range of teaching ideas to develop and reinforce algorithms and concepts.

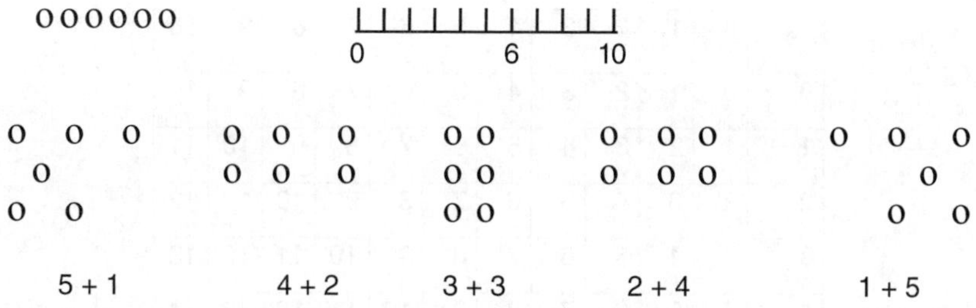

000000 — number line 0 … 6 … 10

5 + 1   4 + 2   3 + 3   2 + 4   1 + 5

Figure 6.1 Visual images for six.

Strategies for Learning/Remembering the Addition and Subtraction Facts

The basic addition facts, which convert to the basic subtraction facts, from 0 to 10 can be arranged in a square (Figure 6.2; see also the times table facts square). This gives the child a task of rote learning 121 addition and 121 subtraction facts or developing strategies for as many of these facts as possible. Viewing this statement in isolation makes it seem a daunting task. Indeed, viewing that density of information as presented in the square at one time can be a daunting task. One of the great characteristics of maths is that you can use the interrelationships between facts and operations to significantly reduce the size of tasks such as this one.

The procedure for addressing the addition/subtraction facts task is similar in technique to the one that will be used for times tables. It uses patterns, the interrelationships between numbers and operations and the ability to break down and build up numbers, using the core/key numbers (0, 1, 2, 5, 10). It builds on strategies that the children themselves sometimes use, but organises and rationalises idiosyncratic ideas. It adds structure and pattern. The presentation as a square of facts gives some motivation in that initial gains can be shown convincingly and as quickly achieved, by shading in 'known' facts. The strategies are widely applicable and mathematical rather than being a collection of one-off 'tricks', rhymes or mnemonics. It is not the purpose to overwhelm the learner by presenting all this information in such a concentrated way at one time. It is to provide motivation by demonstrating progress.

Even though we discuss subtraction after working on the addition aspect of these facts, we feel it is most important to emphasise the subtraction 'side' of the addition fact as each fact is discussed. As ever, teachers use their judgement to decide what constitutes a counterproductive

+	0	1	2	3	4	5	6	7	8	9	10
0	0	1	2	3	4	5	6	7	8	9	10
1	1	2	3	4	5	6	7	8	9	10	11
2	2	3	4	5	6	7	8	9	10	11	12
3	3	4	5	6	7	8	9	10	11	12	13
4	4	5	6	7	8	9	10	11	12	13	14
5	5	6	7	8	9	10	11	12	13	14	15
6	6	7	8	9	10	11	12	13	14	15	16
7	7	8	9	10	11	12	13	14	15	16	17
8	8	9	10	11	12	13	14	15	16	17	18
9	9	10	11	12	13	14	15	16	17	18	19
10	10	11	12	13	14	15	16	17	18	19	20

Figure 6.2 The addition and subtraction facts square.

overload of information. However, this has a developmental attribute, for example leading to early experiences of algebra:

$$15=8+\square \quad (\text{where the algebra form would be } 15=8+y)$$

The zero facts: n + 0 and 0 + n

Many years of experience in the classroom has taught us that zero will create problems.

The collection of facts, $n+0$ and $0+n$, can be demonstrated using, for example, counters in boxes.

- An empty box is shown to the child and, after discussion about the contents and zero, the symbol 0 is written on the screen, white board or a sheet of paper.
- Five counters are added to the box. + 5 is written on the screen/board/paper, giving $0+5$.
- The child counts the number of counters in the box, 5.
- The written form now is $0+5=5$.

A similar procedure may be used to deduce $5+0=5$. Careful and appropriately focused use of language is needed if later confusion with $\times 0$ facts is to be pre-empted.

Much of 'early' maths is better taught when the need to pre-empt future confusion is addressed.

This establishes 21 facts, though, as is ever the case, an unusual or new presentation of a 'known' fact may confuse the child. A typical error occurs in addition sums such as

$$\begin{array}{r} 356 \\ +30 \\ \hline 380 \end{array}$$

The subtraction of zero should be demonstrated, discussed and presented in symbols.

Adding on 1 and 2

This can be introduced by asking the child to look at a number line and handle counters or a bead string (Figure 6.4), so that he sees, say, $4+1$ as one move on the number line, that is, a move to the next number, one counter added (Figure 6.3), one bead moved. For adding one, the child has to 'see' the process as simply moving to the next number by adding one object each time and the reverse by subtracting/taking away one object each time.

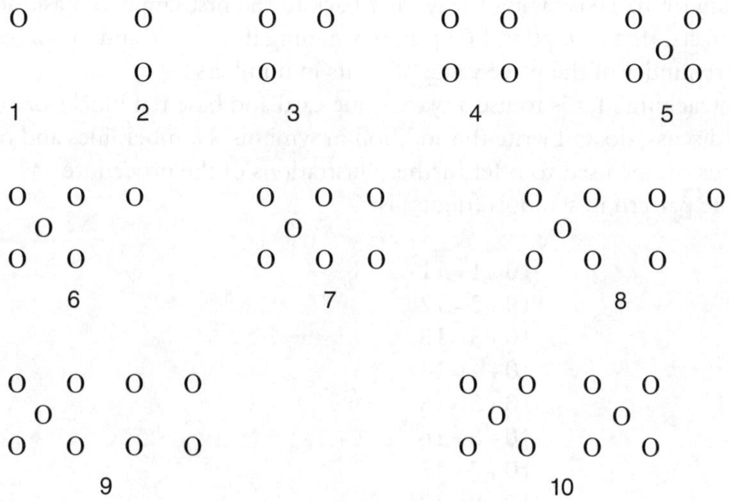

Figure 6.3 The number patterns for 1–10.

Figure 6.4 The bead string set up to show 8 + 2.

A very similar argument applies to adding 2, although the child may have to physically and orally count on the two numbers. This should still be quick and accurate. A knowledge of the even and odd numbers will support this operation and encourage the appraisal of answers. The child can practise counting in twos, starting from different numbers. The child will then need to spend some time looking at facts such as 1 + 9 and 2 + 5, with the teacher leading him into the commutative properties of $1 + n = n + 1$ and $n + 2 = 2 + n$ and teaching that it is quicker, less prone to error and more effective to count the smaller number onto the bigger number.

If this can be accomplished, then 36 more fact squares can be shaded in on the addition square, a total of 57, leaving 64 to go.

Adding to ten; adding on ten

It is often the case when working with dyslexics and dyscalculics that a lesson has more than one goal. The subsidiary goal is usually a review of a previously 'learned', and often 'forgotten', fact or concept. In this case the forgotten concept is likely to be place value. If this is re-established, then adding on to 10 is taking the learner back to the first family of basic addition facts, that is, $n + 0$ and $0 + n$ and extending it to $n + 10$ and $10 + n$ partly as a reminder of the place value of digits in numbers.

A teaching idea is to use a place value card and base ten blocks or coins and discuss, do and write the addition in symbols. Number lines and bead strings can be used to offer further illustrations of the procedure.

The pattern in symbols (digits) is:

10 + 1 = 11
10 + 2 = 12
10 + 3 = 13
10 + 4 = 14
10 + 5 = 15
10 + 6 = 16
10 + 7 = 17
10 + 8 = 18
10 + 9 = 19 and 10 + 10 = 20

The tens digit (1) does not change, but the ones digit becomes the same as the added number, 10 + d = 1d (not an algebra term). An extra difficulty sometimes arises from the inconvenient situation that the names of the numbers from 13 to 19, unlike subsequent decades, have the ones digit named first, for example 17. This makes the oral pattern inconsistent in comparison to the next decades. This is a chance to remind learners to be ready for this inconsistency.

If this series of facts is understood and absorbed then the task has reduced to 49 facts.

Use of doubles

For addition facts, children often know the doubles. Similarly, in multiplication they often know the squares. Many children also use them to derive other addition facts, for example, 8 + 7 is often seen as double 8 less 1 or as double 7 plus 1.

Two sets of counters provide a good representation of the derivation of these facts, using the core patterns for the arrangements, for example, 6 + 6.

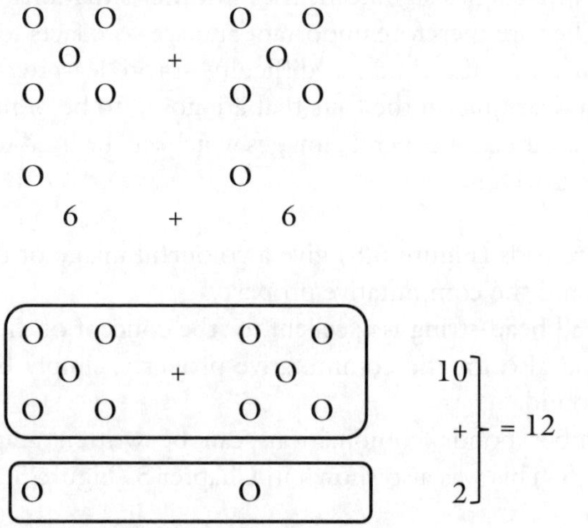

```
O   O       O   O
  O     +     O
O   O       O   O

O           O
  6     +     6
```

```
 ----------------------
| O   O       O   O    |
|   O     +     O      |     10 ┐
| O   O       O   O    |        |
 ----------------------      +  ├ = 12
 ----------------------         |
| O           O        |      2 ┘
 ----------------------
```

Cuisenaire rods are also useful, for example two seven rods are placed side by side and 7 + 7 is written and discussed as being equal to 14. A one rod is placed on the end of a seven rod, increasing the sum to 15 (adding on 1 takes you to the next number). The seven and one rods are exchanged for an eight rod and the addition 7 + 8 = 15 can be discussed, maybe using the ever-useful question, 'Is this bigger or smaller?

$$(2+2)+1=2+3=3+2=5$$
$$(3+3)+1=3+4=4+3=7$$
$$(3+3)-1=3+2=2+3=5$$
$$(4+4)+1=4+5=5+4=9$$
$$(4+4)-1=4+3=3+4=7$$
$$(5+5)+1=5+6=6+5=11$$
$$(5+5)-1=5+4=4+5=9 \quad \text{and so on.}$$

This gives 7 facts for the doubles and 12 facts for doubles ±1. The total task is down to 30 facts, half of which are commutative, so there are 15 different facts to go.

Again there is an opportunity here to look at the concept of odd and even numbers and at the basic rules about combining numbers.

The doubles are core basic facts.

Number bonds/combinations for ten

This family of facts has significant uses in other situations to solve other problems. They are therefore important and are core facts to learn. To put this in another way, if a child has difficulty in rote learning facts, then let him focus his learning on the facts that are going to be of most use.

There are a variety of concrete images which can be used to illustrate the number bonds to ten.

- Cuisenaire rods (Figure 6.5) give a colourful image of the linear relationship and the commutative property.
- A ten-bead bead-string is excellent for the concept of the conservation of ten and also for the commutative property, simply by turning the string around.
- The number bonds/combinations can be written graphically, as in Figure 6.6. This was also shown in Chapter 5 (Figure 5.12).

Note: A learner can be taught to write a normal sized digit version of this series quite quickly, 0 to 10 on top of 10 to 0, with 5 and 5 having to be aligned as a check, at the top of an exam paper, removing stress when the facts are needed within the exam.

0	1	2	3	4	5	6	7	8	9	10
10	9	8	7	6	5	4	3	2	1	0

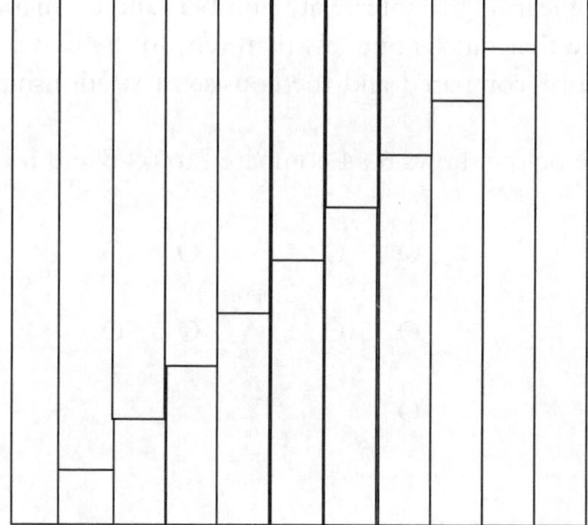

Figure 6.5 Cuisenaire rods.

Figure 6.6 Different font sizes to illustrate the number combinations for ten.

Whatever materials the child handles, or visual images he sees, you must make sure that the digits are presented with each aid so that the link is made between the material or the visual representation and the symbols.

Although this section collects together the number bonds/combinations for 10, only 6 + 4, 4 + 6, 7 + 3 and 3 + 7 are 'new' facts, so, 26 to go out of the 121.

The number bonds/combinations for ten are core facts.

Number bonds/combinations for nine

It is valuable to link these to the number bonds for ten. They are important as part of the strategy for the nine times table facts and for continuing the processes of learning to interrelate numbers and estimation. The child is guided to see that nine is one less than ten, so the two sets of number bonds need to be compared and the consistent relationship and pattern emphasised.

The example below shows 6 + 4 compared to 6 + 3 and 5 + 4

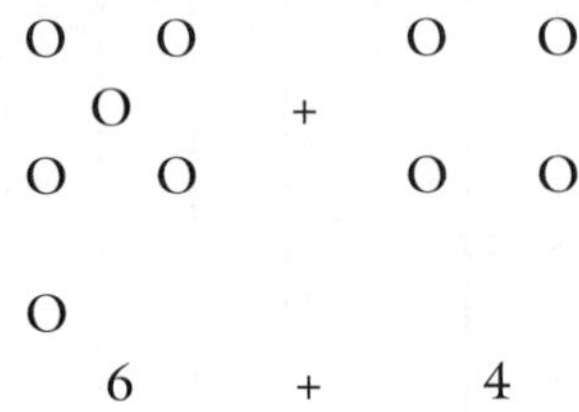

Adding on nine

Adding on nine also follows on from the facts for ten. This collection of facts is also useful as an early example of estimation. The child is learning again that ten is one more than nine and that nine is one less than ten. The question to use when comparing the addition of nine to the addition of ten is again, 'Is the answer bigger or smaller?'

The child can practise the addition with coins, Cuisenaire rods or base ten blocks, comparing adding ten with adding nine, looking at adding nine by adding ten then subtracting one, or using the added number to provide one to make the nine up to ten and thus making the added number one less, for example:

$$9+6=10-1+6 \quad \text{or} \quad 9+6=(9+1)+(6-1)$$

These two groups of nine facts add twelve more facts, leaving fourteen to go.

Sharing doubles

Algebra can be an easy and illustrative way of writing a generalisation, though we are not saying this is a good idea for seven-year-old pupils.

So $n+n$ is the same as $(n-1)+(n+1)$. There are six of these facts left that have not been dealt with elsewhere:

3+5 and 5+3 have the same total as 4+4=8

5+7 and 7+5 have the same total as 6+6=12

8+6 and 6+8 have the same total as 7+7=14

(The others are: 2+4&4+2; 4+6&6+4; 7+9&9+7.)

Again these facts can be experienced by moving counters between two initially equal patterns. The strategy is an example of the conservation of number and is worth inclusion for this learning objective alone.

There are eight facts to go. The commutative property reduces this to four: 8+3, 8+4, 8+5, 7+4.

Adding onto 8 can be achieved via 10, for example 8+5 becomes (8+2)+3.

7+4 can be seen as one more than the number bond 7+3.

Overview

Some of the facts/combinations described in this chapter fall into more than one strategy group. As flexibility is important, this gives the child some choice of method. Shading squares on the addition fact table for families of strategies can emphasise the pattern of each relationship.

In each strategy there is ample scope to enable the child to use concrete manipulative materials and visual images. These materials and images must be used, as ever, in conjunction with the written numbers. The materials and images are of no use if they are not automatically linked in the child's mind to the symbols for the quantities they represent. Also, the child has to learn to progress from the concrete to the visual to the symbolic.

When writing and talking about the addition facts, you must use more than one format and vary the vocabulary without creating confusion, for example, $4 + 6 = 10$ can be phrased as:

- What is 4 add 6?
- What adds on to 4 to make 10?
- Can you find the 'right' number to fit into the boxes?

$$4+6=\square \quad 4+\square=10 \quad \square+6=10$$

The latter two examples are leading the child to see subtraction as 'adding on'. So, $4+6=\square$ is a straight addition fact. The child is, however, learning that ten can be split into two constituent parts, in this case four and six. With $4+\square=10$ and $\square+6=10$ the child still has to know that we are looking at two parts, but he now knows the total and only one of the parts. We are changing the frame of reference, not the knowledge. The child is learning the adaptability of mathematics facts.

Subtraction Facts

Although the subtraction facts should be discussed alongside the addition facts, there will probably be a need to reinforce this material. From informal surveys when lecturing to adults on teaching arithmetic, we know that the perception of subtraction is that it is a harder operation than addition. This has been confirmed with analysis of the data collected to standardise Chinn's (2017a) '15 minute test' from *More Trouble with Maths.*

Further examples and the introduction of the vocabulary of subtraction (minus, subtract, take away, etc.) should help the child to translate his addition facts into subtraction facts. The idea of a total or sum and two parts or addends will be used in 'harder' subtraction problems in the next chapter.

The child needs to learn that addition and subtraction are variations of the same process (Chinn and Ashcroft, 1992; 2004). The ideas above provide the framework which you can use and develop into an instructional format.

Extension

We (Chinn and Ashcroft, 1992; 2004) have long been advocates for the use of patterns and sequences to support memory. For example, the addition fact 4 + 7 can be extended to the sequences/patterns:

4 + 7 = 11	4 + 7 = 11
4 + 17 = 21	14 + 7 = 21
4 + 27 = 31	24 + 7 = 31
4 + 37 = 41	34 + 7 = 41
4 + 47 = 51	44 + 7 = 51, etc.

These patterns show the consistent contribution of 4 + 7 to a sequence of additions. We have found that our dyslexic learners often need the aspects of this pattern (and similar patterns) pointing out. In doing this, you are also leading the child towards more challenging addition problems, where he will be using the addition facts and, it is hoped, reinforcing his knowledge of these facts.

7

The Times Tables Facts/Number Combinations

Introduction

Whenever there is a back-to-basics movement in education, the issue of learning 'times tables' (and other basic facts) arises. This seems to happen very frequently in England, most recently in 2014 with the introduction of a new curriculum. To a large extent this argument about rote learning times table facts is irrelevant for dyslexics and probably many other students, too. In our combined experience of over 50 years of teaching mathematics to dyslexics, we have found that the rote learning of times tables is a frustrating exercise for both learner and teacher (see also Miles 1983; Pritchard *et al.*, 1989; Chinn, 1995a; Turner Ellis *et al.*, 1996; Threlfall and Frobisher, 1999; Geary 2003). Yet still there are unrealistic expectations which should not be applied to *all* children, dyslexic or not.

It is one of our hopes for the future that, as neuroscience becomes increasingly sophisticated, there will be neurological evidence as to why this task is so difficult for so many children, and what solutions are possible.

Rote Learning Strategies

We believe that there is an effective alternative solution to this problem. Although within this chapter we suggest a highly effective rote learning technique, we believe that strategies, or derived fact strategies (Dowker, 2005) based on patterns and the interrelationships of numbers are effective in learning how to work out times table facts, a principle stated some

Mathematics for Dyslexics and Dyscalculics: A Teaching Handbook, Fourth Edition.
Steve Chinn and Richard E. Ashcroft.

18 years ago in the Primary School Mathematics Curriculum Document for Ireland: Teacher Guidelines (1999):

> All children can gain from using strategies for number facts making them, in effect, number combinations. They can learn the 'easy' number facts first (×1, ×2, ×5, ×10) and use these to build up the others using doubles, near-doubles and patterns of odd and even. These strategies are of particular help to children with memory problems, but can also develop a more secure knowledge of these facts in all learners.

These strategies give the learner routes to an answer, as opposed to him or her relying on only using memory, which will give no possibility of obtaining a correct answer when he or she forgets the fact (Chinn, 1994) or a wrong answer inhibits the access to the correct fact. Again, our experience is that many children already use strategies, as others have found (Gray and Tall, 1994; Bierhoff, 1996), which they have devised for themselves, though often these strategies are neither consistent nor organised mathematically.

Siegler (1991) writes that: 'Children often know and use many strategies for solving a class of problems. Knowing diverse strategies adds to the children's flexibility in solving problems.' and: 'Children's strategy choices may be less subject to conscious, rational control than often thought.' Our experience is that strategies need to be taught and organised, through working with what the child already knows and uses. We have tried to use strategies which are developmental, for example the strategy used to work out 7 × 8 by breaking down the single step to 5 × 8 plus 2 × 8 will be used for products such as 23 × 54 and later for algebraic expressions (Wigley, 1995). We are mindful of the Bransford *et al.* (2000) Key Finding 2:

> To develop competence in an area of enquiry, students must:
>
> a. have a deep foundation of factual knowledge,
> b. understand facts and ideas in the context of a conceptual framework, and
> c. organise knowledge in ways that facilitate retrieval and application.

It is the importance of (b) and (c) in supporting (a) that we are demonstrating in this (and other) chapter(s).

McCloskey *et al.* (reported in Macaruso and Sokol, 1998) hypothesise that the process involved in the retrieval of arithmetic facts is separate from those involved in the execution of calculation procedures. This is further support for the principle of not holding a pupil back in maths just because he cannot retrieve basic facts from memory.

Hattie's (2009) meta-analysis of education research found that metacognitive strategies and Piagetian programmes were among the most effective in influencing learning.

Use of music

There are CDs of times tables set to music. The rhythm and the tune help some to learn the tables, but in our experience, it is not the panacea.

Use of 'fun' games

These are rarely fun for very long and still rely on rote learning. If it works then use it, but remember that the ability to retrieve something from memory does not guarantee that you understand it.

The ARROW technique

If the child is to be encouraged to learn by rote, then this technique is powerful, but, as ever, it will not be successful for every child. It does not claim to be 'fun' other than giving some learners the rewards of success.

The learner can use the ARROW technique to rote learn these facts (Lane and Chinn, 1986; Lane, 1990; 2012). This is a multisensory method using the learner's own voice which, in the initial trials in the 1980s, was recorded on audiotape. Now it is possible to record the data onto computer and use visual input via the screen to provide a multisensory presentation.

1. The child types into the computer the table facts he wishes to learn.
2. He records them onto the computer, in his own voice, leaving a 3–5-second gap between each fact.
3. He puts on headphones and listens to and sees just one fact.
4. He listens again to the fact several times.

If the learner sub-vocalises the fact as he hears it this can be a powerful aid to learning. This can be a very effective method for many people, but as with so many interventions, not for all. The process should be repeated several days in a row for the same set of facts. The learner will probably find that 5–10 facts per session are enough, but success has a great motivating effect, so more may be possible. The goal is to achieve long-term retention.

Learning by Understanding

There are many advantages in learning times table facts by understanding. The methods we advocate provide memory 'hooks' on which to hang several connected facts, and some of them are introductions to procedures used later on in mathematics, such as in estimation, long multiplication and algebra. This is part of the developmental aspect of this approach to teaching maths. The strategies suggested here encourage the learner to look for patterns and interrelationships between numbers and operations; they help develop a facility with numbers and an understanding of algorithms. They may also enhance pupil confidence.

It is our experience that the basic structure for the strategy approach links with the times table square, even though initial work is with separate tables. The square gives an overview of the task, encourages interrelating facts, also presents facts as division and can be used to illustrate gains in an encouraging way. Also a student can learn how to fill in a blank table square (partially), a useful technique which makes good use of some of the extra time which may have been allocated for an examination.

There are 121 facts in the table square (Figure 7.1). The size of this task can be reduced quite quickly and easily. This progress can be readily shown to the learner and contrasts with the normal approach of, 'Which times

×	**0**	**1**	**2**	**3**	**4**	**5**	**6**	**7**	**8**	**9**	**10**
0	0	0	0	0	0	0	0	0	0	0	0
1	0	1	2	3	4	5	6	7	8	9	10
2	0	2	4	6	8	10	12	14	16	18	20
3	0	3	6	9	12	15	18	21	24	27	30
4	0	4	8	12	16	20	24	28	32	36	40
5	0	5	10	15	20	25	30	35	40	45	50
6	0	6	12	18	24	30	36	42	48	54	60
7	0	7	14	21	28	35	42	49	56	63	70
8	0	8	16	24	32	40	48	56	64	72	80
9	0	9	18	27	36	45	54	63	72	81	90
10	0	10	20	30	40	50	60	70	80	90	100

Figure 7.1 The times tables square.

tables facts do you know?' It is worth noting that for some children this mass of information, presented at one time may be overwhelming: too much information. You (the teacher) should ask the child to look at the table with you, to see several helpful things.

There are patterns, some easier than others, for example the column and row for the ten times facts is 10 20 30 40 50 60 70 80 90 100, the numbers from 1 to 10 with an extra digit, a 0, at the end (see also place value). If information can be seen to be in patterns or if it can be organised in patterns, it is easier to learn. There is also a pattern in the sound of the words for the ten times facts which links to the numbers one to nine: ten, twenty, thirty, forty, fifty, sixty, seventy, eighty, ninety – one of us (SC) sometimes uses 'tenty' as well as one hundred to reinforce the verbal pattern, to emphasise the place value need for a special word for 100 and to refer to when in subtraction a hundred is renamed as ten lots of ten, 'tenty'.

There are other patterns in the square that the child can look at later. At this stage you are providing an overview. You must use your professional judgement to see how far to go at this stage without becoming counter productive. It is meant to be a supportive and motivating activity, putting a positive perspective on the number of facts that they do know.

Numbers which do not appear

Not all the numbers between 0 and 100 appear, for example 43 and 71. This does not mean they are not important. They are just not part of this collection of numbers.

Limiting the task

The numbers on the square have a lowest value of 0, and a highest value of 100. This gives some limits for the task, making it appear possible and, with a little understanding of how numbers relate to each other, even more possible.

Currently (2015) children in England are expected to learn the 11× and 12× facts. This seems, in our metric world, to be a superfluous requirement. It is worth noting that the 12× table was found to be the most difficult for primary children in Smith and Teague's (2014) study. The use of strategies, particularly combining 10× and 2× facts for 12× facts, makes this an unnecessary rote task.

Remember that each time the child learns a set of facts, shading in known facts on the square shows that the task remaining is getting smaller. Furthermore, when he learns a fact from say the five times table, for example $7 \times 5 = 35$, he also learns $5 \times 7 = 35$, two facts for the price of one. This commutative property can be introduced quite early in the work and, like all interventions, revisited and reviewed frequently until it is thoroughly internalised by the student.

The order in which to learn the facts

It seems sensible to learn first the facts which lead to the quickest and most secure gains and therefore encourage confidence. You may wish to change the order given, but we suggest that the first five remain set as shown. Our order is based on:

1. The facts that a dyslexic or dyscalculic learner is most likely to know (0×, 1×, 2×, 5× and 10×)
2. The type of strategy advocated

0 1 10 2 5 4 3 6 7 9 8

By the time the child has learnt the times tables facts for 0, 1, 2, 5 and 10, he has reduced his task from 121 facts to learn down to 36 (and this can be almost halved to acknowledge the commutative property of $ab = ba$). These first 85 facts are the easiest to learn and you can demonstrate how the child can start to make significant gains.

Check-backs/reviews

Constant reviews are important. You are often dealing with severe long-term memory deficits and incorrect previous learning. It helps to revise and review material with the child quite often and, as with all skills, without practice the skill level decreases. This is especially so with dyslexics and dyscalculics. We maintain that those learning-check charts you see with headings 'Taught, Revised, Learnt' should also have a fourth column, 'Forgotten'. When S.C. lectures, and it is the same response in many countries, he often asks teachers and parents, 'What are the biggest problems you face with children learning maths?' One of the most frequent responses is, 'He learns it that evening, but by the next morning he has forgotten it again.'

The Commutative Property

The commutative property is expressed algebraically as:

$$ab = ba \qquad (a \times b = b \times a)$$

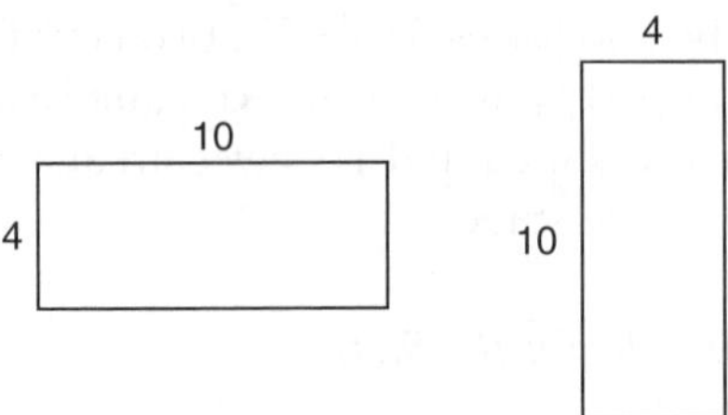

Figure 7.2 Using area.

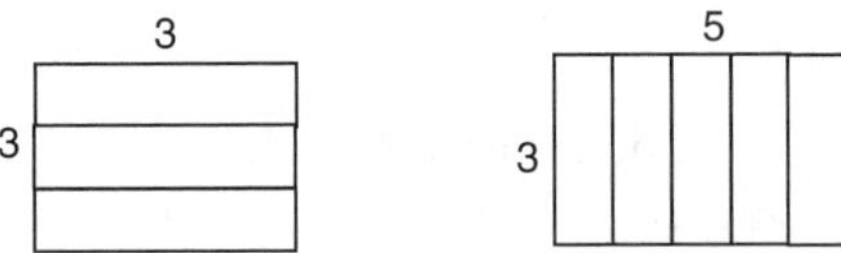

Figure 7.3 Using Cuisenaire rods.

It can be introduced to a child as a way of getting double value for most of the times table facts that he learns. Obviously this is not so for the squares such as 4×4 and 9×9.

One of the models or images used for 'a times b' is area. Base ten (Dienes) blocks, Cuisenaire rods, square counters and squared paper are useful to illustrate this model. To illustrate the commutative property a learner can draw a rectangle of 4×10, oriented to have the side of 10 units horizontal, then he can draw a second rectangle, 10×4, with the side of 10 units vertical. These areas could be representing rooms or carpets. If it is not obvious that the two areas are the same, then the learner can cut out the two rectangles and place them on top of one another to show they are the same size (Figure 7.2).

Another illustration of this property can be achieved with Cuisenaire rods. So for 3×5 and 5×3, three five rods (yellows) can be put down to make a rectangle and then five three rods (light green) can be placed next to them to show that 3×5 and 5×3 cover the same area (and that three lots of five and five lots of three are the same) (Figure 7.3). Area is a powerful model for the developmental aspect of this work, leading ultimately to algebraic expressions.

Another effective demonstration which focuses on the 'lots of' version of 'times' is to use square counters in rows and columns. This additional 'picture' reinforces and develops further understanding of the concept of multiplication. For example, twelve counters can be placed down as three rows of four and a second set of twelve counters placed down as four rows of three (Figure 7.4).

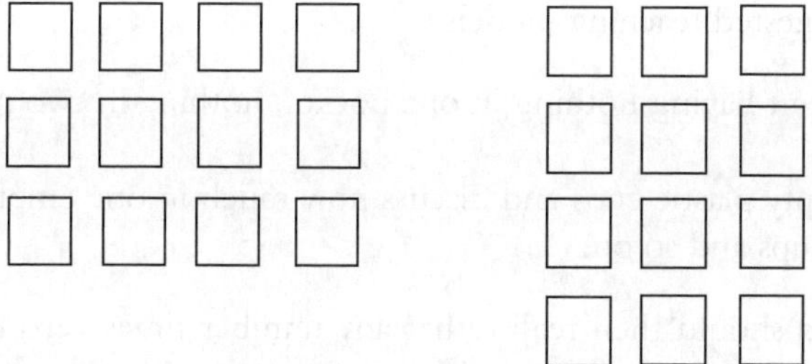

Figure 7.4 Using square counters.

Each of these demonstrations looks at a different facet of multiplication and each has future currency. This suggests that all three should be used to demonstrate and reinforce the concept. Examples of future currency for these demonstrations are using area to provide a picture of multiplications such as $(a+b)(a+3b)$, and extending 5×8 from five lots of eight to six lots of eight.

You have then demonstrated that 4×10 is exactly the same as 10×4, that $5\times 3=3\times 5$, that $3\times 4=4\times 3$ and so on. Each fact the child learns can have the order changed round, giving him another fact – free. You may wish to digress to discuss squares, such as 4×4 – as ever, judge the readiness of the individual.

Learning the Table Square

Zero: 0

Zero is an important concept, so time should be spent establishing that the child has some understanding of zero; zero, nought, nothing – as ever, the language should be varied.

In later numeracy work the child will meet examples like 304×23 or $406 \div 2$, where the process of multiplying a zero, multiplying by zero or dividing into zero is used. The introduction of a zero into any computation increases the number of errors. Zero is not well understood.

You can start by explaining the meaning of 3×0 and so on: 3×0 means:

> 3 times 0
> or three lots of zero gives the answer zero.
> 0×3 is the same as 3×0, zero lots of three is also zero.

This is another example of the need to use varied language to present a comprehensive image of the concept.

Two suggested teaching models

- Talk about having nothing in one pocket, nothing in two pockets and so on.
- Use empty plastic cups and discuss how much in one empty cup, two empty cups and so on.

The child should then realise that any number times zero equals zero and zero times any number equals zero. So:

$1\times0=0$	and	$0\times1=0$
$2\times0=0$		$0\times2=0$
$3\times0=0$		$0\times3=0$
$4\times0=0$		$0\times4=0$
$5\times0=0$		$0\times5=0$
$6\times0=0$		$0\times6=0$
$7\times0=0$		$0\times7=0$
$8\times0=0$		$0\times8=0$
$9\times0=0$		$0\times9=0$
$10\times0=0$		$0\times10=0$

Children like enormous examples such as 'a billion lots of zero' or 'zero lots of a billion' – it impresses much more than 'zero lots of two' even if the result is the same.

Now you can tell the child to look at the table square.

'You will see a row of 0s across the top, and a column of 0s down the left hand side. You have just learnt your first 21 facts.'

Progress check

If you want the child to keep a check on his progress use the table square in Figure 7.1. Copy one and hand it to the child to act as his record of progress. Tell him to shade in all the zero facts – the top row and the first column. You will probably find the child needs a second table square to keep as a 'clean' copy.

One: 1

One is the basic unit.

4×1 means: 4 times 1, or 4 lots of 1, and both give the answer 4.

So, 1×4 has the same answer as 4×1.

Any number times 1 equals that number.

One times any number equals that number.

Multiplying a number by 1 does not change its value. (This pedantic statement is important for work on renaming a fraction, where the fraction's value does not change, but its appearance will.).

Counters are quite a good manipulative aid for demonstration. They can also be used on an interactive screen or via an animated slide with PowerPoint (e.g. as shown in www.mathsexplained.co.uk), or for the child to use to understand 'one lot of n' or 'n lots of one'.

The concept you are introducing here is summed up by the equations:

$$n \times 1 = n \quad \text{and} \quad 1 \times n = n$$

Again, tell the child to look back at the table square and see that the one times table facts appear twice, first written across, second row down; then written down, second column in.

$$\begin{array}{rr} 0\times 1=0 & 1\times 0=0 \\ 1\times 1=1 & 1\times 1=1 \\ 2\times 1=2 & 1\times 2=2 \\ 3\times 1=3 & 1\times 3=3 \\ 4\times 1=4 & 1\times 4=4 \\ 5\times 1=5 & 1\times 5=5 \\ 6\times 1=6 & 1\times 6=6 \\ 7\times 1=7 & 1\times 7=7 \\ 8\times 1=8 & 1\times 8=8 \\ 9\times 1=9 & 1\times 9=9 \\ 10\times 1=10 & 1\times 10=10 \end{array}$$

Again, explain and demonstrate the important fact that the number you multiply by 1 does not change in value. When 1 multiplies a number it leaves the number with the same value as it had before.

The child has now learnt 19 new facts (he had already learnt 0×1 and 1×0), making a total so far of 40 out of 121 – almost a third.

Progress check

The child can now shade in the 1× facts. He can shade in the second row and the second column. These are the numbers 1–10 across and down.

Ten: 10

1, 2, 3, 4, 5, 6, 7, 8, 9 are single digits. 10 has two digits, a 1 followed by a 0. The 0 means zero ones, and the 1 means 1 ten. It is necessary that the child has retained earlier work on place value from Chapter 5. A moment's reinforcement will check this. Because maths is a developmental subject there are many opportunities to review, revisit and revise previous topics.

Ten is a key number in this chapter (and, indeed throughout the book). The ten times table facts will be extended to teach the child how to work out the five times table facts and the nine times table facts (and can also be extended to access the 11×, 12×, 15× and 20× facts). Thus, it is well worth reviewing the child's understanding of ten and place value.

So explain that 20 has a 0 digit for 0 ones and a 2 digit for 2 tens. 2×10 means:

2 times 10 equals 20
2 lots of 10 are 20

There is an easy pattern to show this and the commutative facts:

$$
\begin{array}{rr}
0 \times 10 = 0 & 10 \times 0 = 0 \\
1 \times 10 = 10 & 10 \times 1 = 10 \\
2 \times 10 = 20 & 10 \times 2 = 20 \\
3 \times 10 = 30 & 10 \times 3 = 30 \\
4 \times 10 = 40 & 10 \times 4 = 40 \\
5 \times 10 = 50 & 10 \times 5 = 50 \\
6 \times 10 = 60 & 10 \times 6 = 60 \\
7 \times 10 = 70 & 10 \times 7 = 70 \\
8 \times 10 = 80 & 10 \times 8 = 80 \\
9 \times 10 = 90 & 10 \times 9 = 90 \\
10 \times 10 = 100 & 10 \times 10 = 100
\end{array}
$$

Get the child to listen to the pattern as he says the ten times table and hears the oral connection, for example:

Four tens are *for*ty
Six tens are *six*ty
Nine tens are *nine*ty

Even two tens are twenty gives a two-letter clue. We find that sometimes a brief digression to 'twoten' to 'twoty', 'threeten' to 'threety' and 'fiveten' to 'fivety' reinforces rather than confuses.

It is worth noting that the sounds of twelve and twenty are frequently confused, as are thirteen and thirty.

The auditory and visual clues to each answer within the ten times tables enable the student to access an answer without having to count from 1×10 to the required answer (which many children do to access the answers for the 2× table facts).

This pattern can be practised with trading money, always remembering to have the child say as he trades one 1p coin for one 10p coin, 'one times ten is ten'. He then trades two 1p coins for two 10p coins, and says 'two times ten is twenty'.

And so on, till he trades 10 × 10p coins for ten 10p coins, and says 'ten times ten is tenten or tenty'; there are no such words of course and a special word is used instead – hundred. A hundred, 100, has three digits, the only number with three digits in the table square. A hundred pence has its own coin, a pound. So 10 × 10p = 100p = 1 pound. All this reinforces the special importance of 100.

There are other ways to practise the ones/tens relationship.

- Single straws, and bundles of ten straws:

  1 straw × 10 = 1 bundle = 10
  2 straws × 10 = 2 bundles = 20
  3 straws × 10 = 3 bundles = 30 and so forth.

  Each time 'ten times bigger' means exchanging a ten-straw bundle for a single straw.
- Base ten (Dienes) blocks, a one hundred bead string or a metre rule can be used to add to the development of the idea of the ten times table. Base ten blocks reinforce the place value aspect.

Remember that some materials are proportional in size to their value, for example Cuisenaire rods; some are proportional in quantity, for example bundles of straws; some are proportional by volume and area, for example base ten blocks; some are proportional by length, for example a metre rule; some are representative of value, for example 1p and 10p coins. Using a mixture of these and the numbers/digits ensures development from concrete to symbolic understanding.

Some 'everyday' examples may be used to provide reinforcement:

- How many legs on ten cows?
- How many wheels on ten bikes?
- How many pence in ten 5p coins?
- How many legs on ten spiders?
- How many sides on ten 50p coins?

Progress check

If the child is comfortable in his ability to retrieve the ten times facts from memory then he can shade in the end column and the bottom row of his table square, the ten times facts. Filling in the tens column and the tens row should remind the child that for each times fact he can write the numbers in either order, so, for example, $2 \times 10 = 10 \times 2$. This means that, if he remembers that $10 \times 3 = 30$, then he knows $3 \times 10 = 30$, one fact from the three times table and one fact from the ten times table – one again, two for the price of learning one. The commutative property should be reinforced frequently.

The goal for retrieving these core facts is automaticity.

So far the child has learnt 57 facts, almost half. He has 64 to learn.

Two: 2

First, as for each number, the lessons should look at the concept of the number and its interrelationships with other numbers. There can be some demonstrations, discussions and some information on two, such as:

- Two is one more than one.
- It is twice as big as one.
- It is an even number.
- Even numbers are numbers that share/divide into two equal parts.

Some examples:

Eight divides (shares) into two lots of four:

$$8 \div 2 = 4 \quad \text{or} \quad 8 = 4 + 4.$$

Twenty divides into two lots of ten:

$$20 \div 2 = 10 \quad \text{or} \quad 20 = 10 + 10$$

Each child can try equal sharing with a random pile of pennies, sharing them out, one at a time, into two piles. If the two piles are equal, then he started with an even number. If there is one penny left over, then he started with an odd number.

- The even numbers from 1 to 10 are 2, 4, 6, 8, 10
- The odd numbers from 1 to 10 are 1, 3, 5, 7, 9

A useful extra fact, actually a generalisation, here is that *any* even number ends in 2, 4, 6, 8 or 0, and *any* odd number ends in 1, 3, 5, 7 or 9. Some review/revision questions can be used, such as:

- Which of these numbers is even? 2341, 4522, 57399, 34, 70986, 11112, 335792
- Which of them divide evenly by two?

- If the pattern for even numbers is:

2	4	6	8	10
12	14	16	18	20
22	24	26	28	30

Continue the pattern to 102.

The 2× table and the commutative facts:

$0 \times 2 = 0$	$2 \times 0 = 0$
$1 \times 2 = 2$	$2 \times 1 = 2$
$2 \times 2 = 4$	$2 \times 2 = 4$
$3 \times 2 = 6$	$2 \times 3 = 6$
$4 \times 2 = 8$	$2 \times 4 = 8$
$5 \times 2 = 10$	$2 \times 5 = 10$
$6 \times 2 = 12$	$2 \times 6 = 12$
$7 \times 2 = 14$	$2 \times 7 = 14$
$8 \times 2 = 16$	$2 \times 8 = 16$
$9 \times 2 = 18$	$2 \times 9 = 18$
$10 \times 2 = 20$	$2 \times 10 = 20$

Note that the ones digit pattern repeats: 2, 4, 6, 8, 0.

The first four facts can be learnt as a chant:

'Two, four, six, eight, who do we appreciate?'

This chant brings the child to almost halfway in learning the two times table.

Often it is useful to have reference points in calculations. The child already has a start reference point, $1 \times 2 = 2$, and an end reference point, $10 \times 2 = 20$. The middle reference point has its value on the child's hands – two hands, each with five fingers, two lots of five fingers is ten fingers, $2 \times 5 = 10$ or $5 \times 2 = 10$. It also is illustrated by $5 \times 2\text{p} = 10\text{p}$, a trading operation, where five 2p coins are traded for one 10p coin. So $5 \times 2 = 10$ is the middle reference point on which to build the remaining facts 6×2 to 10×2.

The answers for 6×2 to 9×2 have the same last digits as the first four facts, 12, 14, 16, 18 – show the child the pattern. The numbers have the same digit pattern because 6×2 is one more two than 5×2 and 7×2 is two more twos than 5×2, etc., and because 5×2 has zero in its ones digit column. This is a use of the strategy of a middle reference point, which in this case combines with the strategy of breaking down numbers to build up on known facts ($6 = 5 + 1$, $6 = 5 + 2$ and so on).

So if the child can remember the reference value $5 \times 2 = 10$, he can quickly work out, say, 7×2.

Seven is $5 + 2$

o o o
o
o o o

7×2 is five lots of two plus two lots of two:

$$7 \times 2 = (2+2+2+2+2)+(2+2)$$

$$7 \times 2 = (5 \times 2)+(2 \times 2) = 10+4 = 14$$

There are three useful and regularly occurring strategies here:

1. Breaking down a number into key/core numbers (1, 2, 5, 10) as with breaking down seven into five and two, so that these facts are used and extended.
2. The use of a reference point in the middle of the task. Many children will claim to 'know' the two times table; however, it is often the case that when asked for 7×2 they begin at 2 and work up 2, 4, 6, 8, 10, 12, 14. A middle reference point means that the child can start at 10.
3. The use of 'lots of' for times leads to six lots of two being seen as one more lot (of two) than five lots of two. This image of multiplication as repeated addition of the same number and addition of 'chunks' of that number will be used again later.

However effective they may be eventually, strategies still need practice and reinforcement.

Some practical work can be built around coins and trading, using a 10p coin for tens and 2p coins for two. The learner trades five lots of 2p for a 10p coin to reinforce the middle reference point and the repeating 2, 4, 6, 8 pattern. An example with 8×2 is to take eight 2p coins, take out five of these and trade them for a 10p coin. This leaves one 10p coin and three 2p coins, which combine as 10 and 3×2 to make 16. This reinforces the image of 8×2 breaking into clusters of 5×2 and 3×2.

Trading is a procedure that will be used in addition and subtraction. The issue of consistency arises again here for this procedure, with the range of words in use for trading, including renaming and decomposing.

Four: 4

As always, it is worth starting with an overview, looking at the properties of four and relating four to other numbers. The most useful of these relationships are:

- Four is two times two. $4 = 2 \times 2$
- Four is twice two (be careful as some children interpret 'twice' as 'add two').
- Four is an even number.
- Numbers which are divisible by four can be divided by two twice.
- Four is four ones added together $1 + 1 + 1 + 1$.

Four times facts are accessed by doubling the two times facts. This also has the benefit of revisiting the two times facts. This strategy also introduces the procedure of two-step multiplications. So 4 is used here as 2×2. Later, learners will multiply by numbers such as twenty by using two stages, ×2 and then × 10 (or vice versa). This $\times 2 \times 2$ method is building on knowledge the child has already learnt and makes use of the interrelationships of numbers. The child is taught to double the two times table. You have to establish the strategy, using methods such as 2p coins set out to show the two times table alongside the four times table, for example:

$$2 \times 2 \text{ compared with } 2 \times 4$$
$$3 \times 2 \text{ compared with } 3 \times 4$$

The two times table is shown with single piles of 2p coins and the four times table is shown with double piles of 2p coins. The child can be shown, for example, the piles for 'three lots of' and it should be possible to convince him that he ends up with twice as much from piles with 4p in as he does from three piles with 2p in. (This is a similar strategy to comparing the five times and ten times tables.)

Once the idea of the strategy is established, you can move on to comparing the answers to the 2× and 4× tables in the same way that the 5× and 10× tables will be compared.

$$1 \times 2 = 2 \qquad 4 = 1 \times 4$$
$$2 \times 2 = 4 \qquad 8 = 2 \times 4$$
$$3 \times 2 = 6 \qquad 12 = 3 \times 4$$
$$4 \times 2 = 8 \qquad 16 = 4 \times 4$$
$$5 \times 2 = 10 \qquad 20 = 5 \times 4$$
$$6 \times 2 = 12 \qquad 24 = 6 \times 4$$

$$
\begin{array}{rr}
7\times 2=14 & 28=\ 7\times 4 \\
8\times 2=16 & 32=\ 8\times 4 \\
9\times 2=18 & 36=\ 9\times 4 \\
10\times 2=20 & 40=10\times 4
\end{array}
$$

It is worth reminding the learner that he already knows 0×4, 1×4, 2×4 and 10×4 from the tables he has learned previously.

1×4 to 5×4 are achieved by doubling within the range of the two times table, for example the learner can manage 4×4 as $2\times 4=8$ and $2\times 8=16$ and thus $4\times 4=16$. Some practice to reinforce this 'known' pattern may be needed.

6×4 and 7×4 are relatively easy since there is no carrying to complicate the second doubling:

$$
\begin{array}{ll}
6\times 2=12 & 12\times 2=24 \\
7\times 2=14 & 14\times 2=28
\end{array}
$$

The second doubling for 8×4 and 9×4 can be done via breakdown strategies, using 8 as $5+3$ $(2\times 10+2\times 6)$ and 9 as $5+4$ $(2\times 10+2\times 8)$ or $10-1$ $(2\times 20-2\times 2)$. Alternatively, 9×4 can be done, later, as 4×9 from the nine times table.

It may be good practice for the learner to give you the first step in practice sessions so that 7×4 is delivered in two stages: 14 then 28.

When the four times facts are shaded in on the table square the learner has just 36 facts to learn.

(Note: The eight times facts can be accessed by a triple multiplication of 2× 2× 2×. Although this is a long strategy it does take the learner to an answer instead of them feeling helpless when they have no recall from memory available for this fact.)

Five: 5

As with all the times tables, the first step is to establish a basic understanding of the number.

Some information about five

- A key fact is that five is halfway from zero to ten. The learner can be reminded how five was used as a halfway reference point in the two times table.
- Five is half of ten.
- Ten divided by two is five. $10 \div 2=5$.
- Five is an odd number.

- Even numbers multiplied by five have zero in the ones place.
- Odd numbers multiplied by five have five in the ones place.
- Five can look like: 5 or l l l l l or ~~llll~~ or V or 10/2 or 10 ÷ 2 or

● ●
●
● ●

The five times table and the commutative facts

$0 \times 5 = 0$	$5 \times 0 = 0$
$1 \times 5 = 5$	$5 \times 1 = 5$
$2 \times 5 = 10$	$5 \times 2 = 10$
$3 \times 5 = 15$	$5 \times 3 = 15$
$4 \times 5 = 20$	$5 \times 4 = 20$
$5 \times 5 = 25$	$5 \times 5 = 25$
$6 \times 5 = 30$	$5 \times 6 = 30$
$7 \times 5 = 35$	$5 \times 7 = 35$
$8 \times 5 = 40$	$5 \times 8 = 40$
$9 \times 5 = 45$	$5 \times 9 = 45$
$10 \times 5 = 50$	$5 \times 10 = 50$

Note:

1. The child knows the start reference point $1 \times 5 = 5$, and the end reference point $10 \times 5 = 50$.
2. There is a repeating pattern in the ones digits: 5, 0, 5, 0, 5, 0, 5, 0, 5, 0.
3. This means another pattern/generalisation: an odd number times five gives an answer that ends in five and an even number times five gives an answer which ends in zero, thus providing another example of the concept of odd and even numbers.

It is useful to set up a comparison of the 10× and 5× tables by writing the answers side by side. Looking at the answers illustrates the relationship between them, that is, each 5× answer is half of each 10× answer, for example $6 \times 5 = 30$ and $6 \times 10 = 60$, and 30 is half of 60. It is possible to work out the fives by taking the tens and halving the answers. So, for 8×5, start at $8 \times 10 = 80$ and half of 80 is 40. As a check, eight is an even number, so the answer ends in zero. Again, for 5×5: $5 \times 10 = 50$ and half of 50 is 25. As a partial check, five is odd, so the answer ends in five.

This strategy will be useful later when working out key number percentages.

The strategy of looking at the ones digit also helps to reinforce the child's attention on reviewing answers to check their validity.

Some practical work

The learner can practise halving tens by trading 10p and 5p coins; for each 10p trade one 5p. Each time you can help the child rehearse the process:

> 'Seven times five. Start at seven times ten. Half of seventy is thirty-plus five, that is, thirty-five. Seven was odd. The answer ends in a five. That checks.'

This can be reinforced by taking seven 5p coins and explaining that each coin is worth half as much as a 10p coin and that collectively they are worth half as much as seven 10p coins.

If the child has difficulty in dividing 30, 50, 70 and 90 by 2, remind the child how to break numbers down, for example 50 is $40 + 10$. Halve 40 (answer 20) and halve 10 (answer 5), so that $50 + 2 = 25$.

Again, you may have to remind the child how sometimes it is easier to use two small, quick steps than to struggle with one difficult step.

Other materials may be used to reinforce this relationship between five and ten; these include Cuisenaire rods, and patterns of dots. The digits can also demonstrate the 'lots of' aspect of multiplication, used when extending knowledge of, say five 'lots of' to six 'lots of' or seven 'lots of':

Six lots of five $5 + 5 + 5 + 5 + 5 + 5$
Seven lots of five $5 + 5 + 5 + 5 + 5 + 5 + 5$

As before, the goal is for the learner to be able to recall a five times table fact from memory, or work out an answer quickly and to get as close to automaticity as is possible. The strategy is designed to give security and consistency in the answers and inhibit the influence of incorrect answers. Starting from 1×5 and counting up to the required answer is not the goal. When the learner can remember or work out the five times facts, then he can shade in the five row and column on his table square. The times table task is reduced to 25 facts.

Three: 3, six: 6 and seven: 7

The strategy used for these times table facts is the same and is very much a part of the developmental nature of this programme. The strategy is to break down a 'difficult' number into two 'easier' numbers. So 3 becomes 2+1, 6 is 5+1 and 7 is 5+2. This procedure is used in long multiplications such as 35×78, where the 35 is broken down to 30+5 and the two partial products, 30×78 and 5×78, are then recombined for 35×78. Whilst this example is the procedure advocated by many texts, most people do not need to use it for easier numbers such as 3, 6 or 7. We have extrapolated the method back to help with retrieving basic facts. This also serves as an introduction to the area model for partial products in multiplication and, it is hoped, sets up this concept for future work in other multiplications such as fractions and quadratic equations. The Figures 7.5 to 7.7 illustrate the model and its developmental property.

The language of multiplication can be quite abstract. 'Three times four' or 'three fours' requires the student to know the code. 'Three lots of four' is more closely related to multiplication, hinting at repeated addition. This

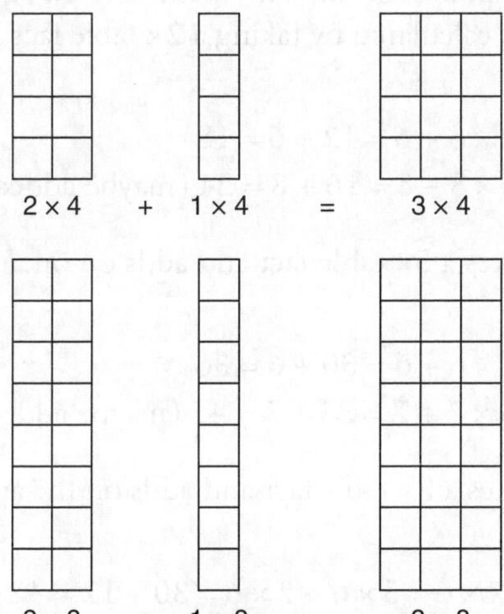

Figure 7.5 *2n + 1n = 3n.*

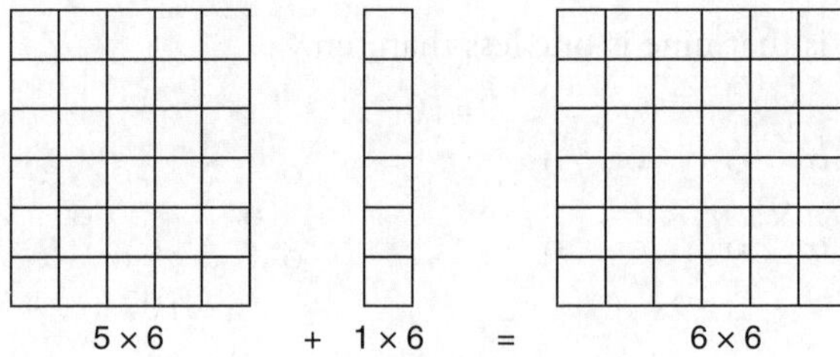

Figure 7.6 *5n + 1n = 6n.*

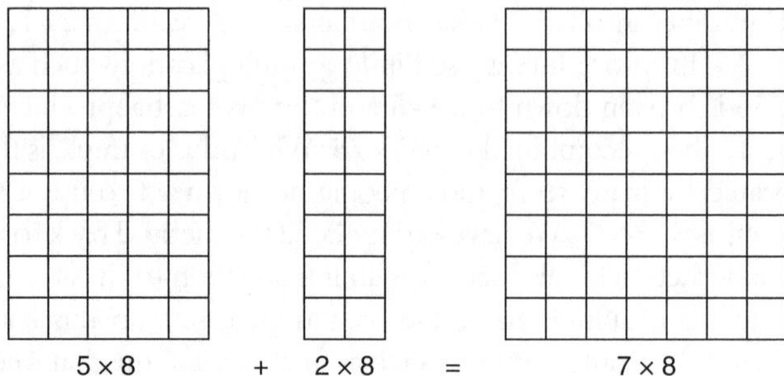

Figure 7.7 $5n + 2n = 7n$.

latter wording also lends itself to the concept of $3n = 2n + n$ again setting the foundations for the development of further maths skills and concepts. The same concept applies for $6n = 5n + n$ and $7n = 5n + 2n$.

So the 3× table is calculated by taking a 2× table fact and adding on one more, for example:

$$3 \times 6 = 2 \times 6 + 6 = 12 + 6 = 18$$
$$3 \times 8 = 2 \times 8 + 8 = 16 + 8 = 24 \text{ (maybe added as } 16 + 4 + 4\text{)}$$

and the 6× table takes a 5× table fact and adds on one more multiplicand, for example:

$$6 \times 6 = 5 \times 6 + 6 = 30 + 6 = 36$$
$$6 \times 7 = 5 \times 7 + 7 = 35 + 7 = 42 \text{ (maybe added as } 35 + 5 + 2\text{)}$$

and the 7× table takes a 5× table fact and adds on the appropriate 2× table fact, for example:

$$7 \times 6 = 5 \times 6 + 2 \times 6 = 30 + 12 = 42$$
$$7 \times 7 = 5 \times 7 + 2 \times 7 = 35 + 14 = 49$$

Nine: 9

The key fact is that nine is one less than ten.

$$9 = 10 - 1$$

o o o o   o o o o
o   o   o
o o o o   o o o o
9   10

There is an easy method to work out the 9 times facts using fingers. If we were being rigidly principled, we might not mention a method which

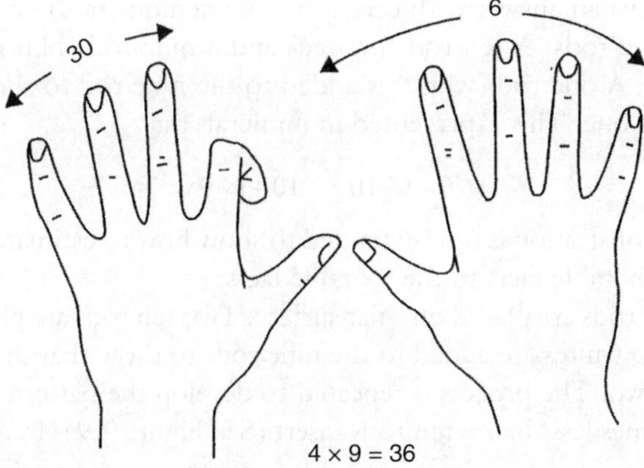

Figure 7.8 Using fingers to find the nine times facts.

is radically different from the other methods and strategies mentioned in this book. However, working with dyslexics can make you very pragmatic and eclectic, on the basis that the gains in the child's self-confidence may outweigh any doubts about the academic validity of a particular technique.

So, if you want to know the answer to 4 × 9, for example, put the fingers of both hands down on a surface and tuck back the fourth (4) finger from the left (Figure 7.8). The answer lies each side of this fourth finger, the tens to the left, three fingers means thirty, and the units to the right, six fingers, giving an answer of thirty-six. Often parents like this method.

However, we prefer a strategy with potential for further use, a developmental strategy. Therefore, the strategy we advocate is based on estimation, the particularly useful estimation of ten for nine, and the subsequent refinement of this estimation. The strategy could also be perceived as a breakdown/partial products method, with a subtraction of the partial products rather than the addition we have used so far.

The first step is to establish the principle of the method, that is, that nine is one less than ten. This is helped by examining nine.

- Nine is nine units.
- Nine is one less than ten.
- $9 = 10 - 1$ and $10 = 9 + 1$.

The closeness in value of nine and ten can be demonstrated by showing the child a pile of ten 1p coins and asking him to say, without counting them, if there are nine or ten. It does not matter which the child guesses. It is the uncertainty that is important; the nearness of nine and ten makes it hard to give an answer with certainty. The demonstration can move on to Cuisenaire rods. A ten rod (orange) and a nine rod (blue) are placed side by side. A one rod (white) is added to the nine rod to show that the difference is one. This is presented in numerals as:

$$9+1=10 \qquad 10-1=9$$

This demonstration is now extended to show how to estimate and refine from the 10× table facts to the 9× table facts.

Two nine rods are placed on a flat surface. Two ten rods are placed alongside and two whites are added to the nine rods to show that the difference in value is two. The process is repeated to develop the pattern that *n* nine rods are *n* ones less than *n* ten rods insert (See Figure 7.9). In numbers:

$$2\times 10=20 \quad 20-2=18 \quad 2\times 9=18$$
$$3\times 10=30 \quad 30-3=27 \quad 3\times 9=27$$
$$4\times 10=40 \quad 40-4=36 \quad 4\times 9=36$$
$$5\times 10=40 \quad 50-5=45 \quad 5\times 9=45$$

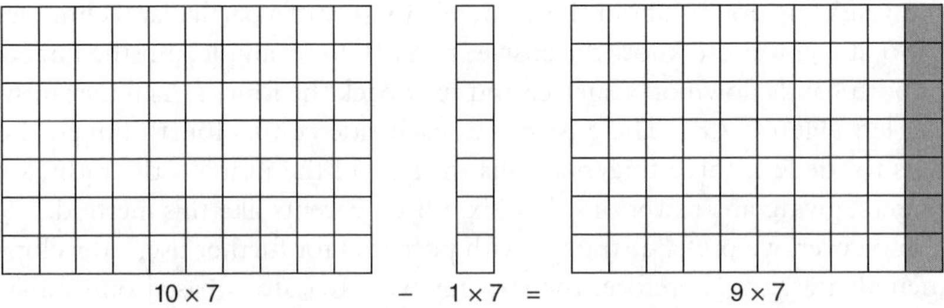

Figure 7.9 *9n = 10n – 1n.*

Thus any nine times fact can be worked out from a ten times fact, for example 8×9 is worked out as:

$$8\times 10=80 \quad 80-8=72 \quad 8\times 9=72$$

This is verbalised as:

> 'Eight times nine is eight less than eight times ten. Eight times ten is eighty, so, eight times nine must be seventy something.'

The 'something', the unit digit, can be found by subtracting eight from eighty, or eight from ten, using number bonds/combinations for ten (another example of revisiting the key facts). It can be found by counting backwards from 80, though this is a very difficult task for some dyslexics, or a further pattern can be used:

$$
\begin{aligned}
1\times 9 &= 9\\
2\times 9 &= 18\\
3\times 9 &= 27\\
4\times 9 &= 36\\
5\times 9 &= 45\\
6\times 9 &= 54\\
7\times 9 &= 63\\
8\times 9 &= 72\\
9\times 9 &= 81\\
10\times 9 &= 90
\end{aligned}
$$

Notice:

The units column digits go from 9 to 0, whilst the tens column digits go from 0 to 9. This results in the sum of the two digits in each answer always being nine, for example for 63, $6+3=9$.

So the child can work through the following process for, say, 4×9.

$4\times 10=40$;
4×9 is smaller and must be 'thirty something';

The 'something' must be the number which adds on to 3 to make 9, that is 6. So the answer is 36. For 8×9, again:

$8\times 10=80$

$8\times 9=7\square$

$7+\square=9$

$\square=2$ so $8\times 9=72$

The child may think that this is a long process, but with regular practice it becomes quicker. Also, as the child becomes more adept, he starts to short-circuit the process and use it to top off a half-known answer. In other words, the strategy provides a memory hook for the child so that he is not left floundering when faced with an 'impossible' question.

When the child has grasped this strategy, he may shade in the nine times column and row. He now has only one fact left to attack.

Eight: 8

8×8 can be accessed by repeated multiplication, that is:

$$8\times 2\times 2\times 2$$

$$
\begin{aligned}
8\times 2 &= 16\\
16\times 2 &= 32\\
32\times 2 &= 64
\end{aligned}
$$

Final notes

The squares, 3×3, 4×4, 5×5, 6×6, 7×7 and 8×8 are connected to the products of the numbers 'each side' of them, that is 2×4, 3×5, 4×6, 5×7, 6×8 and 7×9 respectively by:

$$n^2=(n-1)(n+1)+1$$

$3\times3=(2\times4)+1$	$3\times3=\ 9$	$2\times4=\ 8$
$4\times4=(3\times5)+1$	$4\times4=16$	$3\times5=15$
$5\times5=(4\times6)+1$	$5\times5=25$	$4\times6=24$
$6\times6=(5\times7)+1$	$6\times6=36$	$5\times7=35$
$7\times7=(6\times8)+1$	$7\times7=49$	$6\times8=48$
$8\times8=(7\times9)+1$	$8\times8=64$	$7\times9=63$

Developmental aspects

Multiplication facts are, of course also division facts. For example, when students are factorising equations in algebra or reducing fractions to the simplest form they will need to use the times table facts in division format. The maths vocabulary used is pertinent to the process, for example:

For $30 \div 5$
How many fives in thirty? … 'five' comes before 'thirty'
How many times does five go into thirty? … 'five' comes before 'thirty'
What is thirty divided by five? … 'thirty' comes before 'five'
Share thirty dollars between five people. … 'thirty' comes before 'five'
Five people share thirty dollars equally. … 'five' comes before 'thirty'

Division facts should be linked to multiplication facts and children need to know that whilst multiplication is repeated addition, division is repeated subtraction (of the same number). The multiplication square can be used for division. The student may need guidance in doing this as directional issues are involved.

There are some simple clues as to divisibility and factors for some of the factors. Some are obvious, such as the rules for a number being divisible by two (and thus four and eight) or by ten or by five. The rule for divisibility by nine has already been mentioned, that is, that all the digits will add up to nine, though this may take more than one step. For example, 4914 adds up to 18 and then $1+8=9$.

The rule for divisibility by three is that the digits will add to three, six or nine. If the number is also an even number then it will divide by six.

These simple rules allow the learner to deal with divisibility by 2, 4, 5, 6, 8, 9 and 10.

Times table facts and exams

If a candidate is not allowed to take a times table square into a maths examination it is likely that he will be able to have a sheet of squared paper on which he can make a 12 × 12 grid (needed for the 0× to 10× facts). A student can be taught how to fill in a blank square very quickly, especially if he chooses not to fill in every blank, say filling in only the core facts for 0×, 1×, 2×, 5× and 10×, leaving the others until needed for a specific question. It is good practice and good revision of the facts, and how they are related, to do this exercise reasonably frequently, especially in the run up to an exam. The square, of course, gives factors, too, and equivalent fractions. The square gives security.

Summary

In this chapter we have introduced the idea of teaching strategies to learn/work out the times tables facts, treating them as 'number combinations'. We believe that this approach is pragmatic, since few dyslexics or dyscalculics can rote learn this information. It has the added bonus of introducing and teaching several useful mathematical processes and concepts, which include: estimation, factors, that number values and operations are interrelated, that multiplication is repeated addition and partial products, all via the strategy of breaking down numbers into convenient and appropriate parts. We hope that a child may, by using these strategies, learn to produce quick answers for the times table facts, whilst having a back-up strategy for those occasions when the mind goes blank or is uncertain which of a number of possible answers stored in the brain is the right one. We have also tried to introduce some flexibility in the methods described, ever mindful of our basic premise that not all children learn in the same way.

Finally, it is worth repeating the cautionary note concerning division facts. We think that so many children perceive the multiplication square as the times table facts that they forget that they are also the basic division facts.

Video tutorials of this work are available via www.mathsexplained.co.uk (see Appendix 1).

8

Computational Procedures for Addition and Subtraction

The child's knowledge of basic facts concerning addition and subtraction can now be extended to longer computations. Good, empathetic teaching will always help a dyslexic and dyscalculic to experience fewer classroom acquired difficulties (rather than learning difficulties), but you still need to understand and adjust to your learner to maximise the chances of effective learning (Miles, 1992; Ostad, 1997; Miles and Miles, 2004). An understanding of place value is a key prerequisite (Ho and Cheng, 1997; Ho *et al.*, 2015).

Our experience of dyslexics and dyscalculics leads us to think that some misconceptions occur because a procedure appears to have no reference to previous procedures or any rationale to make the knowledge seem relevant or distinguishable. For example, directions for finding your way on a journey that rely solely on 'left' and 'right' instructions are less likely to be remembered than directions which include landmarks. The landmarks make the directions more 'real' and concrete. There is also the ever-present potential influence of Buswell and Judd's (1925) observation regarding the impact of a child's first experience of learning new material. That first experience will be a dominant memory which is problematic if it is an incorrect experience, for example, as stated before, the child may have been told in early subtraction lessons, 'Take the little number from the big number.'

Again it is worth noting that all too frequently addition is the default operation for many learners (not just dyslexics and dyscalculics). Teachers will have attitude and motivational aspects to address as well as the cognitive ones.

Mathematics for Dyslexics and Dyscalculics: A Teaching Handbook, Fourth Edition.
Steve Chinn and Richard E. Ashcroft.

Addition and subtraction can be taught by multisensory methods and these methods have a double purpose. First, the child has the benefit of input through more than one sense and, second, the child has concrete and visual image experiences to which he can relate the abstract symbols we use for numbers and operations and thus the abstract concepts of addition and subtraction. The goal is that the child may learn to understand an algorithm rather than just apply it mechanically, that is, to use a blend of cognitive styles and approaches. The use of concrete materials and visual images should also enhance estimation skills, by giving a sense of the size of the numbers involved. Kennedy (1975) refers to research that supports the seemingly obvious statement that children perform better when using algorithms which they understand. Madsen *et al.* (1995) refer to the benefits of using conceptual understanding to help the recall and use of procedures. Hattie (2009) has strong words on policy and pedagogies that survive long after they have been found to be ineffective, at best, and damaging, at worst.

The use of multisensory teaching in mathematics makes understanding more likely, especially if the materials are used so as to give concrete meaning to the abstract concept. These materials and images need to be used in a structure. They do not teach by themselves. There is an important role for new technologies here too. There have been dramatic developments in the scope of these tools for explaining mathematics. One of us (S.C.) has recently (2014) produced work making extensive use of these new tools (www.mathsexplained.co.uk).

There have been, however, some cautionary words about the use of these aids to learning. Hart (1989) warns us that children do not always relate the 'bricks' to the 'sums'. Indeed, some may not be ready for this transition. Even the Singapore Model Method (Hong *et al.*, 2009) left some children stuck in the visual image stage, so that further input was then designed to aid the transition to symbols, in particular to progress to algebra. Thus the concrete materials must be accompanied by the written symbols and the teacher must watch his pupils to see if the connection has been taken on board. You must also remember that children do not all have the same cognitive style and therefore you should encourage the use of global overviews, estimates, detailed algorithms, documentation and evaluation (checking), remembering that some of these procedures are more related to one end of the cognitive style spectrum than to the other.

Finally, we believe there is great value in teaching addition and subtraction together. We feel that relating the two operations reinforces understanding of the algorithms used, especially the renaming/regrouping/decomposing process. Linking the operations is as important to developing number sense as linking the numbers. Our hope (and experience) is that the linking might just strengthen confidence and competence with subtraction.

Estimation

Pre-calculation estimates and post-calculation appraisals should be encouraged as they serve several purposes. Many children, and adults, will avoid these steps for at least two reasons. First, they do not have the skill to estimate and appraise. It is not a natural skill for all learners. Second, it is another procedure to add to the one they may already be somewhat reluctant to do.

1. Some dyslexics are likely to transpose the teen numbers so that, for example, 13 becomes 31, particularly when dual tasking, that is retrieving a fact whilst in the process of computation. Estimates and appraisals encourage the good practice of checking answers (before and after they have been calculated) and help the learner to see his possible errors. We have found that often checks made after a brief break from the work are more effective than immediate checks.
2. Estimates and appraisals should be used to check results from calculators, where students are prone to press the wrong keys and sometimes in the wrong sequence.
3. Estimates are often a real-life mathematics calculation. For example, a driver may only need to know roughly how many litres of petrol he can buy for £20 rather than have an answer to three decimal places.
4. Estimates can (and should) use less threatening numbers, requiring the learner to once again make use of the relationships between numbers, for example rounding 395 to 400.

Addition

Work on the computational procedures for addition should be preceded by a review of place value. You need to always have in mind the learner's need for continual reminders and memory refreshers. Overlearning is an important part of any long-term tuition plan and re-establishing the precursors of a new topic reduces the sources of potential failure. An example is in the error shown below:

$$\begin{array}{r} 38 \\ +27 \\ \hline 515 \end{array}$$

The child adds the ones digits to obtain 15, but fails to realise, or forgets, that the one represents a 'ten' and thus should be added into the tens column. Errors such as these are less likely if the child is taught to preview and review the value of his answers. Again, you should be trying to encourage the child to be flexible in his cognitive processes.

The use of concrete materials and visual images adds a multisensory dimension to the teaching. You need to keep in mind the level of abstraction of the materials and images you are using and to remember, as ever, to link these to the symbols and the vocabulary.

A developmental programme for teaching addition and subtraction

The programme is illustrated by two problems:

$$253+312 \quad \text{and} \quad 458+376$$

which are added and then used as examples for subtraction, that is:

$$565-253 \quad \text{and} \quad 834-458$$

The methods described use concrete materials and are thus suitable for one-to-one teaching. The use of animated visuals via computer (as used in www.mathsexplained.co.uk, for example) are suitable for larger groups.

Start with 253+312

Stage 1

You will need a place column card, some base ten blocks and a sheet of paper on which to record the addition as it progresses

Set the numbers up on a place value board in base ten blocks (Figure 8.1). Write the problem on the paper. Tell the child to add (combine/put together) the ones blocks (3+2), which gives him five ones blocks. Write '5' in the ones column of the written record.

Now tell the child to add the tens blocks (5+1), which gives him six tens blocks in the tens column. Write '6' in the tens column of the written record.

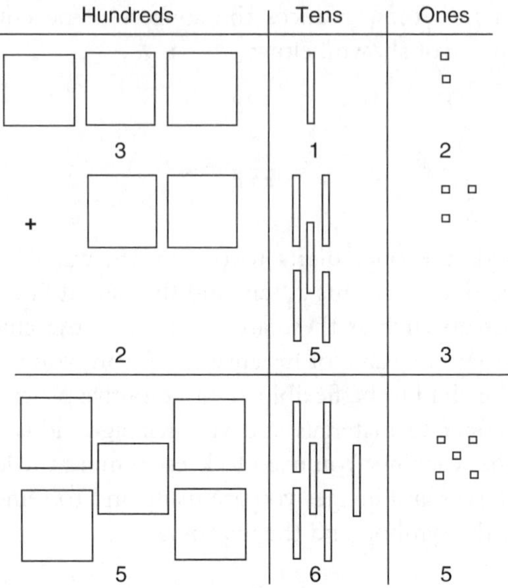

Figure 8.1 Addition with base ten blocks (no trading).

Move to the hundreds blocks and tell the child to add/put together the hundreds blocks (2 + 3), which gives him five hundreds blocks. Write '5' in the hundreds column of the written record.

Look at the whole answer and identify it as 565.

Stage 2

Repeat the process with coins, again writing each step of the procedure on paper, identifying the answer as 565.

You can discuss the idea of adding, putting together, leading the discussion into the idea of taking apart, subtracting the numbers, in this case back to the original two (unequal) parts.

Set up the problem 565 – 253.

Stage 1

Set up the 565 on a place value card in base ten blocks. Tell the child that he is going to take away 253 from the 565. Write the problem on paper. The answer to the subtraction will be the number left behind at the end of the procedure. Take three ones cubes down to the bottom of the card, leaving two ones cubes. Write this on the paper. Now tell the child to take away five tens blocks and place them at the bottom of the card, leaving one tens block. Write down this step. Then the child takes away to the bottom of the card two hundred blocks, leaving three hundred blocks. Write down the step.

The child should look at the card and see that there is 253 in base ten blocks at the bottom and that there is 312 left at the top and that the written addition mirrored this.

Stage 2
The same procedure is followed using coins instead of base ten blocks.

The subtraction problem and its answers should be reviewed and related to the equivalent addition problem.

Now set up the next problem, 258+376

Stage 1
Set the numbers up on a place value board in base ten blocks (Figure 8.2a). Tell the child to add (combine/put together) the ones blocks (8+6), which gives him 14 ones blocks. You can then discuss this, looking at fourteen as four ones and one ten. The ten ones blocks can be traded for one tens block. This is also shown in symbols, so the child relates the written algorithm to the blocks (Figure 8.2b). Write this step on paper.

Then tell the child to add the tens blocks (5+7+1). Encourage the same type of discussion, that is, the child has 13 tens blocks, which should

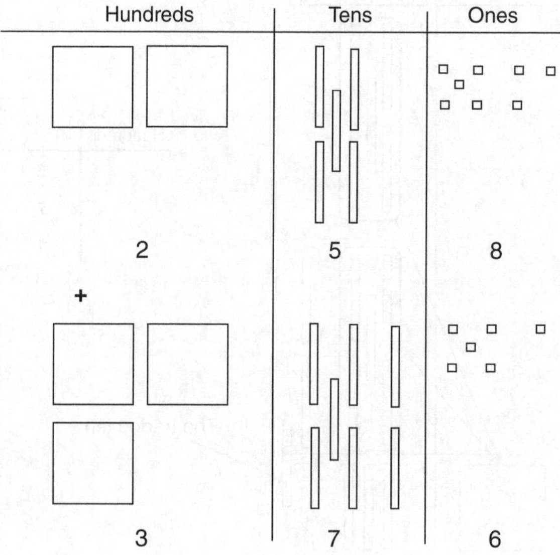

Figure 8.2a 258 + 376. Addition with base ten blocks (with trading).

be viewed as 100 and 30, that is one hundred and three tens. The ten tens blocks are traded for one hundreds block and the operation is written in symbols (digits) so that the child relates the written algorithm to the concrete manipulative aids (Figure 8.2c). Write this step on paper.

Finally, the hundreds column is considered. The blocks show 2 + 3 + 1 in hundreds square blocks, giving a total of five hundreds blocks. Then, take the child through the algorithm again, just in symbols, reminding him of the blocks as each place value is added. Write this step on paper.

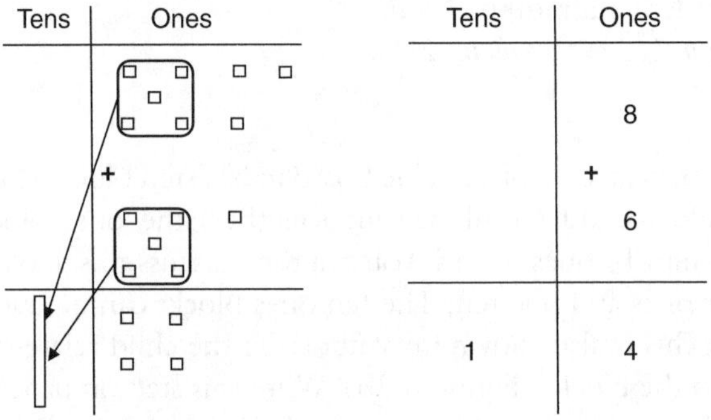

Figure 8.2b Adding and trading the ones.

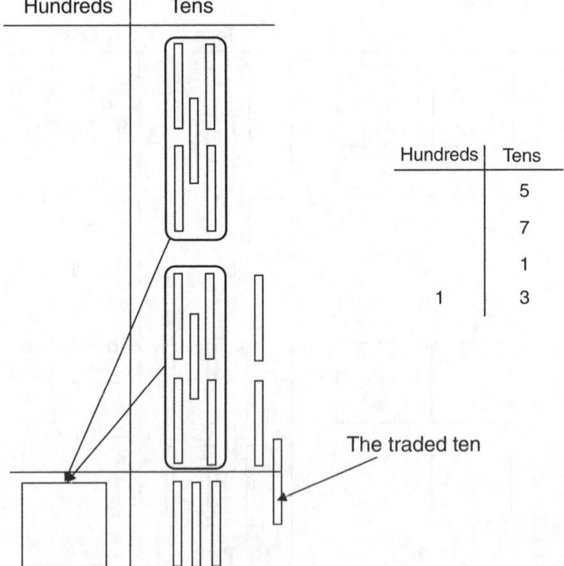

Figure 8.2c Adding and trading the tens.

Look at the answer and identify it as 634.

Stage 2

Repeat the process with coins, explaining how a maximum of nine pennies is allowed in the ones column and the consequent need to trade lots of 10×1p for 1×10p and 10×10p for 1×100p (£1) (Figure 8.3).

Now the addition can be reversed as an example of subtraction. The problem is 634 – 458.

Stage 1

Set up the problem on a place value card with base ten blocks, so there are eight hundreds blocks, three tens blocks and four ones blocks. Tell the child that he has to take away 458, that is four hundreds blocks, five tens blocks and eight ones cubes and identify the number left. Each step with the blocks should be written (as numbers) on paper.

Tell the child to start in the ones column and take away eight ones cubes. Obviously he cannot do this with only four ones cubes available. The subsequent discussion can look back at the addition when ten ones cubes were traded for one tens block and the need to reverse this for this subtraction, which is the reverse of addition. (Sometimes it may help to keep the traded blocks from the addition ready to use in the subtraction, adding further evidence to the interconnection.) Thus, a tens block is traded for ten ones cubes and the written version mirrors this.

A similar process deals with the subtraction in the tens column. The trading is now to take one hundreds block and trade it for ten tens blocks

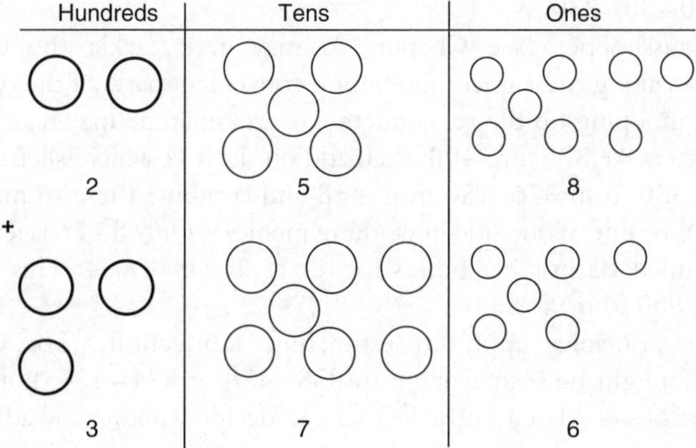

Figure 8.3 Addition with coins.

(a 'tenty'). The subtraction in the hundreds column is straightforward. For both these steps the written version should mirror the concrete materials.

It is also a method which enables the breakdown/conservation of the number to be discussed. So, the 834 has become:

7 hundreds	700
12 tens	120
14 ones	14
which add up to	834

Stage 2

The procedure is followed using coins.

A final example addresses one of the most frequent sources of error, that is, problems that include a zero. For example, 507 + 322 and 603 – 247. The reader will be able to extend the previous examples to cover this important extension.

Estimation in addition

In an addition problem like the one above (458 + 376) the child can be taught various accuracy levels of estimation. At the simplest level the sum is reduced to the hundred digits (400 + 300). A closer estimate will be obtained for 450 + 350. At a more sophisticated level the sum can be presented as 450 + 350 + 30, with the child seeing 458 as approximately 450, but with 8 left over. The 376 is seen as 350 and 25. The 8 from 458 and the 25 from 376 are combined to give an estimate of 30 and the total 450 + 350 + 30 = 830.

The grasshopper (see Chapter 3) may even tackle the complete calculation along these lines, combining convenient parts of the two numbers and mopping up the remainders. For example, he may take 24 from the 458 to make 376 into 400, then add on the 434 which is left. He may take out 350 from 376, 450 from 458 and combine these to make 800, which can be put to one side in working memory. Only 8 + 26 is left, which can be added via number bonds for ten as 26 + 4 + 4 = 34. This is added onto the 800 to make 834.

Similar principles apply to estimating subtractions. For example, 834 – 458 might be seen as close to 858 – 458 or 834 – 434, both giving an answer of 400. Then, if the learner can decide whether the adjustment made the estimate high or low, he can say that the answer is a little less than 400. If an accurate answer is needed, then it could be by looking at

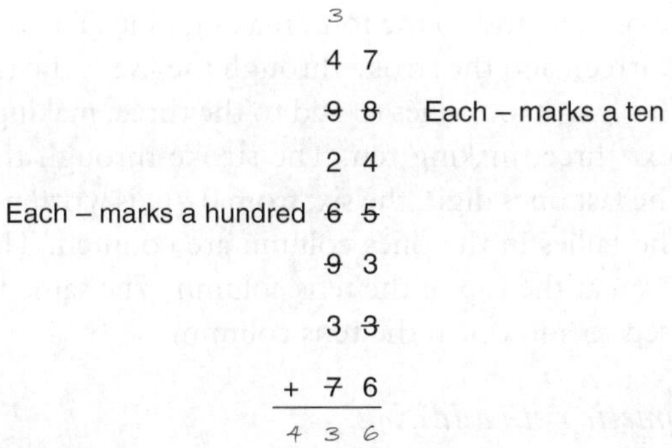

3
4 7
9 8 Each – marks a ten
2 4
Each – marks a hundred 6 5
9 3
3 3
+ 7 6
4 3 6

Figure 8.4 Using tally marks for tens and hundreds, so that additions are focused on 'easy' sub-additions.

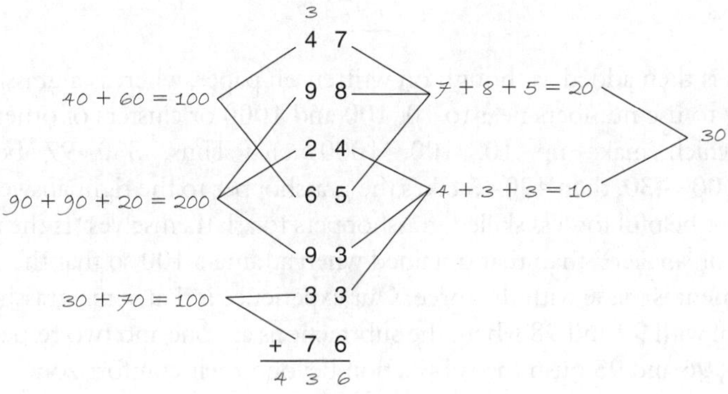

Figure 8.5 Casting out tens (and twenties) using the number bonds/combinations for ten (and twenty).

the adjustment, say, in the 858 – 458 version that the learner adds on 24, then the actual answer is 400 – 24.

These methods illustrate the advantages of breaking down and building up numbers and finding the 'easier' numbers within the 'harder' numbers.

Column addition

The addition of a column of numbers requires somewhat different techniques and can be a daunting task. There are two low-stress algorithms (Ashlock, 2010) which may help. One (Figure 8.4) is more likely to appeal to inchworms and the other (Figure 8.5) to grasshoppers.

In Figure 8.4, addition starts at the top of the ones column with 7 + 8 giving 15. The stroke through the eight is the tally for the ten in fifteen, leaving the five ones to add to the four, making nine. The nine is added to five to make fourteen and the stroke through the five is the tally for the ten in fourteen. This leaves four ones to add to the three, making seven, which is added to next three, making ten. The stroke through the three is the tally for ten. The last ones digit, the six, from 0 + 6, is written at the bottom of the sum. The tallies in the ones column are counted. There are three, so three is written at the top of the tens column. The same tallying procedure is now used to add down the tens column.

Mental arithmetic with addition

An extreme inchworm will probably try to visualise a written procedure, so that 330 + 97 becomes:

$$\begin{array}{r} 330 \\ +97 \\ \hline \end{array}$$

This is then added as though on written on paper, whereas a grasshopper will try to use numbers near to 10, 100 and 1000 or clusters of other numbers which make up 10, 100, 1000, etc. Thus, 330 + 97 becomes 330 + 100 = 430, then 430 – 3 takes the grasshopper to the right answer, 427. It can be helpful for less skilled grasshoppers to ask themselves 'Is the answer bigger or smaller?' than that obtained when adding a 100 so that the correct adjustment is made with the three. Our experience is that some grasshoppers can deal with 99 and 98 where the subtractions are one and two respectively, but 97, 96 and 95 push the subtraction beyond their comfort zone.

The latter process is usually a lesser strain on working memory, and requires less knowledge of basic facts. It does assumes that the student can deal with – 3, either through knowing 10 – 3 or by having enough working memory capacity left to count back three.

The same processes apply to subtraction, for example 578 – 299. The inchworm will visualise the sum rewritten as:

$$\begin{array}{r} 578 \\ -299 \\ \hline \end{array}$$

They then attempt to carry out the written procedure mentally, which is a daunting task for those with working memory problems.

The grasshopper will round the 299 up to 300, subtract to get 278, add on one to obtain the final answer of 279. As with addition, some may need to decide whether the final answer will be 'bigger or smaller?' than the intermediate answer before dealing with the one used for rounding up the 299.

Teaching Subtraction as a Separate Exercise

Even though we feel there are many advantages to teaching subtraction and addition together, there may be situations where subtraction has to be approached separately, even if just to reinforce the understanding of the procedures.

It may be necessary for you to start by providing an overview to remind or re-establish the concept and vocabulary of subtraction before teaching specific algorithms. Some examples to which the child can relate, such as change from shopping and/or examples using manipulative aids, are suitable.

You should be trying to establish in the child's mind a clear picture of the component parts of the subtraction. It is usually unnecessary to use the mathematical terms minuend and subtrahend. However, the child needs to understand the consequences of subtraction and be able to relate it to addition.

Subtraction without regrouping

This is the easiest process and acts as a good introduction as well as reinforcing the concept of subtraction and the identification of the component parts of the sum. Thus a subtraction such as:

$$\begin{array}{r} 79 \\ -34 \\ \hline 45 \end{array}$$

can be used to practise the use of manipulative materials such as money or base ten blocks. Such manipulative work may have to start with the use of a place value card. There is, as ever, a need to teach estimating and to re-emphasise its value as a way to reduce the chance of errors.

Subtraction with regrouping: the decomposition/regrouping/ renaming method

This method is well illustrated by base ten blocks (and coins) as it is very much a method about place value. As with so much in mathematics, the work here relies on previous concepts and therefore these concepts may need attention before starting on the main agenda. The main review is to look again at the regrouping of numbers, for example 72 is also 60 + 12 or at the renaming (a more descriptive term) of numbers such as 742 to the specific format 600 + 130 + 12 (Figure 8.6a).

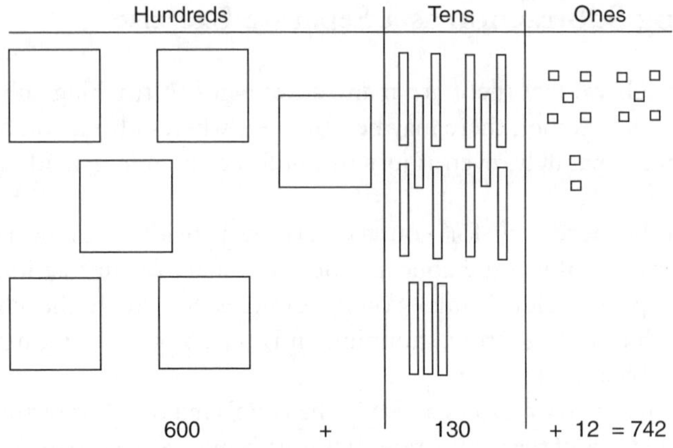

Figure 8.6a Renaming 742 as 600 + 130 + 12.

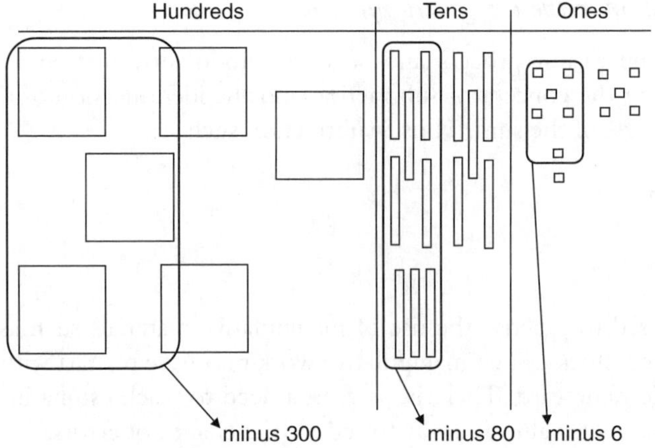

Figure 8.6b Subtracting 386.

100	10	1
7	4	2
6	*13*	*12*
− 3	8	6
3	5	6

Figure 8.6c Including an extra line to show the renaming.

$^{6}\not{7}$	$^{13}\not{4}$	$^{1}2$
− 3	8	6
3	5	6

Figure 8.6d The 'traditional' layout for subtraction.

Note that a number of different words are used for this process. At one school we visited, different classes used different words, so that children had to recognise and readjust to the new word in each class. Whilst children need to be aware of this range of vocabulary, it must not be the source of confusion or misunderstanding for them.

Work on renaming three-digit numbers using this format can be investigated and the consequent generalisation achieved. Examples are:

$$543=400+130+13$$
$$754=600+140+14$$
$$865=700+150+15$$
$$976=800+160+16$$

The application of this renaming process should lead on to subtraction examples set up on a place value card with the teacher talking the child through the algorithm. For example:

$$\begin{array}{r} 742 \\ -386 \\ \hline \end{array}$$

The blocks (Figures 8.6a and 8.6b, used first, followed by money) should be moved by the child. The progression should be from base ten blocks to money, each time writing the numbers as the manipulatives are moved. If the child seems to understand the work, then you may take him to working with just the digits. The child may well need to start this stage with place value columns drawn on the paper.

Spatial and organisational problems may make the traditional layout too confusing, at least at first, so an intermediate presentation may help. A separate middle line is set up with all the renaming done at one time and before the actual subtraction (Figure 8.6c).

Finally the place value columns can be removed and the child works on squared or lined paper (Figure 8.6d).

Examples which include zeros should be demonstrated.

The equal-additions method

The method for the example below is generalised by the equation $a-b=(a+10)-(b+10)$, with 10 added to both a and b, which keeps the difference, $a-b$, the same. It is a harder method to explain to a child than the decomposition method, and Kennedy (1975) quite rightly pointed out that children have more difficulty remembering an algorithm they do not understand. It is also harder to provide multisensory experiences which clearly illustrate this algorithm. Despite these reservations, if the process can be mastered it is easy to reproduce. An 'easy' example may clarify the process, for example:

$$320-90 \text{ becomes} (320+10)-(90+10)=330-100$$

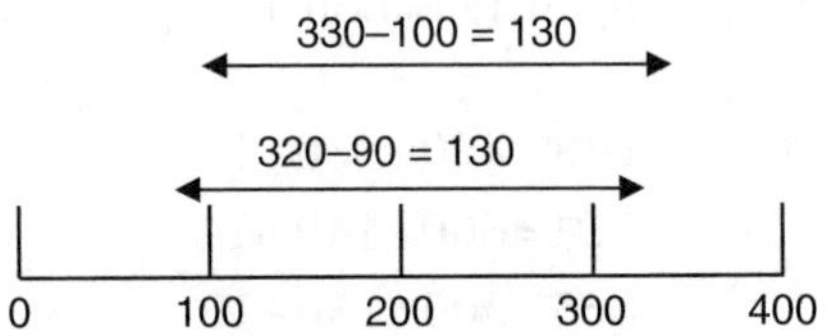

330–100 = 130

320–90 = 130

0 100 200 300 400

A number line can be used to show that the 'difference', 130, shown by the arrow line is the same for the two (and, indeed more) examples.

Subtraction by equal additions is quicker, and probably easier, than decomposition as a mechanical process, but Kennedy's comment should be remembered as being particularly apposite for dyslexics, who often need a concrete base on which to build their understanding and memory.

Mental arithmetic with subtraction

The method of equal additions adjusts the numbers in the calculation and this adjusting strategy can be extended into mental arithmetic. For example, $342-197$ can be made an easier calculation by adding three to both numbers:

$$342-197=345-200$$

This method is easier for some children than a similar procedure where the 197 is rounded up to 200, 200 is subtracted from 342 and 3 is added back onto the resultant 142.

Always take into consideration the load on working memory.

A subtraction such as 411 – 115 does require the latter strategy. The difference is approximately 300 but is less than 300. The question: 'Is the answer bigger or smaller?' comes into play again. This appraisal as to whether the answer is more than 300 or less than 300 is fundamental to the success of this strategy. If 4 is added on to 411, then the subtraction gives an answer of 300. The added-on 4 now needs compensation, so 300 – 4 = 296, the correct answer. In a process such as this, it is easy to assume that subtracting (or counting back) 4 from 300 is a simple and quick task, thus making low demands on working memory. This may not be so for every child. Automaticity is often a key factor for the steps in mental arithmetic.

As before, the ability to perform mental arithmetic with facility is greatly enhanced by an understanding of the interrelationships between numbers and the interrelationship between the operations of addition and subtraction, so that 411 – 115 was seen to be close to, but less than 300 and 197 was seen to be 3 short of 200. Such calculations can also be used to involve and develop estimation skills.

9

Multiplication

Introduction

This topic will be used to illustrate the use of a full programme of instruction. The principles of this structure are applicable to other topics. The work moves from a manipulative aid, which is a direct representation of the problem, to a visual model (in this case, area), to purely written symbols and an algorithm which links back to the concrete model. Whenever possible the structure acknowledges different cognitive styles. The multisensory introduction is used to encourage flexible cognitive processes and to provide an overview.

There are some other methods that are used by some teachers and thus by some children. These include the Napier's Bones method. An overview of the data from the standardisation of Chinn's 15-minute test (Chinn, 2017a) suggests that this method is often only partially remembered. The method makes for an interesting exercise for teachers, that is, to analyse all the prerequisite skills a student needs to make a particular method work, for example here, from spatial organisation to retrieval of basic facts. A failure in even one of the steps will result in a wrong answer. It is hard for a student to understand this method and thus hard to support memory without that understanding. It is also of note from the standardising data that the success rate for a three-digit times three-digit example (541 × 203) in this test was very low, with 15.2% of the 13-year-old cohort and 38.2% of the 15-year-old cohort achieving correct answers.

Mathematics for Dyslexics and Dyscalculics: A Teaching Handbook, Fourth Edition.
Steve Chinn and Richard E. Ashcroft.

The key concepts

Learners need to know and understand that multiplication is about repeated addition of the same number. They also need to understand the role of place value, especially when multiplying by powers of ten.

Multiplying by Ten and Powers of Ten

This procedure is also needed to underpin estimation skills. Estimation skills in multiplication as used, for example, to back up calculator work, centre on an ability to multiply by tens, hundreds, thousands, etc. In our experience this relatively basic skill needs frequent review. It is a skill that depends on an understanding of place value.

The pattern for multiplying by ten must be explained in terms of the basic concept and the implication on place value, rather than solely in terms of the purely mechanical action of 'adding on zeros' or 'moving the decimal point', procedures which generate horror in the minds of many mathematicians, yet are readily adopted by children, who tend to act pragmatically, and are illustrated in some textbooks.

The objective is to explain that multiplying by 10, 100, 1000, and so on, moves numbers up in place value, but that the digits themselves do not change their sequence. To illustrate this, consider 536×10.

- 6×10. Use a place value card and put six ones cubes in the ones column. Remind the child of the ten times table and the exchanging of tens blocks for ones cubes. Then ask the child to exchange each ones cube for a tens block, placing the tens blocks in the tens column. Give the child a sheet of paper with place value columns on it and ask him to write in numerals the 6 and the 60. Discuss the 60 being ten times bigger than the 6 and emphasise that the 6 has moved to a higher place value, that is, from the ones column to the tens column and that this requires writing a zero in the ones column (Figure 9.1a).
- 30×10. Repeat the process, but exchange three tens blocks in the tens column for three hundreds blocks (squares) in the hundreds column (Figure 9.1b).
- 200×10. Repeat the process again exchanging two hundreds squares for two thousands blocks (Figure 9.1c).
- 236×10. Repeat the process all in one example (Figure 9.2). Then discuss what has happened to each digit, the relevance numerically, the

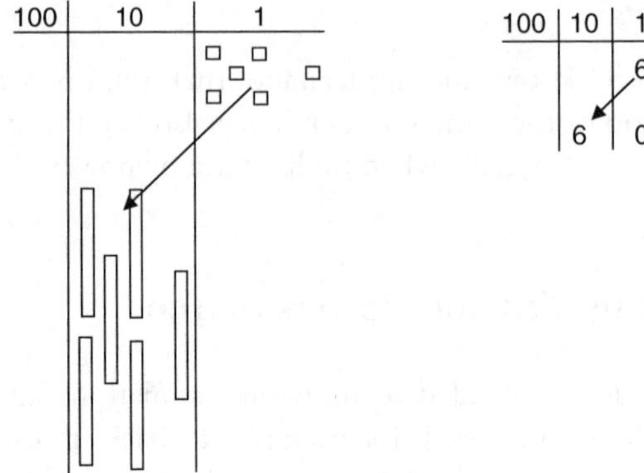

Figure 9.1a Multiplying by 10. 6 × 10 = 60.

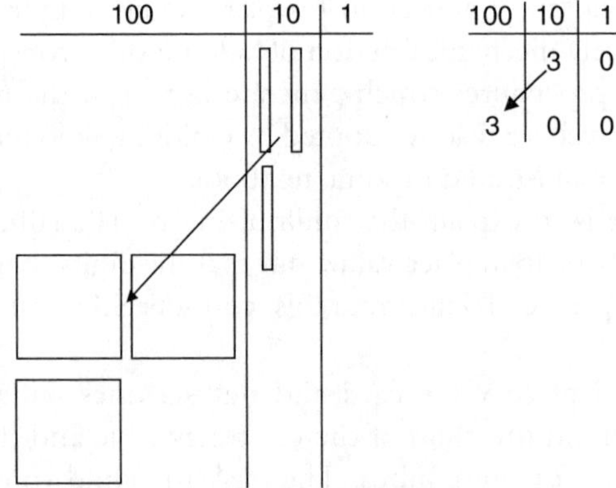

Figure 9.1b Multiplying by 10. 30 × 10 = 300.

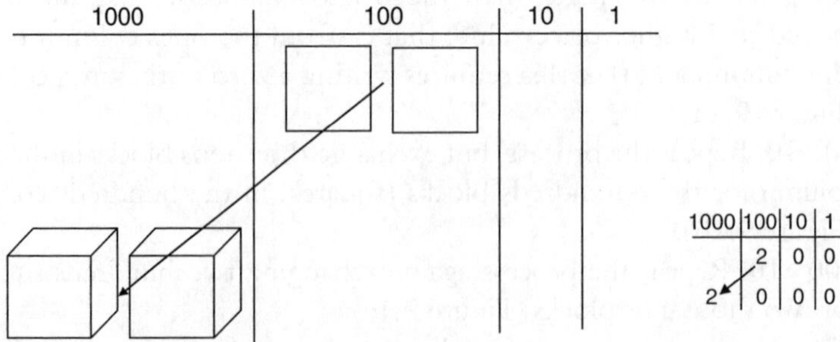

Figure 9.1c Multiplying by 10. 200 × 10 = 2000.

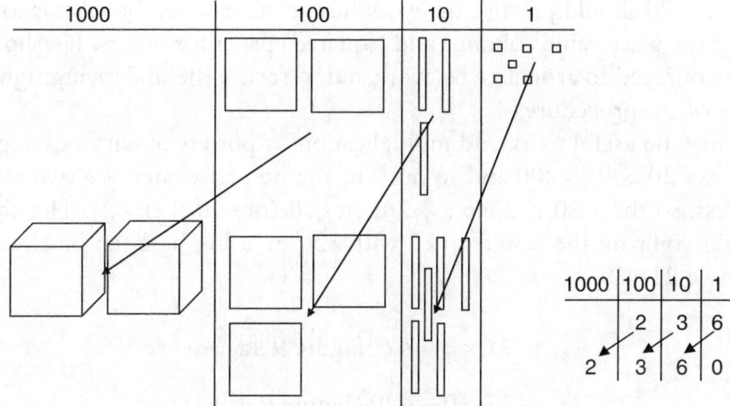

Figure 9.2 Multiplying by 10. 236 × 10 = 2360.

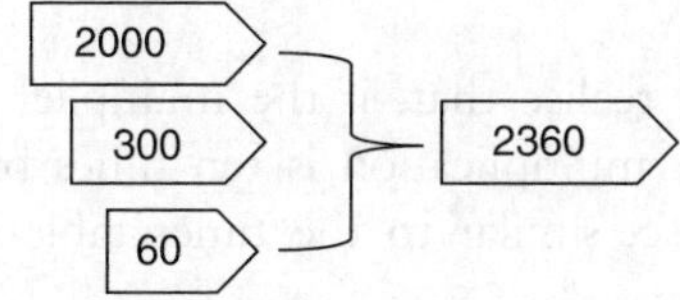

Figure 9.3 2360 = 2000 + 300 + 60

pattern, what has changed and what has not changed in the process. The procedure can be illustrated with place value number arrows (Figure 9.3) as a further reinforcement of the concept.

It should now be possible for the child to explain other calculations such as 849 × 10 = 8490, including the significance of the zero in the ones column, and to restate that the order of digits remains the same. As ever, this work includes a significant element of revisiting previous work and ideas.

A similar process can be used to teach × 100 and × 1000 and other powers of ten. One way of checking the answer is to focus on just one digit, for example in 849 × 100, focus on nine, which will be changed from nine ones to nine hundreds and the remaining digits follow in sequence:

9 × 100 = 900 849 × 100 = 84900

The child should practise the work, using the base ten blocks for some examples, place value columns and (squared) paper for others. He should be encouraged to articulate his work and to review the underlying significance of the procedure.

It may be useful to extend multiplication by powers of ten to examples such as $\times 20$, $\times 50$, $\times 200$ and so on. The method advocated is a two-stage process, so that $\times 20$ is done as $\times 2$ then $\times 10$ (or $\times 10$ then $\times 2$). The child should compare the results of $\times 2$ with $\times 20$ by using base ten blocks, for example 21×20:

$$21 \times 2 = 42 \text{ (Figure 9.4a)}$$

$$42 \times 10 = 420 \text{ (Figure 9.4b)}$$

giving:

$$21 \times 20 = 21 \times 2 \times 10 = 420$$

The child needs to realise that, if the multiplier is ten times bigger, then the result of the multiplication is ten times bigger. This two-step procedure is, of course, similar to the times table strategy of using $\times 2$ twice for $\times 4$.

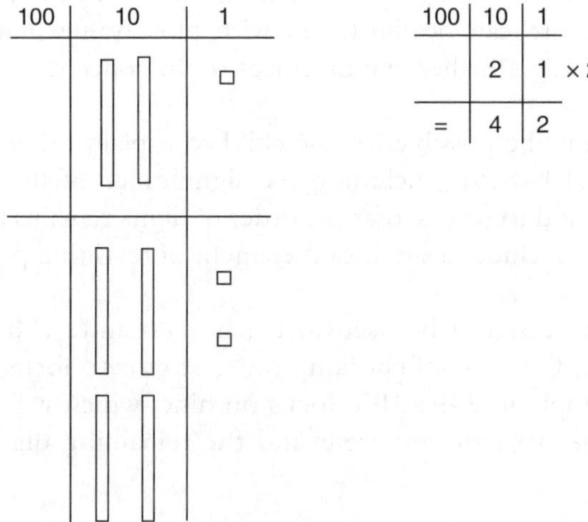

Figure 9.4a Multiplying by 2. 21 × 2 = 42

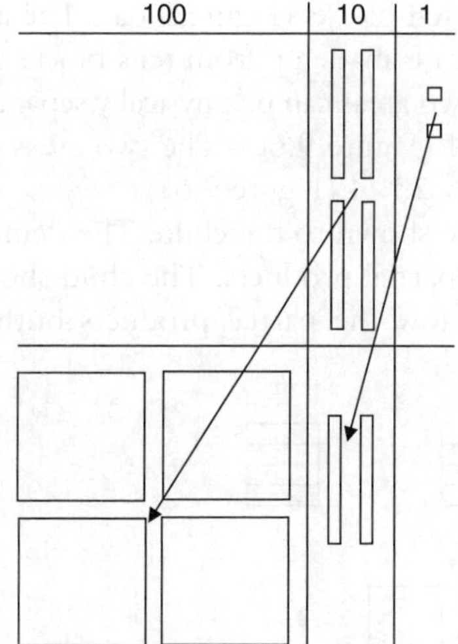

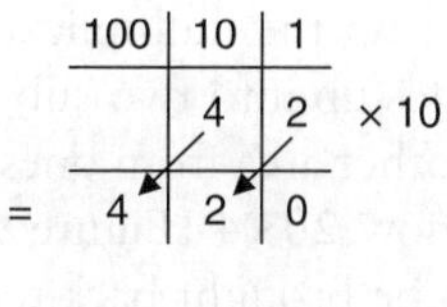

Figure 9.4b Multiplying by 10. $42 \times 10 = 420$.

Multiplication

Times table facts are predominantly one-digit times one-digit operations, but also include $\times 10$. This chapter extends this progressively to two digit times one digit and then to two digit times two digit and thus, by using the same models, to any multiplication. The model of multiplication used is area. This model is advocated because it can be extended into other aspects of multiplication, such as a fraction times a fraction and algebra.

Introducing the model

The child needs some square counters (Figure 9.5). The three piles illustrate three lots of four. This can be discussed as repeated addition, $4+4+4$ leading to the more economical representation 3×4. The counters are then rearranged to represent area.

The concept of $a \times b$, that is, ab, as area can be discussed in real-life terms, such as floor tiles, areas of walls for painting, etc.

Two-digit numbers times one-digit numbers

Consider the example 23×4. The child is going to learn a two-stage procedure. This procedure was used in the times table chapter (Chapter 7), for example, where 7×6 was treated as $(5 \times 6)+(2 \times 6)$, a process of breaking down followed by building up again.

Set up the multiplication with base ten blocks (Figure 9.6a). The area divides up into two sub-areas. One area is made up from tens blocks and the other area from ones blocks. The two areas can be physically separated to show 20×4 (Figure 9.6b) and 3×4 (Figure 9.6c). The two areas can then be brought back together to show 23×4 (Figure 9.6a).

At each step the written symbols are shown to the child. The demonstration shows and separates the two partial products. The child should set up some areas for himself and show the partial products both as blocks and as written digits.

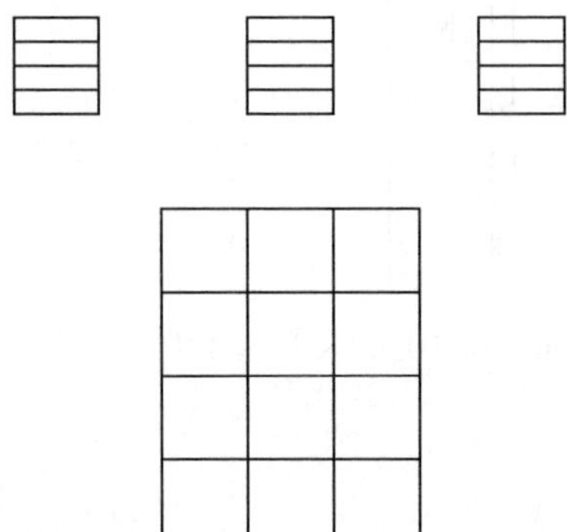

Figure 9.5 Square counters used to show 3×4 as three piles of 4 and as area 3×4.

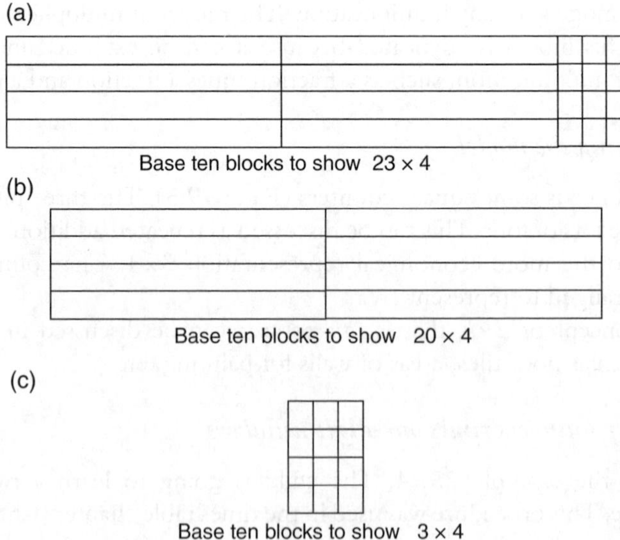

Figure 9.6 Base ten blocks to show the breakdown of 23×4.

Two digit times two digit

The model is again area. Consider the example 22×31. The inefficiency of repeated addition could be reviewed for this example:

$$22+22+22+22+22+22+22+22+22+22+22+22+22+22+22+22+22+22+22+22+22+22+22+22+22+22+22+22+22+22+22.$$

Indeed, this overwhelming presentation would suggest some grouping, or chunking, which could be another route into the area model and the final algorithm.

1. Set up the multiplication in base ten blocks (Figure 9.7a). The blocks illustrate area. They are movable, so that the four sub-areas can be separated (Figure 9.7b). These partial products allow a difficult problem to be broken down into smaller, easier steps. The child can handle the blocks and physically break down the problem with the blocks, as well as with the written digits.
2. The four constituent areas are discussed, starting with the largest area, the area formed by the 'hundred squares'. This offers a first estimate. The blocks provide a very real model of this (Figure 9.7c). The estimation sum is written by the child in digits ($30 \times 20 = 600$).
3. The four areas are examined (Figure 9.8). They are: 30×20 1×20 30×2 1×2

30×20	tens × tens	=	600
1×20	ones × tens	=	20
30×2	tens × ones	=	60
1×2	ones × ones	=	2
	total	=	682

This algorithm is $(a+b)(c+d) = ac + ad + bc + bd$.

The child needs to see and handle each partial product in order to see that the area does break down into constituent parts. Each partial product should be written down in digits.

4. The problem is drawn to scale on squared paper by the child. This will look like Figure 9.8b. The sub-divisions are drawn in, and the relationship between the areas and the numbers in the partial products is explained.

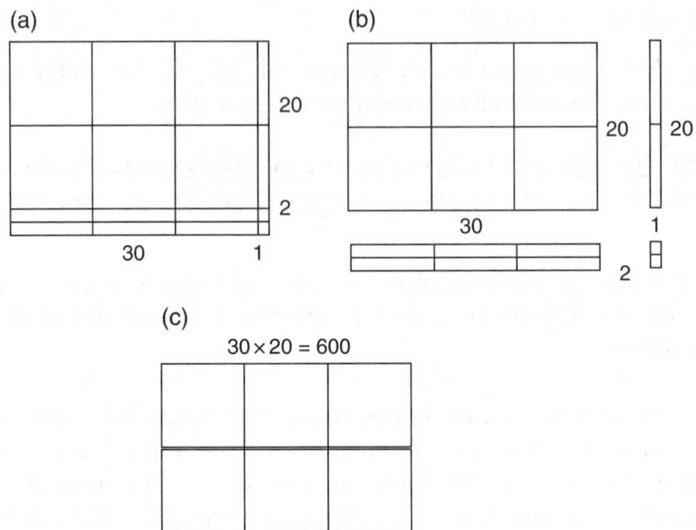

Figure 9.7 Base ten blocks to show 22 × 31.

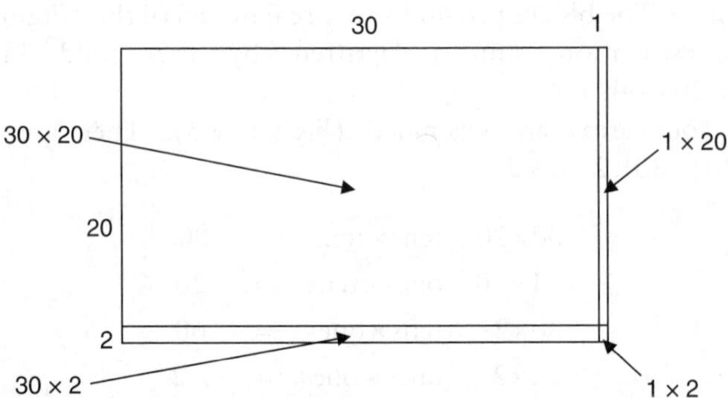

Figure 9.8 An area model for 22 × 31 as four partial products.

5. A problem is presented as numbers, for example 22×31. The partial products are written down and calculated. The child is asked to identify the 'estimate' partial product.
6. The problem is drawn to scale again on squared paper and only one sub-division is made, leaving two areas (Figure 9.9). In numbers the two areas are 20×31 and 2×31. The algorithm is based on $(a+b)c = ac + bc$.

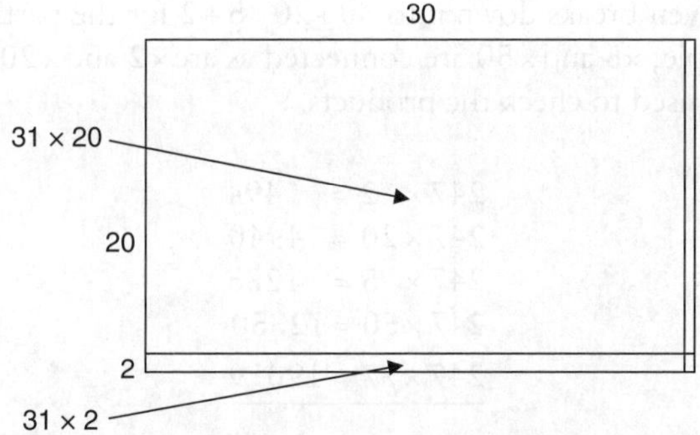

Figure 9.9 An area model for 22 × 31 as two partial products.

The calculation becomes:

$$\begin{array}{r} 31 \\ \underline{\times 22} \end{array}$$

$$\begin{array}{r} 31 \\ \underline{\times 20} \\ 620 \end{array} + \begin{array}{r} 31 \\ \underline{\times 2} \\ 62 \end{array} = 682 \quad (31 \times 22)$$

The child is still doing four multiplications as before, but he is combining two on each line of the calculation.

Compare the two methods as used for another example, 54×23:

$$\begin{array}{rl} 54 & \\ \underline{\times 23} & \\ 1000 & (50 \times 20) \\ 80 & (4 \times 20) \\ 150 & (50 \times 3) \\ \underline{12} & (4 \times 3) \\ 1242 & \end{array} \qquad \begin{array}{rl} 54 & \\ \underline{\times 23} & \\ 1080 & (54 \times 20) \\ \underline{162} & (54 \times 3) \\ 1242 & \end{array}$$

There is a procedure, still using partial products, but as with the times table facts, using the core numbers to create the partial products. For example 247×77.

Seventy-seven breaks down into $50+20+5+2$ for the partial products. In this example, $\times 5$ and $\times 50$ are connected as are $\times 2$ and $\times 20$. Thus place value can be used to check the products.

$$
\begin{aligned}
247 \times 2 &= 494 \\
247 \times 20 &= 4940 \\
247 \times 5 &= 1235 \\
247 \times 50 &= 12350 \\
\hline
247 \times 77 &= 19019
\end{aligned}
$$

Einstein is purported to have said, ‘Everything can be made as simple as possible, but not simpler than that.’ This method restricts multiplications to the core facts. The interrelationships help with place value. However, there are now more partial products and thus more to add.

The same approach as used above will be adopted for division, where the additions of the partial products are replaced by subtractions.

The child should chose the method which best helps his particular strengths and weaknesses, for example organisation of work on the page, knowledge of basic facts and knowledge of place value.

Mnemonics

Mnemonics may help the child with a two-digit times two-digit computation. These will be used again for algebra expressions of the type, $(x+a)(y+b)$. It is hoped that these will only be used once understanding is embedded and not as a substitute for comprehension.

FOIL (Figure 9.10)

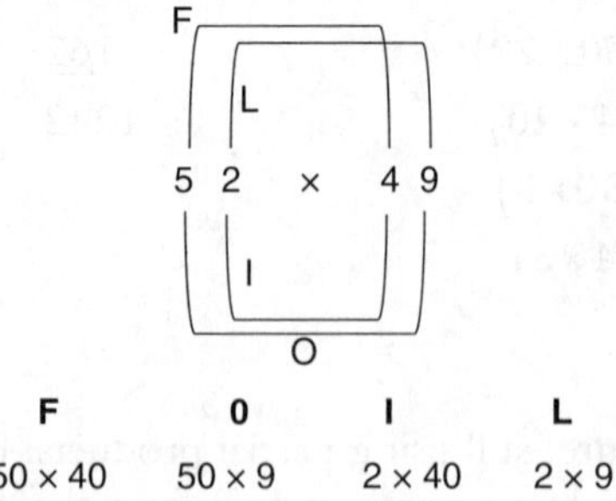

Figure 9.10 The FOIL acronym.

The **F**irst two digits are multiplied together: 50 × 40.
The **O**uter two digits are multiplied together: 50 × 3.
The **I**nner two digits are multiplied together: 2 × 40.
The **L**ast two digits are multiplied together: 2 × 3.

There can, however, be place value problems with this mnemonic.

To reiterate, this 'trick' is merely a mnemonic and is not developing any understanding of the algebra involved. However, a limited use of mnemonics may be a survival skill for some students.

Estimation

Whilst calculators provide a relatively stress-free way of multiplying, dyslexics and dyscalculics have a tendency to press the wrong number keys, get the numbers in the wrong order, use the wrong operation key or use the right operation key at the wrong time. A pre-calculation estimate and a post-calculation evaluation/appraisal are, therefore, important.

The area model provides a good picture of how to estimate, based on the biggest sub-area, plus or minus the other sub-areas. It also allows the child to evaluate his estimate and see if it is high, low or fairly accurate. Some examples will explain this.

- 33 × 54 (Figure 9.11a). This is estimated at 30 × 50 = 1500 and can be seen to be an underestimate, but reasonably close to the accurate answer.
- 42 × 78 (Figure 9.11b). Note that the 78 has been rounded up to 80 so that the length of the rectangle drawn is longer. This, then, is estimated at 40 × 80 = 3200 and can be seen to be very close to the accurate answer with the extra 2 × 40 not quite compensating for the 2 × 78.
- 51 × 92 (Figure 9.11c). Subtract to refine the estimate. Note that the 92 has been rounded up to 100. This is estimated at 50 × 100 = 5000 and can be seen to be an overestimate with 8 × 50 (which has to be subtracted) bigger than 1 × 92 (which has to be added).

Extension

The principle of the algorithm for a two-digit times two-digit calculation can be readily extended to a three-digit times three-digit calculation and so on. The spatial organisation problems may require the child to work on

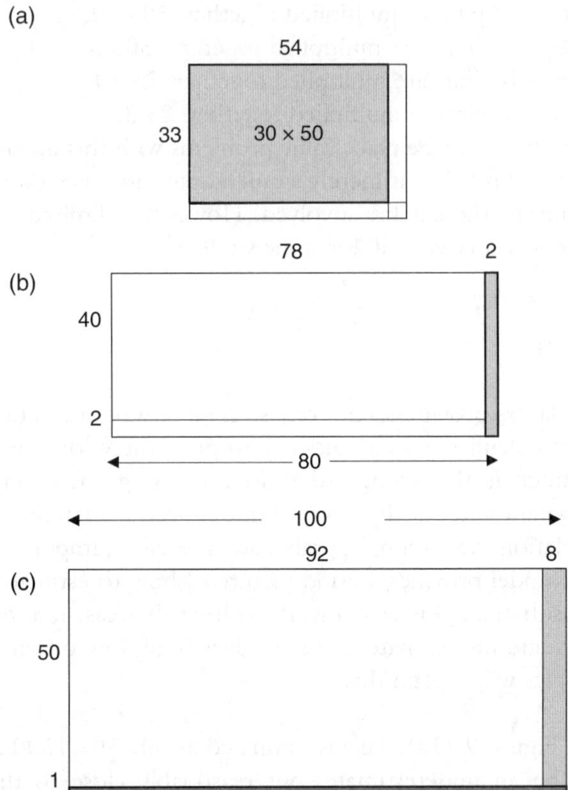

Figure 9.11 Area models to illustrate estimation.

squared paper or paper with vertical lines. In the easier examples the child may benefit from writing or articulating what each partial product means. Equally the principle of developing work from manipulative aids, through visual models, to symbol work is applicable to 'harder' examples.

These procedures integrate multisensory experiences with sound mathematical algorithms and provide the child with some concrete experiences and visual images that will help him to remember what might otherwise seem to him to be a meaningless random process. The structure provided by the identification of the partial products, and the number of partial products involved, helps the child and should help you, the teacher, with the diagnosis of errors and subsequent remedial input.

The area model will be used again in algebra with examples such as $(x+4)(2x-6)$. Much of mathematics has a developmental structure and thus the foundations must be secure to underpin progression.

10

Division
Whole Numbers

Introduction

In this chapter suggestions for teaching the concept of division, then division by single-digit numbers and by powers of ten are discussed. For more complex divisions an alternative algorithm to the traditional one is discussed once again using core number partial products and interrelating the operations.

The 'traditional' procedure for long division is very demanding on many of the skill areas that dyslexic and dyscalculic students find most difficult. The algorithm traditionally used for long division requires good skills in sequencing, memory, knowledge of basic facts and spatial organisation. It is also difficult to model the logic of the traditional algorithm with manipulative materials.

Anghileri (1999) observes that: 'There is now evidence that the procedural approach encouraged by the traditional algorithm leads pupils to ignore the meaning of the numbers as they try to remember complex procedures they have learned without really understanding.' It is worth considering the problems dyslexic and dyscalculic learners face in this particularly challenging topic. The extent of these difficulties may be alleviated by referring back to, and building on, other work the student has covered and by interrelating concepts (such as subtraction and division) so as to try and make old and new work mutually supportive. Once again, the student's existing knowledge makes a good baseline. So, you need to capitalise on this existing knowledge and thus should begin with informal diagnostic work, which is intended to find out what the student knows and which examples and illustrations he relates to.

Mathematics for Dyslexics and Dyscalculics: A Teaching Handbook, Fourth Edition.
Steve Chinn and Richard E. Ashcroft.

The language of division can lead to early problems and can be an initial block to understanding of the concept and processes of division. A typical early question could be, 'divide 36 by 6' or '36 ÷ 6'. The order in which the numbers are stated in these two examples is the opposite to the demands of the traditional 'bus stop' algorithm, 6)36.

The instruction 'divide' might communicate better if it is used as 'divide into n equal parts' which links it more closely to 'share equally between n people'. 'Share' is the better word to use for early, introductory work as it relates more readily to the manipulative materials and their everyday experiences.

The spatial and organisational demands of division algorithms are considerable. The traditional algorithm for 6)378 requires the child to work from left to right, writing the answer at the top, working from the hundreds to the tens and then to the ones and carrying down numbers as the problem proceeds. These requirements are almost directly opposite to those for the standard procedures for addition, subtraction and multiplication. Inconsistencies do not help, though, of course, they cannot always be avoided. Students can, however, be made aware of them.

Furthermore, to help meet these conflicting directional demands, the child may well need support in getting the digits into the correct place values on the answer line. Extra support for this accuracy can be provided by teaching estimating skills and by encouraging the child to overview the question (which may include rephrasing it.)

Introduction to Division

The initial aims are to introduce (or review) division in at least four ways: as sharing out or dividing up into parts; as finding out 'how many numbers in'; as the converse of multiplication; as repeated subtraction. Each of these has a different vocabulary. An introductory activity of taking (small) numbers of counters and dividing them up into groups helps the child to see the processes of division in action and the interrelationship between division and subtraction. You can then extend the child's perception of the activity by structured questions and representations of the 'dividing up' actions.

Example

Take 12 counters and place them randomly on a table (Figure 10.1). Ask the child to count them. (Some children will group the counters automatically when they do this.) Then ask the child to share/divide them into in three groups.

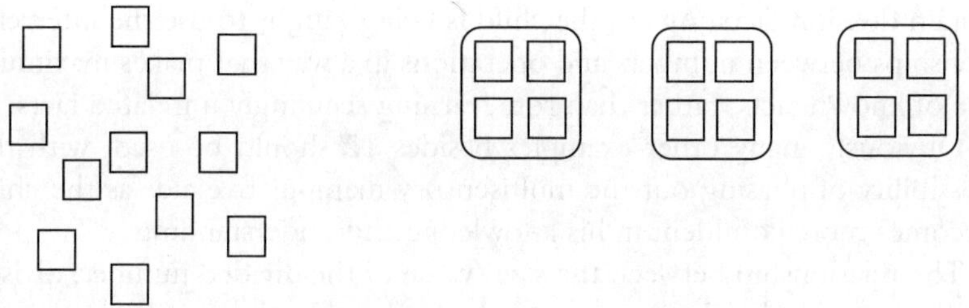

Figure 10.1 Showing twelve as three groups of four.

Ask the child to reorganise the groups into rows and columns. Then the following relationships can be examined as manipulatives and as equations. Again flexibility of language should help strengthen the concept:

Three lots of four (how many fours in twelve?).
Four lots of three (how many threes in twelve?).
Three goes into twelve four times.
Twelve divided by three gives four.
Repeated subtraction, three times, of four from twelve.

This work can be related back to the times table square. Its use as a division square can be taught.

Repeated subtraction relates division to subtraction and acts as a first exposure to a later algorithm. There are a number of ways 'twelve divided by three'can be represented in symbols:

$$12 \div 3 = 4$$

$$3 \times \square = 12$$

$$\frac{12}{3} = 4 \qquad 3\overline{)12}^{\,4}$$

$$12 - 3 = 9$$
$$9 - 3 = 6$$
$$6 - 3 = 3$$
$$3 - 3 = 0$$

The child is being encouraged to see the relationship between division and multiplication, the idea of dividing up, the phrasing, 'How many *x*s in *y*?' as well as the concept of division as repeated subtraction and the idea of sharing equally. Simple division facts can be presented as multiplication facts with 'gaps' and the child can be shown how to use a table square to obtain division facts. Again, the child is being taught to use the interrelationships between numbers and operations in a way that makes maximum use of known facts, rather than rote learning seemingly unrelated facts.

Obviously many other examples besides 12 should be used, with the possibility of phasing out the multisensory manipulative aids as the child becomes more confident in his knowledge and understanding.

The relationship between the size/value of the divided number, divisor and answer can be shown by examples such as dividing 12 by a series of divisors: 12, 6, 4, 3, 2, 1.

$$
\begin{aligned}
12 \div 12 &= 1 \\
12 \div 6 &= 2 \\
12 \div 4 &= 3 \\
12 \div 3 &= 4 \\
12 \div 2 &= 6 \\
12 \div 1 &= 12
\end{aligned}
$$

Work of this type (using, as ever, written presentation alongside manipulative work) leads the child towards estimation skills. At the least, the child is learning that the bigger the divisor, the smaller the answer and the smaller the divisor the bigger the answer (setting the groundwork for division by numbers less than one). Once more the question, ‘Is the answer smaller or bigger?’ comes into play as the precursor to any calculation.

Dividing two-digit numbers by one-digit numbers, with remainder

Although the work described so far could be used to introduce a child to the topic of division, it is best considered as an early stage of intervention. For these early confidence-building stages, remainders provide less confusion than decimal or fraction answers. Thus 14 ÷ 4 is presented with counters (Figure 10.2). It is apparent that the answer is 3 and that there are two counters left over or remaining. ‘Remainder’ seems to be a reasonable name for these counters.

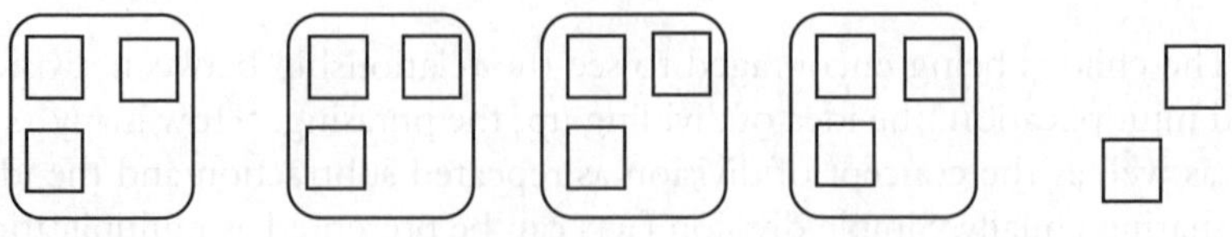

Figure 10.2 Showing fourteen as four groups of three with two ‘left over’.

Dividing two and three-digit numbers with renaming (of tens and hundreds)

Examples

65 ÷ 5

An efficient procedure for dividing 65 into five equal parts requires the student to progress from just counting out 65, sharing one by one, into five groups. He has to learn how to start with: 'How many tens can I place in each of the five parts?' then, 'What do you do with the ten and the five ones left over from the 65?' This is quite a leap in skill and understanding. The demands of the algorithm on areas of difficulty, for example organisation of work on paper and knowledge of division facts, are significant. Again, the teaching principle is to relate the symbols to the concrete and make the algorithm relate to a manipulative and then visual procedure. We advocate a structured approach that pre-empts as many of the difficulties as possible and creates the concrete and visual images for the student:

- Sixty-five is presented in base ten blocks (Figure 10.3a).
- Five tens are taken out, one to each of the five parts (Figure 10.3a).
- The 'left over' ten is traded for ten ones cubes and added to the existing five ones cubes.
- The fifteen ones cubes are shared out, adding three ones cubes to each of the five parts making 10 + 3, an answer of 13 (Figure 10.3b).

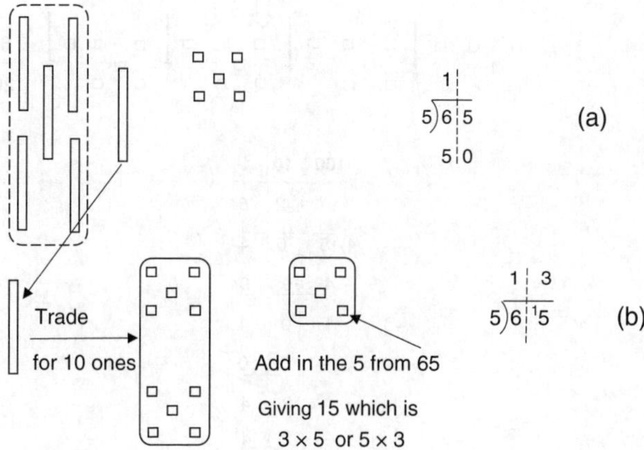

Figure 10.3 Using base ten blocks to demonstrate the division, 65 ÷ 5, as repeated subtraction.

At each stage the written algorithm matches the base ten manipulatives. You can explain the significance of each move and can relate it back to other work. For example, the need to trade tens for ones is used in this subtraction.

504 ÷ 4

- A similar structure is presented, with 504 shown in base ten blocks. This time the first move is to take out four hundreds blocks and place one in each part (Figure 10.4a).

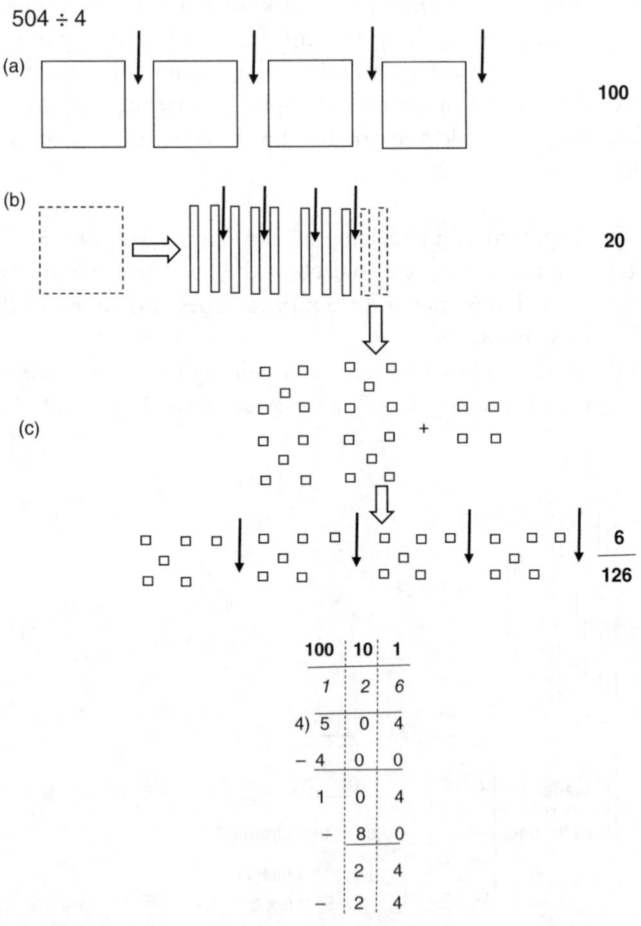

Figure 10.4 Using base ten blocks to demonstrate the division, 504 ÷ 4, as repeated subtraction.

- This leaves one hundreds block, which is traded for ten tens blocks, which are placed in the tens column. This highlights the previously empty tens column and emphasises the need to mark its presence in the answer line. Eight ten blocks are removed, two for each part (Figure 10.4b).
- The two remaining tens blocks are traded for ones cubes, giving twenty-four ones cubes to share into the four parts, six in each (Figure 10.4c).
- The final answer is 126.

Note the use of place value columns in the written version (given alongside the blocks in the parts of Figure 10.4). (Other suitable manipulative aids are money and bundles of cocktail sticks.)

Other examples should be used to consolidate this method. When the manipulative-aid stage is phased out, the use of the place value columns should remain as these tends to eliminate the common errors of starting the answer in the wrong place or missing out a place as in 2)408 which is often erroneously answered as 24.

The principle is to share out the biggest place value equally, trade the left-overs to the next place value down and share those equally, trading down again so that the procedure can be seen as a repeating steps.

Some alternative algorithms

Ashlock *et al.* (1983) offered two interesting alternatives, both based on repeated subtraction. Both require careful presentation. Chinn has adapted one of these algorithms to utilise the facts dyslexics can calculate readily, that is multiples of 1, 2, 5, 10, 20, 50, 100, etc., followed by repeated subtraction. The algorithm also fits into the developmental aspects of the programme. An example is shown in Figure 10.5.

Set up a table of key multiples (Figure 10.5a). These follow patterns, particularly for place value. An appraisal of thee multiples shows that the answer lies between 200 and 500. So, this procedure also provides an estimate. In this case since 5024 is nearer to 3200 than to 8000, the estimated answer must be closer to 200 than 500. Thus, the procedure encourages the pre-evaluation of the answer, too.

The division is then tackled by subtraction of these multiples of 16 (Figure 10.5b). The method is related to our addition of partial products procedure advocated for multiplication, showing division to be the inverse operation and as repeated subtraction.

The authors' experience of this method is that our 11-year-old learners can do this procedure with concrete materials (which act as an introduction to the method), but usually find the digits too difficult. By age 13

5024 ÷ 16

(a)	(b)	
	5024	
16 × 1 = 16	– 3200	200
16 × 10 = 160	1824	
16 × 100 = 1600	–1600	100
16 × 2 = 32	224	
16 × 20 = 320	–160	10
16 × 200 = 3200	64	
16 × 5 = 80	–32	2
16 × 50 = 800	32	
16 × 500 = 8000	–32	2
		314

Figure 10.5 Repeated subtraction of core number partial products.

years the upper groups adapt to it readily. This method provides a good illustration of the 'readiness' of students (see 'Time') and the teacher should watch the class carefully to ensure understanding is achievable.

The student still has to be able to subtract. This remains a key prerequisite skill. There may well be more subtractions involved than in the traditional algorithm. It is the selection of the partial products that is made easier and less prone to error.

Estimating

The ability to multiply the divisor by powers of ten can be used to act as another useful and consistent estimating aid.

Example
1875 ÷ 15

The divisor is multiplied by increasing powers of ten and core numbers. The products are compared with 1875:

15 × 10 = 150
15 × 100 = 1500
15 × 200 = 3000

By comparing them to 1875, these products tell us that the answer will lie between 100 and 200, but closer to 100. Again, the link between division and multiplication is made and there is another chance for the child to reinforce his ability to multiply by powers of ten and the core numbers.

The ability to judge where the answer will lie is an extension of work with number lines, including empty number lines. It may well be beneficial to quickly revisit the skills associated with using these lines before attacking this new skill.

Division by Powers of Ten

This is the converse of setting up partial products for estimating. It requires an understanding of place value, so a review of this concept can be a precursor to the topic. The child needs to remember that the place a digit holds in a number controls its value by a power of ten (e.g. in 58725, the 7 is the third number in, it is in the hundreds column and its value is 7×100 or 700).

Division by powers of ten produces a pattern which can be illustrated by activities where the learner uses base ten blocks to divide numbers into ten parts and thus is drawn to the conclusion that, as with multiplying by powers of ten, the digits do not change, but their place value does change. At this early stage it is advisable to avoid answers that are decimals. A series of base ten block activities leads to series such as:

$$4000 \div 10 = 400$$
$$4000 \div 100 = 40$$
$$4000 \div 1000 = 4$$

$$4000 \div 10 = 400$$
$$4500 \div 10 = 450$$
$$4560 \div 10 = 456$$

It will almost certainly be necessary to use place value columns to emphasise the way the numbers move. A structured programme of manipulative aids (base ten blocks and/or money) and written digits should establish the idea of movement and values in the child's mind and perhaps lead him to some mnemonics once the understanding is established. If this is so, then the move on to quotients that are decimals does not present such a difficult hurdle (see Chapters 11 and 13).

Division by Multiples of Powers of Ten

Examples such as 4000 ÷ 20, 3000 ÷ 2000, 4500 ÷ 50 can be solved by teaching the child to take a two-stage approach: dividing first by 10 and then by 2; by 1000 then by 2; by 10 then by 5 respectively. This can be a multisensory activity with base ten blocks.

It also relates to the making of fractions such as ⅙ by a two-stage process: ÷ 2 and ÷ 3 and back to times table strategies where 4× can be accessed by two stages as 2× and 2×.

Conclusion

Further work may use calculators, providing that the student has an ability to estimate and check the answers. The work outlined in this chapter provides the student with the basic concept and the skills of division by subtraction of 'chunks' and the ability to estimate.

11

Fractions, Decimals and Percentages

An Introduction

Introduction

The mathematics dealt with in the previous chapters has been concerned with using numbers to describe things. This chapter is about describing parts of things with numbers. There are three ways mathematics goes about this task, fractions, decimals and percentages, with important differences and similarities between the three forms. Each form is dealt with in a chapter of its own, but this chapter describes the essential characteristics of each and how they interrelate.

'Fractions' is a topic which causes difficulty for learners across the world and considerable anxiety for adults. In developing the Test of Cognitive Style (1986), we had to take out an item on fractions because it caused so much anxiety in the trials. Subjects would just stop at that item and not attempt any more items, even though they were not about fractions.

However, we do use some fractions, mainly half and quarter, in everyday life; decimals, mainly for money, for example £4.63 or \$13.99; and percentages for example, as interest rates for money and for discounts, for example 'up to 70% off' at sale time in shops.

This chapter will explore the relationship between these formats in an attempt to strengthen an understanding of each format. As ever, we will work from the familiar to the new, so our key relationship will be:

$$\tfrac{1}{2} = 0.5 = 50\%$$

Mathematics for Dyslexics and Dyscalculics: A Teaching Handbook, Fourth Edition.
Steve Chinn and Richard E. Ashcroft.

All three are fractions, but that is only clear when the student knows the code. So, ½ means 'one divided by 2' or 'one of two (equal) parts'. 0.5 requires a knowledge of place value. The 5 has a place value of five tenths, that is 'five out of ten (equal) parts'. 50% requires an awareness that % means 'out of 100', so that 50% means '50 out of 100 (equal) parts'.

$$\frac{1}{2}=\frac{5}{10}=\frac{50}{100}$$

Fractions

Fractions are the most informative way of describing parts of things, but only if you understand the concept. For example, ⅝ tells you that the whole (of something) has been divided into 8 equal parts and that you have 5 of those parts. They are introduced in primary schools with an expectation from teachers and parents that children should be able to understand and work with fractions. Memories tend to be selective here since, as said above, we know that many adults have difficulties dealing with fractions. One of the main reasons for this is that fractions do not appear to do what numbers have previously done. They challenge the learner's sense of consistency.

Fractions use two numbers to describe one quantity, but in a way that is a challenge to previous experiences with numbers. Thus, a half is written as ½, a quarter as ¼ and three-quarters as ¾. The/in effect 'hides' the division sign. Similarly for a two-digit number such as 67, the place value of the 6 'hides' the × 10.

As an example of another apparent inconsistency, the addition of fractions challenges earlier experiences of addition (Skemp, 1971), as is illustrated below:

$$\frac{1}{5}+\frac{2}{5}=\frac{3}{5}$$

The addition sign operates on the 'top' numbers of the two fractions to be added, but not on the two 'bottom' numbers.

A further apparent inconsistency is with the series of fractions:

$$\frac{1}{2},\frac{1}{3},\frac{1}{4},\frac{1}{5},\frac{1}{6}$$

In this series, as the 'bottom' number gets bigger, the fraction value gets smaller.

For the first stage of teaching using concrete materials, we use paper folding to help to illustrate how fractions work. The folded-paper methods described in this book are structured to guide the learner towards understanding fractions and the way we use symbols to represent them. Drawings of folded fractions provide a means of recording and communicating the processes explained by the paper version. They form the intermediate step between folded-paper fractions and written fractions.

We recommend that square or close-to-square shapes be folded and drawn in all cases. We advocate folding in two dimensions, mainly to comply with our ongoing model of using area for (a times b) calculations.

Terminology

A fraction such as 4⁄5 will be referred to as 'part' of a whole thing. The fraction is made up of equal fifths, which will be referred to as 'segments', rather than as parts of the fraction. This avoids the duplicate use of the word 'parts', and children should be familiar with the notion of segments of an orange.

The terms 'denominator' and 'numerator' are confusing for many dyslexic and dyscalculic students. However, if students do wish to have a way of knowing which word means what, then it may help to see the structure of 'de*nom*inator' as having 'nom' or 'name' included (Brown *et al.*, 1989). Denominators such as fifth or tenth or quarter can be seen as the name of the fraction, that is, the name that tells you how many segments.

What is a fraction?

Part of a whole thing

Start by discussing with students what they know about fractions, in particular, the ones they are familiar with in everyday life, which are usually a half and a quarter. Include in the discussion observations and questions such as the following:

> Half of this square (or any object that can be divided exactly into halves and quarters) is bigger than a quarter, yet we write a half as ½ and a quarter as ¼.
>
> Are there other ways we can write the fraction ½? For example, half of a pound (£) could be written as 50⁄100 or half of an hour as 30⁄60.

What do we get when we add a half and a quarter?

What do we get when we halve a half?

How many halves are there in a whole, that is, in one?

How many quarters are there in a half?

How many quarters are there in a whole, that is, in one?

Can you have a bigger half (of a cake or pizza)?

Can you cut an exact half of a pizza or an apple?

These discussions set the basic rules for fractions and can be revisited for checking a procedure or an answer, possibly using the question, 'Is it bigger or smaller?'

- The piece of paper in Figure 11.1a has one-fifth shaded in. It is divided into five equal segments and one is shaded, so the fraction is written as ⅕, one segment out of five segments.
- The fraction in Figure 11.1b shows three-quarters. The written version is ¾, three segments out of four segments.

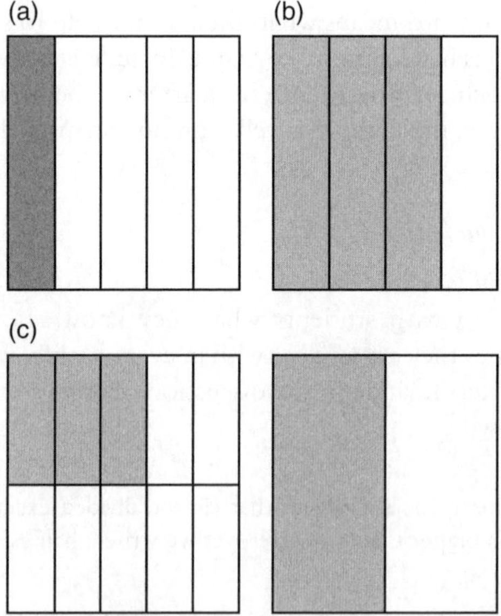

Figure 11.1 Folded paper/area models for fractions.

Children can be asked to give the written form for other fractions, such as those shown in Figure 11.1c.

Whole things divided into equal segments

- Figure 11.2a shows a whole square of paper is ten tenths (that is why they are called tenths). This is written as $^{10}/_{10} = 1$ whole square. The number at the bottom of the fraction indicates both the number of segments and the size of the segments.
- The square in Figure 11.2b has been left as a whole. It can be written as $^{1}/_{1} = 1$ and called one whole.

Children can be asked to write down the fraction for given examples, such as those shown in Figure 11.2c.

- The special name for the segments in Figure 11.3a, halves, should be highlighted.
- The segments in Figure 11.3b are usually known as quarters, but calling them fourths as well at the beginning tells children more about them. A third is also a linguistic exception.
- The version of fourths/quarters shown in Figure 11.3c should also be recognised by the children.

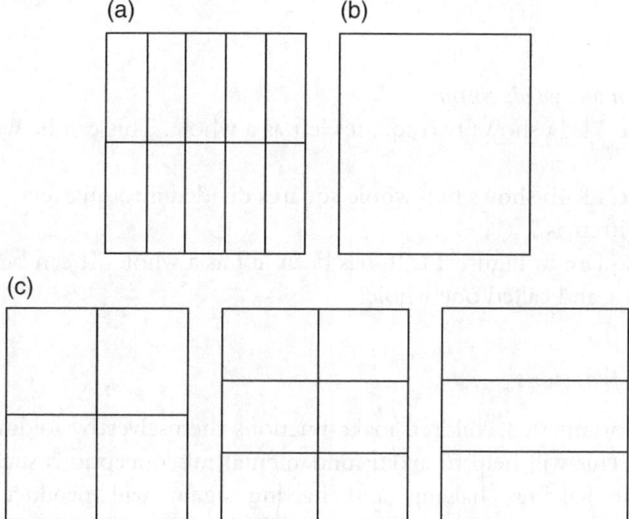

Figure 11.2 Folded paper/area models for fractions.

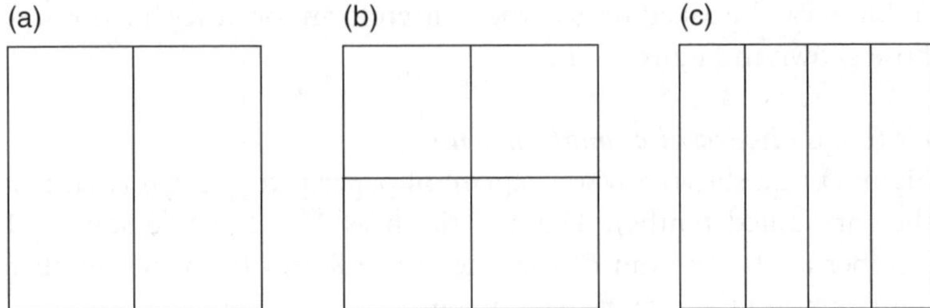

Figure 11.3 Folded paper/area models for fractions.

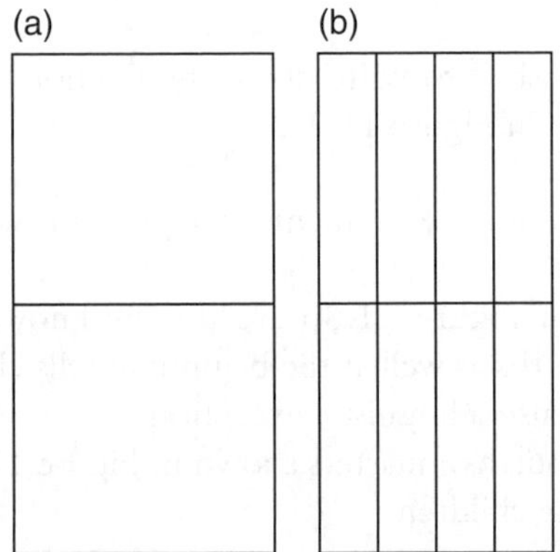

Figure 11.4 Equivalent fractions for 2 : $\frac{2}{1}$ and $\frac{8}{4}$.

More than one whole thing

- Figure 11.4a shows two squares left as a whole. This can be written as $\frac{2}{1}$.
- Figure 11.4b shows two whole squares divided into quarters. This can be written as $2 \times \frac{4}{4} = \frac{8}{4}$.
- The square in Figure 11.2b has been left as a whole. It can be written as $\frac{1}{1} = 1$ and called one whole.

Making fractions

It is important that children make fractions themselves by folding paper squares. This will help to avoid fundamental misconceptions such as the idea that halving, halving and halving again will produce sixths. Demonstrably, it produces eighths. It will also help in case of any future difficulties if children can recall how the fractions were made.

The 'halving' procedure, making halves

Figure 11.5a shows the folding procedure that produces halves. If the procedure is repeated, then it shows that halving and halving again makes quarters (Figure 11.5b). Repeated halving produces a family of fractions, whose subsequent members are eighths, sixteenths, and so on.

The 'thirding' procedure, making thirds

The procedure shown in Figure 11.6a produces thirds. Repeating the procedure will produce a family of fractions, the next member of which is ninths.

The 'fifthing' procedure, making fifths

The procedure shown in Figure 11.6b produces fifths and repeats to produce twenty-fifths, and so on.

Other procedures

A new procedure is required every time the number of segments is prime: $\frac{2}{2}$, $\frac{3}{3}$, $\frac{5}{5}$, $\frac{7}{7}$, and so on.

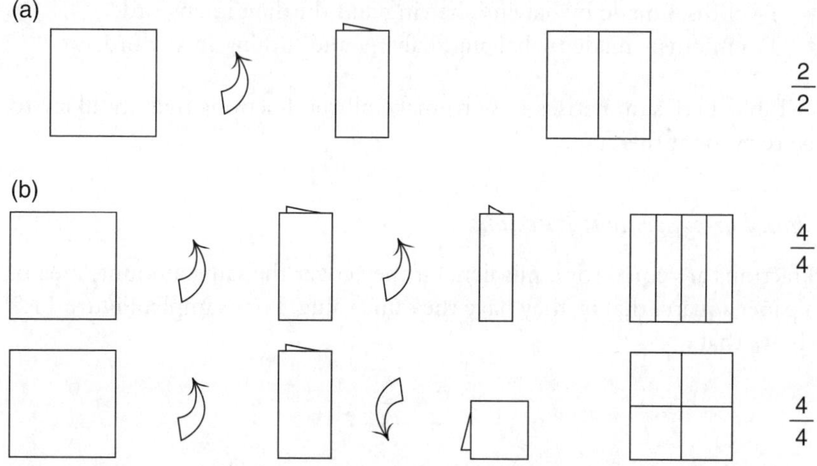

Figure 11.5 Folding paper to show halves and quarters.

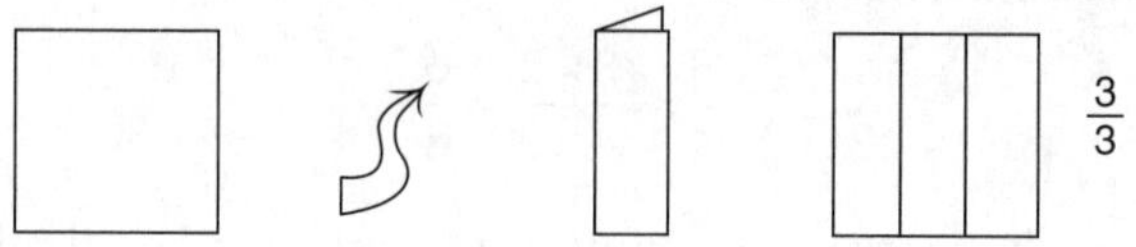

Figure 11.6a Folding paper to show thirds.

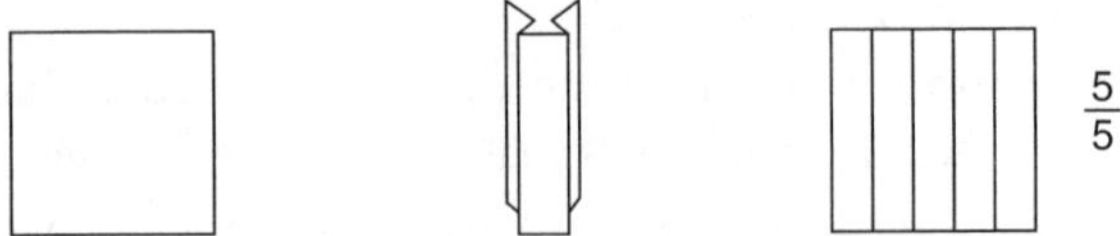

Figure 11.6b Folding paper to show fifths.

In practice, halves, thirds and fifths are sufficient, because sevenths, elevenths, and so on, are very rarely needed, and are undesirable in the early learning stages.

Some teachers refer to these folding procedures as ‘machines’, for example the ‘halving machine’.

Other fractions

Other important fractions can be made using a combination of folding procedures.

- Sixths – made by halving and thirding in either order.
- Tenths – made by halving and fifthing in either order.
- Twelfths – made by halving, halving and thirding in any order.
- Twentieths – made by halving, halving and fifthing in any order.

Table 11.1 summarises how to make all the fractions that are likely to be relevant at this stage

Equal or equivalent fractions

Fractions are equal (or equivalent) if they cover the same amount/area of a paper square, that is, they have the same value. For example, Figure 11.7 shows that:

$$\frac{3}{4}=\frac{6}{8}$$

The extra (horizontal) fold has produced twice as many segments, though the new segments are smaller (half the size). The written format that gives the same effect is:

$$\frac{3}{4}=\frac{3\times 2}{4\times 2}=\frac{6}{8}$$

The image shows that the number of segments has doubled, from four to eight, and the number of shaded parts has doubled, from three

Table 11.1 How to use folding to make the basic fractions.

Fraction	*half*	*half*	*half*	*half*	*third*	*third*	*fifth*
half	*						
third					*		
quarter	*	*					
fifth							*
sixth	*				*		
eighth	*	*	*				
ninth					*	*	
tenth	*						*
twelfth	*	*			*		
sixteenth	*	*	*	*			
twentieth	*	*					*
thirtieth	*				*		*

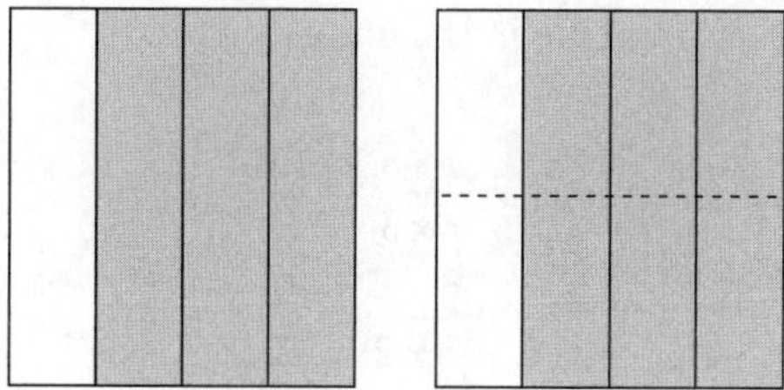

Figure 11.7 Equivalent fractions $\frac{3}{4}$ and $\frac{6}{8}$.

to six. The size or value of the fraction, as shown visually, has remained the same.

The top and bottom numbers of the fraction can be multiplied by the same number without changing the value of the fraction. The procedure is actually multiplying by one. Multiplying by one does not change the value of the fraction. All of the fractions below have a value of 1.

$$\frac{2}{2} = \frac{3}{3} = \frac{5}{5} = \frac{7}{7} = \frac{11}{11} = 1$$

There are many different types of exercise for establishing this concept. Children can be asked the following questions;

- Give the written form for the two equal/equivalent fractions shown in Figure 11.8a.
- Draw in the extra fold lines in Figure 11.8b to show that $\frac{1}{2} = \frac{3}{6}$.

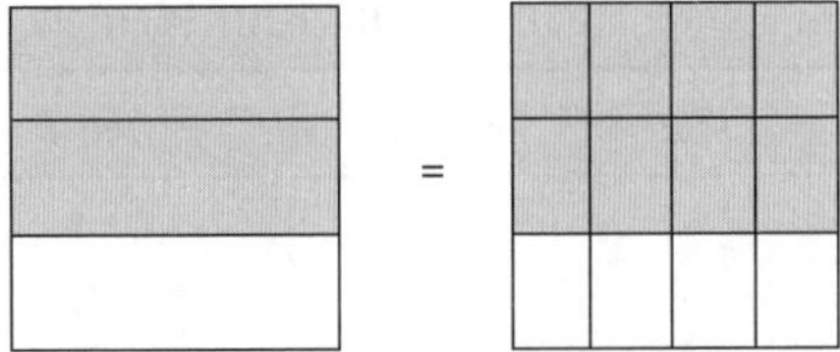

Figure 11.8a Equivalent fractions $\frac{2}{3}$ and $\frac{8}{12}$.

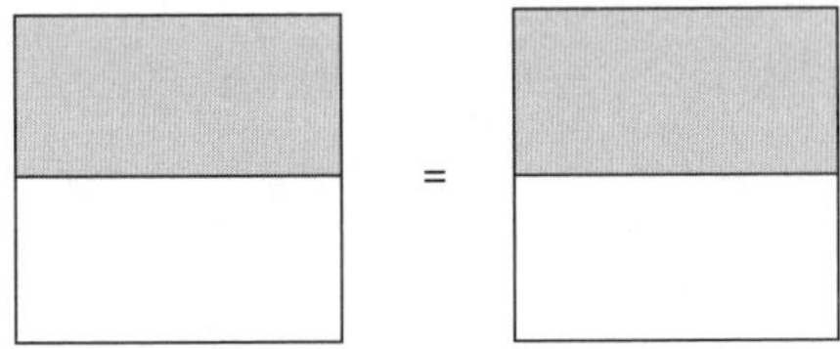

Figure 11.8b Fold to show that $\frac{1}{2} = \frac{3}{6}$.

- Write the correct numbers in the empty boxes:

$$\frac{1}{3} = \frac{1 \times 5}{3 \times 5} = \frac{\square}{\square}$$

$$\frac{3}{5} = \frac{3 \times \square}{5 \times 2} = \frac{6}{\square}$$

$$\frac{3}{8} = \frac{3 \times \square}{8 \times \square} = \frac{9}{\square}$$

$$\frac{3}{4} = \frac{3 \times \square}{4 \times \square} = \frac{\square}{16}$$

Simplifying fractions

Example

In the example shown in Figure 11.9, it is possible to combine the tenths into groups of two, as shown, reducing the number of segments to five. Consequently, the four shaded parts (tenths) are reduced to two (fifths). The written format that gives this effect is:

$$\frac{4}{10} = \frac{4 \div 2}{10 \div 2} = \frac{2}{5}$$

If the top and the bottom of a fraction are divided by the same number it does not change the value of the fraction. This is dividing by one and

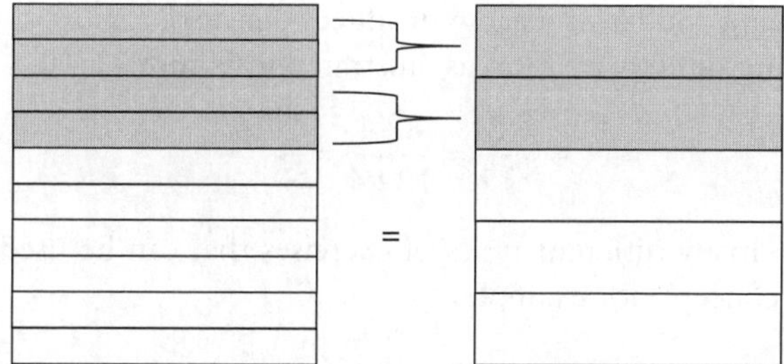

Figure 11.9 Simplifying fractions: $\frac{4}{10} = \frac{2}{5}$.

that operation does not change the value of the fraction, even though it is now composed of different numbers.

A practical problem, here, is to decide what number to use for dividing the top and the bottom, that is, into what size groups can the segments be divided. Prime factors can be used, or trial and error (based on a knowledge of the multiplication/division facts), but the method consistent with the philosophy of this book is to try the numbers used in forming the original segments by folding.

In the example above, tenths would have been formed by folding into halves and fifths. Therefore, dividing into groups of two or five should be tried. Of these, only the groups of two work for the shaded segments, to give the fraction in its 'lowest terms'.

Example

Simplify $\frac{8}{12}$. For this example, if the pupil recognizes that twelfths would be formed by folding into halves, halves and thirds, then dividing by 2, 2 and 3 should be attempted:

$$\frac{8}{12} = \frac{8 \div 2}{12 \div 2} = \frac{4}{6}$$

$$= \frac{4 \div 2}{6 \div 2} = \frac{2}{3}$$

Alternatively, since 8 and 12 are even numbers then dividing by two is possible. This gives $\frac{4}{6}$ where again the numbers are even, so division by two is again possible.

Once $\frac{2}{3}$ has been reached, further dividing of top and bottom numbers by 3 or 2 is not possible, so the fraction is as simple as it can be made.

Since halving and halving again produces quarters, a short cut would be to try dividing directly by four, as illustrated in Figure 11.10.

$$\frac{8}{12} = \frac{8 \div 4}{12 \div 4} = \frac{2}{3}$$

There are many different types of exercises that can be used for establishing this concept, for example:

- What are the folding steps that would make the fraction in Figure 11.11?
- Write the correct numbers in the empty boxes:

$$\frac{5}{10} = \frac{5 \div 5}{10 \div 5} = \frac{\square}{\square}$$

$$\frac{4}{12} = \frac{4 \div 4}{12 \div \square} = \frac{1}{\square}$$

$$\frac{2}{6} = \frac{2 \div \square}{6 \div \square} = \frac{1}{\square}$$

$$\frac{8}{20} = \frac{8 \div \square}{20 \div \square} = \frac{4}{\square} = \frac{4 \div \square}{\square \div \square} = \frac{\square}{5}$$

$$\frac{6}{10} = \frac{6 \div \square}{10 \div \square} = \frac{\square}{\square}$$

Another strategy is to use the times tables square. In Figure 11.12 the columns for four and seven have been italicised. Horizontal pairs show equivalent fractions:

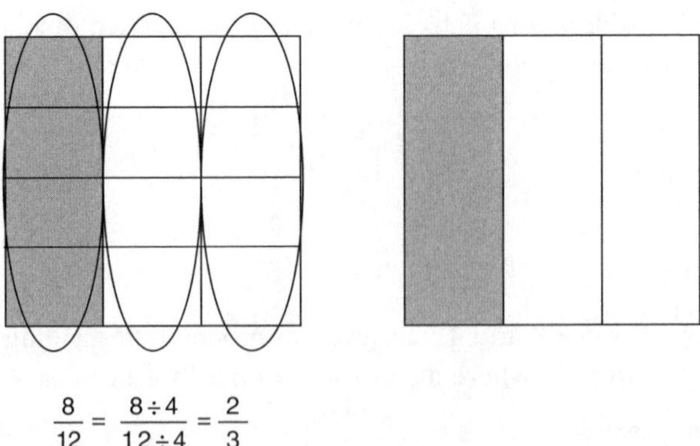

Figure 11.10 Writing 8⁄12 in its simplest form.

Figure 11.11 What folding is needed to make this fraction pattern?

x	0	1	2	3	4	5	6	7	8	9	10
0	0	0	0	0	***0***	0	0	***0***	0	0	0
1	0	1	2	3	***4***	5	6	***7***	8	9	10
2	0	2	4	6	***8***	10	12	***14***	16	18	20
3	0	3	6	9	***12***	15	18	***21***	24	27	30
4	0	4	8	12	***16***	20	24	***28***	32	36	40
5	0	5	10	15	***20***	25	30	***35***	40	45	50
6	0	6	12	18	***24***	30	36	***42***	48	54	60
7	0	7	14	21	***28***	35	42	***49***	56	63	70
8	0	8	16	24	***32***	40	48	***56***	64	72	80
9	0	9	18	27	***36***	45	54	***63***	72	81	90
10	0	10	20	30	***40***	50	60	***70***	80	90	100

Figure 11.12 The times tables square and equivalent fractions.

$$\frac{4}{7} \quad \frac{8}{14} \quad \frac{12}{21} \quad \frac{16}{28} \quad \frac{20}{35} \quad \frac{24}{42} \quad \frac{28}{49} \quad \frac{32}{56} \quad \frac{36}{63} \quad \frac{40}{70}$$

Decimals

Decimals are also used to represent parts of a whole thing.

Where a number is composed of whole and parts, the decimal part is separated by a decimal point, for example 37.651.

tens	ones	. tenths	hundredths	thousandths
10	1	. 1/10	1/100	1/1000
3	7	. 6	5	1

Basically decimals are just specific fractions – the first column after the decimal point representing *tenths*, the second representing *hundredths*, the third representing *thousandths* and so on. However, because of this, each column (tracking right to left) is ten times the place value of the previous column, making decimals a continuation of the place value system. This property is apparent, for example, when a number is carried in an addition, or when a decimal is multiplied by ten.

First decimal place as tenths

This can be demonstrated well with a measuring exercise. Consider the length AB marked against a scale (Figure 11.13).

- Each large unit on the number line is divided into ten smaller units.
- Each smaller unit will be $\frac{1}{10}$ of a large unit.
- The length AB is 53 small units and $5\frac{3}{10}$ large units.
- If AB is written as 5.3 large units, then .3 means $\frac{3}{10}$ and the first number after the decimal point represents tenths.
- 5.3 is five units and three tenths of a unit.

Second decimal place as hundredths

This can be demonstrated with examples using money/coins.

$$100\text{p} = £1$$

$$10\text{p} = £\frac{1}{10}$$

$$1\text{p} = £\frac{1}{100}$$

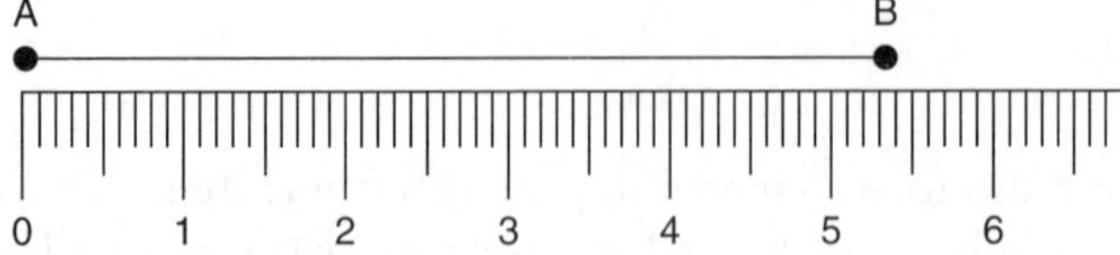

Figure 11.13 Using a rule to show 5.3.

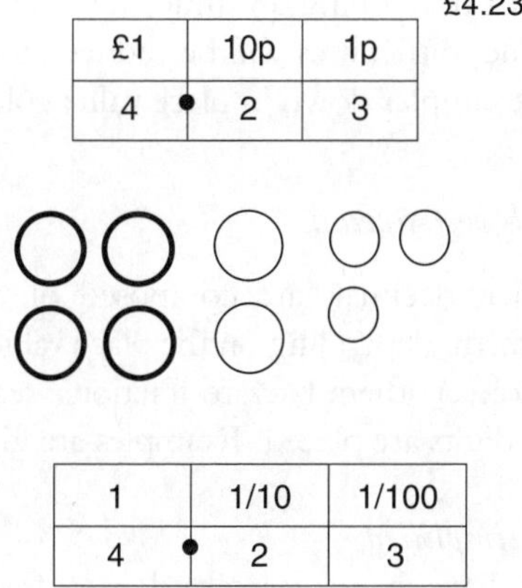

Figure 11.14 Ways to visualise 4.23.

Almost all children will accept and understand the above equivalents for money units. The amount of money illustrated in Figure 11.14 is written in pence at the top and pounds at the bottom.

When the amount of money is in pounds and pence, the decimal point takes up the position we see in prices. Figure 11.14 shows that the first column after the decimal point is for tenths and shows that the second column is for hundredths.

Further decimal places

Once the fraction equivalents are established for the first and second decimal places, it is relatively easy for children to accept the next place as thousandths, and so on. A practical illustration could use a metre rule with millimeter markings. A reminder that the familiar whole-number column headings are: thousands, hundreds, tens, ones is usually helpful. It is worth explaining that the decimal point is not the centre of symmetry in:

Thousands hundreds tens ones. tenths hundredths thousandths

The centre of symmetry is 'ones'.

If the numbers are shown as powers of ten, this puts 1 as 10^0 in the centre of the series.

10^3	10^2	10^1	10^0	10^{-1}	10^{-2}	10^{-3}
1000	100	10	1	1/10	1/100	1/1000

In the early stages of developing an understanding of decimal numbers and decimal place value, difficulties will be reduced if children can be persuaded to write their examples down in place value columns with headings.

Converting decimals to fractions

As was outlined earlier, decimals are composed of the specific fractions $\frac{1}{10}$, $\frac{1}{100}$, $\frac{1}{1000}$, and so forth, depending on the place value column(s) in which they are written. To convert them back to fractions, read off which of these columns in which the digits are placed. Examples are given in Figure 11.15.

Examples that can be simplified

After some decimals have been converted into fractions, they can be simplified.

$\frac{1}{10}$	$\frac{1}{100}$	$\frac{1}{1000}$	
• 8			$= \frac{8}{10} = \frac{8 \div 2}{10 \div 2} = \frac{4}{5}$
• 4	5		$= \frac{45}{100} = \frac{45 \div 5}{100 \div 5} = \frac{9}{20}$
• 0	0	4	$= \frac{4}{1000} = \frac{4 \div 4}{1000 \div 4} = \frac{1}{250}$

1/10	1/100	1/1000	
• 3			3/10
• 4	7		47/100
• 0	9		9/100
• 7	8	9	789/1000
• 0	2	3	23/1000

Figure 11.15 Linking decimal numbers to tenths, hundredths and thousandths.

Use of the number 25

In many cases where decimals have been converted into fractions and are to be simplified, the ability to divide (top and bottom) by 25 is a useful short cut. There are two in 50, three in 75, four in every 100 and so 40 in every 1000. For example:

$$.375 = \frac{375}{1000} = \frac{375 \div 25}{1000 \div 25} = \frac{15}{40} = \frac{15 \div 5}{40 \div 5} = \frac{3}{8}$$

Special decimals

A few decimals can be converted and simplified to very important fractions. It is useful if these can be memorised:

$$.1 = \frac{1}{10} \quad .01 = \frac{1}{100} \quad .001 = \frac{1}{1000}$$

$$.5 = \frac{1}{2} \quad .25\ \frac{1}{4} \quad .75 = \frac{3}{4} \quad .2 = \frac{1}{5}$$

The significance of zeros

Zeros are used to hold digits in their place value position in a number. With decimals, zeros are sometimes used in situations where they have no impact on the value of the number, for example 0.50. Neither zero in 0.50 has an impact on the place value of the five. In the number 0.05, the second zero (after the decimal point) has 'pushed' the five into a hundredths place value position. It does have an effect on the value of the five.

With whole numbers the equivalent situation would be, for example, 8, 08 and 80. We rarely write 08. The zero has no impact on the place value of the 8, but with 80, it moves the 8 from the ones place to the tens place.

When a decimal, such as .92 has no whole-number part, it is usually written in the form 0.92, with an optional zero at the front, as a matter of style and to draw attention to the decimal point. As long as children are having difficulty with decimals, simplicity is more important than style, so it could be argued that this should be avoided. In this chapter, such zeros have been omitted for this reason.

In general, just as for whole numbers, the significant zeros are located between other digits, or between a digit and the decimal point. The unnecessary or optional zeros are to be found beyond those numbers furthest from the decimal point.

The following examples demonstrate the role of zero in decimals:

Tenths	hundredths	thousandths	fraction
.7			7/10
.0	7		7/100
.1	0	8	108/1000
.0	2	9	29/1000

Comparing decimals

'Which decimal is bigger, .87 or .135?' In answer to this question, many children will give the answer .135, because they see 135 as being bigger than 87. Of course, they are not comparing like with like, because the 135 are thousandths whereas the 87 are hundredths. The decimal numbers have challenged their sense of consistency. For whole numbers a three-digit number is bigger, has greater value than a two-digit number. By way of explanation, write the decimals in their place value columns and give them the same number of digits by using zeros that have no influence on value:

1/10	1/100	1/1000
• 8	7	0
• 1	3	5

This process has the same effect as making segment sizes the same for fractions. Now 870 is clearly bigger than 135.

Some children have a similar problem understanding why .25 is halfway between .2 and .3, both of which may seem smaller. The column headings and optional zeros can help again:

1/10	1/100
• 2	0
• 2	5
• 3	0

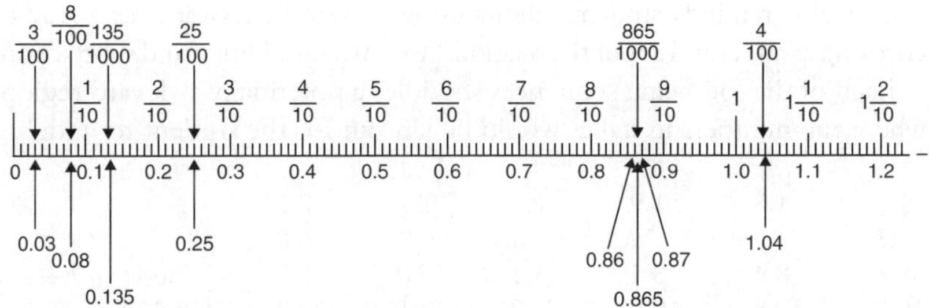

Figure 11.16 A number line for decimals.

This shows that 25 hundredths is halfway between 20 hundredths and 30 hundredths.

This can also be modelled with Dienes blocks. The thousand cube becomes one, the flat becomes a tenth, the long becomes a hundredth and the small cube becomes a thousandth. If, despite explanations, this new interpretation confuses the learner then it will not help.

Another approach to these and other similar problems is to explain with a decimal number line, such as is shown in Figure 11.16. This number line shows that .87 is bigger than .135. The equivalent fractions above the line provide further justification. It also shows that .25 lies halfway between .2 and .3, another such situation being observable at .865, which is halfway between .86 and .87.

Decimal number sequences

Decimal number sequences can be regarded as extracts from a number line, such as in Figure 11.16. If the examples are selected carefully, they can provide a very convincing alternative way of looking at problem areas that may not have been fully understood. One such problem area is tackled below. Consider the following sequence:

.95 .96 .97 .98 .99

Those children who have not properly taken on board the message that decimals follow place value rules, just as whole numbers do, may make the mistake of assuming that the next decimal in the sequence is .100. They have not understood that the 1 digit from 100 has to move up in place value to produce 1.00.

Another explanation can be provided by approaching the sequence from the other direction, working downwards, for example:

1.04 1.03 1.02 1.01 1.00 .99 .98

This also reminds students about using working backwards as a way of checking answers and about the relationship between addition and subtraction.

Each of the following sequences straddles a potentially awkward region, where the numbers in italics would be left out for the student to find:

1.7	1.8	1.9	*2.0*	*2.1*	2.2	2.3	
7.3	7.2	*7.1*	*7.0*	6.9	6.8		
8.8	8.6	8.4	8.4	*8.0*	7.8	7.6	7.4
19.7	19.8	19.9	*20.0*	20.1	20.2	20.3	
20.03	20.02	*20.0*	*20.00*	19.99	19.98	19.97	

Converting fractions to decimals

Some fractions are very simple to convert into decimals, because they are already tenths, hundredths or thousandths. They slot into the decimal columns immediately, like the examples below:

Tenths	hundredths	thousandths	fraction
.3			3/10
.0	9		9/100
.1	0	7	107/1000
.0	2	9	29/1000

There are other fractions that can easily be made into tenths, hundredths or thousandths, as shown with the following examples:

	1/10	1/100	1/1000
$\frac{2}{5} = \frac{2 \times 2}{5 \times 2} = \frac{4}{10} =$ •	4		
$\frac{3}{4} = \frac{3 \times 25}{4 \times 25} = \frac{75}{100} =$ •	7	5	
$\frac{1}{20} = \frac{1 \times 5}{20 \times 5} = \frac{5}{100} =$ •	0	5	
$\frac{7}{8} = \frac{7 \times 125}{8 \times 125} = \frac{875}{1000} =$ •	8	7	5

The final example, $\frac{7}{8}$ in the table above, depends, for its conversion, on the knowledge that $8 \times 125 = 1000$. Lack of this knowledge would push this conversion into the most difficult category, along with fractions such as $\frac{5}{9}$. For such an example, it is necessary to regard $\frac{5}{9}$ as $5 \div 9$, and to perform a decimal division, which is beyond the scope of this chapter, so such conversions are covered in Chapter 13.

Percentages

Percentages are another way of describing parts of whole things. 'Percent' means 'out of a hundred'. For example, 1 percent means 1 out of a 100, which can also be written as $\frac{1}{100}$. In essence, percentages are hundredths. The sign for percent, %, seems to be constructed from a 1, a 0 and another 0, so it behaves as a perpetual and valuable reminder of the importance of 100. Clearly, since percentages are hundredths, it is a simple matter to convert between percentages and fractions. Moreover, since hundredths constitute one of the decimal column headings, it is also easy to convert between percentages and decimals.

Percentages and whole things

Writing down whole things in terms of percentages is slightly more difficult with fractions or decimals, where whole numbers are just written separately, in front. However, there is subsequently much less need to manipulate the percentages, so the difficulty is not carried further. A whole thing is $\frac{100}{100}$, which is 100%. Every whole thing is 100%, and so, for example, a whole number such as 5 is 500%.

An inclusive model for percentages, fractions and decimals

Figure 11.17 shows a whole square divided into 100 equal segments. Each segment is $\frac{1}{100}$, or 1%, or .01 (1 in the hundredths place value column). These can be represented physically by the ones bricks in Dienes apparatus. Each column of ten ones is $\frac{1}{10}$, or 10%, or .1 (1 in the tenths place value column). These can be represented by 'longs'. The whole square is 100%, or 1 whole number, and could be represented by a 'flat'.

Percentages are a rather more palatable or accessible way of expressing parts of whole things for most people, perhaps because it seems easier for most people to visualise, for example, 39% as 39 out of their visual image of 100, rather than the symbols $\frac{39}{100}$ or .39.

Also, the values of percentages are much easier to compare.

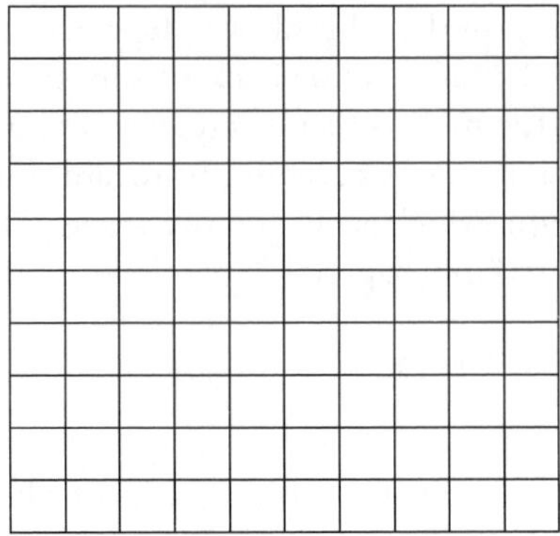

Figure 11.17 A hundred square.

Comparing percentages

Unlike fractions, which can have segments of any size, or decimals, which can be tenths, hundredths, thousandths, and so on, percentages all have the same segment size – they are all hundredths. Their numerical values can therefore be compared in a straightforward way – the bigger the number, the bigger the percentage (and the bigger the part that it represents).

Examples

- 38% is bigger than 26% (by 12%) (Figure 11.18).
- 19% is smaller than 22% (by 3%).
- 31.5% is bigger than 31%.
- 135% is bigger than 125%.

Converting percentages to fractions

If percentages are understood to be hundredths, converting them to fractions is simply a matter of writing them as a fraction, with 100 as the bottom number (denominator).

Examples

$$27\% = \frac{27}{100}\text{(Figure 11.19)}.$$

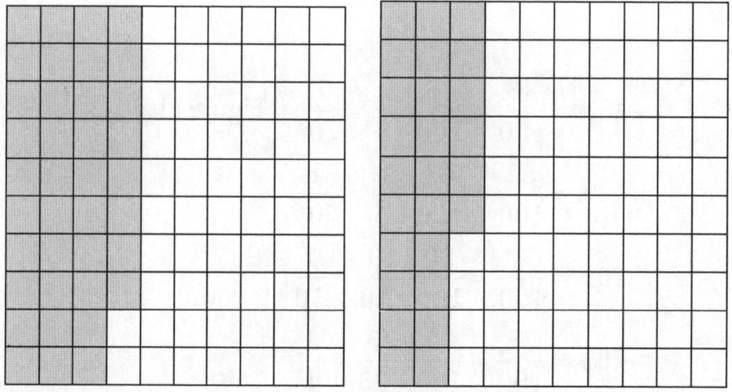

Figure 11.18 A hundred squares used to compare 28% and 26%.

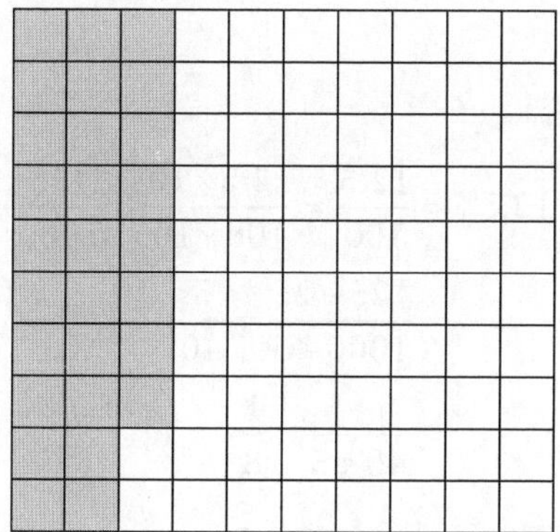

Figure 11.19 27% as $^{27}/_{100}$.

$$127\% = 1\frac{27}{100}$$

$$91\% = \frac{91}{100}$$

$$9\% = \frac{9}{100}$$

Sometimes the fraction obtained can be simplified.

Examples

$$45\% = \frac{45}{100} = \frac{45 \div 5}{100 \div 5} = \frac{9}{20} \quad \text{(Figure 11.20)}$$

$$62\% = \frac{62}{100} = \frac{62 \div 2}{100 \div 2} = \frac{31}{50}$$

$$70\% = \frac{70}{100} = \frac{70 \div 10}{100 \div 10} = \frac{7}{10}$$

$$75\% = \frac{75}{100} = \frac{75 \div 25}{100 \div 25} = \frac{3}{4}$$

$$5\% = \frac{5}{100} = \frac{5 \div 5}{100 \div 5} = \frac{1}{20}$$

Some percentages produce fractions that need many steps to simplify.

Example

$$12.5\% = \frac{12.5}{100} = \frac{12.5 \times 10}{100 \times 10} = \frac{125}{1000}$$

$$= \frac{125 \div 25}{1000 \div 5} = \frac{5}{40}$$

$$= \frac{5 \div 5}{40 \div 5} = \frac{1}{8}$$

(See Chapter 13 for multiplying decimals by 10.)

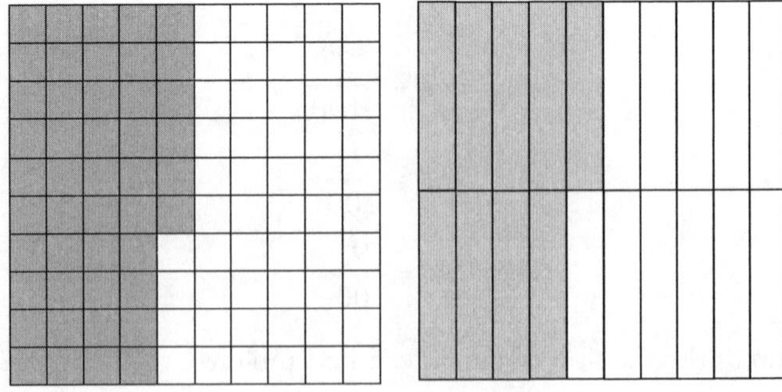

Figure 11.20 45% as $\frac{9}{20}$.

Example

$$33\tfrac{1}{3}\% = \frac{33\frac{1}{3}}{100} = \frac{33\frac{1}{3}\times 3}{100\times 3} = \frac{\frac{100}{3}\times 3}{300}$$

$$= \frac{100}{300} = \frac{100\div 100}{300\div 100}$$

$$= \frac{1}{3}$$

(See Chapter 12 for multiplication of fractions.)

Converting fractions to percentages

When fractions are hundredths, then a % can replace the denominator.

Examples

$$\frac{83}{100} = 83\%$$

$$2\frac{83}{100} = 283\%$$

$$\frac{7}{100} = 7\%$$

Some fractions have to be first changed into hundredths. (A similar step was necessary in converting fractions to decimals.)

Examples

$$\frac{1}{2} = \frac{1\times 50}{2\times 50} = \frac{50}{100} = 50\% \quad \text{(Figure11.21)}$$

$$\frac{2}{5} = \frac{2\times 20}{5\times 20} = \frac{40}{100} = 40\%$$

$$\frac{12}{25} = \frac{12\times 4}{25\times 4} = \frac{48}{100} = 48\%$$

$$\frac{37}{50} = \frac{37\times 2}{50\times 2} = \frac{74}{100} = 74\%$$

At times, children will be unable to change the fraction into hundredths, because they do not know the multiplier that will make the denominator 100. Finding this multiplier becomes the first step. Consider $^{17}/_{20}$:

$$\frac{17}{20} = \frac{17\times ?}{20\times ?} = \frac{?}{100}$$

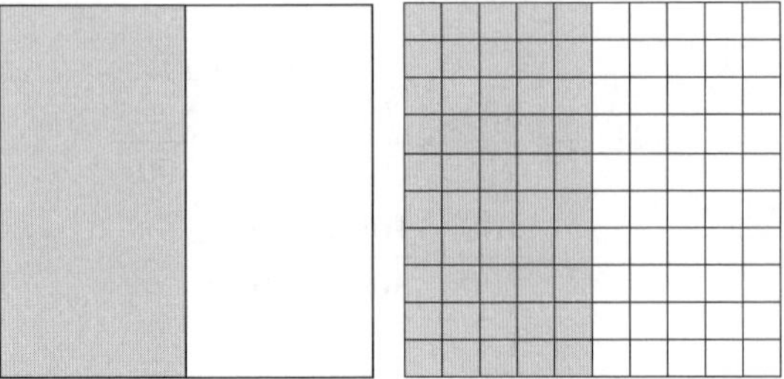

Figure 11.21 Equivalent fractions and percentages $\frac{1}{2} = \frac{50}{100} = 50\%$.

The question is 'How many 20s are there in 100?' This may help the student to realise that the equation needed is $100 \div 20 = 5$. It is now possible to multiply the top and the bottom numbers by 5 and create hundredths:

$$\frac{17}{20} = \frac{17 \times 5}{20 \times 5} = \frac{85}{100} = 85\%$$

Sometimes the numbers that make up the fraction create a division that is sufficiently complex to make the use of a calculator a pragmatic option. This should be backed up by an estimate. For example, $\frac{58}{95}$ can be rounded to 6/100 and thus give an estimate of 0.6.

Converting percentages to decimals

Percentages are hundredths, and the second column of decimals is for hundredths. Therefore, it is a relatively simple task to write a whole-number percentage in the decimal columns of a place value card.

Examples

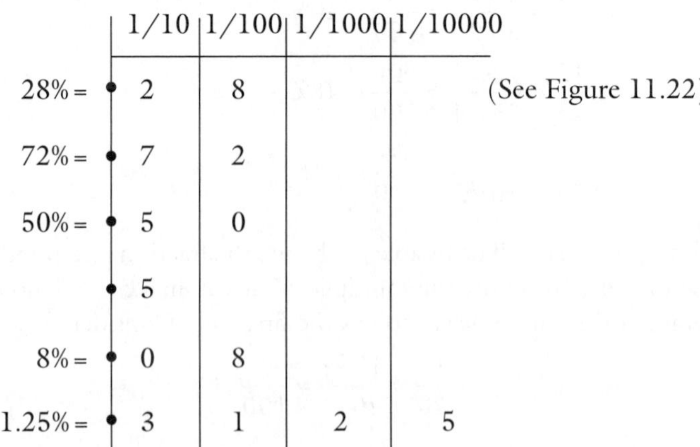

	1/10	1/100	1/1000	1/10000	
28% = •	2	8			(See Figure 11.22)
72% = •	7	2			
50% = •	5	0			
•	5				
8% = •	0	8			
31.25% = •	3	1	2	5	

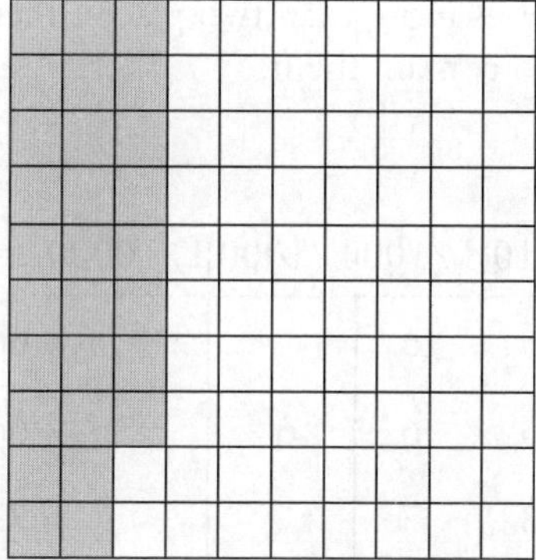

Figure 11.22 28% and 0.28.

The final example above shows a harder decimal percentage. The digits go beyond the hundredths column because of the .25%. This needs extra decimal places, as far as ten thousandths, because:

$$.25\% = \frac{0.25}{100} = \frac{0.25 \times 100}{100 \times 100} = \frac{25}{10000}$$

Converting decimals to percentages

The second place value column for decimals is for hundredths. Therefore, any decimal that can be 'lifted' entirely out of the first two columns for decimals can be written immediately as a percentage.

Examples
Converting decimals to percentages

The second column of decimals is for hundredths. Therefore, any decimal that can be 'lifted' entirely out of the first two columns of decimals can be written immediately as a percentage.

Examples

1/10	1/100
• 2	8 = 28%
• 7	2 = 72%
• 5	0 = 50%
• 0	5 = 5%
• 1	0 = 10%

If the decimal contains more than two places, then the percentage will have to be extended to contain them.

Example

	1/10	1/100	1/1000	1/10000	
•	6	6			= 66%
•	6	6	6	7	= 66.67%
•	3	7			= 37%
•	3	7	5		= 37.5%
4 •	1	8			= 418%
•	1	8			= 18%

Special percentages

The following list shows the equivalent percentages, fractions and decimals for the most important parts of a whole thing:

$$\frac{1}{2} = 50\% = .5$$

$$\frac{1}{4} = 25\% = .25$$

$$\frac{3}{4} = 75\% = .75$$

$$\frac{1}{10} = 10\% = .1$$

$$\frac{1}{5} = 20\% = .2$$

$$\frac{1}{3} = 33\tfrac{1}{3}\%$$

$$= 33.3\% = .333$$

$$\frac{2}{3} = 66\tfrac{2}{3}\%$$

$$= 66.7\% = .667$$

$$\frac{1}{100} = 1\% = .01$$

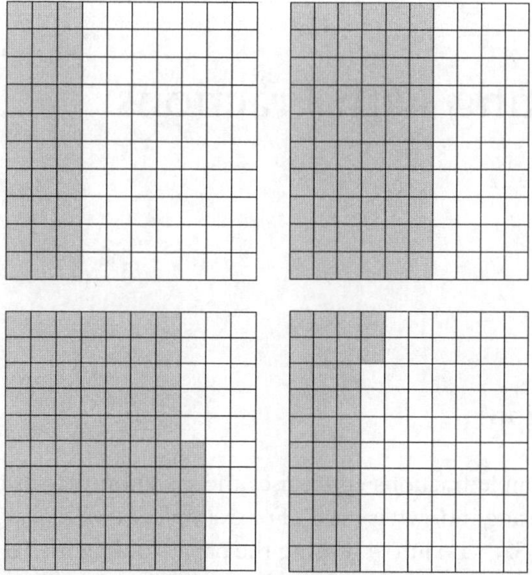

Figure 11.23 Write each of these as percentages, decimals and fractions.

Overview

In order to practise the various conversion processes detailed in this chapter, the learner should convert the shaded parts on diagrams, such as those shown in Figure 11.23, to symbol format. The task should be to write the numbers as percentages, decimals and fractions (simplified where possible).

12

Operating with Fractions

Introduction

Work with simple fractions epitomises the assertion that, 'Mathematics is easy, only writing it down is hard'. For example, as we shall show, it is very easy to make $3\frac{1}{4} + 1\frac{1}{2}$ into $4\frac{3}{4}$ using the paper-folding model advocated in this book for introducing fractions, but the written version, which carries with it a complex and thus difficult to explain algorithm, seems very difficult indeed by comparison. The work in this chapter is designed to link the 'doing' with the 'writing down' with the aim of making them equally easy. The paper-folding model also provides a visual and kinaesthetic image to help the student recall and use the algorithm correctly.

As in Chapter 11, the ideas illustrated and validated by using paper folding show the student what the written version should be, so that the written version of the problem relates directly to the concrete and visual demonstrations. Thus, whenever the written problem proves to be difficult there will be a parallel paper-folding procedure or visual image to support understanding and thus memory.

Here, as elsewhere in this book, the structure brought out by these models and procedures is intended to contribute towards the pupil's overall understanding of the algorithms and concepts. The use of folded-paper fractions is usually a clear enough method for understanding the examples and thus only a minimum amount of explanatory text is needed. As in other chapters, you must use your experience with your students to blend the work to suit each individual. We suggest that the basic structure is, however, best left intact.

Mathematics for Dyslexics and Dyscalculics: A Teaching Handbook, Fourth Edition.
Steve Chinn and Richard E. Ashcroft.

Making Segment Sizes the Same

It will become apparent during the course of this chapter that if two or more fractions are to be compared, added, or subtracted, their segments must be the same size. In mathematical terminology, this is expressed as, 'the denominators must be the same'. Generally, their segments will not be the same size, but there is a method of making them so, which is fully consistent with the philosophy of this book. It depends on the argument that, for segments to be made the same size, the same paper-folding steps must be used for all the fractions involved. Each fraction must be given the folds it does not already share with the others. The folding can be real, drawn, imagined, or written, but the objective will be a situation where for all fractions the same folding steps have been used. The experience gained earlier, in actually making fractions, will be valuable here.

Examples

Consider the fractions ⅞ and ¾ (Figure 12.1a).

	The folding to make the fraction	*Extra folding to create the same denominator (name)*
⅞	halved then halved then halved	none
¾	halved then halved	halved

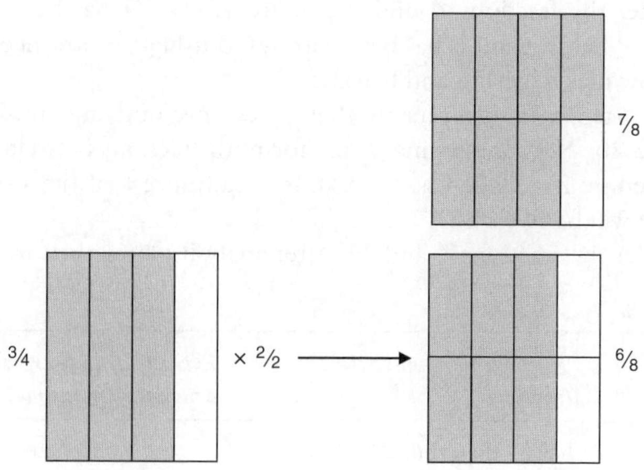

Figure 12.1a ¾ is changed to 6/8, which can now be added to ⅞.

$$\tfrac{7}{8} \qquad = \qquad \tfrac{7}{8}$$

$$\tfrac{3}{4} = \frac{3 \times 2}{4 \times 2} = \tfrac{6}{8}$$

Figure 12.1b Renaming one fraction to create the same denominator.

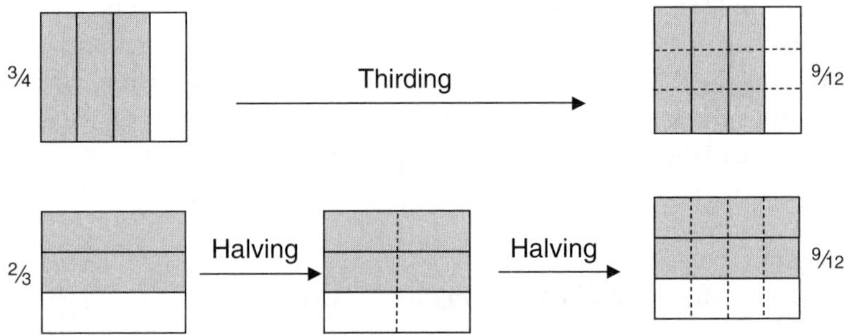

Figure 12.2a Adding fractions with different denominators: $\tfrac{3}{4} + \tfrac{2}{3}$.

The written/symbols version is shown in Figure 12.1b. The folded-paper diagram and the written version are now showing eighths as the segment size for both fractions.

Consider the fractions $\tfrac{3}{4}$ and $\tfrac{2}{3}$ (Figure 12.2a). $\tfrac{3}{4}$ has been through halving and halving and $\tfrac{2}{3}$ has been through thirding. $\tfrac{3}{4}$ now needs thirding; $\tfrac{2}{3}$ now needs halving and halving.

The written/symbols version that gives this outcome is shown in Figure 12.2b. Now the segment size for both fractions is twelfths. With this procedure it is unnecessary to know in advance that the shared segment size will be twelfths.

Consider the fractions $\tfrac{5}{6}$ and $\tfrac{9}{10}$. After analysing how they are formed:

	The folding to make the fraction	*Extra folding to create the same denominator (name)*
$\tfrac{5}{6}$	halved then thirded	fifthed
$\tfrac{9}{10}$	halved then fifthed	thirded

$$\frac{3}{4} = \frac{3 \times 3}{4 \times 3} = \frac{9}{12}$$

$$\frac{2}{3} = \frac{2 \times 2}{3 \times 2} = \frac{4}{6} = \frac{4 \times 2}{6 \times 2} = \frac{8}{12}$$

Figure 12.2b Renaming both fractions to create the same denominator.

it is evident that $\frac{5}{6}$ now needs fifthing and $\frac{9}{10}$ needs thirding. Now by using the written form only, we have:

$$\frac{5}{6} = \frac{5 \times 5}{6 \times 5} = \frac{25}{30}$$

$$\frac{9}{10} = \frac{9 \times 3}{10 \times 3} = \frac{27}{30}$$

In later examples, where this calculation is done, the region of working will be highlighted within a dotted rectangle as it has been in these examples. Of course, this is not necessary beyond this book.

Comparing Fractions

Examples

Which fraction is bigger: $\frac{3}{5}$ or $\frac{2}{3}$?

Some students would say $\frac{3}{5}$, because there are more segments, whereas others would say $\frac{2}{3}$ because the segments are bigger. Even a picture of the folded-paper version leaves some doubt (Figure 12.3a).

Fractions can be compared best when their segments are the same size. This can be achieved by the procedure detailed in the previous section, which involves further folding: real, drawn, imagined or written. Again, the objective is a situation where both fractions have been through the same folding procedure. $\frac{3}{5}$ has been through fifthing. $\frac{2}{3}$ has been through thirding.

Therefore, $\frac{3}{5}$ now needs thirding and $\frac{2}{3}$ needs fifthing (Figure 12.3b).

The written version of this would be as shown in Figure 12.3c. Both the folded and written versions show $\frac{2}{3}$ to be bigger (by $\frac{1}{15}$).

Which fraction is bigger, $\frac{9}{16}$ or $\frac{5}{8}$?

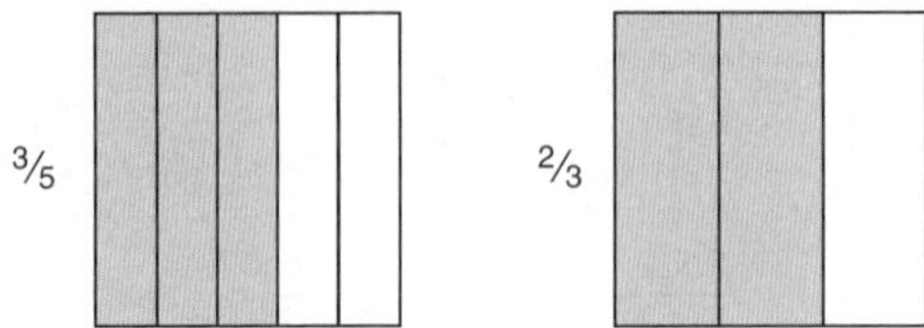

Figure 12.3a Comparing fraction values.

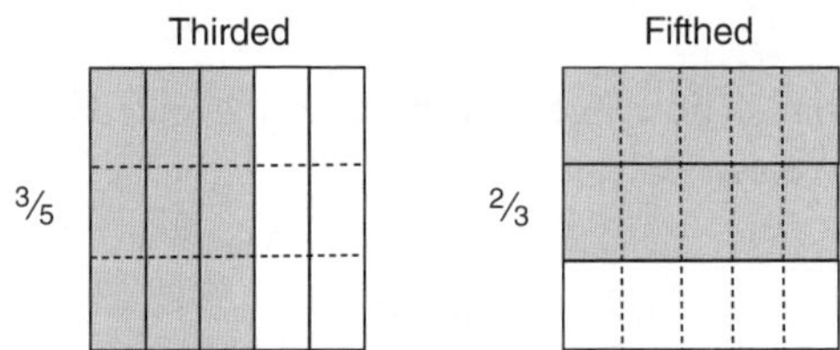

Figure 12.3b Adding fractions with different denominators: 3/5 + 2/3.

$$\frac{3}{5} = \frac{3 \times 3}{5 \times 3} = \frac{9}{15}$$

$$\frac{2}{3} = \frac{2 \times 3}{3 \times 5} = \frac{10}{15}$$

Figure 12.3c Adding fractions with different denominators; written version.

After considering how the paper would have been folded to make these fractions, it is evident that the 5/8 needs to undergo another halving process. Using only the written form:

$$\frac{9}{16} = \frac{9}{16}$$

$$\frac{5}{8} = \frac{5 \times 2}{8 \times 2} = \frac{10}{16}$$

which makes 5/8 bigger (by 1/16).

Converting mixed fractions to top-heavy fractions

2¼ is called a mixed fraction, because it has a whole-number part and a fraction part. It is frequently necessary to convert the mixed fraction into

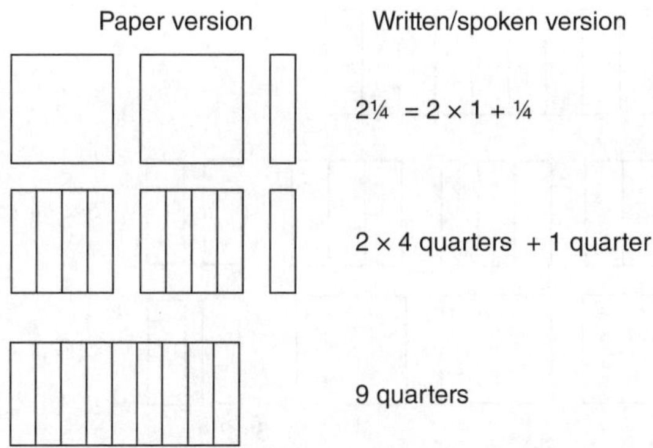

Figure 12.4 2¼s a 'top heavy' fraction: $\frac{9}{4}$.

segments (in this case quarters). Figure 12.4 shows the paper and written/spoken versions. The result is known as a top-heavy fraction for obvious reasons. The careful use of words in the written/spoken version is deliberate and necessary at first. This is because many students who have seen this work before remember incorrect methods. This will inhibit the learning of new methods for the same problems. They remember a rule that says something along the lines of, 'Multiply something by something and add something', but unfortunately mix up their somethings. Until they understand why they are multiplying and adding, they are likely to confuse the steps and write $2 \times 1 + 4$ (giving 5) or $4 \times 1 + 2$ (giving 6) rather than $2 \times 4 + 1$ (giving 9).

Converting top-heavy fractions to mixed fractions

Top-heavy fractions are also called 'improper' fractions, a name that suggests it maybe undesirable to leave them in this form. They can be converted into mixed fractions as follows.

Example
$\frac{10}{3}$

As the segments are thirds, they must be grouped in threes to form whole numbers (Figure 12.5). Any remainders will stay as thirds. The essential working is a division by three:

$$10 \div 3 = 3 \text{ remainder } 2$$

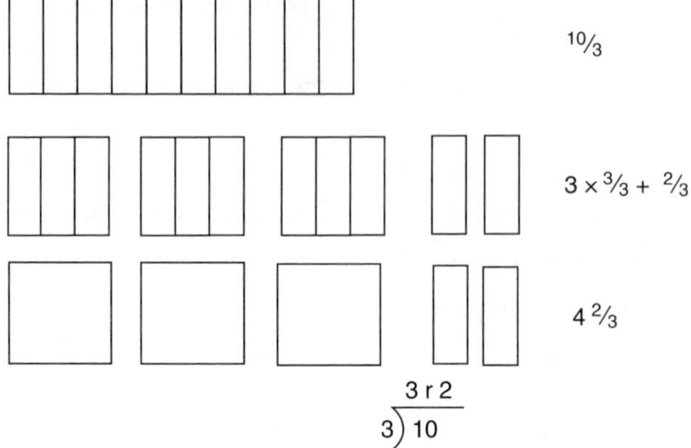

Figure 12.5 Converting $^{10}\!/_3$ to $3\frac{2}{3}$.

The results may be interpreted as follows:

Spoken version:

'Ten thirds

There are three lots of three thirds in ten thirds, with two thirds remaining.

Three lots of three thirds make three ones.

Two thirds left over makes 3 and ⅔.'

Written version

$^{10}\!/_3$

$=3\times{}^3\!/_3+{}^2\!/_3$

$=3\times1+{}^2\!/_3$

$=3\frac{2}{3}$

Combining Fractions

Caleb Gattengno (Brown *et al.*, 1989) in his farewell address to the ATM in 1988 spoke of adding fractions:

> Once at my desk in Addis Abbaba in 1957, I blushed. I was so ashamed of myself. 1957, twenty years after I got my doctorate in mathematics,

> I understood what we do when we add two fractions…I did not know that to add two fractions involves addition. I said it but I didn't know it. I could write it, I could get the answer, but I didn't know what it meant to add two fractions. And suddenly, I realised that, whenever I have pears and apples, two pears and three apples, I don't have five apples or five pears. I have something altered, I have five pieces of fruit. So why did I do that? Because I wanted to find how to get them together, I had to raise myself to another level where pears, pearness and appleness are replaced by fruitness. And at that moment I can say five. And I never realised that 'common denominator' meant 'give the same name' to both. And in the middle of the word 'denominator' I see a French word 'nom' which I knew very well. It didn't strike me, ever, that it is addition that forces me to get denominators, common denominators, not fractions. That was my shame…

There are so many messages in that paragraph, not least, that true understanding of a topic may come after many years of illusory success.

Vertical and horizontal presentations of fraction problems

We believe that a major cause of misunderstanding and confusion with fractions derives from the radical differences between the procedures used for addition and subtraction and those used for multiplication (and division). These differences are summarised in Table 12.1.

Paper folding is used as the (two-dimensional) model to illustrate the combining of fractions. This demonstration can be shown to relate directly to the written algorithm. It simplifies each operation and provides a solution to the problem summarised in Table 12.1. It leads naturally to a vertical

Table 12.1 Combining fractions using paper folding.

Addition/subtraction	*Multiplication*
Addition and subtraction cannot take place until there are common denominators (i.e. equal segment sizes).	Multiplication can take place without common denominators.
The denominators are neither added nor subtracted.	The denominators (and numerators) are multiplied.
Simplification is done at the end.	Simplification is done as early as possible.
Whole numbers are treated separately.	Whole numbers are combined with fractions (to make mixed fractions).

layout for addition and subtraction, which contrasts with the horizontal presentation suggested for multiplication. Further advantages of this will be discussed later in this chapter.

The difficult concept of division of and, especially, division by fractions is discussed later in the chapter. The 'normal' algorithms that are used to solve division problems for fractions must seem totally irrational and bizarre to many students (and adults). Some explanation is given, along with two methods, one vertical and the other horizontal.

Adding Fractions

This section starts with using paper folding to provide a concrete image of the operation. The explanation then moves to a more conceptual/symbolic level to extend the student's performance and streamline his work. The initial descriptions progress from the easiest operation on fractions with the same denominator (segment size) to problems that involve mixed fractions.

Fractions where the segments (denominators) are the same size

Example

$\frac{1}{5} + \frac{3}{5}$

Paper, written and spoken versions are given in Figure 12.6. The reference to a 'spoken version' introduces another two senses, oral and aural, and emphasises that adding fifths to fifths produces fifths, that is, there is no change in segment size (or name), just as adding a number of marbles

Paper version	Written version	Spoken version
(1 of 5 segments shaded)	$\frac{1}{5}$	one fifth
(3 of 5 segments shaded)	$\frac{3}{5}$	three fifths
(4 of 5 segments shaded)	$\frac{4}{5}$	four fifths

Figure 12.6 Adding fractions with the same denominator.

to another set of marbles still produces marbles. Thus, examples of this type are used to establish that segments must be the same size before addition can proceed. You can judge how many examples of this type are needed to establish this fundamental precept.

Adding fractions where the segments are of different size

Example

$\frac{1}{2} + \frac{2}{5}$

Again the different versions are given (see Figure 12.7). The paper-folding version signals a problem since the segments of the two pieces of paper in this type of problem are of different sizes. The spoken version confirms that like is not being added to like. You could discuss this problem with the student, 'What would be the segment size of the result?' if such an addition were to proceed.

The student's attention should be focused on the segments, which are not the same size (and do not have the same name). This is the reason addition cannot proceed without some modification to one or both of the segment names. The modification is to make the segments the same size (or give them the same name). So, the half is fifthed to make tenths and the fifths are halved to make tenths. In this example, the new segment size is tenths, because both halves and fifths can be modified to this segment size (see Chapter 11). Both existing segments can be folded again. The written version is given below:

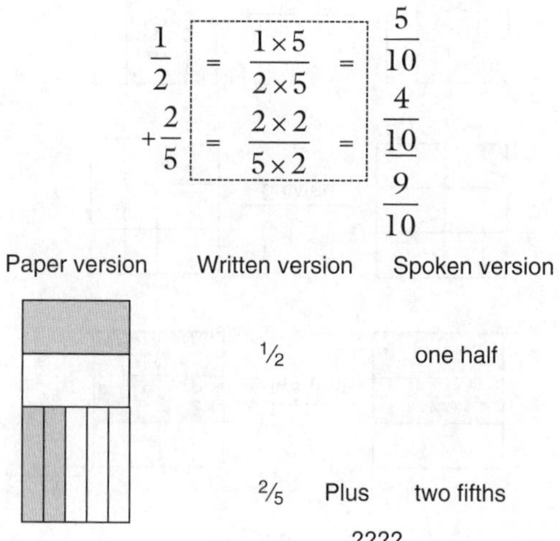

Figure 12.7 How do we add fractions with different denominators?

This follows the steps with the paper folding and extends the method described in Chapter 11, which made segments the same size.

Adding more than two fractions

The same method, of making segment sizes the same, can be extended. Again the principle is to obtain the same segments (names) for each fraction. Since more fractions are being added there is a likelihood of larger answers, possibly resulting in a top-heavy fraction.

Example

$\frac{3}{4}+\frac{1}{6}+\frac{2}{3}$

The common segment size is twelfths (Figure 12.8).

The written version is as follows:

$$\frac{3}{4} = \frac{3\times3}{4\times3} = \frac{9}{12}$$

$$\frac{1}{6} = \frac{1\times2}{6\times2} = \frac{2}{12}$$

$$+\frac{2}{3} = \frac{2\times4}{3\times4} = \frac{8}{12}$$

$$\frac{19}{12} = \frac{12}{12} + \frac{7}{12} = \frac{19}{12} = 1\frac{7}{12}$$

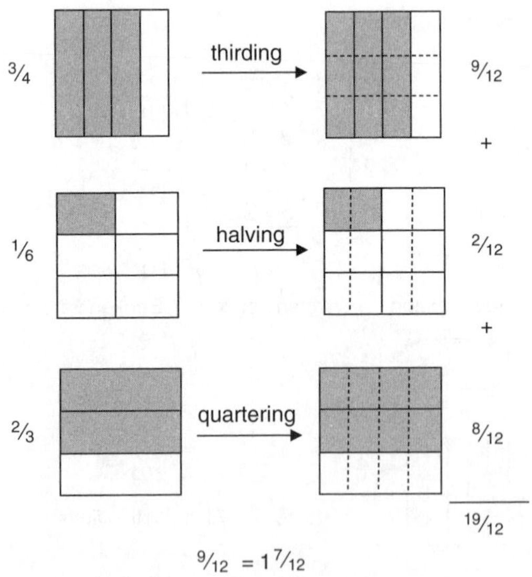

3/4 thirding 9/12

+

1/6 halving 2/12

+

2/3 quartering 8/12

19/12

9/12 = 1 7/12

Figure 12.8 Adding fractions resulting in a 'top heavy' fraction.

Adding mixed fractions

Mixed fractions with segments that are the same size
The procedure is similar to the addition of simple fractions, but the student is learning to treat the whole numbers and fractions separately.

Example
$2\frac{1}{5} + 3\frac{2}{5}$

The folded-paper version (Figure 12.9) shows the answer clearly and also relates well to the written version:

$$\begin{array}{l} 2\frac{1}{5} \\ 3\frac{2}{5} \\ \hline 5\frac{3}{5} \end{array} \quad \text{compare with} \quad \begin{array}{l} 21 \\ 32 \\ \hline 53 \end{array}$$

It demonstrates the need to deal separately with the whole numbers and the fractions in the same way that tens and units are dealt with separately in whole-number addition.

Mixed fractions with different segment sizes
Once again, the student has to focus on the size of the segments and remember from the example above to deal with the whole numbers and fractions separately. Thus, the exercise can be used to reinforce previously learnt skills.

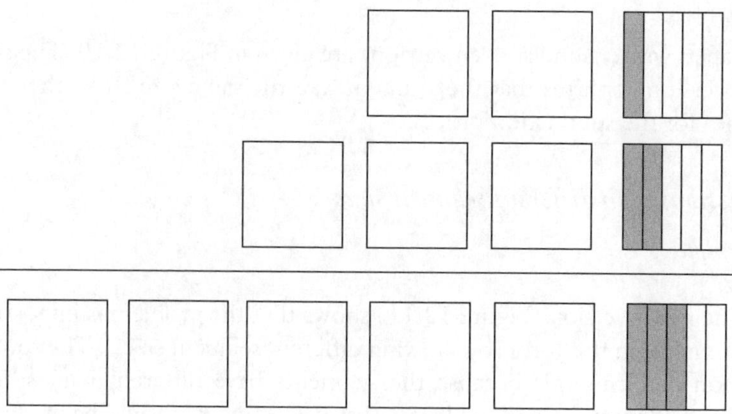

Figure 12.9 Adding mixed numbers: $2\frac{1}{5} + 3\frac{2}{5}$.

Example

$2^1/_4 + 1^2/_3$

The written version is:

$$
\begin{array}{cccccccccc}
2 & \frac{1}{4} & = & \frac{1\times 3}{4\times 3} & & & & & = & \frac{3}{12} \\
\underline{+1} & \frac{2}{3} & = & \frac{2\times 2}{3\times 2} & = & \frac{4}{6} & = & \frac{4\times 2}{6\times 2} & = & \frac{8}{12} \\
3 & & & & & & & & & \frac{11}{12}
\end{array}
$$

It would be simple to use paper folding to demonstrate the above steps, confirming the algorithm and the answer:

$$2\tfrac{1}{4} + 1\tfrac{2}{3} = 3\tfrac{11}{12}$$

Subtracting Fractions

The basic principle is the same as for addition. The student has to learn that the segments have to be the same size (same name) before subtraction can proceed. As with addition, a series of progressively more complex examples is given.

Fractions where the segments are the same size

Example

$\tfrac{3}{5} - \tfrac{1}{5}$

Paper, written, and spoken versions are given in Figure 12.10. The spoken version confirms that the segments are the same size (have the same name) for the subtraction process.

Fractions with different segment sizes

Example

$\tfrac{4}{5} - \tfrac{2}{3}$

The paper version (Figure 12.11) shows that the problem is impossible to complete in this form (by showing different segment sizes). The spoken version confirms this because the segments have different names. The problem requires, as with addition, that the segments should be made the same size, in this case, fifteenths. Again, the concrete example of paper

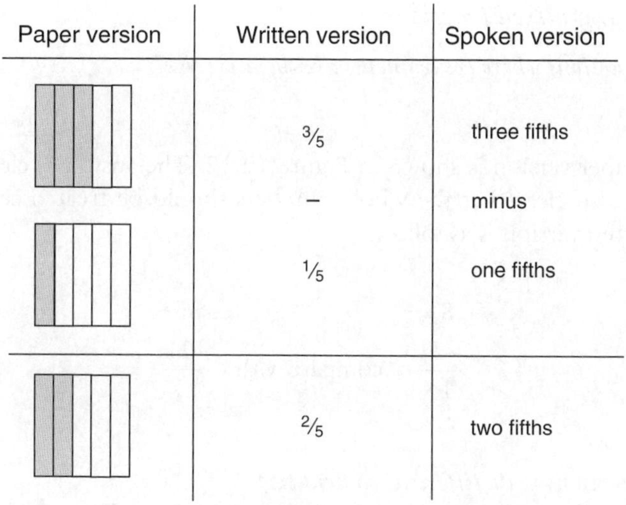

Paper version	Written version	Spoken version
	$3/5$	three fifths
	–	minus
	$1/5$	one fifths
	$2/5$	two fifths

Figure 12.10 Subtracting fractions with the same denominator.

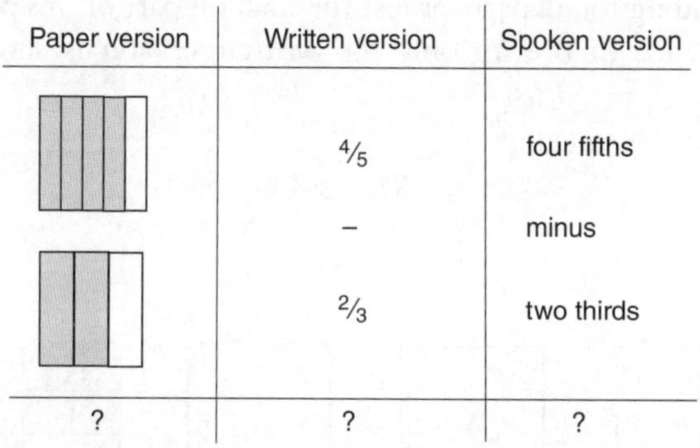

Paper version	Written version	Spoken version
	$4/5$	four fifths
	–	minus
	$2/3$	two thirds
?	?	?

Figure 12.11 How do we subtract fractions with different denominators?

folding focuses on the critical part of the algorithm, the need to work with segments that are the same size:

$$\begin{array}{rcccl} \frac{4}{5} & = & \frac{4\times 3}{5\times 3} & = & \frac{12}{15} \\ -\frac{2}{3} & = & \frac{2\times 5}{3\times 5} & = & \frac{10}{15} \\ & & & & \frac{2}{15} \end{array}$$

Subtracting mixed fractions

Mixed fractions where the segments are the same size

Example

$3\frac{5}{9} - 2\frac{1}{9}$

The paper version is shown in Figure 12.12. The answer is clearly $1\frac{4}{9}$, and it is also clear that the whole numbers should be treated separately. The written version is as follows:

$$\begin{array}{r} 3\frac{5}{9} \\ -2\frac{1}{9} \\ \hline 1\frac{4}{9} \end{array} \quad \text{compare with} \quad \begin{array}{r} 35 \\ -21 \\ \hline 14 \end{array}$$

Mixed fractions with different segment sizes

Again, the student has to focus on the segment sizes. The segments must be adjusted to be the same size (and to have the same name) and the whole numbers and parts must be dealt with separately. The student can use paper folding for all parts or just the fraction part of this problem. For the convenience of brevity only the written version is shown for this example:

$$5\frac{5}{6} - 2\frac{1}{4}$$

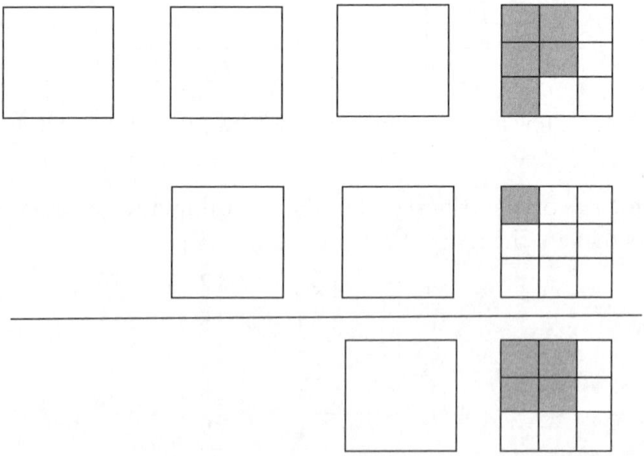

Figure 12.12 Subtracting mixed numbers: $3\frac{5}{9} + 2\frac{1}{9}$.

$$
\begin{array}{rcccc}
5 & \frac{5}{6} & = \frac{5 \times 2}{6 \times 2} & = & \frac{10}{12} \\
\underline{-2} & \frac{1}{4} & = \frac{1 \times 3}{4 \times 3} & = & \underline{\frac{3}{12}} \\
3 & & & & \frac{7}{12}
\end{array}
$$

Mixed fractions where a bigger fraction part is subtracted from a smaller fraction part

Example

3½ − 1⅔

Since ⅔ is bigger than ½, the problem requires an adjustment not dissimilar to a whole-number subtraction such as 374 − 158, where 8 is bigger than 4. The solution to this difficulty with fractions is very similar to that used with whole numbers. The student has to use a whole number and convert it to a fraction in the same way as a student doing a whole-number subtraction has to use the tens column to obtain ones.

Thus, the algorithm is not another new, unrelated idea to learn. You are showing the student the wide applicability of mathematical procedures. The action of paper folding provides a concrete model for the algorithm and a multisensory input to the memory. The paper-folding procedure also confirms for the student that ⅔ is bigger than ½. The paper version is given in Figure 12.13.

The written version is as follows:

$$
\begin{array}{rr}
3\tfrac{1}{2} = 3\tfrac{3}{6} = 2 + \tfrac{6}{6} + \tfrac{3}{6} = & 2\tfrac{9}{6} \\
-1\tfrac{2}{3} = & \underline{1\tfrac{4}{6}} \\
 & 1\tfrac{5}{6}
\end{array}
$$

Combined Additions and Subtractions

Both addition and subtraction of fractions require:

- Segments of the same size (same name) and
- Whole numbers to be treated separately from parts.

Consequently, it is possible to perform both operations in the same calculation without a change of procedure. The student may need to use paper folding, but by now he may be able to move straight to the written algorithm.

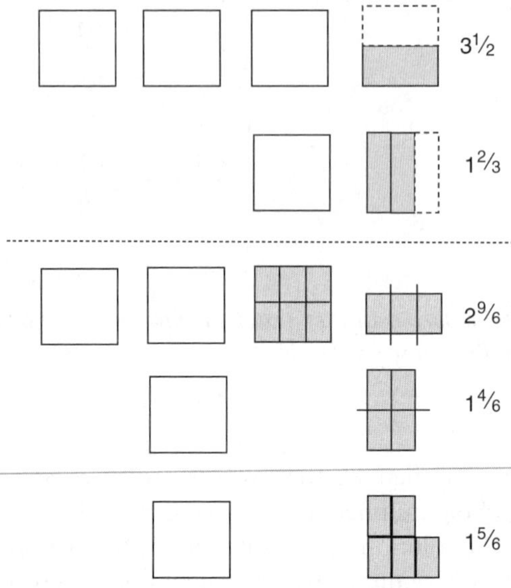

Figure 12.13 Subtracting mixed numbers where the fractions have different denominators.

Example

$$2\tfrac{1}{8} + 3\tfrac{1}{2} - 1\tfrac{1}{4}$$

$$\begin{array}{rlcccc}
2 & \dfrac{1}{8} & & & = & \dfrac{1}{8} \\[2ex]
+3 & \dfrac{1}{2} & = & \dfrac{1 \times 4}{2 \times 4} & = & \dfrac{4}{8} \\[2ex]
\underline{-1} & \dfrac{1}{4} & = & \dfrac{1 \times 2}{4 \times 2} & = & \underline{\dfrac{2}{8}} \\[2ex]
4 & & & & & \dfrac{3}{8}
\end{array}$$

It may be advantageous to explain to the student why the addition and subtraction of fractions have been presented in a vertical format. The following summarises the advantages.

Advantages of the vertical layout for addition and subtraction of fractions

- It signals the need to make segment sizes the same.
- There is less likelihood of adding or subtracting the denominators.
- It allows room horizontally to change the segment sizes.
- It lines up fractions and whole numbers separately and encourages the student to deal with them separately.
- Numbers are added and subtracted vertically, which is a more familiar and easier method for most students.

Multiplying by Fractions

The language of multiplication should be established first. As with percentages, the word 'of' is frequently used to denote multiplication. For example $\frac{3}{4}$ of 8 means $\frac{3}{4} \times 8$. If the student needs to be convinced of this use, then refer back to whole-number examples such as, 'How many sweets are there in seven packets **of** ten?' or, 'If one pen costs 20p, how much do I pay for eight **of** them?'

The question, 'Is the answer going to be bigger or smaller?' is particularly useful when evaluating the answers for fraction questions.

Fraction times fraction

For multiplication of a whole number by a whole number (Chapter 8) area was used as a model. Area is a two-dimensional model. The paper-folding model for fraction times fraction does the same.

The method of finding the fraction of a square of paper was explained earlier. Multiplication repeats the process in a second dimension. So, one dimension represents a and the other dimension represents b in $a \times b$.

Example 1

$\frac{1}{2} \times \frac{1}{3}$

This multiplication is carried out by using a square of paper to find one-half of one-third of the square.

Figure 12.14 shows $\frac{1}{3}$ shaded. A vertical fold gives one-half of this third. The part shaded twice is one-half of one-third. There are six segments in all, so one segment is $\frac{1}{6}$.

The application of two fraction operations to the same square has two major implications:

- The change in segment size is seen to be inevitable. It should be obvious to the student that the answer will have a new segment size (and that it will be smaller).

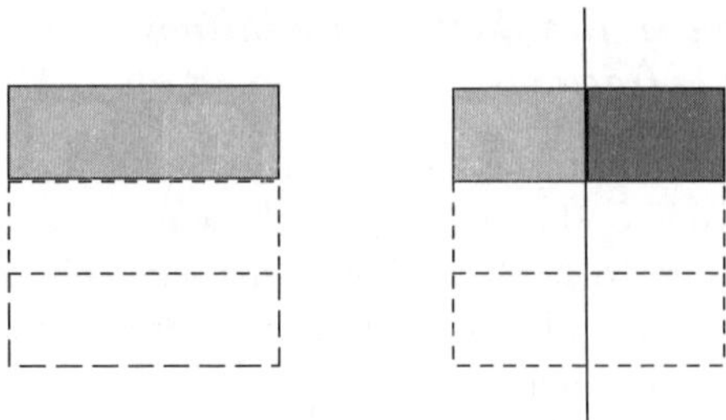

Figure 12.14 Multiplying fractions: $\frac{1}{3} \times \frac{1}{2}$.

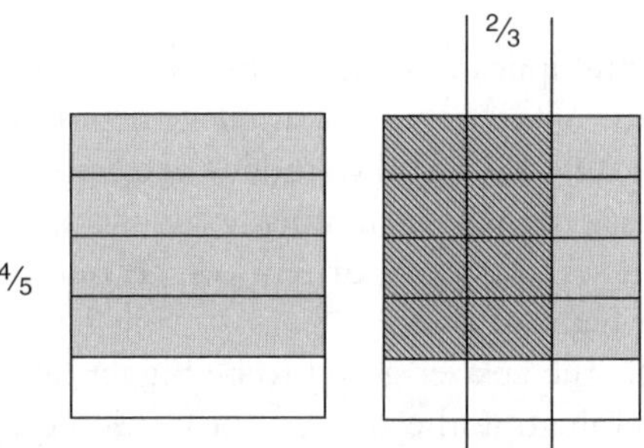

Figure 12.15 Multiplying fractions: $\frac{4}{5} \times \frac{2}{3} = \frac{8}{15}$.

- The *horizontally* written layout of this multiplication reflects the difference between this operation and its model to that used for addition and subtraction.

The written form of the example above is as follows:

$$\frac{1}{2} \times \frac{1}{3} = \frac{1}{6}$$

Example 2

$\frac{2}{3}$ of $\frac{4}{5}$

The square is folded into fifths in one direction and four of these fifths are shaded (Figure 12.15). The square is then folded into thirds in the opposite direction to give a grid with $\frac{8}{15}$, shaded twice.

The concrete operation of folding and shading the square relates directly to the written form:

$$\frac{2}{3} \text{ of } \frac{4}{5} = \frac{2}{3} \times \frac{4}{5} = \frac{2 \times 4}{3 \times 5} = \frac{8}{15}$$

The student is multiplying the top and bottom parts of the fractions, which is easier to remember if the fractions are written side by side. The folding shows why three and five are multiplied together to make fifteen segments and why two and four are multiplied together to give eight of these segments.

Example 3
½ of ⅘

This results in an answer that can be simplified or reduced. The paper-folding procedure is the same as in Example 2, leading to an answer of 4⁄10 . Although this is not wrong, it would be more elegant to obtain ⅖.

The written version may be used to explain cancelling before and after the multiplication. This offers an opportunity to remind the student that fractions are about division and that a fraction may have more than one 'name'.

Fraction times whole number

Example 1
¼ of 1 (Figure 12.16a)

Example 2
¼ of 3 (Figure 12.16b)

The student should see that ¼ of 3 is ¼ three 'times', relating 'times' and 'of' once again. The written version relates exactly to fraction times fraction if 3 is written as 3⁄1:

$$\frac{1}{4}\text{of } 3 = \frac{1}{4} \times \frac{3}{1} = \frac{1 \times 3}{4 \times 1} = \frac{3}{4}$$

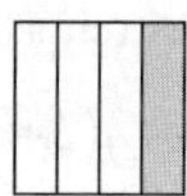

Figure 12.16a ⅕ × 1.

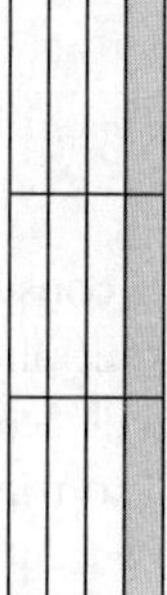

Figure 12.16b ⅕ × 3.

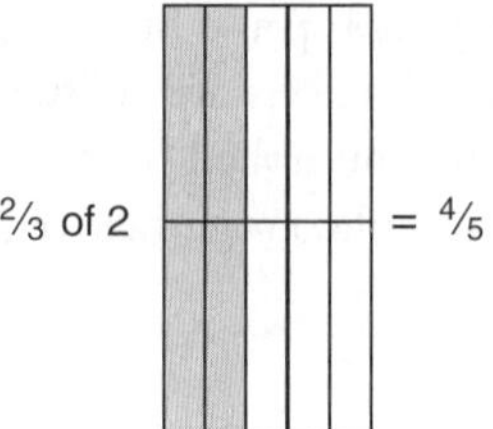

Figure 12.16c $\frac{2}{5} \times 2$.

Example 3
$\frac{2}{5}$ of 2 (Figure 12.16c)

The written version is:

$$\frac{2}{5}\text{of } 2 = \frac{2}{5} \times \frac{2}{1} = \frac{2 \times 2}{5 \times 1} = \frac{4}{5}$$

Multiplying Mixed Fractions

Example
$3\frac{1}{2} \times 2\frac{1}{4}$

The most probable error in this type of calculation arises when the student separates the fractions from the whole numbers, following an addition algorithm, and simply multiplies 3×2 and $\frac{1}{2} \times \frac{1}{4}$.

A consistent application of the area model for multiplication shows the need for four separate multiplications (see Chapter 9).

$3\frac{1}{2} \times 2\frac{1}{4}$ gives four areas, *A*, *B*, *C* and *D* (Figure 12.17).

This multiplication could be written as:

$$(3 + \tfrac{1}{2})(2 + \tfrac{1}{4})$$

A is $3 \times 2 = 6$ (which provides a simple estimate)
B is $2 \times \frac{1}{2} = 1$
C is $3 \times \frac{1}{4} = \frac{3}{4} = \frac{6}{8}$
D is $\frac{1}{2} \times \frac{1}{4} = \frac{1}{8}$
Total $= 7\frac{7}{8}$

Although this provides a method consistent with that used for two-digit times two-digit whole-number multiplications, it is more complex for fractions. So a procedure that is usually less open to errors is recommended. The mixed fractions are converted to top-heavy fractions, which can then be multiplied together as for simple fractions:

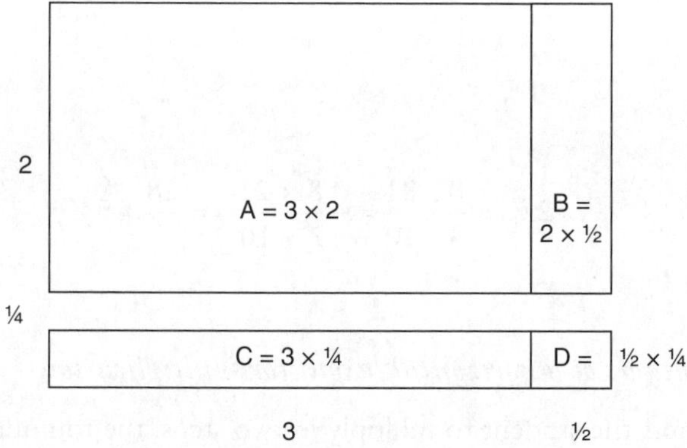

Figure 12.17 Multiplication using the area model.

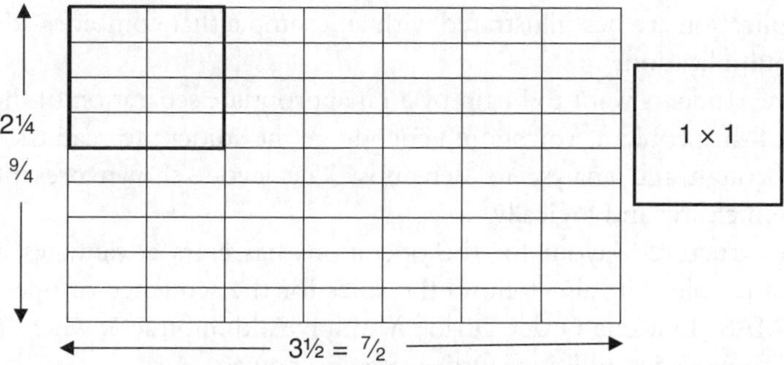

Figure 12.18 Multiplication using the area model.

$$3\tfrac{1}{2} \times 2\tfrac{1}{4} = \frac{7}{2} \times \frac{9}{4} = \frac{7 \times 9}{2 \times 4} = \frac{63}{8} = 7\tfrac{7}{8}$$

A new diagram can be drawn to illustrate this written method (Figure 12.18). This rectangle shows there are halves (seven of them) and that there are fourths (nine of them). The unit square shows the answer will be in eighths and the 7×9 grid shows there are 63 of these eighths.

With these larger numbers, cancellation may be done prior to multiplication in examples where this is possible.

Example
$2\frac{2}{3}\times 2\frac{1}{10}$

$$2\tfrac{2}{3}\times 2\tfrac{1}{10} = \frac{8}{3}\times\frac{21}{10} = \frac{{}^{4}\cancel{8}\times\cancel{21}^{7}}{{}_{1}\cancel{3}\times\cancel{10}_{5}} = \frac{28}{5} = 5\tfrac{3}{5}$$

The advantages of a horizontal layout for multiplication

- It prompts the student to multiply in two steps: the top numbers first and then the denominators.
- It encourages simplifying by cancelling at the beginning.
- There is less temptation to treat whole numbers in isolation.
- It distinguishes between addition/subtraction and multiplication.

The advantages of different presentations for addition/subtraction and multiplication are best illustrated with an example that combines addition and multiplication.

Some students want to begin by an inappropriate separation of the portions of the problem. You should encourage the student to read the problem through and analyse its demands. The layout shown presents the problem clearly and logically.

The structured layout for the operations has extra advantages in this type of problem. It also follows the rules for the sequence of operations BODMAS (Brackets Order Divide Multiply Add Subtract), where multiplication precedes addition. Order refers to powers.

Example
$\left(3\tfrac{1}{2}\times 1\tfrac{1}{2}\right)+\left(1\tfrac{2}{3}\times 2\tfrac{1}{5}\right)$

$$\begin{array}{rcccccccl}
3\tfrac{1}{2}\times 1\tfrac{1}{2} = & \frac{7}{2}\times\frac{3}{2} & = & \frac{7\times 3}{2\times 2} & = & \frac{21}{4} & = 5 & \frac{1}{4} & = \frac{3}{12} \\
+1\tfrac{2}{3}\times 2\tfrac{1}{5} = & \frac{{}^{1}\cancel{5}}{3}\times\frac{11}{\cancel{5}_{1}} & = & \frac{1\times 11}{3\times 1} & = & \frac{11}{3} & = 3 & \frac{2}{3} & = \frac{8}{12} \\
 & & & & & & \overline{8} & & \ \ \frac{11}{12}
\end{array}$$

Multiplication →
Addition ↓

Multiplying with fractions, an overview

This brief overview makes use of the question, 'Is the answer smaller or bigger?' In this case we also need, 'Is the answer the same value?'

When we multiply a number by a fraction whose value is smaller than one, then the answer will be smaller than the number, but bigger than the fraction.

When we multiply a fraction that is smaller than one by another fraction that is smaller than one, then the answer will be smaller than either fraction.

When we multiply a fraction by one it stays the same value. This seemingly obvious statement is less obvious when renaming fractions, for example:

$$\frac{5}{8} \times \frac{2}{2} = 10/16$$

The outcome, $\frac{10}{16}$ does not *look* the same as $\frac{5}{8}$, but it does have the same value.

Dividing with Fractions

A sequence of divisions may be used to introduce the student to this difficult concept (Ashcroft and Chinn, 1992):

$$20 \div 4 = 5$$
$$20 \div 2 = 10$$
$$20 \div 1 = 20$$
$$20 \div \frac{1}{2} = 40$$

This may help the student to rephrase the question, a strategy that has quite extensive value. Thus, $20 \div \frac{1}{2}$ can be re-phrased as 'How many halves are there in 20?' A square of paper may be folded to make two halves, followed by the question 'How many halves are there in one?' It can be halved again, leading to the question 'How many quarters are there in one?' The process can be continued through $\frac{1}{8}$, $\frac{1}{16}$, $\frac{1}{32}$ to show the answer becoming bigger as the fraction becomes smaller.

Division by fractions

Two methods are described here. The first deals with simple examples and establishes a concrete image for this difficult concept. It is harder to explain the second method in this way, but it is an expedient way for those who progress to algebra.

The first method is set out vertically, whereas the second method is presented horizontally (it being more akin to multiplication).

Division by making the segments the same size

Example
$\frac{7}{10} \div \frac{1}{10}$

The spoken version of this problem needs flexibility for mathematical vocabulary again. It could be read as 'seven-tenths divided by one-tenth', but the student is more likely to understand, 'How many one-tenths are there in seven-tenths?' Again, the ability to rephrase a question can take the student a long way towards the answer of seven.

Example
$\frac{3}{4} \div \frac{1}{8}$

The use of the same spoken version leads to, 'How many one eighths are there in three-quarters?' This makes about as much sense as, 'How many cars are there in a pencil?' However, the alternative interpretation: 'Divide three-quarters into eighths' indicates more clearly that the segment sizes (denominators) should be made the same. So, that is the first step. Figure 12.19 shows the paper, written, and spoken versions.

Paper version	Written version	Spoken version
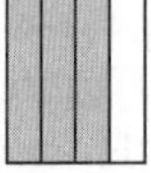	$\frac{3}{4} \div \frac{1}{8}$	three quarters divided by one eighth
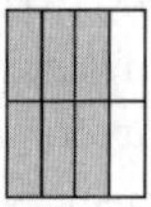	$\frac{6}{8} \div \frac{1}{8}$	= six eighths divided by one eighth
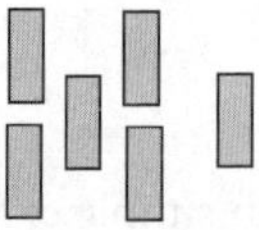	6	six

Figure 12.19 Dividing with fractions by changing denominators.

Example
$\frac{3}{5} \div \frac{7}{10}$

This is shown in the written version only:

$$\begin{aligned} & \frac{3}{5} = \frac{6}{10} \\ \div\ & \frac{7}{10} = \frac{7}{10} \\ & \phantom{\frac{7}{10}} = \frac{6}{7} \end{aligned}$$

Examples with mixed fractions

The initial step for the method advocated is to convert the mixed fraction into a top-heavy fraction.

Example
$3\frac{3}{4} \div \frac{3}{4}$

Since the segments are already the same, the division can be done immediately. The three versions are shown in Figure 12.20. The question is interpreted and illustrated as, 'How many groups of three quarters are there in fifteen quarters?'

Example
$5\frac{2}{3} \div 2\frac{1}{2}$

This is shown in written version only, for the student who has a well-established model of fractions:

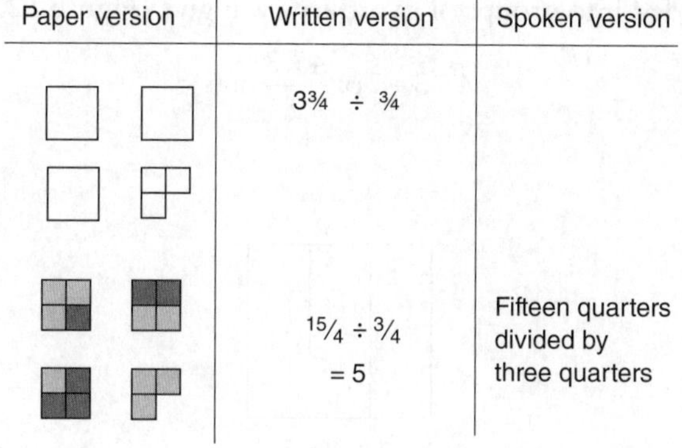

Paper version	Written version	Spoken version
	$3\frac{3}{4} \div \frac{3}{4}$	
	$\frac{15}{4} \div \frac{3}{4}$ $= 5$	Fifteen quarters divided by three quarters

Figure 12.20 Comparing the visual, symbol and written versions of division with fractions.

$$5\tfrac{2}{3} = \frac{17}{3} = \frac{17 \times 2}{3 \times 2} = \frac{34}{6}$$

$$\div 2\tfrac{1}{2} = \frac{5}{2} = \frac{5 \times 3}{2 \times 3} = \frac{15}{6}$$

$$\frac{34}{15} = 2\tfrac{4}{15}$$

Dividing fractions by inverse multiplication

This method is quicker, but requires the student to remember a seemingly inexplicable rule. So $4 \div \frac{2}{3}$ is calculated as $4 \times \frac{3}{2}$. In our experience this is one of the best recalled 'rules' of maths, even by adults who have long since left the maths classroom. Perhaps it is the seemingly bizarre instruction to 'Turn upside down and multiply' that makes it so. Some students will be happy enough to accept the explanation, or rationalisation, that since multiplication is the opposite of division then there is a need to do an opposite thing with the fraction, that is, to turn it upside down.

An explanation for the algorithm can be developed for the student by a series of paper-folding exercises.

- $1 \div \frac{1}{2}$
  By definition, one whole number divided into thirds gives 3 (Figure 12.21a).
- $3 \div \frac{1}{3}$
  Four whole numbers divided into thirds will give $3 \times 3 = 9$ (Figure 12.21b).
- $4 \div \frac{2}{3}$
  Four divided into groups of two-thirds will give (Figure 12.21c):

$$4 \times 3 \div 2 \text{ or } \frac{4 \times 3}{2} \text{ or } 6$$

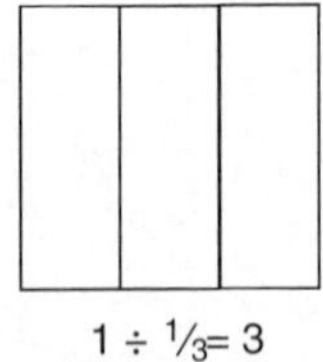

Figure 12.21a Whole numbers divided by a fraction.

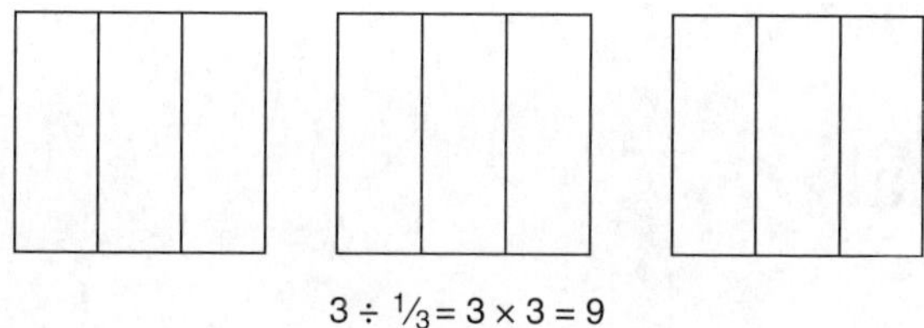

Figure 12.21b Whole numbers divided by a fraction.

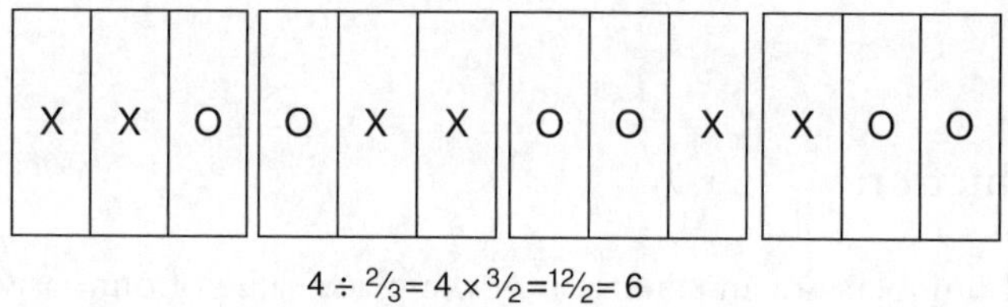

Figure 12.21c Whole numbers divided by a fraction.

Since $^2/_3$ is twice as big as $^1/_3$, the student should expect the answer to be half that of the previous example, that is, the previous answer has to be divided by two. However you choose to justify the rule, the pragmatics are that the fraction is inverted and then multiplied:

$$y \div \frac{a}{b} = y \times \frac{b}{a}$$

13

Decimals

Introduction

Decimal numbers are an extension of the place value of our base ten system. They follow the same logic, but often the perceived inconsistencies block understanding. The processes of addition, subtraction, multiplication and division are identical to those covered for whole numbers in Chapters 8–10, but the decimal point confuses learners. This is not helped by books that suggest, for some calculations, 'Move the decimal point.'

As with all chapters in this book, we will try to encourage an understanding of the work, partly by relating it to and building on previous concepts and knowledge.

Addition and Subtraction

Addition

Common errors tend to be due to misalignment of the decimal point, that is, incorrectly lining up the place values of the numbers involved (Ashlock, 2010). The tendency persists to line up the numbers from the right, irrespective of place value. Reinstating place value column headings can help.

An example of a common error pattern is:

$$1.23 + 5 \quad \text{becoming} \quad \begin{array}{r} 1.23 \\ +\ 5 \\ \hline 1.28 \\ \hline \end{array}$$

Mathematics for Dyslexics and Dyscalculics: A Teaching Handbook, Fourth Edition.
Steve Chinn and Richard E. Ashcroft.

The correct process can be illustrated by using Dienes base ten blocks or similar apparatus. Effective help can also be provided with the use of money. For example, students who begin by adding £1.23 + £5 with coins will rarely try to add the 5 and the 3, as in the written version above. Reinforcement can be by using the suggestion that £5 may be written as £5.00, writing the .00 because it has no pence, and so the written version becomes:

$$\begin{array}{r} £1.23 \\ +\ £5.00 \\ \hline £6.23 \\ \hline \end{array}$$

If written examples are linked with the student handling the equivalent money, then generally it becomes clear that pounds are added to pounds, pence are added to pence, and so on. The student can then be guided to write them under each other, a step which automatically puts the decimal points, which separate the pounds and pence, under each other. This gives the student a focus so that £0.09 + £0.5(0) is written as:

$$\begin{array}{r} £0.09 \\ +\ £0.50 \\ \hline £0.59 \\ \hline \end{array}$$

Coins provide the concrete memory hook for the student. The pragmatics are to use the decimal point as the marker of place value and to line up the numbers based on lining up the decimal points.

Another common error with decimal addition, 3.97 + 1.04 is shown below:

$$\begin{array}{r} 3.\overset{1}{9}7 \\ +1.04 \\ \hline 4.101 \\ \hline \end{array}$$

A student who makes this error has been content to carry a 1 from the hundredths to the tenths column, but has not carried a 1 from the tenths to the ones column, which requires him to cross over the decimal point. There is a lack of understanding here that the decimal columns are simply an extension of the whole-number columns, that they are related in the same way, that is, increasing and decreasing in powers of ten and that they must follow the same rules. This problem was anticipated in

Chapter 11, where the issue was clarified by the use of decimal number sequences. A demonstration with money can be used to provide further reinforcement. The example above can be viewed as £3.97 + £1.04 and written as:

$$\begin{array}{rr} \pounds & \overset{1}{3}.\overset{1}{9}7 \\ +\pounds & 1.04 \\ \cline{2-2} \pounds & 5.01 \\ \cline{2-2} \end{array}$$

Thus 7 + 4 is 11 pence, which is changed (traded) for a single ten pence, carried to the ten-pence column, and one penny which is retained as the answer in the one pence column. Similarly, in the ten pence column, the carried over one (a ten pence coin) is added to the nine and zero to give ten lots of ten pence. These can be traded for £1, which is carried into the pounds column.

Subtraction

Subtraction of decimal numbers presents students with virtually the same problems as addition. For example 24.38 – 0.6 might generate the error:

$$\begin{array}{r} 24.38 \\ -0.\ 6 \\ \hline 24.32 \\ \hline \end{array}$$

Here, the tendency, again, is to line up numbers from the right regardless of place value, compounded by the fact that 6 is easier to subtract from 8 than 3. The pragmatic solution to this problem is, as for addition, to use the decimal points as markers of place value and to line up the decimal points. Once again, a good manipulative material to illustrate and develop this procedure is coins.

Another common error pattern is illustrated by the example 48.5 – 2.36. This tends to generate two types of errors:

- Lining up from the right:

$$\begin{array}{r} 47.5 \\ \underline{-2.34} \\ 24.1 \end{array} \quad \text{or } 2.41 \quad \text{or } 2.4.1$$

- Setting up correctly, but:

$$\begin{array}{r} 48.5 \\ -2.36 \\ \hline 6 \\ \hline \end{array}$$

The 6 is just transferred to the answer line, before the rest of the calculation is completed correctly.

$$\begin{array}{r} 48.5 \\ -2.36 \\ \hline \underline{46.26} \end{array}$$

The use of an optional zero to 'square off' the calculation reminds the student that the 6 has to be subtracted, and gives him something to subtract from.

$$\begin{array}{rcr} 48.50 & & 48.\overset{4}{\cancel{5}}{}^{1}0 \\ -2.36 & \text{then} & -2.36 \\ \hline \\ \hline \end{array} \qquad \begin{array}{r} \\ \\ \hline \underline{46.14} \end{array}$$

This can be practised with coins and place-value columns.

Errors in the addition and subtraction of decimals can be reduced by reminding students of the ever-present need to preview and review a question; to absorb some meaning and value for the numbers, and produce an estimate; and then check their answers against the estimate. This is likely to reduce the incidence of errors due to misalignment.

Multiplication and Division by Powers of Ten

Multiplication by ten

As with so much work in mathematics, place value is important here, so a review of the topic may be an advisable precursor to the next work.

Confronted by the question 4.62×10, if the student can remember that $4 \times 10 = 40$ then this can help him to see that 4.62×10 (as '4 and a bit' times 10) should be forty-something. Focusing on one digit from the number can reduce confusion and generate security. Alternatively,

4.62×10 can be interpreted as ten lots of 4.62 and can be evaluated the 'long' way (as a repeated addition):

$$\begin{array}{r} 4.62 \\ 4.62 \\ 4.62 \\ 4.62 \\ 4.62 \\ 4.62 \\ 4.62 \\ 4.62 \\ 4.62 \\ +4.62 \\ \hline 46.20 \\ \hline \end{array}$$

Many students will notice that the digits 4, 6 and 2 have not changed, nor has their sequence in the number. This observation is, of course, an extension of the ten times table pattern. The digits have moved along *one* place value, so that each digit now represents a value that is ten times bigger. Most students can appreciate this pattern when it is pointed out to them. Base ten blocks or money can be used for manipulative work. The pattern and the procedure can be shown by considering each of the digits separately, using the base ten blocks or money.

As always, a multiplication is more efficient, quicker and less prone to error than the repeated addition of ten numbers.

When the calculation is written as $4.62 \times 10 = 46.2$, some students will imagine that the decimal point has moved rather than the digits. While this is mathematically incorrect, it is a simplification that is often the only way some students can remember what to do, especially if the computation is part of a longer calculation, when dual tasking can create problems. Actually, the digits move relative to the decimal point in order to have new place values. We would rather that this understanding preceded any pragmatic short cuts.

Multiplication by hundred

There are students who will be able to predict the effect of multiplying by hundred and they will conclude that the digits will move two place values.

As with multiplying by ten, an example that relates to known facts can provide an initial understanding of the operation, as well as a valuable estimation procedure (also useful when calculators are used). For example, if it is known that $2 \times 100 = 200$, then 2.375×100 (which is two and a bit times one hundred) should be expected to be two hundred and something. Then, if the digits and their sequence are not to change, then the two hundred and a bit must be 237.5. This result can alternatively be justified by treating $\times 100$ as $\times 10 \times 10$ in two stages (compare with $\times 4$ as $\times 2 \times 2$ in Chapter 7), and by using the same materials to demonstrate this.

$$\begin{aligned} & 2.375 \times 100 \\ = \; & 2.375 \times 10 \times 10 \\ = \; & 23.75 \times 10 \\ = \; & 237.5 \end{aligned}$$

Multiplication by thousand

At about this stage, students will usually see the pattern that the number of zeros in the (10^n) multiplier dictates the number of places moved:

Multiplying by ten	one place value
Multiplying by hundred	two place values
Multiplying by thousand	three place values

For example, $27.1875 \times 1000 = 27187.5$. For justification, $\times 1000$ is equivalent to $\times 10 \times 10 \times 10$. Again a focus on a digit, say seven, which is seven ones, tells the student that it will become seven thousands. Again the other digits retain their sequence.

Multiplication by other powers of ten

The pattern can be extended, using similar arguments, illustrations and materials.

Division by ten

The initial goal is to show that division by ten is the opposite of multiplication by ten. The answer becomes ten times smaller rather than ten times bigger. The topic could be introduced using money or base ten blocks and the student asked to show coins or blocks that are ten times bigger or ten times smaller. The answers can be written on place value column cards.

For an example of the inverse relationship, $3p \times 10$ becomes 30p and conversely $30p \div 10$ becomes 3p. The movement of the numbers is demonstrated by their place values on the card. A good demonstration of the required rule uses the argument that a division by ten and a multiplication by ten will cancel each other out, because they are opposites:

$$37.62 \times 10 = 376.2$$

$$376.2 \div 10 = 37.62$$

The second line above shows that division by ten causes a movement of one place, a movement which is in the direction opposite to that caused by a multiplication by ten.

Direction of movement

A decision about convention is now needed for describing the direction of a movement. Referring to the direction as left or right would be ambiguous, because if the digits move left, the decimal point moves right, and vice versa. Furthermore, terms such as left and right, forwards and backwards, in front and behind are all likely to confuse dyslexics, if they have laterality problems (Miles, 1983). We suggest that a safer and more meaningful practice is to describe the movement of the digits in accordance with whether the answer is bigger or smaller than the original number.

- Multiplication by powers of ten produces answers that are bigger than the original number.
- Division by powers of ten produces answers that are smaller than the original number.

This convention encourages overviews, estimates and reviews.

Division by hundred, thousand and other powers of ten

Divisions follow the same pattern as multiplications, in that the number of zeros in the divisor dictates the number of places moved, but now in a direction that produces smaller answers:

- Division by ten causes a movement of one place value
- Division by hundred causes a movement of two place value,
- Division by thousand causes a movement of three place values, and so on

This work can be justified, if necessary, by arranging divisions as repeated divisions by ten, or as reverse multiplications.

Examples

$46.2 \div 10 = 4.62$	40 becomes 4
$346.5 \div 100 = 3.465$	300 becomes 3
$1872.3 \div 1000 = 1.8723$	1000 becomes 1
$985.3 \div 1000 = 0.9853$	900 becomes 0.9

The last example illustrates inserting a leading zero and the need to explain this to a student. Again, there is the importance of using and appreciating place value.

Rationalisation (1)

It is worth anticipating student's potential problems when trying to apply these procedures to whole numbers – only decimal numbers have been used so far in this chapter. Whole numbers do not display a decimal point, so three is written as 3 and not 3.0. Many calculators will change an entry of 3.0 to 3 as soon as an operation key is pressed. Students often tend to simplify the multiplication and division of whole numbers by powers of ten into a process of gaining or losing zeros. For example:

$$2 \times 10 = 2\underline{0}$$

$$3000 \div 1000 = 3\cancel{000} = 3$$

It is important that students do not see the treatment of whole numbers and decimals as two different processes. The two situations can be rationalised by again focusing on a digit:

$3.6 \times 10 = 36$ three ones become three tens

Here there is a movement of one place value to make the answer bigger:

$4008 \div 1000 = 4.008$ four thousands become four ones

Here, there is a movement of three place values to make the answer smaller.

These procedures should rationalise all multiplications and divisions by powers of 10.

Multiplication of decimals by decimals

There is an expectation that multiplying a whole number will produce an answer that is bigger than the original number. Multiplying by powers of ten has been an example of this. However, for the example 0.6×0.8 this will not be the case (see Chapter 12 Summary). Often such outcomes are very difficult for students, still in the earlier stages of developing this concept, to understand unless they apply the procedure of focusing on a digit as well as recognising that 0.6 and 0.8 are smaller than 1.

The outcome can be first established using the area model (Figure 13.1) for multiplication, as in other chapters of this book. Within the unit square, divided into hundredths, as in the figure, the answer is shown by the area of the shaded rectangle. The small squares, each $\frac{1}{100}$, show the answer to be $\frac{48}{100}$ or 0.48, which is less than either of the original numbers, 0.6(0) and 0.8(0). Of course, this is because the answer represents part of a part.

With or without the area model shown in Figure 13.1, the rule is best presented through fractions (Chapter 11 deliberately interrelated fractions, decimals and percentages), so 0.6×0.8 becomes:

$$\frac{6}{10} \times \frac{8}{10} = \frac{48}{100} = 0.48 \quad \text{Note that } \frac{6}{10} \text{ is also } \frac{60}{100} \text{ and } \frac{8}{10} \text{ is also } \frac{80}{100}$$

In this example, the decimal places for 0.6 and 0.8 are treated as tenths. The tenths become, by multiplication, hundredths, so any rule for the

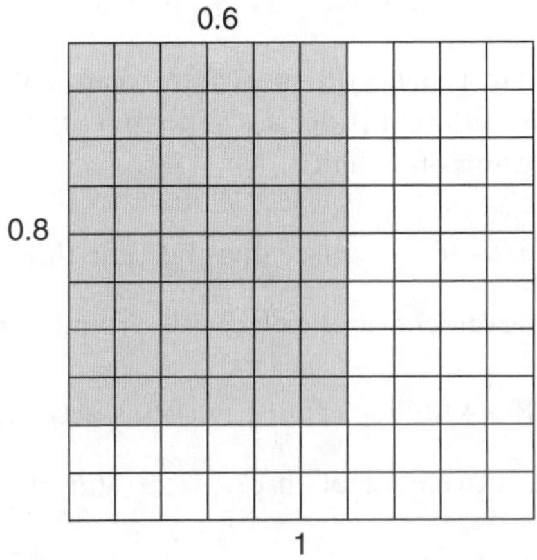

Figure 13.1 The area model for 0.6×0.8.

decimal places must reflect this progression. A pragmatic rule for overviewing the process is:

0.6	1 decimal place
× 0.8	1 decimal place
0.48	2 decimal places

The rule for the position of the decimal point can be stated as follows: 'The number of decimal places in the answer is equal to the total number of decimal places in the numbers of the question'. The digits in the answer (48) are the result of multiplying together the numbers in the question (6 and 8), and are obtained independently of the decimal places. Therefore, the digits in the answer and the position of the decimal point are two separate considerations.

Examples

0.0003	4 decimal places
×0.02	2 decimal places
0.000006	6 decimal places

3.2	1 decimal place
×0.05	2 decimal places
0.160	3 decimal places

21.09	2 decimal places
×3	0 decimal places
63.27	2 decimal places

The final example shows that multiplication of a decimal by a whole number does not increase the number of decimal places. Quoting a special example such as this too early may lead to the over-generalisation that the decimal points do line up. Taken with other examples, this can be shown to occur only when there is whole-number multiplier.

Rationalisation (2)

In this chapter, it has been suggested that students are taught to expect a larger answer after multiplying by a power of ten or indeed any number greater than one, but to expect a smaller answer after multiplying by a decimal number with a value less than one. There is no ambiguity here, and the following explanation can be used to rationalise the situation, and also to encourage good estimations and checking strategies. A sequence such as the following is used:

$$
\begin{aligned}
45 \times 100 &= 4500 \\
45 \times 10 &= 450 \\
45 \times 1 &= 45 \\
45 \times 0.1 &= 4.5 \\
45 \times 0.01 &= 0.45
\end{aligned}
$$

The pivotal value of the multiplier is one, because any number times one remains unchanged in value. A multiplier bigger than one gives an answer bigger than the original number, whereas a multiplier less than one gives an answer less than the original number. This leads to the basic estimate/check procedure: 'If the multiplier is bigger than one, expect the answer to be bigger, and if the multiplier is less than one, expect the answer to be smaller'. The overview is, once again, an important ingredient of the procedure.

An interesting sidetrack concerns students' intuitive estimation of questions such as 0.4×0.002. Given that the choice of the answer may be:

- Bigger than 0.4,
- A middle value between 0.4 and 0.002, or
- Smaller than 0.002,

many students choose the middle value. A discussion as to the correct answer, with further examples, helps students understand the concept of multiplication by numbers less than one and acts as a useful reference/estimate for similar problems.

Division of Decimals

Division by a whole number

This work builds on the work of Chapter 10, with the added dimension of a decimal point, so a comparison with a whole-number example is a good lead-in. The traditional presentation for the problem 81 ÷ 3 is

$$\begin{array}{r} 27 \\ 3\overline{)81} \\ \underline{60} \\ 21 \\ \underline{21} \\ 0 \end{array}$$

A pre-estimate of 81.6 ÷ 3 might be 'less than 30, but more than 25'. The calculation could then be presented as:

$$\begin{array}{r} 27.2 \\ 3\overline{)81.6} \\ \underline{60.0} \\ 21.6 \\ \underline{21.0} \\ .6 \\ \underline{.6} \\ 0 \end{array}$$

The result compares well with the pre-estimate. For division by a whole number, the decimal points and place values line up with each other. The place value rules continue into the decimal digits. This algorithm sets the model for other decimal divisions.

Division by a decimal A question such as 8.64 ÷ 2 follows the procedure above, because it is a division by a whole number. The question 8.64 ÷ 0.2 will often be set out (erroneously) in the same way, as follows:

$$\begin{array}{r} 4.32 \\ 0.2\overline{)8.64} \\ \underline{8.} \\ .64 \\ \underline{.6} \\ 4 \\ \underline{4} \\ 0 \end{array}$$

Of course, division by 0.2 should produce a different answer to division by 2 and thus there will need to be a modification to the method for division by 2. It could be worth discussing why the answer is ten times bigger.

A rephrasing of the language of the question can help. Instead of '8.64 divided by 0.2', the question can be understood as 'How many 0.2 s are there in 8.64?' or 'How many £0.20s are there in £8.64?' with the extra help of examining the value of 0.2(0) and of using money to set up the question. A pre-estimate is then unlikely to suggest anything like four for the answer. As a lead into this argument, the student could ask 'How many 0.2 s in 1?' Since the answer is 5, the answer 4.32 cannot be correct.

For the written, exact version, a solution to the problem lies in modifying the question so that it becomes a division by a whole number. This can be explained using the procedure used for equivalent fractions: 8.64 ÷ 0.2 may be written as:

$$\frac{8.64}{0.2} = \frac{8.64 \times 10}{0.2 \times 10} = \frac{86.4}{2} \text{ or } 86.4 \div 2$$

Multiplying the top and bottom of the fraction alters the division to 86.4 ÷ 2, without changing the final result (as in renaming fractions).

The division can then proceed as in earlier whole number examples:

$$\begin{array}{r} 43.2 \\ 2\overline{)86.4} \\ \underline{80.0} \\ 6.4 \\ \underline{6.0} \\ 4 \\ \underline{4} \\ 0 \end{array}$$

Further examples

- 0.695 ÷ 0.05 becomes 69.5 ÷ 5 (moving the digits in both numbers two place values by multiplying both by hundred). The traditional algorithm follows:

$$\begin{array}{r} 13.9 \\ 5\overline{)69.5} \\ \underline{50.0} \\ 19.5 \\ \underline{15.0} \\ 4.5 \\ \underline{4.5} \\ 0 \end{array}$$

- 13.2 ÷ 0.006 becomes 13200 ÷ 6 (multiplying both numbers by a thousand and thus moving the digits in both numbers three places).
- 0.13 ÷ 0.8 becomes 1.3 ÷ 8 (moving the digits in both numbers one place value).

```
     0.1625
  8)1.3000
     .8
     .50
     .48
      20
      16
       40
       40
        0
```

Note that in the final example 1.3 was written as 1.3000. The extra zeros are optional (see Chapter 11) and do not affect the value, but do help with the setting out of the question and lining up the digits in the correct places.

Approximations/rounding

Sometimes it is desirable to give an approximate answer in round figures. For example, £8.28 might be described as 'nearly £8.30(£8.3)', or 'about £8'.

- For rounding to one decimal place (tenths) view 8.28 as being between 8.20 and 8.30. It is nearer to 8.30, because it is above the halfway position of 8.25. Therefore, rounded to 1 decimal place, 8.28 would be written as 8.3.
- For rounding to the nearest whole number, an analysis of 8.28 shows that it lies somewhere between 8 and 9. It is nearer to 8, because it is below the halfway position of 8.50. Therefore, rounded to the nearest whole number, 8.28 would be written as 8.
- A number line (Figure 13.2) shows quite clearly which approximation is nearer.

A numerical policy is more readily applicable, however. The accepted policy is demonstrated in Table 13.1 through rounding a complete set of numbers to 1 decimal place (nearest tenth). The place to be retained is separated by a line from the place to be removed.

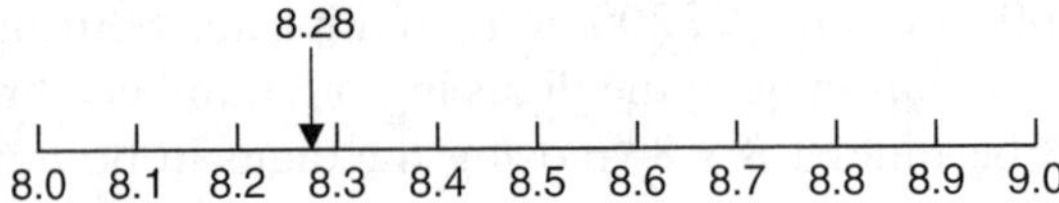

Figure 13.2 Using a number line to round decimal numbers.

Table 13.1 Rounding decimal numbers.

		Nearer to	*Rounded to*
.60 = .6	0	.60*	.6
.61 = .6	1	.60	.6
.62 = .6	2	.60	.6
.63 = .6	3	.60	.6
.64 = .6	4	.60	.6
.65 = .6	5	.70*	.7 by convention
.66 = .6	6	.70	.7
.67 = .6	7	.70	.7
.68 = .6	8	.70	.7
.69 = .6	9	.70	.7

- When the place to be removed contains a five or more, the number retained is rounded up. This is a convention and thus a rule.
- When the place to be removed contains a four or less, the number retained is rounded down 0.

This is the policy that is normally applied, because it is even-handed: half of the numbers are rounded up and half are rounded down.

Sometimes a division will produce an answer that is too long, and will have to be shortened, by rounding off excess/unnecessary places. Indeed, some divisions, such as 39.5 ÷ 7 would carry on forever. The early part of this calculation is shown:

$$39.5 \div 7 = 5.6428571$$

The answer to this division is now given in various approximations:

- 6 to the nearest whole number, because a 6 creates a rounding up
- 5.6 to 1 decimal place, because a 4 creates a rounding down
- 5.64 to 2 decimal places, because a 2 creates a rounding down
- 5.643 to 3 decimal places, because an 8 creates a rounding up

Some decimals are particularly awkward to round. For example, approximating 9.999 to two decimal places. When rounding off the 9 in the second decimal place, then it is affected by the 9 in the third decimal place. This dictates that the 9 in the second decimal place, the hundredths now becomes ten hundredths, one tenth.

$$\begin{array}{r} 9.99 \\ \underline{+0.01} \\ 10.00 \end{array}$$

The act of rounding up has a knock-on effect for the other digits. The two zeros after the decimal point must be retained even though they are normally regarded as optional. They are needed here to show the approximation to the required number of decimal places.

Rounding must be performed in a single step, for accuracy. Rounding in stages can produce errors. For example:

6.247 becomes 6.2 correct to 1 decimal place

But, using stages:

6.247 becomes 6.25 to 2 decimal places and then
6.25 becomes 6.3 to one decimal place, which is incorrect.

Converting harder fractions to decimals

In this chapter, it is possible to cover the types of example like $\frac{5}{9}$, which were beyond the scope of the methods used in Chapter 11. The diagrams in Figure 13.3 are intended to show that $\frac{5}{9}$ is the same as 5 ÷ 9.

The conversion of $\frac{5}{9}$ to a decimal can now be achieved by calculating 5 ÷ 9 as a decimal division, and rounding the answer to, say, three decimal places. It will be necessary to work out four decimal places, so that the size of the fourth decimal place, and its consequent effect on the third decimal place, can be determined.

$$\begin{array}{r} 0.5555,\text{etc.} \\ 9\overline{)5.0000} \\ \underline{4.5} \\ 50 \\ \underline{45} \\ 50 \\ \underline{45} \\ 50 \\ 45 \end{array}$$

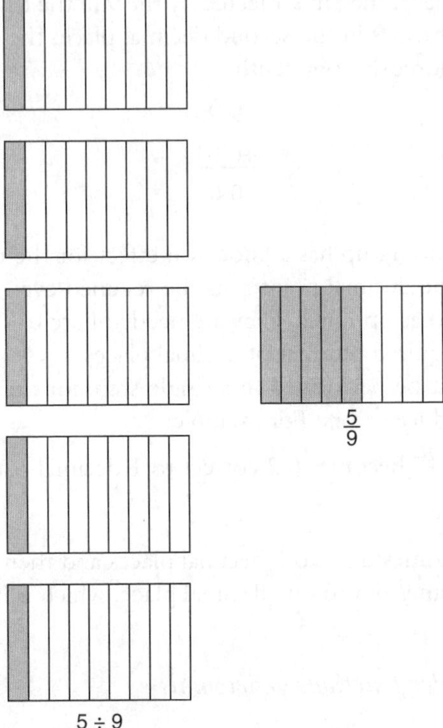

Figure 13.3 Converting fractions to decimals.

0.5555 = 0.556 correct to three decimal places.

$\frac{5}{9}$ = .556 correct to three decimal places.

This method of conversion works for any fraction, even the earlier easy examples. Furthermore, in Chapter 11, it was seen that the conversion of ⅞ to a decimal requires some special knowledge. Now it can be carried out mechanically as 7 ÷ 8.

```
   0.875
8)7.000
  6.4
    60
    56
     40
     40
     00
```

$\frac{7}{8}$ is equivalent to the exact decimal .875.

Of course, such divisions can be carried out using by calculators, with the ever-present caveat, that the student can find an approximate answer beforehand.

Summary

In this chapter we have tried to explain and rationalise the methods used. We have also given some pragmatic rules to remember. Our hope is that the underlying understanding supports the memory for the rules.

- For addition or subtraction, all the decimal points of the question and the answer line up vertically.
- Modify the numbers in a division by making the divisor a whole number. This is achieved by multiplying both numbers by the same appropriate power of ten.
- The decimal points in a multiplication do not line up. The number of decimal places in the answer is given by the total number of decimal places from the numbers in the question. Then the actual numbers can be multiplied together in the normal way.
- Multiplication and division of decimals by ten, hundred, thousand, and so on, never changes the digits, nor their sequence – they merely move them to new place values. The number of places moved is dictated by the power of the ten used, whereas the direction of movement gives a bigger answer for multiplication, and a smaller answer for division.

Because addition, subtraction and multiplication ultimately follow the same rule, some teachers prefer to teach them first, in the given order. Division, often perceived as the odd one out, is then dealt with last.

Finally, and leaving out much of the detail, the policy for approximating when rounding is summarised by the following:

- Five or more means round up.
- Four or less means round down.

14

Percentages

Introduction

In Chapter 11, percentages were related to decimals and fractions in an attempt to show the pattern of relationships between these concepts and, it is hoped, to make them mutually supportive in the development of the concept of numbers less than one. In this chapter, the work will be extended to all numbers, including those greater than one, but the key reference values of 50%, 20%, 10%, 5%, 2% and 1% will be used to build pre-and post-estimates and to check if an answer and/or the process used to solve the problem make sense. The main objective of this chapter is to provide concrete and visual images of percentages so that the formulae and algorithms are understood and that the understanding acts as an anchor for memory. This is achieved by focusing on a hundred and on one.

An Image of Percentage

Since percentage relates to 100, the image presented to the learner should involve a clear demonstration of 100. Further, it should demonstrate dividing the quantity up into 100 parts, thereby identifying one part out of the hundred parts. The 100 square (Figure 14.1) has been used throughout this book in several applications.

Mathematics for Dyslexics and Dyscalculics: A Teaching Handbook, Fourth Edition.
Steve Chinn and Richard E. Ashcroft.

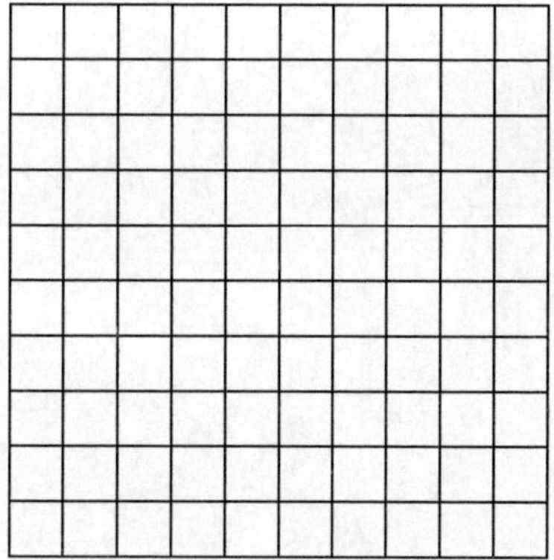

Figure 14.1 100%.

This chapter will deal with three types of percentage problems:

- Type 1 is 'What is x% of N?' This is finding the percentage of a quantity.
- Type 2 is 'What percentage of y is x?' This is expressing one quantity as a percentage of another.
- Type 3 is 'x is n% of which number?' This is finding the original number.

Each type is explained in turn.

Type 1: 'What is x% of N?'

An example can be used to show the hundred square in use. Start with an example where the pupil is likely to know the answer from the introductory work done in Chapter 11. The question chosen to set the procedure in familiar territory is, 'What is 5% of 300?'

A general method that will be applicable to any percentage of any number uses 1%. So the first step is to calculate 1%. This is done by dividing the number by 100, so a knowledge of the role of place value when dividing by 100 is essential.

Example 1 5% of 300

1% is computed by using one hundredth, $\frac{1}{100}$, that is, dividing by 100

300 ÷ 100 is 3

5% of a number will be 5 times the 1% value

5% of 300 is 5×3.

5% of 300 is 15 (Figure 14.2)

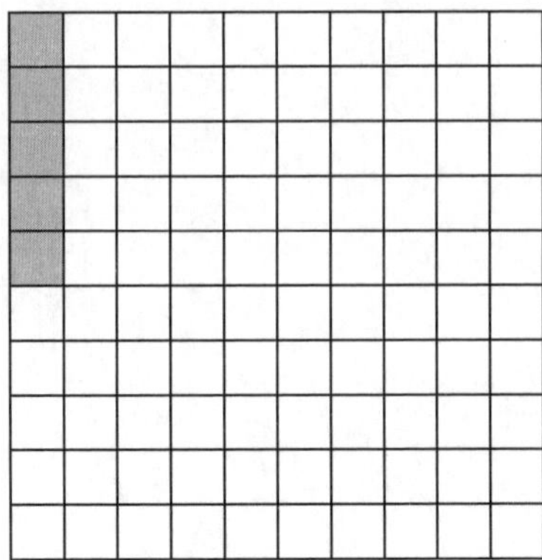

Figure 14.2 The whole square represents 300. One square is 3. Five squares are 15. 5% of 300 = 15.

The 100 square can be pictured as representing the 100% of the number, in this example, 300. So each single square represents 3.

Alternatively the visual image could be of three 100 squares, where each single square represents 1.

Example 2 *'What is 12% of 400?'*

Again, start by finding 1%

1% is one hundredth, so divide 400 by 100

$400 \div 100 = 4$

1% is 4

12% will be 12 times the 1% value

$12\% = 12 \times 4 = 48$

This could be written as a flow chart (Figure 14.3):

The process is: dividing up into 100 (equal) parts to obtain 1 part (1%), use the 1% value to find any other percentage.

The answer can be checked against key values (see later).

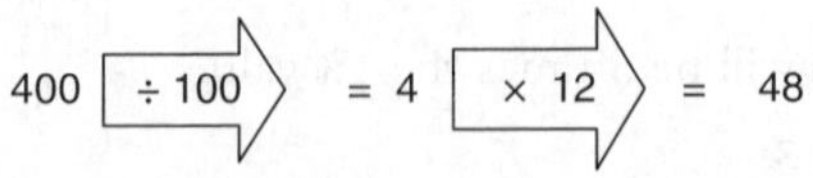

400 [÷ 100] = 4 [× 12] = 48

Figure 14.3 Flow chart for 12% of 400.

Example 3 'What is 15% of 60?'
Again, start by finding 1%

1% is one hundredth, so divide 60 by 100

$60 \div 100 = 0.6$

15% will be 15 times the 1% value

$15\% = 15 \times 0.6 = 9$

(15×6 could be computed as 10×0.6 plus 5×0.6, where 5×0.6 gives half the answer of 10×0.6)

This could be written as a flow chart:

60 [÷ 100 ⇨] = 0.6 [× 15 ⇨] = 9

The work can be extended, depending on the age and ability of the learner, to lead to the general formula for the following question:

$$\text{'What is } n\% \text{ of } N\text{?'} \quad n(N \div 100) \quad \text{or} \quad \left(\frac{N}{100}\right)n$$

Whatever the question, learners should be encouraged to compare their answers with estimates based on the 'easy' numbers of 1%, 2%, 5%, 10%, 20%, 25%, 50% and 75%.

Type 2: 'What percentage of y is x?'
This type of percentage is often presented as an examination-score type of question such as the following:

'If a learner gets 46 out of 85 in his maths examination, what is his percentage mark?'

A simple exemplar can be used to illustrate the procedure and act as a check, should the learner forget the procedure. So we could start with the following question:

What percentage mark is 40 out of 80?

The pupil should know that this is 50%, but is asked to write out the fraction, $^{40}/_{80}$ ('40 out of 80') and convert it (by dividing) into a decimal:

$$^{40}/_{80} = ^{1}/_{2} = 1 \div 2 = 0.5$$

The pupil should convert this to a percentage, that is, a fraction out of 100, by multiplying by 100/100.

$$0.5 \times \frac{100}{100} = \frac{50}{100} = 50\%$$

This format requires the learner to convert a fraction, *x/y*, into a decimal and then into a percentage. The decimal gives the score out of 1. To make this a score out of 100, that is, a percentage, multiply by 100.

So, in the example above, 46 out of 85 becomes 46/85 = 0.5412, or 0.5412 out of 1, which converts to a percentage of 54.12% or 54.12 out of 100.

Again the first step uses one percent.

If we refer back to Chapter 11, the procedure could also be seen as one of changing the fraction *x/y* to an equivalent fraction with a denominator 100. The learner has to appreciate that a percentage is a fraction with a denominator of 100, but where the convention is that only the value of the numerator is quoted and the symbol % tells us that this value is 'out of 100'.

Again the result can be compared with key values. In this example, 46/85 is a little over a half and thus a little over 50%.

Type 3: 'x is n% of which number?'

Again the focus is on 1%. So, in an example such as, '36 is 12% of which number?' the first operation is to calculate 1%. Using the 100 square image again, the question is, 'What goes into one small square?'

The student is asked, 'If there are 36 objects shared into 12 small squares, can you work out how many there are in one square?' The answer should be found by computing 36 ÷ 3, giving an answer, 'three in each square'. The calculation of 100% is then a matter of multiplying three by a 100, providing the answer 300.

As another example, '10.5 is 15% of what number?'

If 10.5 is 15%, then 1% is 10.5 ÷ 15

$10.5 \div 15 = 0.7$

1% is 0.7, so 100% is

$0.7 \times 100 = 70$

In all three types, 1% is the key to finding the answer.

Estimates from key values

In Chapter 11 we explained the relationship between fractions, decimals and percentages. In Chapter 7 we showed how all basic multiplication facts could be accessed by using the key numbers, 1, 2, 5 and 10. This principle can be extended to percentages for estimating and for many everyday applications.

The key facts are the following:

100% is 1, that is, all of the quantity.*

50% is ½, that is, half of the quantity, obtained by dividing by 2.

10% is $\frac{1}{10}$, that is, one-tenth of the quantity, obtained by dividing by 10.

1% is $\frac{1}{100}$, that is, one-hundredth of the quantity, obtained by dividing by 100.

These can then be extended by relationships such as:

2% is twice 1%

5% is half of 10%

2.5% is half of 5%

20% is twice 10%

25% is half of 50%

75% is 50% + 25%

Once again, interrelating these numbers to the target number can make many calculations much easier, provide estimates and enhance the learner's understanding of the concept of percentages. It is yet another example of working from (and using) what the learner knows to take him to what he can know. In doing this, you are returning to previously taught facts and procedures and reinforcing work that has been covered earlier.

Consider the problems of the format 'What is *n*% of *N*?'

*It is worth explaining to pupils that there can be percentage values above 100% (as in football managers asking their players for 110%). So, 200% is 2×, 500% is 5×, 150% is 1.5× and so on. And for pay-day loans these can be over 1000%.

Example What is 50% of £88?

$$£88 \div 2 = £44$$

This value can be halved again to give 25% of £88 as £22.

50% gives a reasonable estimate for values from 45% to 55%.

Example What is 10% of £88?

£88 ÷ 10 = £8.80 (You may have to explain that .8 translates to .80 for money and vice versa, that is, .80 keyed into a calculator will be displayed on the screen as .8).

The two values, 10% and 50%, can be combined to give 40% and 60%, for example 40% of £88 is 50% – 10%.

$$£44 - £8.80 = £35.20$$

The 10% value can be doubled to give 20%:

and halved to give 5%;

and halved again to give 2.5%.

To obtain 1% of £88, divide by 100:

$$88 \div 100 = 0.88$$

This can be doubled for 2%.

So several key values have been obtained with just basic calculations, allowing the learner to combine values from a selection of: 1 %, 2 %, 5 %, 10 %, 20 %, 25 % and 50 %.

Summary

The one hundred square provides images of 1% and 100% in a way that allows the algorithm to be related directly to the image. The learner has to evaluate the data in each question and form a mental image of what goes into each one square in order to understand this concept and its procedures.

The estimation procedure allows the learner to check if his calculation is reasonable and also acts as a simple method for calculating percentages in daily life such as discounts in sales, which tend to be easy values, and tipping in restaurants.

15

Time

This chapter addresses two aspects of work with time: telling the time and simple problems involving time. We feel that the topic is often underrated in terms of its difficulty. This is probably because time is pervasive in everyday life and we take the skill of 'telling' the time for granted. Copeland (1984) observed that at age ten some pupils are still not ready for a true understanding of this concept. If the pupil is dyslexic or dyscalculic, even at the age of ten he may not be ready for mastery of time. In fact, being unable to tell the time is a classic weakness for many dyslexics. The advent of the digital watch and smart phone has enabled more pupils to 'tell' the time, but this does not mean they have any understanding of what they 'tell'.

Telling the time or, preferably, understanding the time is an important life skill. Understanding the 24-hour clock is an essential skill when travelling, but for many learners dealing with time in a 24-hour context is much more challenging than using a.m. and p.m. and a 12-hour clock. Time also shifts the number bases we use to 12 and 60. It also has a time line, as contrasted to a number line, that is a circle. There are other challenging differences, for example the number of words related to time (Haylock and Cockburn, 1997).

Our comments about the paucity of research into dyscalculia and dyslexia and mathematics pale into insignificance when we look for research into time.

Mathematics for Dyslexics and Dyscalculics: A Teaching Handbook, Fourth Edition.
Steve Chinn and Richard E. Ashcroft.

What are the Potential Problems with Time?

Time is complicated by the large number of apparent inconsistencies that learners have to address (Chinn, 2001). Time involves new numerical ideas, for example using number bases of 12, 24 and 60. The language of time can be misleading, for example we say, 'Five past one' and write 1:05 or even more challengingly, 'Ten to nine' and write 8:50. The language of time itself has to be carefully explained and the language we use to explain time has to be carefully chosen to be as unambiguous as possible. For example, a classic mistake that American pupils make is to write 'Quarter past four' as 4:25, using the familiar money/dollar interpretation of 'quarter' as 25 cents. However, an analysis of the data used to standardise a 15-minute test (Chinn, 2017a) revealed this as a common error in the UK, too. Another potential ambiguity is with 24-hour time, where 08:00 is pronounced as 'O eight hundred', which does not reinforce the concept of 60 minutes in an hour.

There are directional complications, for example, we count on in minutes after the hour until we reach thirty minutes past the hour and then we countdown the minutes to the next hour, for example, 'twenty minutes to six' (Figure 15.2). Fractions are used, but only half and quarters (Figure 15.1). The numbers on a clock face only refer to hours. The user has to work out the minutes. A time may be written in a way that looks like a decimal, but 8.30 is in fact half past eight and 8.50 is not half past eight.

After working over the years with dyslexic pupils, we got used to being greeted with, 'Good afternoon' at breakfast time.

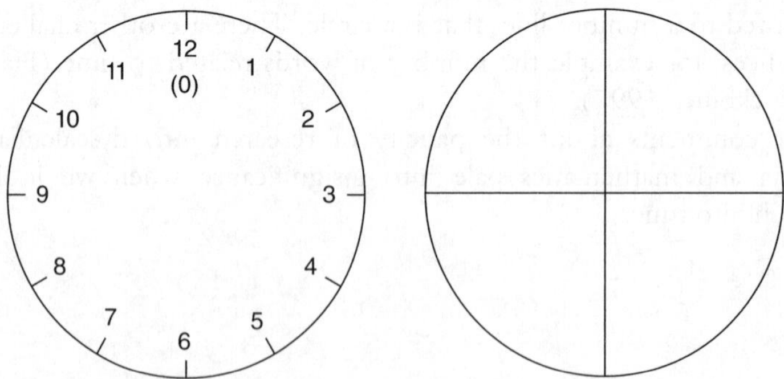

Figure 15.1 The clock face and quarters.

Setting the scene: the overview

The adage, 'working from what the pupil knows to what he can know' applies, of course, to time. Although digital watches, digital clocks and mobile phones are now common, the analogue clock face is still a familiar sight. The advantage of the analogue clock face is that it provides a context for time. It gives 12 a prominent place and 12 is an important part of many calculations involving time. It gives a visual image of time past and time to go.

So, a clock face is a good visual aid. A cheap cardboard play clock has the disadvantage of not having synchronised hand movements. It is possible to buy geared demonstration clocks where the hour hand moves as the minute hand is moved (see Appendix 2, Resources). Watching a working clock gives some idea of the relative values/speeds of second, minute and hour hands.

The clock face allows teachers to explain the key facts: that there are 12 hours, used twice in a day for a.m and p.m. (**a**nte **m**eridian/before midday and **p**ost **m**eridian/after midday), that there are 60 minutes in an hour and 60 seconds in a minute, and that each hour mark also represents a five-minute interval for the minute hand and a five-second interval for the second hand.

Starting with the assumption that the pupil has some awareness of time, a few questions will determine how large or how little that knowledge base is. Questions that use the pupil's experiences should be used, such as what time school finishes, what time lunch break starts, or what time a favourite programme begins on television. As pupils give each time, the teacher writes them on the board and shows them on a clock. Work of this kind focuses on showing the pupil the use of hours and minutes to identify the time, without the pupil having to find and read them from a clock.

Work can be focused on terms such as 'o'clock', 'quarter past', 'half past' and 'quarter to' in order to fix some key reference times and introduce the concepts of a mix of hours and minutes and of using 'to' and 'past'. So, half past can also be expressed as '30 minutes past'. There is this flexibility in the language used for time and it needs to be introduced to the learner. For example, the relationship between morning and a.m. and between afternoon and evening and p.m. should be taught, highlighting the significant times, 12 noon and 12 midnight. If learners can grasp these key reference times they will be on the first step towards accuracy, but will also have an acceptable level of accuracy for many everyday needs. This acceptable level in everyday life often means saying, for example, 'almost quarter past' rather than 'thirteen minutes past', which can sound pedantic.

Other key ideas that need to be introduced in an overview are the circular nature of the clock, that is, for example, everyday has a 1:00 a.m. and a 1:00 p.m., and time moves in cycles. Also, there is our convention of counting the minutes after an hour only until we reach half past the hour and then counting down the minutes to the next hour (29, 28, 27, 26), so we start to name a particular hour 30 minutes before we reach it and cease using it 30 minutes after we pass it. There is an old conundrum, 'How far can you walk into a wood? Halfway, and then you are walking out.'

Reading the Time

Times may sometimes be written as though they were a decimal number, for example, 6.21. This can create confusion with pupils writing 'one and a half hours' as 1.30 hours. This confusion between the 60-minute nature of time and decimal notation may also encourage pupils to enter the time into a calculator as a decimal. We would recommend using the colon, as in 5:43 for example, to avoid this potential confusion in early experiences of learning about time.

Digital time is easy to read, but may not give the meaning of reading the analogue time. Older learners may be more comfortable with 'Five to eight' rather than '7:55', possibly because it seems more relevant to everyday experiences, possibly because it sounds less pedantic, precise and formal or possibly because it gives them a better sense of their location in time.

Quarter past, half past and quarter to

These key reference times, phrased in the way we use them in the UK, should be relatively easy to master. Pupils may refer back to previous base ten experiences of quarters and half. First we divide a circle to show the hours and then mark the 60-minute intervals. Pupils can then practise estimation skills by judging the time as being closer to one of these, for example 6:40 could be expressed as 'almost quarter to seven'. The convention of counting on the minutes up to half past an hour and counting down the minutes to go to the next hour after half past an hour can be reviewed by focusing on quarters. As ever, the structure of any topic should incorporate as many reviews as possible and it is better if these are from slightly different perspectives each time. This strategy can be practised with a clock face. The pupils are shown a time, say 4:11 and need to say the nearest quarter, half or o'clock ('quarter past four').

There is some rationalisation in the use of 'past' and 'to' (Figure 15.2) in that we only refer to the nearest hour, so the nearest hour at 38 minutes past an hour is the next hour. Half past, that is 30 minutes past is the changeover point. There is a similarity here to rounding up and rounding down (Figure 15.3).

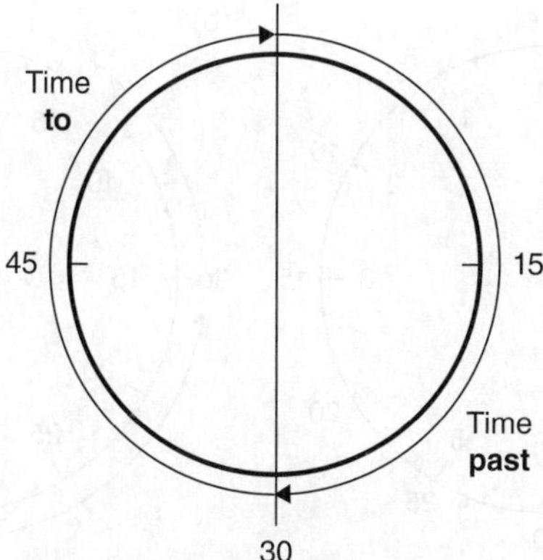

Figure 15.2 The clock face and halves: counting 'past' and 'to'.

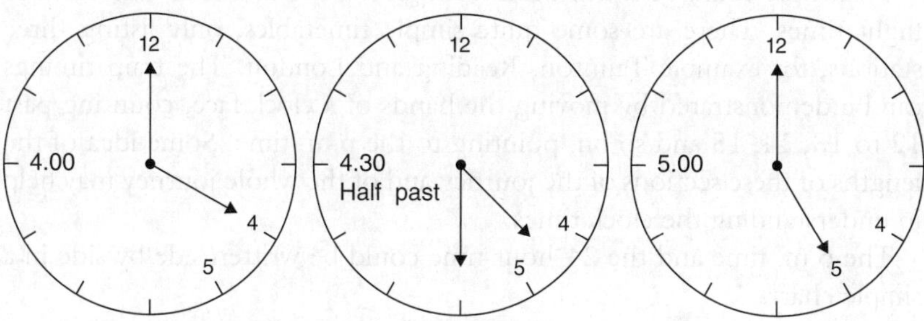

Figure 15.3 Four o'clock, half past four, five o'clock.

Minutes past and minutes to

This topic extends the work done on quarters and half. The first 30 minutes after an hour are normally referred to as 'past the hour'. The next 29 minutes are normally used to count down to the next hour. The quarters can be used for mid-point check values. So, the further the minute hand goes past the hour, the greater the number of minutes … counting up. The closer the hand goes to the (next) hour, the fewer the number of minutes … counting down (Figure 15.4a and 15.4b).

The 24-hour clock

While pupils come across times such as 8:30 a.m. and 10:15 p.m. on a daily basis, they will be less familiar with the 24-hour clock. They may know, and should revisit this anyway, that there are 24 hours in a day, that analogue clocks almost always show only 12 hours and that digital clocks show either 12 hours or 24 hours when programmed to do so.

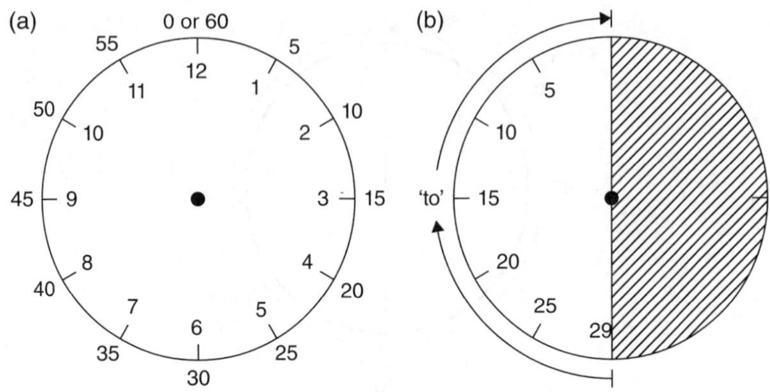

Figure 15.4 (a) Hours and minutes. Figure 15 (b) 'Minutes to'.

This topic could be introduced through the use of a train timetable or flight times. There are some quite simple timetables, only listing three stations, for example Taunton, Reading and London. The train timings can be demonstrated by moving the hands of a clock face, counting past 12 to 13, 14, 15 and so on, pointing to the p.m. time. Some idea of the lengths of these sections of the journey and of the whole journey may help in understanding the clock times.

The p.m. time and the 24-hour time could be written side by side in a simple chart.

12:00 p.m. 12:00
1:00 p.m. 13:00
2:00 p.m. 14:00
3:00 p.m. 15:00
4:00 p.m. 16:00
5:00 p.m. 17:00
6:00 p.m. 18:00
7:00 p.m. 19:00
8:00 p.m. 20:00
9:00 p.m. 21:00
10:00 p.m. 22.00
11:00 p.m. 23:00
12:00 a.m. 24:00 (see Figure 15.5)

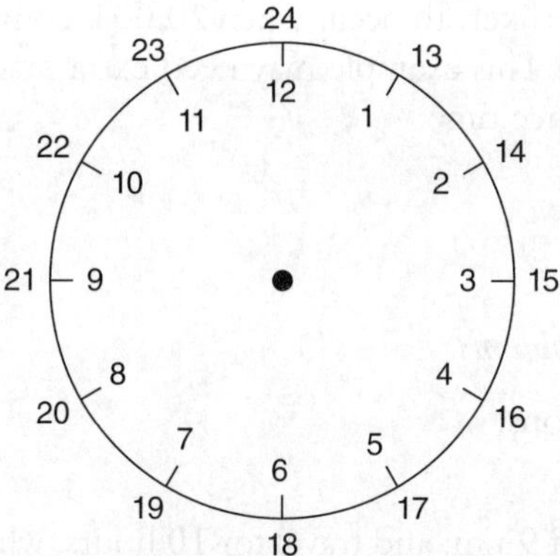

Figure 15.5 The 24-hour clock.

The pattern should be clear from this chart, but the additions of time with the 12-hour clock and the 24-hour clock produces some strange looking results when viewed with base ten experiences in mind:

$$6 + 3 = 9$$

$$7 + 4 = 11$$

$$8 + 7 = 15 \quad \text{(24-hour clock)}$$

$$8 + 7 = 3 \quad \text{(12-hour clock)}$$

$$10 + 8 = 18 \quad \text{(24-hour clock)}$$

$$10 + 8 = 6 \quad \text{(12-hour clock)}$$

Explaining this inconsistency in the rules of addition (because we are using base 12) as applied to the 24-hour clock may help the pupil's understanding of its relationship to the 12-hour clock. This is another example of inhibition, the student has to inhibit their base ten interpretation, and another example of the tendency of first learning experiences, base ten, to be dominant.

A similar chart could be set up by the pupil for a typical day in his life, starting with waking up time, through school time, to dinner time and evening time. The conversion from p.m. to 24-hour time requires the pupil to add 12 to the p.m. time. The conversion from 24-hour clock to p.m. time requires the pupil to subtract 12 from the former time. Thus, this is another example of reversible operations.

The classic error is likely to occur when 20:00 is converted to 10:00 p.m. instead of 8:00 p.m. This example may need extra practice or can even be used as a key reference time.

Time Problems

Finishing-time problems

Some typical questions:

Problem A:
If I start a journey at 9 a.m. and travel for 10 hours, when do I arrive at my destination? or, the more difficult:

Problem B:
If I start a journey at 8:45 p.m. and travel for 2 hours 37 minutes, when do I arrive at my destination?

Several alternative methods are available for these problems, which are essentially addition, but not with base ten. Once again, the use of alternative methods addresses the individual needs of learners and also provides a means for checking an answer.

Using the clock face as a number line and bridging the 12 boundary Problem A (Figure 15.6):
Use 12:00 noon as the key intermediate stage, so:

9:00 to 12:00 = 3 hours
This leaves 10 – 3 = 7 hours left to travel
12:00 + 7 = 7 p.m. is the finishing time

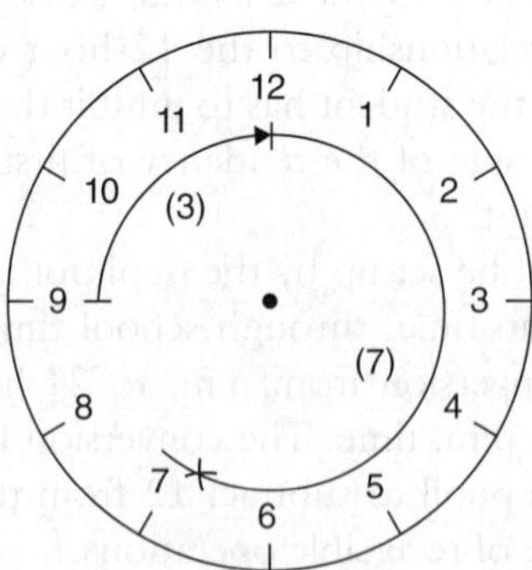

Figure 15.6 Using the clock as a circular number line.

Using a linear time line Problem B:

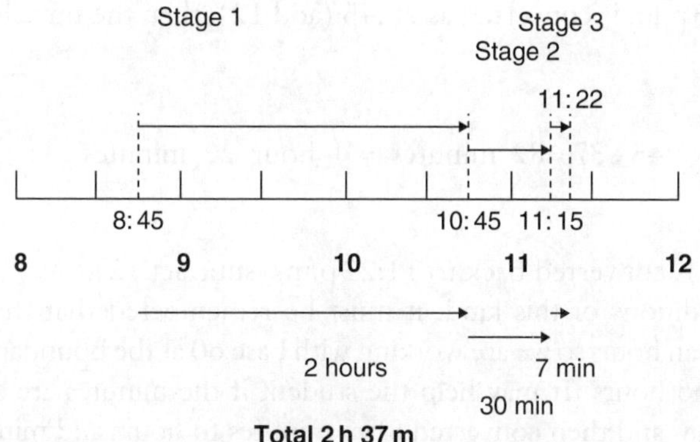

The numbers on a clock face are rolled out to make a 'time line' and the journey is represented in stages.

Stage 1. Move 2 hours down the time line, 8:45 to 10:45 p.m.
Stage 2. Move 30 minutes down the time line, 10:45 to 11:15 p.m.
Stage 3. Move the remaining 7 minutes, 11:15 to 11:22 p.m.

The method encourages the pupil to work with easy chunks of time. The principle of 'easy' chunks was used for both long multiplication and division (see Chapters 9 and 10). It may be necessary to discuss and identify what are 'easy' chunks. These are likely to be hours and half hours, and in some 'moves' there may be a back move to compensate for an over addition, for example while adding 55 minutes it may be effective to move down the line by 60 minutes and then back by 5 minutes.

This is another example of the use of the same strategies being used throughout the arithmetic curriculum, for example when nine was added by adding ten and subtracting one.

Conversion to the 24-hour clock

If time can be converted to the 24-hour clock format, then the travelling time is simply added to the starting time. This time can then be converted back into the 12-hour format if required.

Problem A:

When 9:00 a.m. is converted as 09:00, then the travelling time is added on:

$$\begin{array}{r} 09{:}00 \\ \underline{+10{:}00} \\ 19{:}00 \end{array}$$

and 19:00 is converted back to 7:00 p.m. (subtract 12)

Problem B:
When 8:45 p.m. is converted as 20:45 (add 12), then the travelling time is added on:

$$\begin{array}{r} 20{:}45 \\ \underline{+2{:}37} \\ 23{:}22 \end{array} \qquad 45+37=82 \text{ minutes} = 1 \text{ hour } 22 \text{ minutes}$$

and 23:22 is converted back to 11:22 p.m. (subtract 12).

With additions of this kind, it must be remembered that there are 60 minutes in an hour, so we are working with base 60 at the boundary between minutes and hours. It may help the student if the minutes are added as a separate sum and then converted from minutes to hours and minutes.

Elapsed time problems

These are questions such as the following:

Problem C:
A woman works from 10:00 a.m. until 3:00 p.m. How long does she work?

Problem D:
A journey begins at 7:35 a.m. and ends at 1:27 p.m. How long is the journey?

Problems C and D can be solved by using modified versions of the methods used to solve problems A and B.

Problem C:
This could be solved by using the clock face as a number line and bridging the 12 boundary (see Figure 15.7).

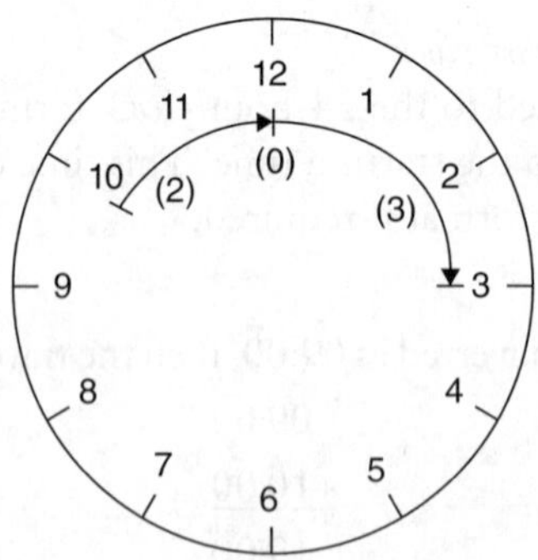

Figure 15.7 Using the clock as a circular number line.

Or Problem C can be solved by bridging 12 noon without the use of the drawing of a clock:

Time worked up to 12:00 noon, 12:00 – 10:00 = 2 hours
Time worked after 12:00 noon, 3:00 – 0:00 = 3 hours
Total time worked = 2 + 3 = 5 hours

The pupil has to understand that 12:00 noon also acts as zero for p.m. and a.m. time. 12:00 noon and 12:00 midnight are where 12-hour day time returns to 0:00. It is a key fact in the use of a circular time line that is used for the analogue clock face.

Problem D:
Using a linear time line:

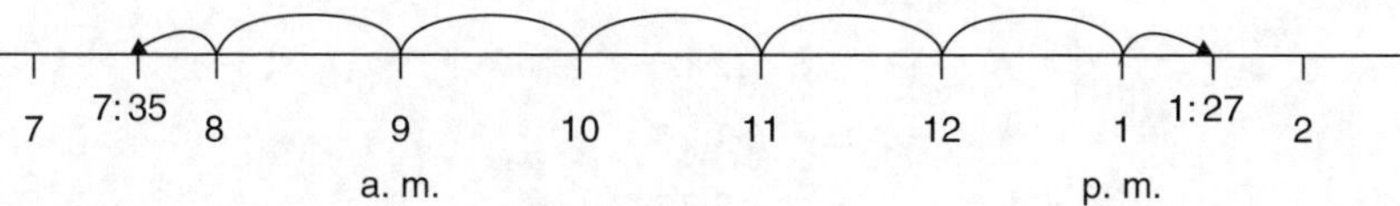

Without the time line:

Time travelled from 7:35 to 8:00 = 25 minutes
Time travelled from 8:00 to 12:00 = 4 hours
Time travelled from 12:00 to 1:00 = 1 hour
Time travelled from 1:00 to 1:27 = 27 minutes
Total time travelled = 5 hours 52 minutes

Conversion to the 24-hour clock
This transforms both the problems into time subtractions, where again the pupil must remember that he is using a 60-minute number base for one hour.

Problem C:
Convert the finishing time

3:00 p.m. + 12 = 15:00

Subtract the starting time

−10:00

Time worked (elapsed) 5:00 hours

Problem D:
Convert the finishing time <1:27, 13:27, 7:35>

$$1{:}27\text{ p.m.} + 12 = 13{:}27$$

Subtract the starting time

$$-7{:}35$$

At this stage, there are more options, for example estimating that the answer is approximately 6 hours (slightly less) and a refinement of this estimate could be used to arrive at an accurate answer (comparing 27 minutes with 35 minutes, the adjustment is to take off 8 minutes from 6:00 hours).

Alternatively, we could take an hour from the 13 and change it to 60 minutes, using a decomposition/renaming method, but trading for 60 rather than the 10 used in a base ten number calculation

```
 12:87
 1̸3̸:2̸7̸
 –7:35
 -----
  5:52
```

Summary

The language and vocabulary used for time is full of inconsistencies that will confuse many learners, so the language and vocabulary used to explain this concept must be exceptionally clear and cognisant of the potential problems. Once again, the principles of starting with 'easy' examples that can be referred to as exemplars of methods and for estimations may be followed. The bridging strategy and the traditional subtraction algorithm of decomposition/renaming are also used, where 60 and 12 are used instead of 10. The clock face and the time line can be used to provide visual images for the calculation procedures. It is worth reiterating: 'Telling the time' is a task where difficulty is frequently underestimated (and may well be taught to children when they are too young to cope with the peculiar challenges).

16

Teaching the Full Curriculum

Introduction

Faced with a dyslexic or dyscalculic child who at a young age is experiencing great difficulty with mathematics, many teachers will feel it is best to persevere with the basics of numeracy until the child has mastered them. The teacher might regard these basics as so fundamentally important that to proceed to other topics would not seem to represent the best use of time or effort. As time passes, and the child continues to experience many of the same difficulties, the temptation is to concentrate even harder on a narrow range of activities. Such a situation can continue over a period of years, during which the child is enduring constant failure and losing all confidence in himself and the learning process. The loss of confidence is a serious additional problem in a subject where confidence in performance is so important – mathematics is like walking a tightrope, in the sense that if you think you are going to fall, then you will probably fall.

Varying the mathematical diet for such a child is a course of action that may have beneficial effects of three kinds:

- It may provide him with experience of some success and bring back some confidence.
- Even more importantly, it may begin a process that gives him an alternative way of looking at the subject – a way around his problems, when there may be no way through them. If building a wall can be used as a metaphor for the learning of mathematics, then the wall of a dyslexic or dyscalculic child will have many bricks missing for parts of the subject

Mathematics for Dyslexics and Dyscalculics: A Teaching Handbook, Fourth Edition.
Steve Chinn and Richard E. Ashcroft.

he has not mastered. Of course, a wall can remain standing despite a few gaps, with the support of the bricks around the gaps. The wider the wall, the more missing bricks it can bridge. If the maths wall of a child with learning difficulties cannot be built directly upwards, it should be built across and then upwards, by widening his mathematical experience, especially at the foundation levels.

- It may give him abilities, such as telling and understanding the time, which can be regarded as social or 'survival' skills (Copeland, 1984), the lack of which can be embarrassing for the child or his parents. Widespread access to digital displays of time via mobile phones now makes it possible to read the time (but not necessarily understand it).

Maths is a wide mixture of skills and knowledge, far beyond arithmetic. Topics such as graphs and geometry may be far more encouraging.

The introduction of mathematical topics other than number can be achieved in such a way that it also reinforces numerical work by using different contexts. In a single chapter, it is impossible to cover much curricular ground, but it is possible to describe some general principles and give a number of illustrative examples.

Some General Principles

Sound foundations

'Children who start behind, stay behind' (Geary, 2013).

In an ideal world we would not have children who 'start behind', but we do. Early learning sets the foundations for a subject that is developmental. The early curriculum should be about understanding and not just about pouring information and facts into brains.

If those foundations are missing, or weak, future progress will be handicapped. Hence the need to build reviews and revisits into the curriculum.

Plan for the long term

It is extremely important that long-term success should not be jeopardised for the sake of early gains through the use of short cuts that are not conceptually based. This can be taken to include reliance on special cases, mnemonics or too many rules, which dyslexics and dyscalculics are likely to forget, or remember inaccurately.

Examples

- When faced with the mixed fraction 3½, many secondary-aged dyslexics will feel they know how to convert it into a top-heavy fraction, because they remember a rule 'multiply that by that and add that'. When challenged which 'that' should be multiplied by which, and which 'that' should then be added, some will choose three times one add two, some will choose two times one add three, and some will choose two times three add one (the correct version). That most of them remember the rule inaccurately is bad enough, but what is even more dangerous is when they have a total conviction that they can rely on what they remember.
- In Chapter 12, the division of a fraction by another fraction was dealt with in two ways. One way was to make segment sizes the same and then divide the 'like with like'. The other way suggested, which initially seems bizarre, was to invert the divisor fraction and then multiply. It may be the bizarre nature of this rule, but it is one rule that adults seem to retrieve from their school day memories of maths. For students who do progress mathematically, this particular rule extends much further and has great value in algebraic fractions such as:

$$\frac{a^2b^3c}{w^2y^2z} \div \frac{abc}{wy^2z} = \frac{a^{\cancel{2}}b^{\cancel{3}2}\cancel{c}}{w^{\cancel{2}}\cancel{y}^{\cancel{2}}\cancel{z}} \times \frac{\cancel{w}\cancel{y}^{\cancel{2}\cancel{z}}}{\cancel{a}\cancel{b}\cancel{c}} = \frac{ab^2}{w}$$

Use illustrations of wide applicability

Once children understand the concept of area, and can fluently calculate the areas of rectangles, the area model can help in many ways. Towards the end of Chapter 9, the use of blocks for multiplications transforms into the use of scale drawings and then area sketches. For example, the single multiplication 38×14, viewed as $(30+8)(10+4)$, performed as the four partial products 30×10, 30×4, 8×10 and 8×4 can be illustrated using the areas in Figure 16.1.

38×14 is the area of the whole shape
$= \text{area A} + \text{area B} + \text{area C} + \text{area D}$
$= 30 \times 10 + 8 \times 10 + 30 \times 4 + 8 \times 4$
$= 300 + 80 + 120 + 32$
$= 532$

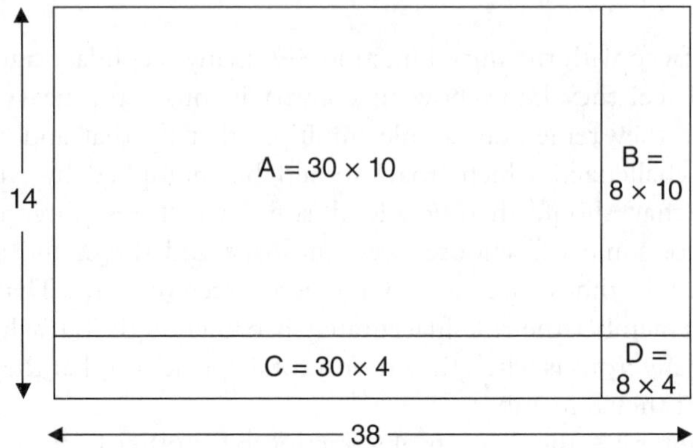

Figure 16.1 The area model for multiplying numbers.

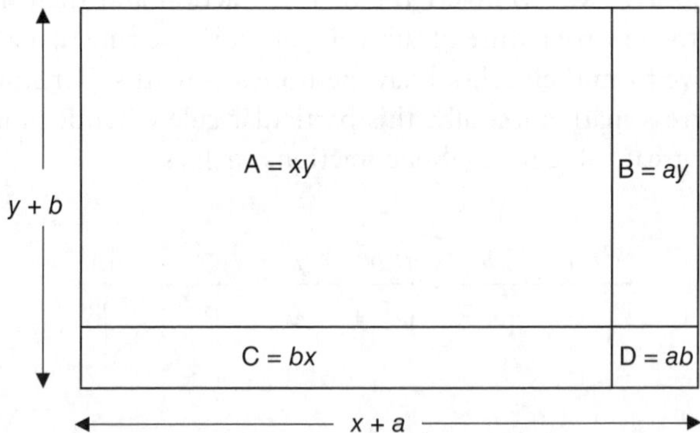

Figure 16.2 The area model for multiplying in algebra: $(x + a)(y + b)$.

This idea can be exploited in a very similar way, to perhaps even greater benefit, in algebraic multiplication. Figures 16.2 and 16.3 show how to work out two problems:

$$(x+a)(y+b) \text{ and } (x-a)(y-b)$$

For $(x+a)(y+b)$:
$(x+a)(y+b)$ is the area of the whole shape
$=$ area A + area B + area C + area D
$= xy + ay + bx + ab$

For $(x - a)(y - b)$:
This is done in stages:

Stage 1. Area (1) xy Figure 16.3a
Stage 2. Area (2) $y(x-a) = xy - ay$ Taking area B off area 1. Figure 16.3b
Stage 3. Area (3) $xy - ay - bx$. Taking area C off area 2. Figure 16.3c
Stage 4. Area (4) $(x-a)(y-b)$. Adding back area D, which has been taken off twice.

Area (4) is for $(x-a)(y-b) = xy - ay - by + ab$

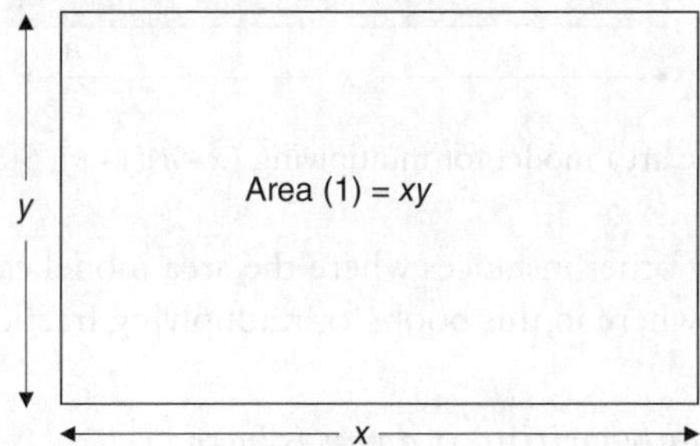

Figure 16.3a The area model for multiplying $(x-a)(y-b)$. Stage 1.

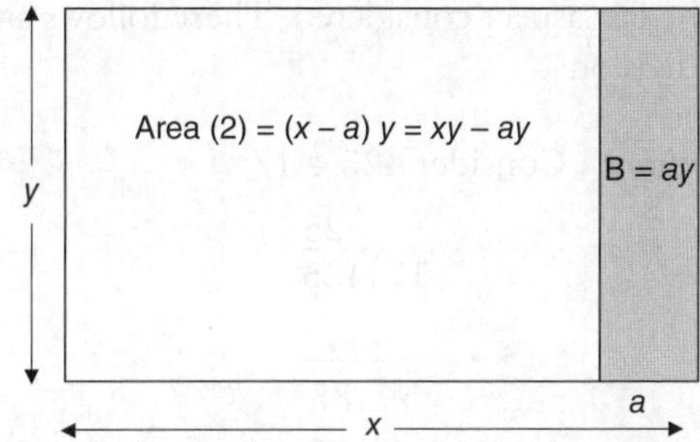

Figure 16.3b The area model for multiplying $(x-a)(y-b)$. Stage 2.

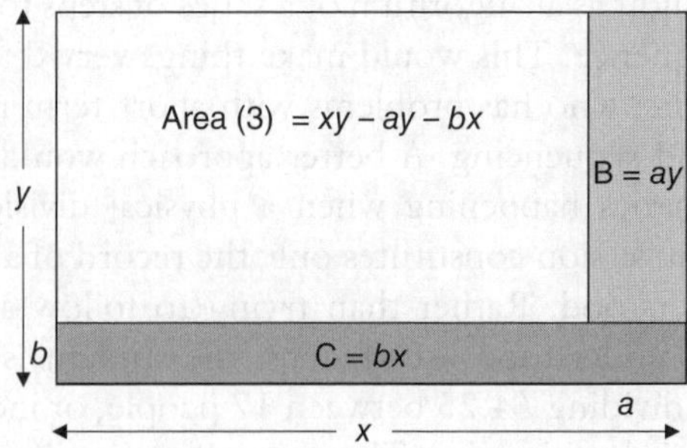

Figure 16.3c The area model for multiplying $(x-a)(y-b)$. Stage 3.

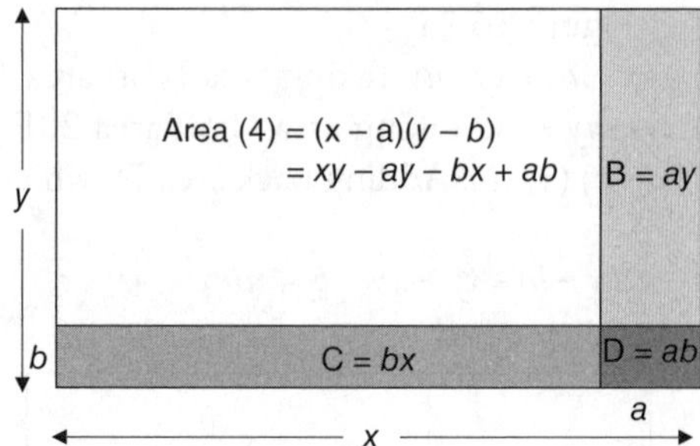

Figure 16.3d The area model for multiplying $(x-a)(y-b)$. Stage 4.

There are many other instances where the area model can prove invaluable. It is used elsewhere in this book, for multiplying fractions, for example.

'Maths is easy – only writing it down is hard'

It is all too common to consider only the written form of mathematics, the most difficult form for many dyslexics and dyscalculics. In fact, the written form should be the last aspect considered. There follows another variation of algorithm for division:

Example: long division Consider 425 ÷ 17:

$$\begin{array}{r} 25 \\ 17\overline{)425} \\ \underline{-34} \\ 85 \\ \underline{-85} \\ 0 \end{array}$$

It might be taught as an algorithm or a series of steps to be learned and performed in sequence. This would make things very difficult for a dyslexic or dyscalculic, who has problems with short-term memory, multiplication facts and sequencing. A better approach would be to consider the real mathematics happening when a physical division takes place. Then, the written version constitutes only the record of a common event that is well understood. Rather than trying to follow a badly remembered and badly understood list of steps, the student is better encouraged to imagine dividing £4.25 between 17 people, or indeed to actually perform the division with coins. The written steps *will* match the physical steps.

Consider the £4.25 as 425p, in the form of 4 one pound coins, 2 ten pence coins and 5 one penny coins. First, we would attempt to divide the 4 £1 coins between the 17 people:

$$17\overline{)4}$$

Clearly there are not enough even to have one each, so the 4 pounds would be changed into 40 ten pence pieces, which would added to the existing 2 to give 42:

$$17\overline{)42}$$

Now we would attempt to divide the 42 ten pence coins between the 17 people (a separate problem in itself). They would receive 2 each, and this would use up 34 of the ten pence coins:

$$\begin{array}{r} 2 \\ 17\overline{)42} \\ \underline{34} \end{array}$$

This would leave 8 ten pence coins that could not be divided between the 17 people:

$$\begin{array}{r} 2 \\ 17\overline{)\;42} \\ \underline{-34} \\ 8 \end{array}$$

These would be changed into 80 one penny coins, which is added to the existing 5 to give 85:

$$\begin{array}{r} 25 \\ 17\overline{)425} \\ \underline{-34} \\ 85 \end{array}$$

Now we would attempt to divide the 85 one penny coins among 17 people. They would receive 5 each and this would use up all 85, with none remaining:

$$\begin{array}{r} 25 \\ 17\overline{)425} \\ \underline{-34} \\ 85 \\ \underline{-85} \\ 00 \end{array}$$

The written form, obtained here by recording the physical steps, is identical with the version achievable using a difficult algorithm. The difference is that this teaches the child how to understand what has happened, and how to repeat it.

Example: a rule for equations Equations are a very important theme, a theme that runs all the way through maths. The highly stylised procedures to be followed for solving them are very likely to confuse many dyslexics and dyscalculics. Therefore it is necessary for a teacher to be extremely alert, sensitive and responsive as well as very careful about how this work is presented. Once again, the method that will be best understood is the method derived from physical experience.

For solving an equation like $x+3=8$, there are various schools of thought. Pupils can be taught with flow charts. They can be taught that equations are like balance scales, pivoted about the = sign, and that any operation must be done to both sides to maintain the balance. For this example, it is possible to subtract 3 from both sides to leave $x=5$. Although this method can be physically demonstrated with a special pair of balance scales, we have found that it can seem 'artificial' and lead to some awkward subtractions at times. Some pupils prefer another method, which they sometimes discover for themselves. The teacher covers up an 'unknown' number of counters, adds three more and then shows the result to be eight. If the pupils are then asked to describe how to find the original number, none of them have any doubt that the extra three must be subtracted (revealing the original five). In its written form, this appears as follows:

$$x + 3 = 8$$

then $x = 8 - 3$

and therefore $x = 5$

It looks as though the three has crossed over the = symbol and the + sign has changed to –. As the pupils describe it, the number that was added must now be subtracted. The written form has reflected what the pupils found self-evident.

For solving the equation:

$$\frac{x}{2} = 5$$

the teacher again covers up the 'unknown' number of counters, this time explaining that they are being divided into two equal groups and then showing one group to contain five. Now if the pupils are asked to suggest how to find the original number, they will suggest that the five should be doubled (multiplied by two) giving ten for the result. In its written form this appears as follows:

$$\frac{x}{2} = 5$$

$$\text{then} \qquad x = 5 \times 2$$

$$\text{and therefore } x = 10$$

It looks as though the two has crossed over the = symbol and its sign changed from division to multiplication, as the pupils suggested. Again the written form reflects the pupils' way of thinking.

Almost incidentally, the pupils have derived for themselves a rule (a mnemonic), which is easily remembered as:

Change the side. Change the sign

Although there is insufficient space here to demonstrate further examples, this is the rule pupils will usually carry with them throughout their mathematical careers, no matter how far they advance in the study of equations, and they will remember it all the better because they have understood it by having related it to a multisensory experience.

Teaching the Other Parts of the Curriculum

Some examples of other topics from a typical maths curriculum are explained. They often involve arithmetic still, but in different contexts.

Using and applying mathematics

Two uses for this kind of work are dealt with in this chapter. The work helps by combining different skills and knowledge from different mathematical areas. The other use is in investigations, where children examine a new piece of curricular work and derive a hypothesis for themselves. This use is not as daunting for the children as it sounds, particularly if careful and empathetic guidance is given.

The first example is the angle-sum of a triangle. This can start with a class activity where each child in the class draws a triangle, measures the angles and adds them up, then the result will be about 180° for all those who have not made a gross error. The gross errors might include mistakes in addition, or use of the wrong scale on the protractor. Once these have

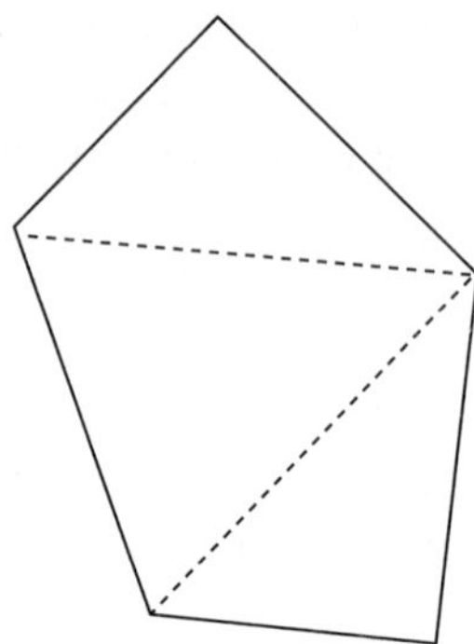

Figure 16.4 A pentagon divided as three triangles.

been corrected, there should be enough answers just above 180° to balance those just below 180° and persuade the children that 180° is the right answer. If the triangles are of many different shapes, then this will confirm the universal application of the result.

A more difficult, though related, example concerns the angle-sum for any polygon. This used to be taught as $2n-4$ right angles, which is a difficult formula to remember and employs less familiar units. When asked to investigate this polygon problem, instead of being given the formula, children might need the hint that they should divide the polygon into triangles (preferably all from one corner). If they all draw several polygons, they can be guided to the generalisation that you can always draw two triangles less than the number of sides of the polygon.

For the pentagon in Figure 16.4, this would be $5-2=3$ triangles. From what they already know, children would be able to work this out as $3\times 180^\circ = 540^\circ$. Having worked on the theory for themselves, they are more likely to have understood it. They are also more likely to remember it, either using the easier formula $(n-2)\times 180^\circ$, or in a form of words like 'two triangles less than the size', or simply resolving always to divide their polygons into as many triangles as it takes.

Algebra

It can be argued that for older children a significant portion of the study of mathematics involves not so much of an intellectual challenge as the acceptance and acquisition of conventions of mathematical syntax. Nowhere is this truer than in algebra. Of course, effective acquisition and retention requires thorough explanation and practice of every possible type of problem, based on understanding.

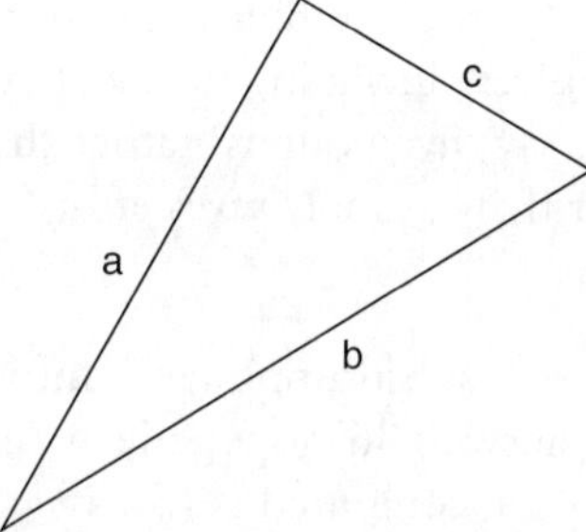

Figure 16.5 The perimeter of a triangle: $a+b+c$.

Two areas of major importance within algebra concern formulae and equations (Kitz and Nash, 1995).

Children will be expected to be able to derive formulae for simple situations. This is the skill of generalising. They will subsequently be expected to substitute values into given formulae, often to 'find' an unknown number. Algebra is often about generalising and finding. Many people only associate it with 'finding'.

When a problem finishes with a formula, for example, $a+b+c$ as the perimeter of the triangle in Figure 16.5, there are children who will be dissatisfied, based on their previous experiences in maths, with the lack of a numerical answer.

They can usually be convinced by the argument that a formula is an 'instruction' or a 'generalisation' about what to do when the values of a, b and c become known. In this sense a formula is superior because it applies to every triangle, while a numerical answer is only correct for one specific triangle. It is a generalisation for all triangles.

Example $y=5n$ In this example, $5n$ represents '5 times n', even though the multiplication sign is not shown (another one of the perceived inconsistencies of maths). If the question is to substitute $n=4$ into the formula $5n$, then the multiplication sign should be included before the substitution takes place, otherwise the common incorrect answer, 54, may be generated.

$$\begin{aligned} &5n \\ &= 5\times n \\ &= 5\times 4 \\ &= 20 \end{aligned}$$

Children often ask why the multiplication sign is missed out, and a range of reasons can be given, including the fact that it resembles the letter x too closely or that we say 'five pounds' rather than 'five times a pound' in everyday language or that it simply saves effort.

Example $y=3n^2$ Children substituting $y=2$ into the formula $3n^2$ can produce the incorrect answer 36, especially with casual use of certain calculators. What they have computed is $(3\times2)^2$ rather than $3\times(2)^2$. The 'squared' applies only to the n and not to the three.

An earlier passage described how to arrive at the rule for solving equations. There are further problems implementing the rule. At the beginning of the work on this topic, the numbers in an equation must be kept simple to avoid clouding the main issue, that is, understanding algebra. They allow the student to focus on the procedure and not be blocked by the computations. However, some children confronted with the equation $x+3=8$ will often rush to guess the answer 5, and then be unhappy when their teacher insists (appearing pedantic) that they must set out all the steps properly. Ironically, using simple numbers can limit the children's acceptance of the need for a careful procedure. It is necessary to convince them that the need will soon increase, and one way is to show them an equation, such as $31.2x - x(2.5 - x) = 0.654$, which they cannot solve mentally but may have to solve in later years. This can be followed up by adopting the motto: 'Look after your equations when they are young, and they will look after you, when you are older.'

Shape and space

Application of the Test of Cognitive Style in Mathematics (Chinn, 2017a) has indicated that the mathematical style adopted in this branch of the subject, which covers topics such as angles, volume and symmetry, can be different from the style adopted for arithmetic.

Furthermore, the misconceptions experienced by dyslexics and dyscalculics in this branch can produce some of the most confusing mistakes. For example, we have met children who argue long and hard that in the diagram in Figure 16.6 '$y=40$, because both angles are the same'.

Our discussions about this with children have shown that the misconception seemed to derive from the perception that both angles were formed with the same pair of straight lines.

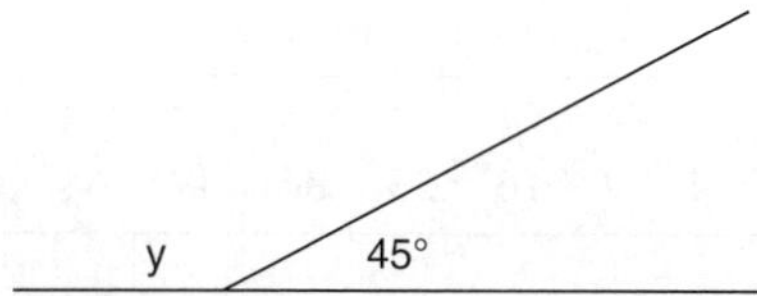

Figure 16.6 Angles on a straight line add to make 180°.

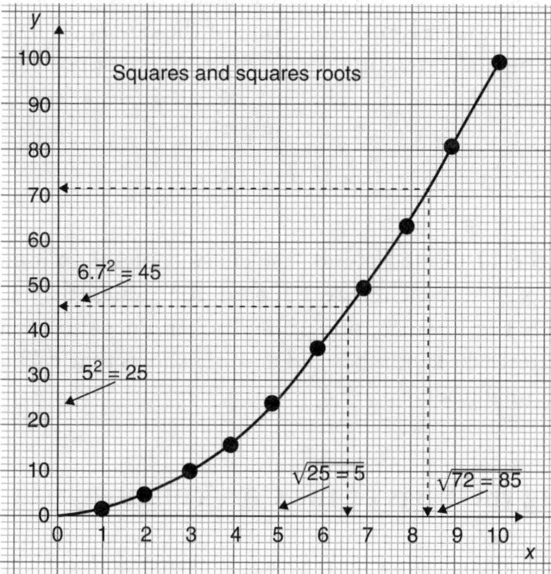

Figure 16.7 The graph for $y = x^2$.

Handling data

The calculation of means, medians and modes always seems to be a very numerical process. Pie charts and histograms require visual presentations as well as numerical work. For example, we felt that dealing graphically with a table full of coordinates (from a quadratic equation, for example) is an example of handling and presenting data. The graph in Figure 16.7 for squares and square roots is such an example.

When covering squares and square roots, a curved graph may be plotted for the easy, whole number square root values (x) and the single digit whole number square values (y) in Table 16.1.

When read from one scale to the curve and then from the curve to the other scale, the graph can provide much more data than the list of values. Broken lines on the graph show how this is done. Additional data is obtainable in at least two ways.

Table 16.1 Table of values for $y=x^2$.

x	0	1	2	3	4	5	6	7	8	9	10
y	0	1	4	9	16	25	36	49	64	81	100

- Reading from the x scale to the y scale gives squares, while reading from the y scale to the x scale gives square roots. In view of this dual capability, the graph is providing one of the best ways to demonstrate that squaring and extracting the square root are opposite processes.

$$25 = 5^2$$
$$\text{so } \sqrt{25} = 5$$

- Between the 11 plotted points, the curve contains an infinite number of other points, which may be used for values between those in Table 16.1. For instance, one of the broken lines shows that $6.7^2=45$ to the nearest whole number and another shows that $\sqrt{72}=8.5$ correct to one decimal place.

Combining the Parts of the Curriculum

This final section contains a short series of examples that increase in complexity, to show how different parts of maths combine. Arithmetic is a frequent contributor.

Examples 16.8.a and b Addition in two digits can be illustrated by putting that operation in the context of combining of angles, as, for example, those shown in Figure 16.8a.

$$\begin{array}{r} 25 \\ +\underline{50} \\ 75 \end{array}$$

The idea of combining angles can be extended to the case where angles are represented by letters (Figure 16.8b). It should be a small increase in level of difficulty for children to add the above angles and obtain $x+35$. It is also an option to create the equation $x+35=90$, since the outer angle has been chosen as a right angle.

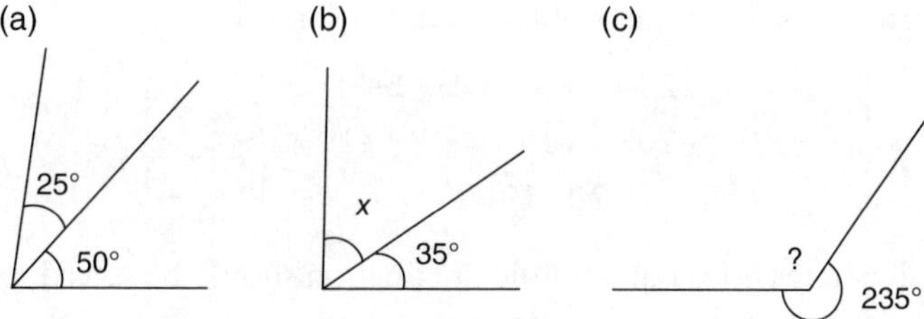

Figure 16.8 Working with angles.

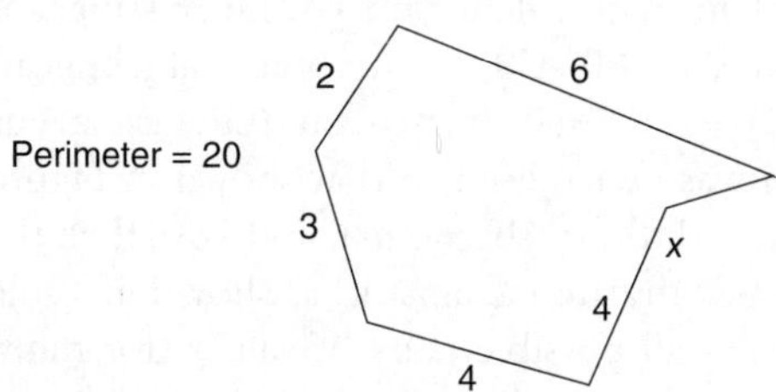

Figure 16.9 'Finding' *x*.

Example 16.8.c When children are practising subtraction of hundreds, tens and units, its application to an example such as that in Figure 16.8c can provide context and motivation.

$$\begin{array}{r} 360 \\ -\underline{235} \\ 125 \end{array}$$

Example 16.9 Sometimes a carefully chosen example from one part of the curriculum can help children to derive or confirm rules for another. If the topic of perimeter has been studied, the diagram in Figure 16.9 could lead to more topics.

If asked, 'How would you find a value for *x*?' many children would have no difficulty in deciding that the sides with given values should be added, and the total subtracted from 20.

A written version of the problem and its solution:

$$20 = x + 4 + 6 + 3 + 2 + 4$$
$$20 = x + 19 \quad or \quad x + 19 = 20$$
$$x = 20 - 19 = 1$$

This illustrates how a quite difficult equation should be solved, and uses the rule derived earlier in this chapter.

Change the side. Change the sign

Example 16.10 The problem illustrated in Figure 16.10 can be regarded as a spatial problem. The calculation of the missing angle can be performed numerically, as 180 – 70, or interpreted algebraically in the form of the equation $x + 70 = 180$. An estimate would suggest an answer above 100.

If the problem was generalised to that shown in Figure 16.11 and the value of x was allowed to vary, between 0 and 180, then the corresponding values of y could be tabulated against it, as shown in Table 16.2.

Table 16.2 shows all possible pairs of values, for multiples of 20 that could be generated from the relationship $y = 180 - x$. The graph in Figure 16.12 shows a backwards-sloping straight line, which can be used

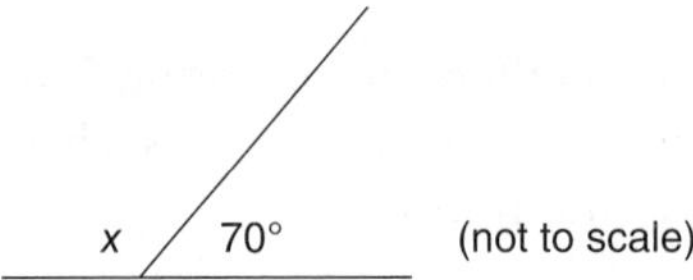

Figure 16.10 'Finding' x.

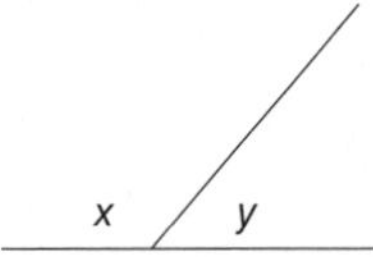

Figure 16.11 Working out the relationship between $x°$ and $y°$.

Table 16.2 Table of values for y = 180 – x.

x	0	20	40	60	80	100	120	140	160	180
y	180	160	140	120	100	80	60	40	20	0

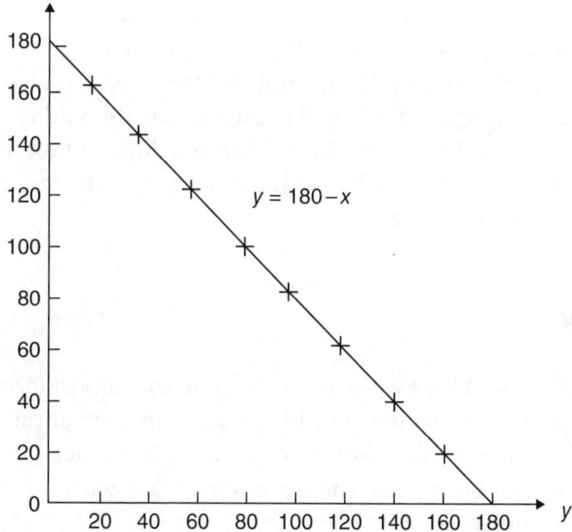

Figure 16.12 The graph for $x+y=180$.

to show every possible pair of values, and thereby demonstrate the problem-solving power of graphs.

Work on using and applying mathematics can, as mentioned earlier, bring together many parts of the curriculum.

An investigative and speculative example Investigating the question, 'Could a person walk a million miles?' turns a child's thoughts to distances and time, and requires him to make various judgements and estimates. The thoughts on time could range from how many minutes to eat a meal, through hours for sleep, how many days for a holiday, weeks, months and years, to decades and centuries. He may wonder how many times you would need to go around the world to travel a million miles or if it is a million miles to the moon. He will have to make judgements about how long the person would live and their walking speed or how far they could reasonably be expected to walk in a day. Children with a poor sense of quantity can give estimates that show wild misconceptions, which can then be discussed very profitably.

An example of a maths challenge Using a challenge for a child to draw a square and a circle with the same area is an example of meta-cognition. If a child chooses a radius, draws a circle first and works out its area, then to draw the square only requires him to take the square root of this area to find the length of the square's sides. This exercise involves choosing a radius and drawing a circle, remembering and evaluating the formula for the area of a circle, reversing the formula for the area of a square to obtain the length of its sides, and then drawing the square. Should the child draw the square first he will have a considerably more difficult task reversing the formula for the area of the circle, but that is part of the learning experience students get from challenges.

Summary

The purpose of this chapter has been to argue the importance of a structure that organises the widest possible range of mathematical experiences for dyslexic and dyscalculic children. While complete coverage of this topic would take several books, the chapter covers some general principles and includes some illustrative examples.

17

Attacking and Checking Questions

Mathematics is an activity that has to be ‘performed’. A certain amount of theory must be committed to memory, but a pupil must be able to *apply* it to produce methodical solutions to questions asked. This will form the evidence that he is proficient in the subject.

It is now accepted that for dyslexics and dyscalculics the process of acquiring knowledge and understanding in mathematics should be structured to their particular needs and be multisensory. However, the provision of help with the application of the subject needs just as much thought. It would be hazardous at worst, and unproductive at best, to expect dyslexic and dyscalculic pupils to work it out for themselves without guidance and training.

This chapter is concerned with helping pupils cross the barrier between knowing the subject and successfully applying it.

The transitional stage of *practicing* must, especially in the first stages of practice, make sure the student is not developing incorrect procedures.

Practice Examples

For thorough understanding and preparation, a pupil needs to understand any topic ‘forwards, backwards, sideways, upside down and inside out’, because this is the way questions will be asked, for example:

$$7 = 5 + \_\_$$

can be seen as $5 + \_\_ = 7$ backwards

or $7 - 5 = \_\_$ inside out

Mathematics for Dyslexics and Dyscalculics: A Teaching Handbook, Fourth Edition.
Steve Chinn and Richard E. Ashcroft.

For reasons such as lack of time and the pupils' often limited concentration spans, it is probably not possible to cover all these viewpoints when first explaining an idea. Indeed this might actually confuse a pupil. The objective is to give valid, reliable and consistent information that can be picked up on later, as many times as is necessary, as the pupil encounters them again through practice examples.

There is a danger that should be recognised here. The number of questions a pupil completes for practice may be limited, for many reasons, such as lack of motivation or slowness in working. The consequence may be that he reaches only the earliest and the most straightforward examples in the exercises, never seeing the later, more searching questions. The result can be the worst of both worlds. If the simple questions are done correctly, he may think that he understands the topic totally, while the reality is that understanding is only superficial. Part of the teaching structure, the differentiation, for every topic should be a carefully chosen series of practice examples, which would not put all the questions that might enhance understanding at the end. One of the useful activities that maths department teachers and their learning support specialists can undertake is to create a resource of question sheets that have been selected to meet the needs of those students whose pace of work is slower, but whose potential level of achievement is high.

Although they are generally discussed separately in this chapter, attacking questions and checking them are interdependent processes, something best exemplified in the 'trial and improvement' methods, mentioned later. Indeed there are some checks that ought to be carried out before a question is attempted.

Preliminary Checks

1. Recall/look up the relevant information/formula.
2. Use the information given to check proposed/initial working.
3. Make a rough estimate. If you can, a mental estimate will probably be the quickest.

1. Recall/look up the correct formula and then check it

Faced with a problem about a circle, many pupils remember the formula:

$$\text{Area} = \pi r^2$$

Unfortunately, they will go ahead and apply it even to questions involving the circumference of the circle, when they should use the (much less frequently remembered) formula:

$$\text{Circumference} = 2\pi r$$

Some pupils will find the area of a triangle by multiplying **base × height**. In fact, the answer obtained should then be halved. Since a triangle is not a rectangle it is sensible to assume that the formula for its area will be different to that for the rectangle.

$$\text{Area of a triangle} = \frac{\text{base} \times \text{height}}{2}$$

One way to help ensure that the correct formula is chosen is to check its *dimensions*. Formulae for lengths must contain only one length, one dimension, for example, *4r* for the circumference perimeter of a square. Note that because π is a constant, the formula for circumference, $2\pi r$ has only one dimension (one variable).

Because areas are two-dimensional, formulae for areas must contain two lengths, two dimensions, multiplied together. For example, the area of a rectangle of sides a and b is given by $A = ab$, and the area of an ellipse by πab (again, because π is a constant this is still only two dimensions).

Because volumes are three-dimensional, formulae for volumes must contain three lengths multiplied together. For example, the area of a cuboid of sides a, b and c is given by $A = abc$, and the volume of a cone by $\frac{1}{3}\pi r^2 h$.

2. *Use given information to check proposed/initial working*

Example

Complete the following table for $R = 3\,V^2$ and then draw a curve with the values in the table:

V	0	1	2	3	4	5	6
R	0					75	

In the question shown, by using core numbers, pupils should first ensure that:

when $V = 0$ they can make the formula produce $R = 0$, and
when $V = 2$ they can make the formula produce $R = 12$, and
when $V = 5$ they can make the formula produce $R = 75$.

Then they can be confident that their method will be right for the values they have to work out and, therefore, that the graph will be correct.

3. Make a rough estimate first

Later, check that the exact answer is close to the rough estimate.

Example
For 12×145, we might estimate $10 \times 150 = 1500$.

We have decreased the 12 to 10, but roughly compensated by increasing the 145 to 150. This estimate could be done mentally by many pupils. Some examination questions explicitly test pupils' ability to think this way, because this is often how we calculate in everyday life.

Attacking Questions

After the processes of understanding, learning and practising, there comes the point when maths has to be applied to problem questions, most significantly in test or examination situations. These will be different from practice situations in the level of pressure they bring and in the extraordinary wide variation in the questions that can appear, which rules out the possibility of rehearsing them all.

At this point, a structured approach is even more necessary than before. Dyslexic and dyscalculic students need to be taught the following:

1. Not just to take a question at face value, for example in word problems don't simply seek out an operation word, such as 'fewer' and assume the question can be solved correctly by a subtraction.
2. How to examine a question, so as to enable the use of their preferred style of working, exploit their strengths and circumnavigate their weaknesses.
3. How connections are made between the various techniques and items of knowledge needed for a question to be answered.
4. How to draw some sort of illustration to help the comprehension as with the Singapore bar method (Kho *et al.*, 2009).

The variety of approaches needed when attacking a question can be compared to guessing what a present is before you are allowed to unwrap it. You might (using most of your senses):

- Pick it up and feel its weight, squeeze it or shake it
- Turn it over

- Smell it
- Tap it to see what sound it makes

Methods of Attacking Questions

This section will describe a number of practical suggestions for 'attacking questions'. The idea here is to give the pupil something to do to start. Starting is often the biggest hurdle. Pupils should carry out as many of the following steps as required:

1. Use a refined estimate.
2. Do not be afraid to take the long way round.
3. Do what you are told by the question.
4. Draw a diagram.
5. Draw a graph.
6. Try to interpret (decimal) numbers as money, which everybody understands better.
7. Temporarily replace awkward numbers with easy numbers to clarify the method (then replace the actual numbers).
8. In multipart questions, answer the later parts even if you cannot answer the earlier parts.
9. When using a formula, consider whether you prefer to rearrange it before you substitute your values, or vice versa.

1. Use a refined estimate

After working out a rough estimate, we can often see ways of refining it to calculate the exact answer.

Example

For calculating 12×145, the estimate is	$10 \times 145 = 1450$
And for the exact answer we add on	$\underline{2 \times 145 = 290}$
So the accurate answer is	1740

Example

Find the cost of 24 square metres of carpet at £17.60 per square metre.

We might estimate by finding the cost of 25 square metres, because it is close and it is a quarter of 100 at £18 per square metre.

$$25 \times £18 = 100 \times 18 \div 4 = 4.5 \times 100 = £450$$

The accurate cost can be worked out by using 2×17.6 and 20×17.6

$$\begin{array}{r} 2\times17.6 = \ 35.2 \\ 2\times17.6 = \ 35.2 \\ 20\times17.6 = 352.0 \\ \hline 24\times17.6 = 442.4 \end{array}$$

2. *Do not be afraid to take the long way round*

It is worth remembering that a long way is better than no way.

Example 1
Faced with a multiplication like the above, that is 12×145, if all else fails it is better to take a long way around than do nothing. It is legitimate to add 145, 12 times. It is highly undesirable to add 12, a 145 times. It is better to do those additions in easy chunks, for example 10×145 and 2×145.

Example 2
A division such as $5202 \div 17$ would cause many (or even most) pupils to give up because they do not know the 17-times table. In these circumstances, the repeated subtractions can be in 'chunks' of 17.

Set up some partial products or chunks to get the calculation started:

$17\times100=1700$

$17\times2=34$

$17\times200=3400$

Now some repeated subtractions:

$$\begin{array}{rr} 5202 & \\ \underline{-3400} & \mathbf{200} \\ 1802 & \\ \underline{-1700} & \mathbf{100} \\ 102 & \end{array}$$

Set up an extra partial product:

$17\times5=85$

$$\begin{array}{rr} \underline{-85} & \mathbf{5} \\ 17 & \\ 17 & \underline{\mathbf{1}} \\ \text{The answer is} & \mathbf{306} \end{array}$$

Example 3

Even with a calculator, a longer way around can be beneficial. With a question such as:

$$\frac{25.49 \times 1.745}{61.52 - 43.1}$$

it is possible to do the entire sum using the calculator and come out with a single, complete answer (=2.415). However, calculating the top and bottom separately and then putting them together is clearer and shows the working, which will earn marks in case of any errors. It also allows for generating an estimate for this intermediate step.

$$\frac{25.49 \times 1.745}{61.52 - 43.1} = \frac{44.48005}{18.42} = 2.415$$

3. *Do what you are told*

Apart from the obvious need to avoid doing otherwise, sometimes following the instructions will lead pupils to places they would not have reached themselves.

Example

Complete this pattern, and find the answer for 26×16:

$$\begin{array}{rcr} 26 & \times & 16 \\ 52 & \times & 8 \\ 104 & \times & 4 \\ \_\_\_ & \times & \_\_\_ \\ \_\_\_ & \times & \_\_\_ \end{array}$$

208×2 and then 416×1 complete the pattern.

Recognition that all the multiplications are equivalent shows that $26 \times 16 = 416$

Pupils will be led to the answer if they follow the given steps.

Some students would have given up at the beginning, because they think that they cannot work out the answer for 26×16.

4. *Draw a diagram*

If 'a picture is worth a thousand words', then there is an (almost) equivalent benefit to be gained in mathematics by using simple diagrams/drawings.

The picture will give strong hints about how to move forwards. How many pupils would be stuck, or make errors such as 21×21 for the first example, if they drew the diagrams for the following two examples?

Example
What is the perimeter of a square whose side is 21 cm?

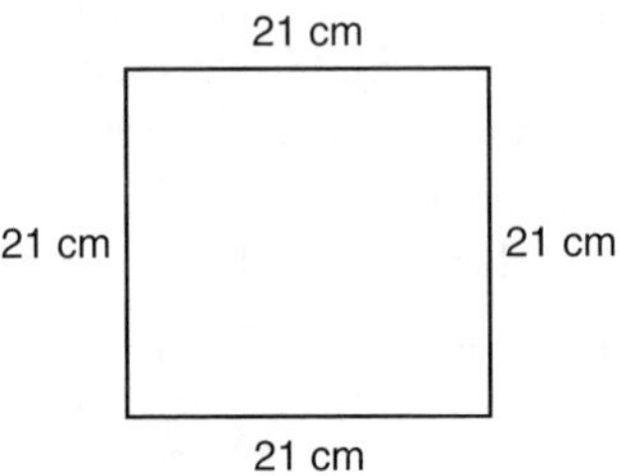

The likely mistake here is failure to realise we are talking about a *square*, although the word is there in the question. The act of drawing is likely to bring this into awareness. The danger of adding two sides instead of four is greatly reduced, as is the lure of multiplying the length by the width.

Example
What is the bearing of a ship travelling south-east?

While a pupil might feel he knows what direction south-east is, the picture (Figure 17.1) allows him to ensure that he is measuring 'from the north, clockwise', even if he does not use a protractor. It also gives him the reminder that his answer should be between 90° and 180°.

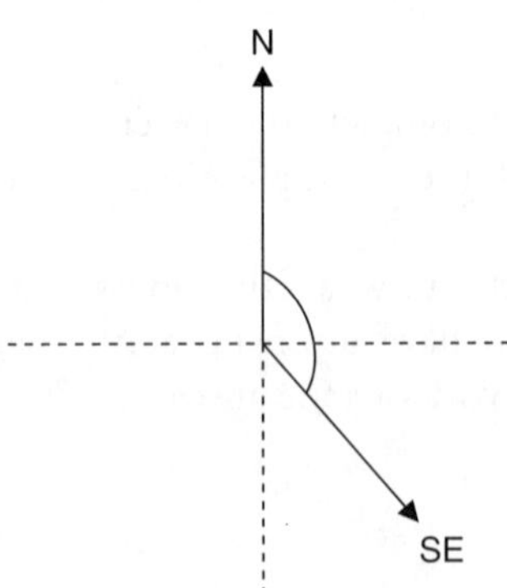

Figure 17.1 Bearing SE.

5. *Draw a graph*

A graph is another form of picture, of course.

For the effort expended on drawing and joining a few points on a graph, what is gained are all the points in between (an infinite number) and any points where the graph can be extended.

Example

Consider the problem of how to use 24 m of fencing in a rectangular shape to enclose the biggest possible area.

As the length increases (and the width decreases), the area changes one length + one width = 1/2 × perimeter = 1/2 × 24 = 12.

Length	*Width*	*Area*
1	11	11
2	10	20
3	9	27
4	8	32
5	7	35
6	6	36
7	5	35
8	4	32
9	3	27
10	2	20
11	1	11

From the table, it is evident that the biggest area is obtained with a square whose sides are 6 m, but consider the situation if we were forced to deal with decimal sides. In an examination, we might be asked to *prove* we have found the biggest arrangement. The graph of length against area are (Figure 17.2), especially with its symmetry, shows that no other value will give a greater area (even if the key decimal values are not calculated).

6. *Try to interpret (decimal) numbers as money, which is usually understood better*

Example

Put the following decimals in order, smallest first:

0.95, 0.905, 0.102, 0.9, 0.85

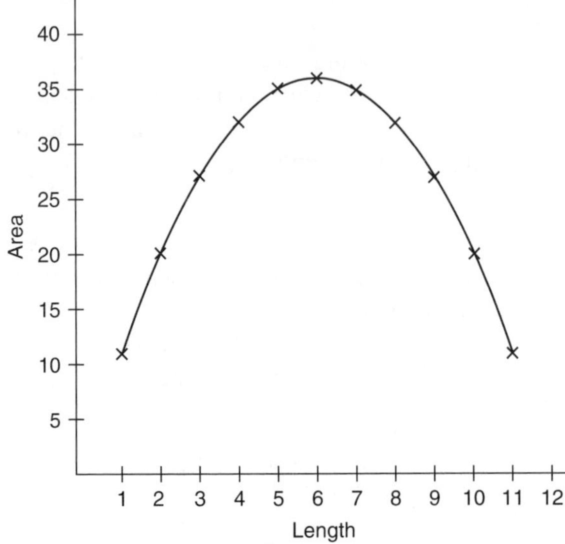

Figure 17.2 Graph for area versus length for rectangular shapes.

Pupils who do not fully understand place values will have the tendency to see 0.102 as bigger than 0.95, because '102 is bigger than 95'. Seeing the numbers as amounts of money can help, especially if they are lined up one below the other and zeros added to make them all three-digit numbers:

£0.950
£0.905
£0.102
£0.900
£0.850

They can then recognise the correct order as:

0.102, 0.85, 0.9, 0.905, 0.95

7. *Temporarily replace awkward numbers with easy numbers to clarify the method (then replace the actual numbers)*

Given the problem:

'Find the average speed of a car that travels 82.3 km in 1 hour 45 minutes', many pupils would be put off by the numbers rather than by the concept.

If the problem is temporarily changed to:

> 'Find the average speed of a car that travels 80 km in 2 hours',

then the method becomes obvious and the answer is clearly seen to be $80 \div 2$, that is, 40 km/hour.

Pupils can now see that the distance must be divided by the time, and careful steps can now be taken to divide with the more awkward figures of the original problem.

8. *In multi-part questions, answer the later parts even if you cannot answer the earlier parts*

Example
Using the following diagram

- Write down a formula for the area of the triangle
- Given that the area of the triangle is 35, show that $x^2 - 3x - 70 = 0$
- Solve the equation $x^2 - 3x - 70 = 0$

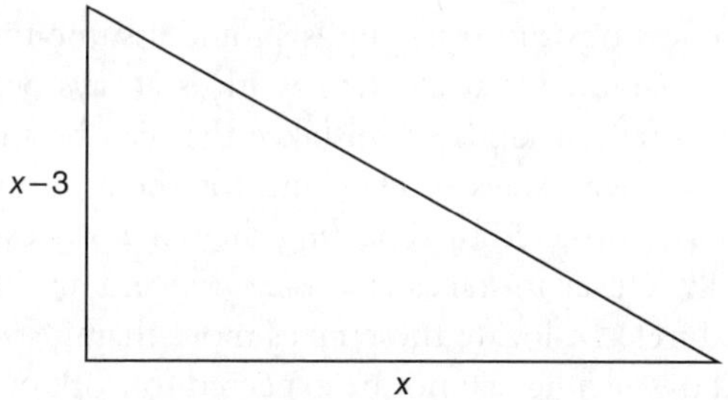

It may be impossible for pupils to write down the required formula for (a) or form the equation for part (b), but that need not prevent them from solving the more mechanical equation in (c) and earning the marks available for that part of the question.

9. *When using a formula, consider whether you prefer to rearrange before you substitute your values, or vice versa*

Example
Use the formula $v = u + at$, to find the value of a when $v = 40$, $u = 30$ and $t = 5$.

Rearranging the formula first:

$$u + at = v$$
$$at = v - u$$
$$a = \frac{v - u}{t}$$

Now substitute the numbers:

$$a = \frac{40 - 30}{5} = \frac{10}{5} = 2$$

Checking

Pupils should recognise the need to check for mistakes, so it is important to emphasise how easily and frequently mistakes are made, and how costly they are. Left to their own devices, or, worse still, *forced* to check their work, many pupils will begin a desultory, and perhaps ill-humoured, process of *repeating* their work. This is probably the least effective method of checking, and it is so boring that most will discontinue it, long before all their answers are checked.

Some mistakes are obvious and will stimulate an immediate check. Other errors are less obvious, but pupils should assume they are present, unless they can guarantee that all their work is always perfectly correct. There are many different kinds of mistakes that can be made, and there need to be just as many ways of checking for them. Some mistakes are *random* and can be corrected by repeating the same process, perhaps a little more carefully. Other mistakes are *systematic* and are caused by using incorrect procedures. To locate these takes more than just repetition.

Dyslexics and dyscalculics cannot be expected to work out how to do all this on their own. There is a need to structure the process or it will be confusing, tedious, ineffective and consequently omitted.

Methods of checking

1. Ask, 'Is the answer sensible?'
2. Repeat the operations.
3. Reverse the operations (work back from the answer).
4. Use an entirely different method.
5. Substitute the answer back into the question, especially if it is an equation.
6. Some questions are self-checking, for example pie charts.

1. Is the answer sensible?

Sometimes pupils are very confident about their answers, especially if they found the question easy to work out or were able to use a calculator. However, if they have worked out that a budgie weighs 10 tonnes, or that a car costs 34p, then they should be alert enough to see something is wrong.

2. Repeat the operations

Repeating the operations carries with it the risk of repeating errors made the first time, even with a calculator. Of course, some errors will be found, and this method is certainly better than not checking at all.

3. Reverse the operations

Example
To check a subtraction, we might add back the number subtracted.

The subtraction 137
−25
112

The addition 25
+112
137

4. Use an entirely different method

This ensures that *none* of the same errors will be made.

Example
A train journey begins at 10:20 and finishes at 12:05. How long does the journey take?

This could be calculated by subtracting the start time and the end time, remembering that time is not expressed in decimals (base ten), and that there are 60 minutes in an hour.

1 6
1~~2~~:05 (12:05 becomes 11:65)
−10:20
1:45

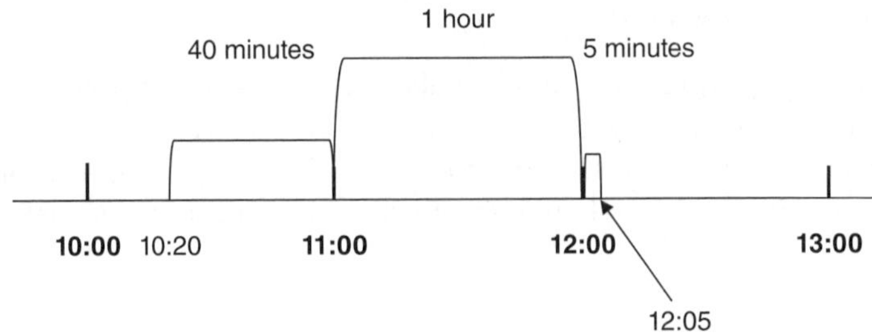

Figure 17.3 A time line for "A train journey begins at 10:20 and finishes at 12:05".

A completely different method could use a 'time line' (Figure 17.3).

$$\text{Time taken} = 40\ \text{minutes} + 1\ \text{hour} + 5\ \text{minutes} = 1\ \text{hour}\ 45\ \text{minutes}$$

5. *Substitute the answer back into the question, especially when using an equation*

This method checks whether the answer really 'works'.

Example

$$\begin{aligned} \text{Solving the equation} \quad 2y+3&=7 \\ 2y&=7-3 \\ 2y&=4 \\ y&=4/2 \\ \text{gives} \quad y&=2 \end{aligned}$$

If y is really equal to 2, then the 2 should fit back into the equation instead of the y.

$$\begin{aligned} &2y+3 \\ &=2\times 2+3 \\ &=4+3 \\ &=7 \qquad \text{as it should be.} \end{aligned}$$

This idea forms the basis for iterative or 'trial and improvement' methods to solve equations. A first guess is made at the answer, perhaps from a hint in the question, and this is checked by substituting it back into the equation. This will not only identify a wrong guess, but it will indicate whether it is too big or too small, and possibly by how much.

Example
The equation $5x+3=15$ has a solution close to 2. Find the exact solution by trial and improvement.

Starting with a guess of 2 (from the estimate), the procedure is best set out in a table:

Guess for x	*Calculate 5x+3*	*Should be 15*
2	13	Too small
3	18	Too big
2.5	15.5	Too big
2.3	14.5	Too small
2.4	15	Correct

The correct answer is 2.4. Of course, it is possible to use a calculator to achieve an answer.

This method will be even more useful for harder quadratic and cubic equations.

6. *Some questions are self-checking*

Example 1
Members of the public were asked to say which of the five TV channels, BBC1, BBC2, ITV1, Channel 4 and Channel 5 was their favourite. The responses are shown in the table.

Draw a pie chart to show the information in the table.

Channel	*Percentage*	*Angle*
BBC 1	25	90
BBC 2	10	36
ITV 1	50	180
Channel 4	10	36
Channel 5	5	18

A pupil produced the pie chart in Figure 17.4.

Inaccurate drawing of the first four angles (slightly too small) implies that there was space left over after the Channel 5 sector. This is a signal that should not be ignored. For another pupil, drawing the angles slightly too big would leave insufficient space for the Channel 5 angle. Gross errors like using the percentage figure as the angle (e.g. 25 degrees for

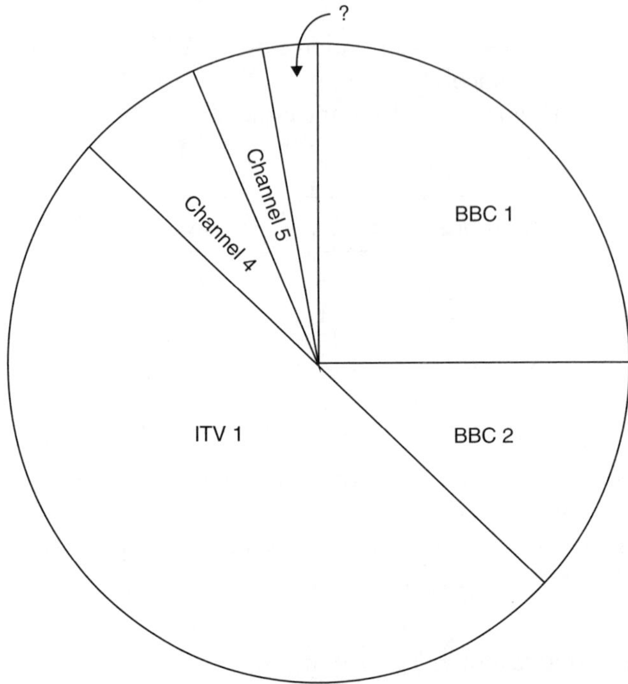

Figure 17.4 An inaccurate pie chart for the TV question.

BBC1) would reveal a more dramatic amount of unused space, and should signal an error in the method.

Example 2

Using the example described earlier in the chapter, that is, requiring a curve to be drawn for $R = 3\ V^2$, if the points plotted do not form a perfect curve, then the error is with either the plotting or, more likely, the calculations. This should not be ignored, even for one point. It will be fairly easy to guess where the point should be, and correct the mistake accordingly.

18

Important Elements of a Teaching Programme

Introduction

In this final chapter, it is our intention to show how we, as teachers and organisers, put our ideas into practice. If in many instances we seem to repeat what has been written earlier, this is because we regard it as sensible to take our own advice. However, we have avoided the repetition of examples at every point in order to reduce the amount of text, while attempting to make this chapter a useful summary of the whole book.

We hope that some of our ideas are applicable in all of the different environments where dyslexic and dyscalculic pupils are taught mathematics. However, it is the principal aim of this chapter to help in the complex situation where they are taught inclusively in classes with similar students, following a mainstream curriculum that is as normal as possible.

Consider the Pupils' Needs

It is almost certain that the mathematical achievements of pupils diagnosed as dyslexic or dyscalculic will not match their potential. They may be from a wide range of backgrounds: social, economic and educational. In many cases, a child will present with significant problems in the affective domain. Although it is hard to prioritise interventions, the need to address anxieties, motivation and negative beliefs will be at least as important as intervention for cognitive development.

Mathematics for Dyslexics and Dyscalculics: A Teaching Handbook, Fourth Edition.
Steve Chinn and Richard E. Ashcroft.

The curriculum should be directed towards creating a relaxed, encouraging, empathetic and low-stress atmosphere, where children can take learning risks. When this is achieved, the pupils should start to feel confident that they can communicate their difficulties and have their questions answered sensitively. Setting up an ethos where the fear of negative evaluation is minimised is a worthy challenge.

The early stages of the course should provide work that is relatively easy, in order to restore a sense of success in pupils who may have experienced many failures, or indeed may have been labelled as failures. It is equally important that the work must not be perceived as too easy and patronising. It must be developmental and efficient if these vulnerable learners are not to fall further behind their peers. Catch-up is another major challenge.

Pupils may have varying abilities and levels of achievement. There is not one common profile of difficulties. In their previous years of education, many will have survived by adopting idiosyncratic methods and/or an impressive range of avoidance strategies and may possess only a piecemeal understanding and knowledge of the subject. The aim is to build upon pupils' strengths and extend what they do know and understand, trying to avoid imposing arbitrary changes, which will only add to their confusion. Teaching should provide the structure, pattern and organisation that their learning difficulty denies them and enable the full spectrum of learning styles to function and, it is hoped, broaden.

Against this background of intentions, it is crucial to maintain the rigour and integrity of the subject. Mathematics is a precise means of communication across the curriculum and in everyday life. It is important to resist the temptation to try and reduce it to a set of tricks. Even within the constraints of a national curriculum and the pressures for success in public examinations (and the PISA tables), it is possible to build a sound base for the further studies many pupils will pursue.

The Structure of the Course

In a world that would suit these learners, a structure based on a spiral with a small pitch allows regular revisits to the same topics (see Figure 18.1). This provides opportunities for essential over-learning and acknowledges the difficulty in achieving mastery of some topics. A spiral with numeracy as its axis recognises the importance of numerical concepts as building blocks for the whole subject and as obstacles when they are not well understood. Topics should be changed frequently to promote and sustain interest. It is the objective that each topic is revisited before it has been forgotten. At each revisit, the topic is reviewed and then pushed to a

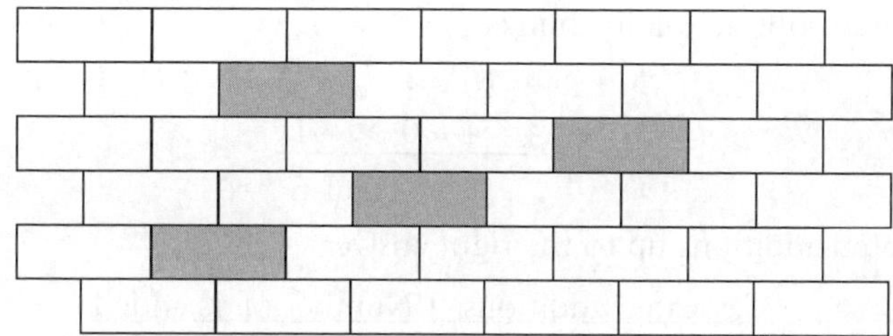

Figure 18.1 The missing bricks in the wall.

slightly higher level, allowing for progress and giving time for 'digestion', but moving on before the pupil loses interest.

Numeracy

The vertical axis of the course begins with the following topics:

- Sorting and classifying
- Counting with whole numbers and using them to measure and draw
- Adding with whole numbers
- Subtracting with whole numbers
- Multiplying with whole numbers
- Dividing with whole numbers
- Understanding about parts of whole numbers
- The four operations for money
- The four operations for decimals
- The four operations for fractions

The axis of the spiral of progress is regarded as a continuum, rather than sets of skills to be acquired separately. The pupils' own characteristic approaches are encouraged. For example, a pupil is encouraged to view a division such as $24 \div 4$ as:

- A reverse multiplication, giving 6, because $6 \times 4 = 24$
- A repeated subtraction down to zero:

Repeated subtractions	Number of 4s subtracted
$24 - 4 = 20$	1
$20 - 4 = 16$	2
$16 - 4 = 12$	3
$12 - 4 = 8$	4
$8 - 4 = 4$	5
$4 - 4 = 0$	6

- Repeated subtraction in chunks:

24 – 20 = 4	5
4 – 4 = 0	1
Total	6

- Repeated additions up to the right answer:

Repeated additions	Number of 4s added
0 + 4 = 4	1
4 + 4 = 8	2
8 + 4 = 12	3
12 + 4 = 16	4
16 + 4 = 20	5
20 + 4 = 24	6

Note that special attention should be given to the number facts for single-digit addition, subtraction, multiplication and division, since knowing these facts, or having quick and reliable strategies with which to work them out, reduces the load on working and short-term memories during calculations. This knowledge helps not only computation but also understanding of numbers.

General mathematical topics

Topics such as perimeter, area, equations, angle sums and graphs are introduced only when an appropriate level of numeracy has been reached. By using core numbers, this can be achieved relatively soon.

The mathematical variety needs to be as wide as possible as early as possible in order to maintain motivation and extend experience. It is particularly useful to introduce algebra very early, in the form of simple formulae at the conclusions of pieces of fully understood work. Algebra is a useful vehicle for developing the generalisation of skills, concepts and knowledge. For example, when working out a perimeter has been grasped for numbers, it is not a large conceptual leap for a pupil to understand that $a + b + c$ is the formula or generalisation for the perimeter of a triangle with sides a, b and c.

Besides maintaining the students' interest, dealing with a wide variety of topics has an even greater value in helping build foundations that are wide, so that difficult areas can be spanned just as missing bricks can be spanned in a wall (see Figure 18.1). Furthermore, relationships between mathematical topics are revealed and alternative paths are explored and developed. In this way, it becomes possible to put into practice the earlier claim to 'build upon pupils' strengths and extend what they do know and understand.

Using and applying mathematics

Investigational and practical work are sometimes viewed as 'bolt-ons' to the curriculum when the student is struggling with the basics, but they are integral to the pupils' understanding of the reasons for studying the subject and how it all works collectively. These activities help pupils with the organisation of their work and offer experiences with which to strengthen their concepts. Pupils usually respond with strong motivation for this alternative kind of work.

The use of patterns

The authors have long advocated the use of patterns in mathematics, as part of its structure. Patterns act as the mortar that holds the bricks of the subject together (Chinn and Ashcroft, 2004). We consider that patterns and their recognition can help in the following ways:

- Streamline and secure the learning of related facts
- Add interest and motivation (as puzzles and games can)
- Help with conceptual problems, by providing another way of looking at things
- Rationalise idiosyncrasies
- Provide structure
- Encourage generalisation skills
- Help long term memory

Mental arithmetic

Throughout the course, pupils should be encouraged and shown how to develop methods of calculating answers mentally, something most of us need to do in everyday situations. They should not be expected to create these methods by themselves, but any methods they have already adopted should be welcomed and discussed. Whether the expectation is for a correct answer or merely an estimate, pupils should be encouraged to use mental calculations as their first resort and then as their last resort when verifying or checking an answer.

However, the problems of weak short-term and working memories are likely to make mental arithmetic very challenging. The pupil is likely to need appropriate differentiation if he is not to be seriously demotivated by this activity. One example of differentiation is to show the problem, for example, written on a white board, so that the pupil can at least focus on the computation.

Classroom Management: Making the Lessons Suit the Pupils

In general, the short attention spans and memory deficits of dyslexic pupils require that a lesson should be divided into short subsections, alternating exposition, demonstration, practical work, discussions, practice and so on. Also remember the saying,

> 'Tell me and I will forget.
> Show me and I will remember.
> Involve me and I will understand.'

Perceptual and organisational difficulties dictate the need for clarity of presentation and thorough lesson preparation. Despite the work involved in the latter, there is also a seemingly opposing need for the teacher to be flexible enough to change direction in response to problems or opportunities as they present themselves during the course of a lesson. Hence the need to have a range of manipulative materials on hand for all lessons.

Board/screen work must be clear and uncluttered, preferably without too much information on display at any one time. Work should be presented both orally and visually. Memory overload must be avoided. Teachers should check that work is copied and copied correctly. Some pupils will need handouts.

Teachers should avoid talking (especially about important parts of the work) while the pupils are writing. A dyslexic pupil finds it hard enough to copy without this added distraction, which may be further compounded by worrying about what he is not hearing because he is trying to write. Dual tasking is not always a skill for this population.

Spread of ability

A teacher's organisation and preparation should enable both faster and slower pupils to make progress. If he is devoting time to slower pupils, then faster pupils should have selected extra work to cover. Pupils can often learn well from each other, so faster pupils can sometimes be given the opportunity to develop their 'communication level of understanding' (Sharma, 1988), by helping slower pupils.

Pupils' mathematical cognitive styles

Chapter 3 explains the two extremes of thinking style. Pupils will lie somewhere on this spectrum. At one extreme is the pupil described as an inchworm learner, who works part-to-whole, and at the other extreme is the pupil described as a grasshopper learner, who works whole-to-part. The inchworms follow a rigid, step-by-step, formula/algorithm-based style when tackling mathematics. This is usually the way this type of learner is best taught. Conversely, grasshoppers work more intuitively and are very answer-oriented. They may have been stifled and demotivated by being taught in the first style, to which many mathematics teachers arguably belong. A good mathematician needs to be flexible and make appropriate use of a mixture of the styles, so pupils need to be encouraged to consider more than one method when appropriate.

Pupils can be helped to find their own best way of working if the teacher:

- Begins each lesson with an overall picture of its contents, using both oral and visual stimuli
- Thoroughly explains the logic behind each method (as overview and then detail)
- Offers alternative methods
- Puts the work into a familiar context, or relates it to the pupils' own experiences and existing knowledge
- Reviews the outcomes of the lesson

Evolving Expectations and Emphases

The nature of a pupil's difficulties and his previous experiences in a classroom situation have often produced poor levels of achievement and an antipathy for the subject. It is essential to begin by taking the time to help the pupil rebuild confidence and develop a positive attitude. Create experiences of meaningful success for him. These successes, progressively gained, will lead the pupil to recognise his real abilities and raise his expectations, while equipping him with the knowledge and skills that will enable him to fulfil his true potential.

The initial aim of restoring pupils' belief in their ability to succeed in mathematics is best met by building on what they already know, because they often know much more than they realise. Their knowledge just needs rationalisation and organisation. Much of the work should continue to cover the basics, in a manner that allows the teacher and pupils to:

- Revise important work
- Fill in as many gaps as possible
- Rationalise established ideas, which may be right, wrong, confused or inefficient

As confidence is developed, pupils' attitudes will become more internalised, positive and motivated. The teacher should encourage the resulting acceleration.

Lesson management

To be taught in a whole class by an empathetic teacher offers some advantages over the individual help some dyslexic pupils receive. The members of the class should work together, share problems and accept mistakes, safe in the knowledge that few learners are perfect. They are encouraged to lose their fear of being wrong and thereby gain confidence. There should be a risk-taking ethos in the classroom.

As pupils improve their mathematics at different paces, the differences between them will grow and become more evident. Each will have his own expectations and require these expectations to be met. Allowing and guiding them to work individually for some of the time encourages them to fulfil more of their potential. Class lessons may remain the main learning mode, but individual routes can be provided, where pupils choose from the following:

- Help or further practice with troublesome current work
- Revision of recent or seemingly mastered topics
- Extension work at higher levels

Published schemes, texts and carefully chosen work from the Internet are becoming increasingly valuable to support this way of working.

Teaching materials

A relevant teaching philosophy can be summarised simplistically as, 'Mathematics is easy, only writing it down is hard'. Sometimes we explain by copying Figure 18.2 onto the board and ask pupils what they think it is.

Pupils will inevitably guess that it is a bike or a moped or a motorcycle or a scooter, and then become annoyed when this is refuted. It is possible to tease them even further by saying, 'If it's a bike, ride it down to the shop'. Eventually they are realise that we are showing something that it is not a bike, but *a picture of a bike*. In many ways, the mathematics we study is not real life, but only a written representation of a real problem. Sharing money between people is a real problem, which we can all do, while the usual written version of, for example, £12.48 ÷ 4 is just a picture, a theoretical version. If the written version can be shown to mimic the actual

Figure 18.2 'Is it a bike?'

processes of dividing up the money, then more pupils will understand. This philosophy suggests the following sequence of steps:

- New topics are introduced through practical work, demonstrations, investigations, discussions and physical experiences. The use of a variety of these will facilitate the development and understanding of each concept. It can put them in a context.
- The next step is to try and translate the concept into a written form, linking the concrete experiences directly to the symbolic representation.
- This will lead into the use of worksheets or textbooks. The worksheets written and used by the authors start with worked examples, which are related to the earlier experiences. Then questions provide practice and revision. The worksheets are thus the third stage of the procedure and not the sole source from which the pupils are expected to learn.

Worksheets can follow a structured course and can be designed to enable the following:

- Present an advance overview of the section of work to be followed
- Eliminate the need for taking down notes, with its inherent risks of slow progress, mistakes, lack of clarity and readability
- Start at the most appropriate point
- Cover only a single concept, so that any point of difficulty can be readily identified, isolated and dealt with (that is, be diagnostic)

- Contain no more information than can be comfortably digested in one bite
- Present work clearly
- Use the fewest possible and simplest words, yet introduce the necessary technical terms carefully
- Incorporate exercises
- Provide a practical revision aid (used as ready-made and organised notes)
- Carefully relate to other sheets
- Be designed to be criterion referenced, at least with some of the questions

As stated earlier, later on there will be a point when the differences between individual pupils begin to outweigh their similarities. Short worksheets, answered together at the same rate, are no longer ideal. At this point, it is also important for pupils to begin to use mainstream materials, as they must eventually face public examinations. An appropriate textbook or a series of textbooks, which becomes familiar and trusted, can provide help and reassurance, especially at the time of examinations. Textbooks provide different viewpoints and a variety in language, to which pupils must acclimatise when they are ready. The presentation of work in textbooks has become more and more appealing, with good graphics, uncluttered pages and well-structured sets of examples. Textbooks must be chosen with great care, so as not to risk a reversal of the changes in attitude previously achieved. New approaches, as used in Singapore for example, are now being introduced.

Writing paper

If the responses of younger, newer pupils need more space than a worksheet allows, there are considerable benefits in using squared paper, either in loose form, to file with their worksheets, or in exercise book form. If centimetre squares are too large for many written answers, half-centimetre (5 mm) squares offer invaluable help with:

- Lining up calculations vertically and horizontally
- Setting out tables and charts
- Doing measurements and diagrams, especially those in centimetres and/or using right angles
- Working out area problems

It is our view that dyslexic and dyscalculic pupils should be coached specifically through the transition from squared paper to lined (vertical lines can help with the alignment of calculations) and blank paper. The transition can take place when the value of the squared paper becomes outweighed by the need to prepare for public examinations, or at a time of the pupil's choosing.

Calculators

With a course that initially has numeracy as its axis, the use of a calculator would be counterproductive. Unless there is another purpose to the work and it involves repetitive calculations, calculators should be discouraged at first.

Mental arithmetic is necessary for everyday life and for checking answers that are worked out using a calculator. Premature over-reliance on a calculator could well delay the acquisition of these mental arithmetic skills, particularly estimation skills.

Furthermore, many of the later mathematical processes, such as $(a+x)(b+y)$, are based on the early numerical processes, for example 35×24, which therefore need to be thoroughly understood.

There will be a point when pupils have learned all they can about manual calculations. Powerful calculators can be bought cheaply, but some have too many functions that will never be used and that make the machine difficult to operate. A simple solar-powered calculator can be sufficient, with scientific functions, including fractions, percentages, and degrees/minutes/seconds, and which does not resort to scientific form in unnecessary cases.

A calculator is an ideal aid for the short-term memory and can help compensate for a pupil's remaining computational difficulties (which might only be a matter of speed). Logic and keying errors can be filtered out using checking methods (see Chapter 17). Specific calculator functions should be introduced on the basis of need, as with the trigonometric functions, for example. Specific time can be set aside for the exploration of other functions, such as $n!$ (n factorial), which are of investigational interest.

Internal Assessment

Pupils need to be assessed regularly for the following purposes:

- Monitoring progress
- Diagnosis of difficulties
- Distinguishing mathematical cognitive style

Most dyslexic pupils will have a long history of 'being tested', but are usually reassured to be told that the results are for the above purposes only, and will have limited circulation. Ironically, yet usefully for examinations, the more the pupils are tested, the less they fear the process, which may be no more distasteful than any other mathematics lesson.

Monitoring progress

Standardised tests are called so because they have been given to a standard sample or population, before publication. The performance of any child can then be compared with this standard population. The results can be expressed in various ways.

Some tests produce a 'mathematical age', which can be compared with a child's chronological age to give an idea of how far behind his attainment is in years and months. The results of subsequent repeat tests will show how much improvement has been made. This can be related to the time that has elapsed to give a 'value-added' factor. For example, 18 months' progress in a year could be defined as a value-added factor of 1.5.

Some tests produce a mathematical 'quotient', which resembles IQ, and relates performance to an average figure of 100. For example, 96 is just below average, but within an average band.

Other tests produce a 'centile' or 'percentile' figure, which shows a child's position in the standard population as a percentage. For example, a percentile figure of 20 would indicate that 20% of the population would be expected to perform at or below the child's level.

Ideally, standardised tests should be repeated at similar times in the year for comparison purposes. Test results should be considered in conjunction with progress in class, and any other changes that may have occurred, to obtain a real picture of progress. Single test results should be treated with caution, as leaps in progress may not coincide with test dates. There is always the possibility that the test may have occurred on a bad day. Many pupils are labile in their performances.

Diagnosis of difficulties

Some tests are designed to assess mathematical sub-skills separately, so that particular problem areas can be identified. The results can be used to direct subsequent teaching towards the areas of weakness. In an ideal classroom teaching and diagnosis should go hand-in-hand.

Pupils' mathematical styles

The Test of Cognitive Style in Mathematics (Chinn, 2017a) can be used to determine mathematical learning/cognitive style. It distinguishes between the step-by-step 'inchworm' and the intuitive, holistic 'grasshopper'. This test is for use with individual pupils and provides a measure of the pupil's position on the continuum of styles from extreme inchworm to extreme grasshopper (see Chapter 3). It encourages discussion as to 'How'.

Summary

Throughout all our years of experience teaching mathematics to dyslexics and dyscalculics, we have tried many things, filtered out what does not work and retained those ideas that have been successful. Therefore, the suggestions in this chapter and elsewhere in the book are included because they have worked for us. The application of the advice should be given careful thought, as other situations involving other factors may require different responses.

It has been our experience that the methods that work for dyslexic and dyscalculic pupils work for all pupils. This has implications for inclusion.

Appendix 1

Books, Journals, Tests and Games

Books

The following list collects some useful titles together.

Background

Berch, D.B. and Mazzocco, M.M.M. (eds) (2007) *Why is Math so Hard for Some Children? Grand Rapids, Michigan.* Paul H. Brookes Publishing Co.
Boaler, J. (2009) *The Elephant in the Classroom.* London. Souvenir Press.
Bransford, J.D., Brown, A.L. and Cocking, R.R. (eds) (2000) *How People Learn.* Washington, DC. National Academy Press.
Butterworth, B. (1999) *The Mathematical Brain.* London. Papermac.
Chinn, S (ed.) (2015) *The Routledge International Handbook of Dyscalculia and Mathematical Learning Difficulties.* London. Routledge.
Copeland, R.W. (1984) *How Children Learn Mathematics: Teaching Implications of Piaget's Research.* New York. Macmillan.
Crawley, J.F. (1985) *Cognitive Strategies and Mathematics for the Learning Disabled.* Rockville, MD. Aspen Systems Corporation.
Datta. D.K. (1993) *Math education at its best: The Potsdam model.* Framingham, Mass. CT/LM.
Dehaene, S. (2011) *The Number Sense.* Oxford. OUP.
Devlin, K. (2000) *The Maths Gene.* London. Weidenfeld and Nicolson.
Donlan, C. (ed.) (1998) *The Development of Mathematical Skills.* Hove. Psychology Press.
Dowker, A. (2005) *Individual Differences in Arithmetic.* Hove. Psychology Press.
Easterway, R. and Wyndham, J. (2005) *Why do Buses Come in Threes?* London. Portico.

Mathematics for Dyslexics and Dyscalculics: A Teaching Handbook, Fourth Edition.
Steve Chinn and Richard E. Ashcroft.

Hattie, J. (2009) *Visible Learning*. Abingdon. Routledge.

Hughes, M. (1986) *Children and Number*. Oxford. Blackwell.

Krutetskii, V.A. (1976) *The Psychology of Mathematical Abilities in Schoolchildren*. Chicago. University of Chicago Press.

Miles, T.R. and Miles, E. (eds) (2004) *Dyslexia and Mathematics* (2nd edn). London. RoutledgeFalmer.

Mortimore, T. (2008) *Dyslexia and Learning Style* (2nd edn). London. Wiley.

Orton, A. (ed.) (1999) *Pattern in the Teaching and Learning of Mathematics*. London. Cassell.

Polya, G. (1990) *How to Solve It*. London. Penguin.

Skemp, R.R. (1986) *The Psychology of Learning Mathematics* (2nd edn). Harmondsworth. Pelican.

Westwood, P. (2000) *Numeracy and Learning Difficulties*. London. David Fulton.

Teaching

Ashlock, R.B. (2010) *Error Patterns in Computation: Using Error Patterns to Help Each Student Learn* (10th edn). Boston. Allyn and Bacon.

Ashlock, R., Johnson, M., Wilson, J. and Jones, W. (1983) *Guiding Each Child's Learning of Mathematics*. Columbus, OH. Charles E. Merrill.

Babtie, P. and Emerson, J. (2015) *Understanding Dyscalculia and Numeracy Difficulties. A Guide for Parents, Teachers and Other Professionals*. London. Jessica Kingsley.

Bird, R. (2007) *The Dyscalculia Toolkit*. London. Paul Chapman.

Bird, R. (2009) *Overcoming Difficulties with Number*. London. Sage.

Bley, N. and Thornton, C. (2000) *Teaching Mathematics to the Learning Disabled* (4th edn). Austin, TX. Pro-Ed.

Brown, T. and Liebling, H. (2005) *The Really Useful Maths Book: A Guide to Interactive Teaching*. Abingdon. Routledge.

Butterworth, B. and Yeo, D. (2004) *Dyscalculia Guidance*. London. NFER-Nelson.

Chinn, S. (2009) *What to do when you can't… series*. Wakefield. Egon.

… Learn the Times Tables

… Add and Subtract

… Multiply and Divide

… Tell the Time

… Do Fractions, Decimals and Percentages

Chinn, S. (2017) *The Trouble with Maths. A Practical Guide to Helping Learners with Numeracy Difficulties* (3rd edn). Abingdon. Routledge (Winner of 'Books for Learning and Teaching' Award, TES/NASEN 2004).

Chinn, S. (2017) *More Trouble with Maths. A Complete Guide to Identifying and Diagnosing Mathematical Difficulties* (2nd edn). Abingdon. Routledge.

Chinn, S. (2011) *The Fear of Maths. How to Overcome It. Sum Hope3.* London. Souvenir Press.
Clausen-May, T. (2005) *Teaching Maths to Pupils with Different Learning Styles.* London. Paul Chapman.
Clayton, P. (2003) *How to Develop Numeracy in Children with Dyslexia.* Wisbech, Cambs. LDA.
Deboys, M. and Pitt, E. (1988) *Lines of Development in Primary Mathematics* (3rd edn). Belfast. Blackstaff Press.
French, D. (2002) *Teaching and Learning Algebra.* London. Continuum.
French, D., Connolly, W., Gardner, H., *et al.* (1992) *Mental Methods in Mathematics: A First Resort.* Leicester: The Mathematical Association.
Gallow, C. (2009) *Getting to Grips with Word Problems.* Stafford. Qed.
Grauberg, E. (1998) *Elementary Mathematics and Language Difficulties.* London. Whurr.
Haggarty, L. (ed.) (2002) *Teaching Mathematics in Secondary Schools.* London. RoutledgeFalmer.
Hannell, G. (2013) *Dyscalculia. Action Plans for Successful Learning in Mathematics* (2nd edn). London. Routledge.
Haylock, D. (2001) *Numeracy for Teaching.* London. Paul Chapman Publishing.
Henderson, A. (2012) *Dyslexia, Dyscalculia and Mathematics: A Practical Guide* (2nd edn). Abingdon. Routledge.
Henderson, A. and Miles, E. (2001) *Basic Topics in Mathematics for Dyslexics.* London. Whurr.
Hornigold, J. (2015) *The Dyscalculia Pocketbook.* Alresford. Teachers' Pocketbooks.
Martin, H. (1996) *Multiple Intelligences in the Mathematics Classroom.* Arlington Heights, IL. RI/SkyLight.
Molina, C. (2012) *The Problem with Math is English.* San Francisco. Jossey-Bass.
Yeo, D. (2003) *Dyslexia, Dyspraxia and Mathematics.* London. Whurr.

Journals

The Journal of Learning Disabilities. The Hammill Institute on Disabilities. USA.
Equals Online – Mathematics and Special Educational Needs. The Mathematical Association. UK.

Suppliers of Software

AVP, School Hill Centre, Chepstow, Monmouthshire NP16 5PH.
mailto:info@avp.co.uk
www.avp.co.uk

Granada Learning, Granada Television, Quay Street, Manchester M60 9EA.
info@granada-learning.com
www.gl-education.com

iANSYST, Cambridge,
sales@dyslexic.com
www.dyslexic.com

www.jellyjames.co.uk

www.nessy.com

R-E-M, Unit 7 Dunball Industrial Estate, Dunball, Bridgwater, Somerset TA6 4TP.
www.r-e-m.co.uk

White Space, 41, Mall Rd, London W6 9DG
sales@wordshark.co.uk
www.wordshark.co.uk (for Numbershark)

Video tutorials

www.mathsexplained.co.uk
A collection of online video tutorials from Steve Chinn

Tests

Basic Number Screening Test (2001) W. Gillham and K. Hesse. Sevenoaks. Hodder Murray.

The Dyscalculia Assessment (2010) J. Emerson and P. Babtie. London. Continuum.

The Dyscalculia Screener. (2003) B. Butterworth. www.gl-assessment.co.uk/products/dyscalculia-screener

Key Maths 3 UK (2014) Austin J. Connolly. www.pearsonclinical.co.uk/keymaths3uk

Mathematics Competency Test (1995) P. Vernon, K. Miller and J. Izzard. London: Hodder Murray.

Dynamo Profiler. Available online: http://dynamoprofiler.co.uk/(ages 6–9).

DysCalculiUM (2010) Iansyst/Tribal https://dyscalculia.advancelearningzone.com/An online screening tool for 16 years and over.

More Trouble with Maths. A Complete Guide to Identifying and Diagnosing Mathematical Difficulties. 2nd edn. (2017) S. Chinn. Abingdon. Routledge (which contains a range of 'free-to-photocopy' tests, including tests normed in the UK).

Sandwell Early Numeracy Test www.gl-assessment.co.uk/products/sandwell-early-numeracy-test

Wide Range Achievement Test 4 (2006) G. Wilkinson and G. Robertson. Psychological Assessment Resources Inc. (available from Ann Arbor, www.annarbor.co.uk).

Games

A huge range is available via the Internet from suppliers such as Amazon.

Appendix 2
Teaching Materials

Some materials can be made, whilst others have to be bought. Unless a supplier is specified, the material is available from educational suppliers such as those listed under 'Suppliers'.

Walton, M. (1994) Maths Words. From SEN Marketing (see Suppliers)

0–5 six-sided dice
1p to 50p six-sided dice
Blank playing cards
Money (plastic or real)
Base ten (Dienes) blocks
Poker chips (buy 'real' ones, or buy 'stackers' from www.crossboweducation.com)
Large (2 cm+) counters
Cocktail sticks (in boxes of 100, bundles of 10 and singly)
Squared paper
Place value cards (make your own)
Vocabulary and symbol cards (make your own)
Abacus
Geo boards
Dice (various shapes and values; blank six-sided dice are obtainable)
Cuisenaire rods
Numicon
Flexitable (www.flexitable.co.uk)
Multi-link cubes
Uni-fix cubes
Square counters (from www.crossboweducation.com)
Beadstrings

Mathematics for Dyslexics and Dyscalculics: A Teaching Handbook, Fourth Edition.
Steve Chinn and Richard E. Ashcroft.

Metre rules: mm divisions, cm divisions and dm divisions
Number square, 1–100, with counters
Clock faces (with synchronised hands), for example the Helen Arkell Teaching Clock (www.arkellcentre.org.uk)
Talking calculators
Pie chart scales
10 dm cube (to hold one litre of liquid)
Stern pattern boards
Tape measure
Trundle wheel
Kitchen scales

The Dyscalculia/Maths Intervention Kit contains a wide range of materials and is available from Crossbow Education

Suppliers

Crossbow Education. 41 Sawpit Lane, Brocton, Staffordshire ST17 0TE
www.crossboweducation.com

Cuisenaire Company. www.cuisenaire.co.uk

Hope Education.
www.hope-education.co.uk
enquiries@hope-education.co.uk

Learning Resources, 5 Merchants Close, Oldmeadow Road, King's Lynn, Norfolk PE30 4JX.
www.learningresources.co.uk

Learning Development Aids. www.ldalearning.com

www.learningmaterials.co.uk for 'Living Maths' books

Magic Whiteboard, 95C Blackpole West Trading Estate, Worcester WR3 8TJ.
www.magicwhiteboard.co.uk

Partners in Education UK Ltd.
www.partnersineducation.co.uk

SEN Marketing (for a large range of special need books)
www.senbooks.co.uk

Special Direct @ TTS Group Ltd, Park Lane Business Park, Kirkby-in-Ashfield, Nottinghamshire NG17 9GU.
www.specialdirect.com

Stern Maths
www.store.sternmath.com/early-number-sense/1-manipulative

Taskmaster Ltd.
www.taskmasteronline.co.uk

Coloured overlays

Crossbow Education
www.crossboweducation.com

Institute of Optometry Sales Ltd (iOO Sales Ltd)
www.ioosales.co.uk

References

Ackerman, P.T. and Dykman, R.A. (1996) The speed factor and learning disabilities: the toll of slowness in adolescents. *DYSLEXIA*, 2 (1), 1–22.

Ackerman, P.T., Anhalt, J.M. and Dykman, R.A. (1986) Arithmetic automatization failure in children with attention and reading disorders: associations and sequela. *Journal of Learning Disabilities*, 19 (4), 222–232.

Al Hakeemi, A. (2015) The Yemen Dyslexia Association. *Perspectives*, 41 (1), 51.

American Psychiatric Association (2013) *Diagnostic and Statistical Manual of Mental Disorders* (5th edn). Arlington, VA. American Psychiatric Publishing.

Anghileri, J. (1999) Issues in teaching multiplication and division. In Thompson, I. (ed.) (1999) *Issues in Teaching Numeracy in Primary Schools*. Buckingham. Open University Press.

Ashcroft, J.R. and Chinn, S.J. (1992) In Miles, T.R. and Miles, E. (eds) *Dyslexia and Mathematics*, p.98. Routledge. London.

Ashcraft, M.H. and Krause, J.A. (2007) Working memory, math performance and math anxiety. *Psychonomic Bulletin and Review*, 14 (2), 243–248.

Ashcraft, M. Kirk, E.P. and Hopko, D. (1998) On the cognitive consequences of mathematics anxiety. In Donlan, C. (ed.) (2000) *The Development of Mathematical Skills*. Hove. The Pyschological Corporation.

Ashcraft, M.H., Krause, J.A. and Hopko, R.H. (2007) Is maths anxiety a learning disability? In Berch, D.B. and Mazzocco, M.M.M. (eds). *Why is Math so Hard for Some Children?* Grand Rapids, Michigan. Paul H. Brookes Publishing Co.

Ashlock, R., Johnson, M., Wilson, J. and Jones, W. (1983) *Guiding Each Child's Learning of Mathematics*. Columbus, OH. Merrill.

Ashlock, R.B. (2010) *Error Patterns in Computation: Using Error Patterns to help each Student Learn* (10th edn). Boston. Allyn and Bacon.

Askew, M. and William, D. (1995) *Recent Research in Mathematics Education 5–16*. London. HMSO.

Mathematics for Dyslexics and Dyscalculics: A Teaching Handbook, Fourth Edition.
Steve Chinn and Richard E. Ashcroft.

Badian, N.A. (1999) Persistent arithmetic, reading or arithmetic and reading disability. *Annals of Dyslexia*, 49, 45–70.

Bath, J.B. and Knox, D.E. (1984) Two styles of performing mathematics. In Bath, J.B., Chinn, SJ. and Knox, D.E. (eds) *Dyslexia: Research and its Application to the Adolescent*. Bath. Better Books.

Bath, J.B., Chinn, S.J. and Knox D.E. (1986) *The Test of Cognitive Style in Mathematics*. East Aurora, NY. Slosson (now out of print, see Chinn, 2017).

Berch, D.B. (2005) Making sense of number sense: Implications for children with mathematical disabilities. *Journal of Learning Disabilities*, 38 (4), 333–339.

Bierhoff, H. (1996) *Laying the Foundations of Numeracy: A Comparison of Primary School Textbooks in Britain, Germany and Switzerland*. London. The National Institute of Economic and Social Research.

Boaler, J. (2015) *The Elephant in the Classroom*. London. Souvenir Press.

Borst, G. And Houde, O. (2014) Inhibitory control as a core mechanism for cognitive development and learning at school. *Perspectives on Language and Literacy*, 40 (2), 41–44.

Bransford, J.D., Brown, A.L. and Cocking, R.R. (eds) (2000) *How People Learn*. Washington DC. National Academy Press.

Bronner, A.F. (1917) *The Psychology of Special Abilities and Disabilities*. Boston. Little, Brown and Co.

Brown, L., Hewitt, D. and Tahta, D. (eds) (1989) *A Gattegno Anthology*. Derby. Association of Teachers of Mathematics.

Bryant, B.R. and Rivera, D.P. (1997) Educational assessment of mathematical skills and abilities. *Journal of Learning Disabilities*, 30 (1), 57–68.

Bryant, D.P., Bryant, B.R. and Hammill, D.D. (2000) Characteristic behaviours of students with LD who have teacher identified math weaknesses. *Journal of Learning Disabilities*, 33, 168–173.

Bynner, J. (1997) Basic skills in adolescents' occupational preparation. *Career Development Quarterly*, 45, 305–321.

Bugden, S. and Ansari, D. (2015) How can cognitive developmental neuroscience constrain our understanding of developmental dyscalculia? In Chinn S.J. (ed.) (2015) *The Routledge International Handbook of Dyscalculia and Mathematical Learning Difficulties*. London. Routledge.

Buswell, G.T. and Judd, C.M. (1925) *Summary of Educational Investigations Relating to Arithmetic*. Supplementary Educational Mongraphs. Chicago. University of Chicago Press.

Butterworth, B. (1999) *The Mathematical Brain*. London. Papermac.

Butterworth, B. (2003) *The Dyscalculia Screener*. London. GL Assessment.

Butterworth, B. (2005) The development of arithmetical abilities. *Journal of Child Psychology and Psychiatry*, 46 (1), 3–18.

Butterworth, B. (2010) Foundational numerical capacities and the origins of dyscalculia. *Trends in Cognitive Sciences*, 14, 534–541.

Chan, W.W.L., Au, T.K. and Tang, J. (2014) Strategic counting: A novel assessment of place value understanding. *Learning and Instruction*, 29, 78–94.

Chasty, H.T. (1989) The challenge of specific learning difficulties. *Proceedings of the First International Conference of the British Dyslexia Association*. Reading. BDA.

Chinn, S. (1992) Individual diagnosis and cognitive style. In Miles, T.R. and Miles, E. (eds) *Dyslexia and Mathematics.* London. Routledge.

Chinn, S.J. (1994) A study of the basic number fact skills of children from specialist dyslexic and normal schools. *Dyslexia Review*, 2, 4–6.

Chinn, S.J. (1995a) Learning difficulties in mathematics. *Learn*, 17, 26–35.

Chinn, S.J. (1995b) A pilot study to compare aspects of arithmetic skill. *Dyslexia Review*, 4, 4–7.

Chinn, S.J. (1996) The relationship between the grades achieved in GCSE mathematics by 26 dyslexic male students and their scores on the WISC. *Dyslexia Review*, 7, 8–9.

Chinn, S.J. (2001) It was just a matter of time. *Mathematics Teaching*, 175, 12–13.

Chinn, S.J. (2003) Multiplication table facts… a quest. *Dyslexia Review*, 15 (1), 18–21.

Chinn, S.J. (2004) Individual diagnosis and cognitive style. In Miles, T.R. and Miles, E. (eds) (2004), *Dyslexia and Mathematics* (2nd edn). London. Routledge.

Chinn, S.J. (2009) Mathematics anxiety in secondary school students in England. *DYSLEXIA*, 15, 61–68.

Chinn, S.J. (2012) 'Beliefs, anxiety and avoiding failure in mathematics' *Child Development Research.* 10.1155/2012/396071

Chinn, S.J. (2013) Is the population really woefully bad at maths? *Mathematics Teaching*, 232, 25–28.

Chinn, S.J. (2017a) *More Trouble with Maths: A Complete Guide to Identifying and Diagnosing Mathematical Difficulties.* (2nd edn) Abingdon. Routledge

Chinn, S.J. (2017b) *The Trouble with Maths* (3rd edn). Abingdon. Routledge.

Chinn, S.J. (ed.) (2015) *The Routledge International Handbook of Dyscalculia and Mathematical Learning Difficulties.* London. Routledge.

Chinn, S.J. and Ashcroft, J.R. (1992) The use of patterns. In Miles, T.R. and Miles, E. (eds) (1992), *Dyslexia and Mathematics* (1992). London. Routledge.

Chinn, S.J. And Ashcroft, J.R. (2004) The use of patterns. In Miles, TR and Miles, E (eds) (2004), *Dyslexia and Mathematics* (2nd edn). London. Routledge.

Chinn, S.J. and Kay, J. (2003) Multiplication facts. Paper presented at the 50th IDA Conference. Atlanta. IDA.

Chinn, S.J., Mcdonagh, D., Van Elswijk, R., *et al.* (2001) Classroom studies into cognitive style in mathematics for pupils with dyslexia in special education in the Netherlands, Ireland and the UK. *British Journal of Special Education*, 28 (2), 80–85.

Choat, E. (1982) Understanding in young children's mathematics. *Mathematics in Schools*, 10 (2), 3–6.

Cialdini, R.B. (2007) *Influence: The Psychology of Persuasion.* New York, NY. Harper Collins.

Cirino, P.T., Fuchs, L. S., Elias, J.T., Powell, S.R. and Schumacher, R.F. (2015) Cognitive and mathematical profiles for different forms of learning disabilities. *Journal of Learning Disabilities*, 48 (2), 156–175.

Cobb, P. (1991) Reconstructing elementary school mathematics. *Focus on Learning Problems in Mathematics*, 13 (2), 3–32.

Cockcroft, W.H. (1982) *Mathematics Counts.* London. HMSO.

Copeland, R.V. (1984) *How Children Learn Mathematics. Teaching Implications of Piaget's Research.* New York. Macmillan.

Cragg, L. and Gilmore, C. (2014) Skills underlying mathematics: The role of executive function in the development of mathematics proficiency. *Trends in Neuroscience and Education*, 3, 63–68.

De Bono, E. (1999) *Six Thinking Hats.* London. Penguin.

Department for Education (2013) *Mathematics programmes of study: Key stages 1 and 2.* National Curriculum in England. DfE.

Department for Education and Skills (2001) *The National Numeracy Strategy. Guidance to Support Learners with Dyslexia and Dyscalculia.* London. DfES 0512/2001.

Department of Education and Science (1999) *Primary School Curriculum Document: Mathematics. Teacher Guidelines.* Dublin. The Stationery Office (DES).

Desoete, A. (2015) Predictive indicators for mathematical learning disabilities/dyscalculia in kindergarten children. In Chinn, S.J. (ed.) (2015), *The Routledge International Handbook of Dyscalculia and Mathematical Learning Difficulties.* London. Routledge.

Desoete, A. and Stock, P. (2011) *Can we Predict Mathematical Disabilities for Abilities in Kindergarten?* New York. Nova Science.

Desoete, A., Roeyers, H. and Declercq, A. (2004) Children with mathematics learning disabilities in Belgium. *Journal of Learning Disabilities*, 37, 50–61.

Devine, A., Fawcett, K., Szucs, D. and Dowker, A. (2012) Gender differences in mathematics anxiety and the relation to mathematics performance while controlling for test anxiety. *Behavioural and Brain Functions*, 8, 33.

Doidge, N. (2007) *The Brain that Changes Itself.* London. Penguin.

Donlan, C. (2015) Linguistic factors in the development of basic calculation. In Chinn, S.J. (ed.) (2015), *The Routledge International Handbook of Dyscalculia and Mathematical Learning Difficulties.* London. Routledge.

Dowker, A. (2001) Numeracy recovery: A pilot scheme for early intervention with young children with numeracy difficulties. *Support for Learning*, 16 (1), 6–10.

Dowker, A. (2005) *Individual Differences in Arithmetic.* Hove. Psychology Press.

Duffin, J. (1991) Oh yes you can. *Times Educational Supplement*, 10 May, p. 49.

Duffin, J. and Simpson, A. (2006) The transition to independent graduate studies in mathematics. In Hitt, F., Harel, G. & Selden, A. (eds), *Research in Collegiate Mathematics Education VI* (pp. 233–246). Oxford. Oxford University Press.

Duncan, G.J., Dowsett, C.J., Claessens, A., *et al.* (2007) School readiness and later achievement. *Developmental Psychology*, 43, 1428–1446.

Emerson, J. and Babtie P. (2010) *The Dyscalculia Screener.* London. Continuum.

Engelhardt, J.M. (1977) Analysis of children's computational errors: A qualitative approach. *British Journal Educational Psychology*, 47, 149–154.

Faber, H. (2014) *Dyscalculia. A Mathematics Disorder and Mathematical Difficulties in Singapore.* Singapore. D-MD Assessment and Intervention.

Fawcett, A.J. and Nicholson, R. (1999) Performance of dyslexic children on cerebellar and cognitive tasks. *Journal of Motor Behavior*, 31, 68–78.

Fuchs, L. and Fuchs, D. (2002) Mathematical problem-solving profiles of students with mathematics disabilities with and without comorbid reading disabilities. *Journal of Learning Disabilities*, 35 (6), 563–573.

Gallaburda, A.M. (1989) Ordinary and extraordinary brain development: Anatomical variation in developmental dyslexia. *Annals of Dyslexia*, 39, 67–80.

Gardner, H. (1999) *Intelligence Reframed. Multiple Intelligences for the 21st Century.* New York. Basic Books.

Gathercole, S. and Alloway, T.P. (2008) *Working Memory and Learning. A Practical Guide for Teachers.* London. Sage.

Geary, D.C. (1990) A componential analysis of an early deficit in mathematics. *Journal of Experimental Child Psychology*, 49, 363–383.

Geary, D.C. (1994) *Children's Mathematical Development.* Washington, DC. American Psychological Association.

Geary, D.C. (2000) Mathematics disorders: An overview for educators. *Perspectives*, 26 (3), 6–9.

Geary, D.C. (2003) Learning disabilities in arithmetic: Problem solving differences and cognitive deficits. In Swanson, H.L., Harris K. R. and Graham, S. (2003) *Handbook of Learning Difficulties.* New York. The Guilford Press.

Geary, D.C. (2004) Mathematics and learning disabilities. *Journal of Learning Disabilities*, 37, (1), 4–15.

Geary, D.C. (2013) Early foundations for mathematics learning and their relation to learning disabilities. *Current Directions in Psychological Science*, 22 (1), 23–27.

Geary, D.C., Hoard, M.K., Nugent, L. and Bailey, H.D. (2013) Adolescents' functional numeracy is predicted by their school entry number system knowledge. *PLoS ONE*, 8 (1), e54651.

Gersten, R., Jordan, N.C. and Flojo, J.R. (2005) Early identification and interventions for students with mathematics difficulties. *Journal of Learning Disabilities*, 38 (4), 293–304.

Gersten, R., Clarke, B. and Mazzocco, M.M.M. (2007) Historical and contemporary perspectives on mathematical learning disabilities. In Berch, D.B. and Mazzocco, M.M.M. (eds) (2007), *Why is Math so Hard for Some Children?* Grand Rapids, Michigan. Paul H. Brookes Publishing Co.

Gillum, J. (2012) Dyscalculia: Issues for practice in educational psychology. *Educational Psychology in Practice: theory, research and practice in educational psychology*, 28 (3), 287–297.

Gillum, W., Hesse, K. and McCarty, C. (2012) *Basic Number Screening Test* (4th edn). Sevenoaks. Hodder and Stoughton.

Gowramma, I.P. (2015) Arithmetic difficulties of children with hearing impairment. In Chinn, S.J. (ed.) (2015), *The Routledge International Handbook of Dyscalculia and Mathematical Learning Difficulties.* London. Routledge.

Grauberg, E. (1998) *Elementary Mathematics and Language Difficulties.* London. Whurr.

Gray, E.M. and Tall, D.O. (1994) Duality, ambiguity and flexibility: A proceptual view of simple arithmetic. *Journal for Research in Mathematics Education*, 26 (2), 115–141.

Harries, T. and Sutherland, R. (1999) Primary school mathematics textbooks: an international comparison. In Thompson, I. (ed.) (1999), *Issues in Teaching Numeracy in Primary Schools.* Buckingham. Open University Press.

Hart, K. (1978) *Children's Understanding of Mathematics 11–16.* London. John Murray.

Hart, K. (1989) There is little connection. In Ernest, P. (ed.), *Mathematics Teaching: The State of the Art.* Lewes. Falmer Press.

Harvey, R. (1982) 'I can keep going up if I want to': One way of looking at learning mathematics. In Harvey, R., Kerslake, D., Shuard, H, and Torbe, M. (eds), *Language Teaching and Learning. 6. Mathematics.* London. Ward Lock Educational.

Hattie, J. (2009) *Visible Learning.* Abingdon. Routledge.

Haylock, D. and Cockburn, A. (1997) *Understanding Mathematics in the Lower Primary Years.* London. Paul Chapman Publishing.

Hein, J., Bzufka, M.W. and Neumarker, K.J. (2000) The specific disorder of arithmetic skills. Prevalence studies in a rural and an urban population sample and their clinic-neuropsychological validation. *European Child and Adolescent Psychiatry*, 9 (2), 87–101.

Henderson, A. (1989) *Maths and Dyslexics.* Llandudno. St David's College.

Ho, C.S. and Cheng, F. (1997) Training in place value concepts improves children's addition skills. *Contemporary Educational Pyschology*, 22, 495–506.

Ho, C.S., Wong, T.T. and Chan, W.W.L. (2015) Mathematics learning and its difficulties among Chinese children in Hong Kong. In Chinn, S.J. (ed.) (2015), *The Routledge International Handbook of Dyscalculia and Mathematical Learning Difficulties.* London. Routledge.

Hoffman, B. (2010) 'I think I can, but I'm afraid to try.' The role of self-efficacy, beliefs and mathematics anxiety in mathematics problem-solving efficiency. *Learning and Individual Differences*, 20 (3), 276–283.

Hong, K.T., Mei, Y.S. and Lim, J. (2009) *The Singapore Model Method for Learning Mathematics.* Singapore. Ministry of Education.

Houssart, J. (2005) Count me out: Task refusal in primary mathematics. In Watson, A, Houssart, J and Roaf, C. (eds) (2005), *Supporting Mathematical Thinking.* London. David Fulton.

Hughes, M. (1986) *Children and Number: Difficulties in Learning Mathematics.* Oxford. Blackwell.

Hunt, T.E., Clark-Carter, D. and Sheffield, D. (2014) Exploring the relationship between mathematics anxiety and performance: The role of intrusive thoughts. *Journal of Education, Psychology and Social Sciences*, 2 (2), 69–75.

Jitendra, A.K., Dupuis, D.N. and Lein, A.E. (2015) Promoting word problem solving performance among students with mathematics difficulties. In Chinn, S.J. (ed.) (2015), *The Routledge International Handbook of Dyscalculia and Mathematical Learning Difficulties*. London. Routledge.

Joffe, L. (1980a) Dyslexia and attainment in school mathematics: Part 1. *Dyslexia Review*, 3 (1), 10–14.

Joffe, L. (1980b) Dyslexia and attainment in school mathematics: Part 2, Error types and remediation. *Dyslexia Review*, 3 (2), 12–18.

Joffe, L. (1983) School mathematics and dyslexia… a matter of verbal labelling, generalisation, horses and carts. *Cambridge Journal of Education*, 13 (3), 22–27.

Kahneman, D. (2011) *Thinking, Fast and Slow*. London. Penguin

Kane, N. and Kane, M. (1979) Comparison of right and left hemisphere functions. *The Gifted Child Quarterly*, 23 (1), 157–167.

Karagiannakis, G.N. and Cooreman, A. (2015) Focused MLD Intervention based on the classification of MLD subtypes. In Chinn, S. (ed.) (2015), *The Routledge International Handbook of Dyscalculia and Mathematical Learning Difficulties*. London. Routledge.

Kaufmann, L., Handl, P. and Thony, B. (2003) Evaluation of a numeracy intervention program focusing on basic numerical knowledge and conceptual knowledge. *Journal of Learning Disabilities*, 36 (6), 564–573.

Kaufmann, L., Mazzocco, M.M., Dowker, A., *et al.* (2013) Dyscalculia from a developmental and differential perspective. *Frontiers of Psychology*, 4, 516 (available on-line: 10.3389/fpsyg.2013.00516).

Kavanagh, J.K. and Truss, T.J. (eds) (1988) *Learning Disabilities: Proceedings of the National Conference*. Parkton, MD: York Press.

Keeler, M.L. and Swanson, H.L. (2001) Does strategy knowledge influence working memory in children with mathematical difficulties? *Journal of Learning Disabilities*, 34 (5), 418–434.

Kelly, B., Gersten, R. and Carnine, D. (1990) Student error patterns as a function of curriculum design: Teaching fractions to remedial high school students and high school students with learning disabilities. *Journal of Learning Disabilities*, 23 (1), 23–29.

Kennedy, L.M. (1975) *Guiding Children to Mathematical Discovery*. Belmont, CA. Wadsworth.

Kibel, M. (2004) Linking language to action. In Miles, T.R. and Miles, E. (eds) (2004), *Dyslexia and Mathematics*. London. RoutledgeFalmer.

Kitz, W.R. and Nash, R.T. (1995) Applying effective instructional strategies for teaching dyslexic students in a remedial college algebra course. *Annals of Dyslexia*, 45, 143–160.

Kosc, L. (1974) Developmental dyscalculia. *Journal of Learning Disabilities*, 7 (3), 46–59.

Kosc, L. (1986) Dyscalculia. *Focus on Learning Problems in Mathematics*, 8 (3, 4), 48–127.

Krutetskii, V.A. (1976) trans Kilpatric, J. and Wirszup, I. (eds), *The Psychology of Mathematical Abilities in School Children*. Chicago. University of Chicago Press.

Kubrick, S. and Rudnick, J.A. (1980) *Problem Solving – A Handbook for Teachers*. Needham Heights, NY. Allyn and Bacon.

Kubiszyn, T. and Borich, G. (2007) *Educational Testing and Measurement*. Hoboken. Wiley.

Landerl, K., Bevan, A. and Butterworth, B. (2004) Developmental dyscalculia and basic numerical capacities: a study of 8–9-year-old students. *Cognition*, 93, 99–125.

Landerl, K. and Moll, K. (2010) Comorbidity of learning disorders: Prevalence and familial transmission. *Journal of Clinical Child Psychology and Psychiatry*, 51, 287–294.

Lane, C. (1992) Now listen hear. *Special Children*, 54, 12–14.

Lane, C. (2012) *Self-Voice. A Major Rethink*. Bridgwater. ARROW Tuition Ltd.

Lane, C. and Chinn, S.J. (1986) Learning by self-voice echo. *Academic Therapy*, 21, 477–481.

Leong, C.K. and Jerred, W.D. (2001) Effects of consistency and adequacy of language information on understanding elementary mathematical word problems. *Annals of Dyslexia*, 51, 277–298.

Lewis, C., Hitch, J.G. and Walker, P. (1994) The prevalence of specific arithmetical difficulties and specific reading difficulties in 9–10-year-old-boys and girls. *Journal Child Psychology and Psychiatry*, 33 (2), 283–292.

Light, J.G. and Defries, J.C. (1995) Comorbidity of reading and mathematics disabilities: Genetic and environmental etiologies. *Journal of Learning Disabilities*, 28, 96–105.

Luchins, A.S. (1942) Mechanisation in problem solving: The effect of Einstellung. *Psychological Monographs*, 54 (6).

Lundberg, I. and Sterner, G. (2006) Reading, arithmetic and task orientation – How are they related? *Annals of Dyslexia*, 56 (2), 361–377.

Lyons M.L. and Beilock, S.L. (2012) When math hurts: Math anxiety predicts pain network activation in anticipation of doing math. *PLoS ONE*, 7 (10), 1–6. www.plosone.com

Mabbott, D.J. and Bisanz, J. (2008) Computational skills, working memory and conceptual knowledge in older children with mathematics learning disabilities. *Journal of Learning Disabilities*, 41 (1), 15–28.

Macaruso, P. and Sokol, S.M. (1998) Cognitive neuropsychology and developmental dyscalculia. In Donlan, C. (ed.) (2000), *The Development of Mathematical Skills*. Hove. The Psychology Press.

Mackay, D. (1994) Show your working – and fail. *Times Educational Supplement*, 4072, p. 22.

Madsen, A.L., Smith, P. and Lanier, P. (1995) Does conceptually oriented instruction enhance computational competence? *Focus on Learning Problems in Mathematics*, 17 (4), 42–64.

Magne, O. (1996) *Bibliography of Literature on Dysmathematics. Didakometry.* Malmo, Sweden. School of Education.

McDougal, S. (1990) *Table Time. The Exciting New Way to Learn Multiplication Tables.* Bromley. Harrap.

McLeish, J. (1991) *Number*. London. Bloomsbury.

Marolda, M.R. and Davidson, S.D. (2000) Mathematical learning profiles and differentiated teaching strategies. *Perspectives*, 26 (3), 10–15.

Marshall, R.M., Schafer, V.A., O'Donnell, L., Elliot, J. and Handwerk, M.L. (1999) Arithmetic disabilities and ADD subtypes. *Journal of Learning Disabilities*, 32 (3), 239–247.

Miles, E. (1992) Reading and writing in mathematics. In Miles, T.R. and Miles, E. (eds) (1992), *Dyslexia and Mathematics.* London. Routledge.

Miles, T.R. (1983) *Dyslexia: The Pattern of Difficulties.* Oxford. Blackwell.

Miles, T.R. (1993) *Dyslexia: The Pattern of Difficulties* (2nd edn). London. Whurr.

Miles, T.R. and Miles, E. (eds) (1992) *Dyslexia and Mathematics.* London. Routledge.

Miles, T.R. and Miles, E. (eds) (2004) *Dyslexia and Mathematics* (2nd edn). London. RoutledgeFalmer.

Molina, C. (2012) *The Problem with Math is English.* San Francisco. Jossey-Bass.

Moll, K., Gobel, S. and Snowling, M.J. (2014) Basic number processing in children with specific learning disorders: Comorbidity of reading and mathematics disorders. *Child Neuropsychology: A Journal on Normal and Abnormal Development in Childhood and Adolescence.* DOI: 10:1080/09297049.2014.899570.

Morgan, C. (1999) Communicating mathematically. In Johnson-Wilder, S., Johnston-Wilder, P., Pimm, D. and Westwell. J. (1999), *Learning to Teach Mathematics in Secondary School.* London. Routledge-Falmer.

Morsanyi, K. and Szucs, D. (2015) The link between mathematics and logical reasoning. In Chinn, S.J. (ed.) (2015), *The Routledge International Handbook of Dyscalculia and Mathematical Learning Difficulties.* London. Routledge.

Mortimore, T. (2008) *Dyslexia and Learning Style. A Practitioner's Handbook* (2nd edn). Chichester. Wiley.

Mtetwa, D. and Garofalo, J. (1989) Beliefs about mathematics: an overlooked aspect of student difficulties. *Academic Therapy*, 24 (5), 611–618.

Murray, E., Hillaire, G., Johnson, M. and Rappolt-Schlitmann, G. (2015) Representing, Acting, and Engaging: UDL and Mathematics. In Chinn S.J. (ed.), *The Routledge International Handbook of Dyscalculia and Mathematical Learning Difficulties.* London. Routledge

National Mathematics Advisory Panel (2008) *Foundations for Success: Final Report of the National Mathematics Advisory Panel.* Washington, DC. United States Department of Education.

Nunes, T., Bryant, P. and Watson, A. (2007) *Key Understanding in Mathematics Learning*. London. Nuffield Foundation.

OFSTED (2008) *Mathematics Report: 'Mathematics: Understanding the Score' (Report on Primary and Secondary Mathematics)*. www.childrens-mathematics.net/continuity_ofsted_maths.pdf

Ostad, S.A. (1997) Developmental differences in addition strategies. A comparison of mathematically disabled and mathematically normal children. *British Journal of Educational Psychology*, 67, 345–357.

Parsons, S. and Bynner, J. (1997) Numeracy and employment. *Education and Training*, 39, 43–51.

Pieters, S., Roeyers, H., Rosseel, Y., Waelvelde, H. and Desoete, A. (2015) Identifying sub-types among children with development coordination disorder and mathematical learning difficulties. *Journal of Learning Disabilities*, 48 (1), 83–95.

Polya, G. (1990) *How to Solve It*. London. Penguin.

Pringle-Morgan, W. (1896) A case of congenital word blindness. *British Medical Journal*. 7 Nov.1896; reprinted in *The Dyslexia Handbook* (1996), Julia Crisfield (ed.). Reading. British Dyslexia Association.

Pritchard, R.A., Miles, T.R., Chinn, S.J. and Taggart, A.T. (1989) Dyslexia and knowledge of number facts. *Links*, 14 (3), 17–20.

Ramaa, S. (2015) Arithmetic difficulties among socially disadvantaged children and children with dyscalculia. In Chinn, S.J. (ed.) (2015), *The Routledge International Handbook of Dyscalculia and Mathematical Learning Difficulties*. London. Routledge.

Ramaa, S. and Gowramma, I.P. (2002) Dyscalculia among primary school children in India. *Dyslexia*, 8 (2), 67–85.

Ramirez, G., Gunderson, E.A., Levine, S.C. and Beilock, S.L. (2013) Math Anxiety, Working Memory, and Math Achievement in Early Elementary School. *Journal of Cognition and Development*, 14 (2), 187–202.

Rashid, S. and Brookes, G. (2010) *The Levels of Attainment in Literacy and Numeracy of 13–19-Year-Olds In England*. London. National Research and Development Centre for Adult Literacy and Numeracy.

Rawson, M.B. (1984) Developmental stages and patterns of growth of dyslexic persons. In Bath, J.B., Knox, D.E. and Chinn, S.J. (1984), *Dyslexia: Research and its Applications to the Adolescent*. Bath. Better Books.

Reeve, R.A. and Gray, S. (2015) Number difficulties in young children. Deficits in core number? In Chinn, S.J. (ed.) (2015), *The Routledge International Handbook of Dyscalculia and Mathematical Learning Difficulties*. London. Routledge.

Reigosa-Crespo, V., Valdes-Sosa, M., Butterworth, B., *et al.* (2012) Basic numerical capacities and prevalence of developmental dyscalculia: the Havana Survey. *Developmental Psychology*, 48 (1), 123–135.

Reigosa, V. and Castro, D. (2015) Dots and digits. How do children process the numerical magnitude? Evidence from brain and behaviour. In Chinn,

S.J. (ed.) (2015), *The Routledge International Handbook of Dyscalculia and Mathematical Learning Difficulties.* London. Routledge.

Reyna, V.F., Nelson, W.L., Han, P.K. and Dieckmann, N.F. (2009) How numeracy influences risk comprehension and medical decision making. *Psychological Bulletin*, 135, 943–973.

Richardson, F.C. and Shuinn, R.M. (1972) The Mathematics Anxiety Rating Scale. *Journal of Counseling Psychology*, 19, 551–554.

Riding, R. and Cheema, I. (1991) Cognitive styles – an overview and integration. *Educational Psychology*, 11 (3 & 4), 193–215.

Riding, R.J. and Rayner, S. (1998) *Cognitive Styles and Learning Strategies.* London. David Fulton.

Ritchie, S.J. and Bates, T.C. (2013) Enduring links from childhood mathematics and reading achievement to adult socioeconomic status. *Psychological Science*, 24, 1301–1308.

Rivera-Batiz, F. (1992) Quantitative literacy and the likelihood of employment among young adults in the United States. *Journal of Human Resources*, 27, 313–328.

Rose, J. (2009) *Identifying and Teaching Children and Young People with Dyslexia and Literacy Difficulties An independent report from Sir Jim Rose to the Secretary of State for Children, Schools and Families.* UK Rose Report on dyslexia and literacy difficulties, 2009 (accessed 15 July 2015).

Rothman, R.W. and Cohen, J. (1989) The language of math needs to be taught. *Academic Therapy*, 25 (2), 133–142.

Seligman, M. (1998) *Learned Optimism.* New York. Pocket Books.

Shalev, R.S., Manor, O., Kerem, B., *et al.* (2001) Developmental dyscalculia is a familial learning disability. *Journal of Learning Disabilities*, 34, (1), 59–65.

Sharma, M.C. (1985) Mathematics as a second language. *Math Notebook*, 4 (1–4).

Sharma, M.C. (1986) Dyscalculia and other learning problems in arithmetic: a historical prospective. *Focus on Learning Problems in Mathematics*, 8 (3, 4), 7–45.

Sharma, M.C. (1988) Levels of Knowing Mathematics. *Mathematics Notebook*, 6 (1, 2).

Sharma, M.C. (1989) Mathematics learning personality. *Mathematics Notebook*, 7 (1, 2).

Shin, M. and Pedrotty Bryant, D. (2015) A synthesis of mathematical and cognitive performances of students with mathematics learning disabilities. *Journal of Learning Disabilities*, 48 (1), 96–112.

Siegel, M. and Fonzi, J.M. (1995) The practice of reading in an inquiry-oriented mathematics class. *Reading Research Quarterly*, 30 (4), 632–673.

Siegler, R.S. (1991) How domain-general and domain-specific knowledge interact to produce strategy choices. In Light, P., Sheldon, S. and Woodhead, M. (1991) *Learning to Think.* London. Routledge.

Siegler, R.S., Duncan, G.J., Davis-Kean, P.E., *et al.* (2012) Early predictors of high school mathematics achievement. *Psychological Science*, 23 (7), 691–697.

Skemp, R.R. (1971) *The Psychology of Learning Mathematics.* Harmondsworth. Penguin.

Skemp, R.R. (1986) *The Psychology of Learning Mathematics* (2nd edn). Harmondsworth. Pelican.

Smith, R. (1996) An investigation into the effects that dyslexia has on children in mathematics. Professional development project for BSc(Ed), University of Exeter.

Smith, M.J. And Teague, S. (2014) Why is 48 so hard to remember? *Mathematics Teaching.* 241, 41–43.

Springer, S.P. and Deutsch, G. (1993) *Left Brain, Right Brain.* New York. Freeman and Co.

Stanovich, K.E. (1991) The theoretical and practical consequences of discrepancy definitions of dyslexia. In Snowling, M and Thomson, M. (eds) (1991), *Dyslexia: Integrating Theory and Practice.* London. Whurr.

Steeves, J. (1979) Multisensory math: an instructional approach to help the LD child. *Focus on Learning Problems in Mathematics,* 1 (2), 51–62.

Sutherland, P. (1988) Dyscalculia. Sum cause for concern? *Times Educational Supplement,* 18 March 1988.

Thompson, I (ed.) (1999) *Issues in Teaching Numeracy in Primary Schools.* Buckingham. OUP.

Threlfall, J. and Frobisher, L. (1999) Patterns in processing and learning addition facts. In Orton, A. (ed.) *Pattern in the Teaching and Learning of Mathematics.* London. Cassell.

Torbeyns, J., Verschaffel, L. and Ghesquiere, P. (2004) Strategy development in children with mathematical disabilities. *Journal of Learning Disabilities,* 37 (2), 119–131.

Turner Ellis, S.A., Miles, T.R. and Wheeler, T.J. (1996) Speed of multiplication in dyslexics and non-dyslexics. *Dyslexia,* 2, 121–139.

Vernon, P.E., Miller, K.M. and Izard, J.F. (2002) *Mathematics Competency Test.* London. Hodder and Stoughton Educational.

Vukovic, R.K., Kieffer, M.J., Bailey, S.P. and Harari, R.R. (2013) Mathematics Anxiety in Young Children: Concurrent and Longitudinal Associations with Mathematical Performance. *Contemporary Educational Psychology,* 38 (1), 1–10.

Watson, A. (2005) Low attaining students can think mathematically. In Watson, A., Houssart, J. and Road, C. (eds) (2006), *Supporting Mathematical Thinking.* London. David Fulton.

Wheatley, G.H. (1977) The right hemisphere's role in problem solving. *The Arithmetic Teacher,* 25, 36–39.

Wheatley, G.H., Frankland, R.L., Mitchell, O.R. and Kraft, R. (1978) Hemispheric specialization and cognitive development: implications for mathematics education. *Journal for Research in Mathematics Education,* 9, 20–32.

Wigley, A. (1995) Minding one's Ps and Qs. *Mathematics Teaching,* 153, 30–33.

Wilkinson, G.S. and Robertson, G.J. (2006) *The Wide Range Achievement Test – 4.* London. Pearson.

Wilson, J. and Sadowski, B. (eds) (1976) *The Maryland Diagnostic Test and Interview Protocols.* Arithmetic Center, University of Maryland. USA.

World Health Organisation (2010) The ICD-10: Classification of Mental and Behavioural Disorders *F81.2 Specific disorder of arithmetical skills* World Health Organisation [online] http://www.who.int/classifications/icd/en/bluebook.pdf (accessed 13 March 2015).

Yeo, D. (2003) *Dyslexia, Dyspraxia and Mathematics.* London. Whurr.

Young, R.M. and O'Shea, T (1981) Errors in children's subtraction. *Cognitive Science*, 5 (2), 153–177.

Young, C.B., Wu, S.S. and Menon, V. (2102) The neurodevelopmental basis of math anxiety. *Psychological Science*, 23 (5), 492–501.

Zarzycki, P. (2001) In the clutches of algorithms: A view from Poland. *Mathematics Teaching*, 174, 8–11.

Zhou, X. and Cheng, D. (2015) When and why numerosity processing is associated with developmental dyscalculia. In Chinn, S.J. (ed.) (2015), *The Routledge International Handbook of Dyscalculia and Mathematical Learning Difficulties.* London. Routledge

Index

Mathematics for Dyslexics and Dyscalculics: A Teaching Handbook, Fourth Edition.
Steve Chinn and Richard E. Ashcroft.